FUNDAMENTAL
GREEK
GRAMMAR

FUNDAMENTAL
GREEK
GRAMMAR

Second Edition

FRiz
Quadrata

James W. Voelz

CONCORDIA

PUBLISHING HOUSE

Job. no. 43549

Copyright © 1986, 1993 Concordia Publishing House
3558 South Jefferson Avenue, St. Louis, MO 63118-3968
Manufactured in the United States of America

Library of Congress Cataloging-in-Publication Data

Voelz, James W., 1945–
    Fundamental Greek grammar/James W. Voelz.—2nd ed.
       p. cm.
    Includes index.
    ISBN 0-570-04252-6
    1. Greek language, Biblical—Grammar. 2. Bible. N.T.—Language, style. I. Title.
PA817.V64 1993   93-22218
487'.4—dc20   CIP

1 2 3 4 5 6 7 8 9 10 BB 02 01 00 99 98 97 96 95 94 93

Contents

Preface

"The name of this book, *Fundamental Greek Grammar*, reveals the philosophy on which it is built, namely, that one must learn the fundamentals first, then build on this foundation for the mastery of more complex material. Now more than ever before is such an approach demanded. Many of today's students of New Testament Greek do not bring with them a liberal arts background (not to mention a previous knowledge of Latin or classical Greek). Others, though trained in the humanities, embark on their study later in life and are handicapped by the ravages of time. Still others are poorly trained in English, whatever their discipline or age—due, perhaps, to the sorry state of American education over the last 20 years—and as such find it difficult to master any language, even their own.

"What does such a 'fundamental' approach mean in instructional-terms? Simply this: moving from what is known to what is unknown—and assuming that what is known is, in fact, very little. Practically speaking, this means beginning with English—explaining English forms and structures in quite some detail—so that students can understand the explanations of and illustrations for the Greek in their own language. A 'fundamental' approach also means proceeding from what is easy to what is hard (all exercises, translations, and Bible passages are so ordered) and from what is regular to what is irregular or an exception (thus the presentation of a given item may be split into two rather widely separated chapters). This makes learning as simple and effective as possible."

So began the preface to the first edition. And the present second edition in no way overturns that philosophy or approach. What, then, has been changed? Revisions have occurred in three areas:

1. Typesetting errors, regrettably too frequent in the previous edition, have been corrected.

2. The presentation of material has been upgraded

    a. by the addition of further explanations (see, e.g., chapter 20, section G, "Another View");

    b. by the reordering of practice sentences (see, e.g., chapter 14) and Bible passages (see, e.g., chapter 12);

    c. by modifying practice sentences (see, e.g., chapter 28) and substituting better Bible passages (see, e.g., chapter 21);

    d. by introducing several verbs in slightly later chapters to aid overall comprehension (see, e.g., ἔρχομαι [now in chapter 8] and ἀπόλλυμι [now in chapter 34]);

    e. by substituting more accurate and more fully developed explanations, especially those related to the "aspect" of the Greek verb (see chapter 9 [cf. chapter 16]).

3. The contents of the book as a whole have been expanded greatly by the addition of several items requested by students and teachers alike:

    a. A complete set of noun, adjective, and verb paradigms gathered in one place for easy reference (pages 318–66)

    b. A Greek-English dictionary (pages 371–89)

Included in this latter section of the book is a special chart to aid in the identification of the stems of the principal parts of irregular verbs (page 370).

"The author wishes to express his appreciation to his wife, Judy, and son, Jonathan, who have graciously consented to his all-too-considerable absences in the preparation of this work; to his colleagues Harold Buls and G. Waldemar Degner for help along the way; to Rev. Geoffrey M. Styler, Corpus Christi College, Cambridge (England), for valuable comments and criticisms; to the students of Concordia Theological Seminary, Fort Wayne, Ind., who have served as 'testers' of this approach for over five years; to Mr. Mark Sell, who helped in the preparation of the answer key; and to Tammy Raymer and Beth Thompson, who succeeded in typing a most difficult manuscript."

These expressions of appreciation from Epiphanytide 1985, related to the first edition, still stand. The author would further express appreciation to the personnel of Concordia Publishing House for their outstanding work in producing this second, revised and expanded, edition; to his hundreds of students since 1985, who have helped to refine the text's presentation and detect its errors; to the program committee of the international New Testament society *Studiorum Novi Testamenti Societas* for allowing him to present a detailed paper on Greek verbal aspect at its 1992 annual meeting in Madrid, Spain, which became the basis for the revisions of chapter 9 and elsewhere; to Don Schneider for assistance with the paradigms and dictionary; to graduate assistant Jeffrey A. Kloha for help of every kind; and to his colleagues at Concordia Seminary, St. Louis, Mo., who give him daily intellectual stimulation and honest, constructive critique.

Epiphany 1993

1

The Rudiments of Greek
Part 1: Alphabet
and Pronunciation

A. Introduction

In this first chapter we will introduce the basic components of Greek: the letters, their pronunciation, and the reading and accenting of words. The importance of this lesson cannot be overestimated. Students who never really master the alphabet or who fail to learn to pronounce words correctly are forever handicapped and never really learn the language in which God's Word of the New Covenant was written.

B. The Alphabet

1. The Letters

Small	Capital	Name	Pronunciation
α	A	Alpha	a, as in father
β	B	Beta	b
γ	Γ	Gamma	g, as in got (not as in generous)
δ	Δ	Delta	d
ϵ	E	Epsilon	e, as in get
ζ	Z	Zeta	dz, as in adds
η	H	Eta	ā, as in gray
θ	Θ	Theta	th, as in thing (not as in this)
ι	I	Iota	i, as in hit (long ι = ee as in machine)
κ	K	Kappa	k
λ	Λ	Lambda	l

11

μ	M	Mu	m
ν	N	Nu	n
ξ	Ξ	Xi	x, as in axe
ο	O	Omicron	o, as in ought
π	Π	Pi	p
ρ	P	Rho	r
σ	Σ	Sigma	s
τ	T	Tau	t
υ	Υ	Upsilon	ü, as German ü (cf. *grün*)
φ	Φ	Phi	ph, as in *phi*loso*phy*
χ	X	Chi	ch, as in Lo*ch* (German A*ch*!)
ψ	Ψ	Psi	ps, as in I*ps*wich
ω	Ω	Omega	o, as in n*o*te

Note: ς is used in place of σ at the end of a word only.

2. Making the Letters

C. Classification of Letters and Further Principles of Pronunciation

1. Vowels

a. Seven Greek letters are classified as vowels. These are as follows:

$$\alpha \quad \epsilon \quad \eta \quad \iota \quad o \quad \upsilon \quad \omega$$

(1) The seven vowels may be arranged thus:

Short	Variable	Long
	α	
ϵ		η
	ι	
o		ω
	υ	

ϵ and o are short vowels; η and ω are long vowels (the counterparts of ϵ and o); α, ι, and υ are variable, i.e., they may be either long or short. If α and υ are long, there is no change in pronunciation. The long ι is pronounced ēē.

(2) We may further note that α, ϵ, η, o, and ω are *open* vowels, while ι and υ are *close* vowels.

b. Diphthongs

(1) Type

(a) A *proper diphthong* is a pair of vowels pronounced as one syllable. The *second* vowel of a diphthong is always *close*, i.e., ι or υ. The first letter is always open, except for the combination $\upsilon\iota$. The common diphthongs and their pronunciation are as follows:

$\alpha\iota$ = ai, as in *ai*sle
$\epsilon\iota$ = ay, as in h*ay*[1]
$o\iota$ = oi, as in *oi*l
$\alpha\upsilon$ = ow, as in c*ow*
$\epsilon\upsilon$ = (y)ou, as in f*eu*d[1]
$o\upsilon$ = oo, as in s*ou*p
$\upsilon\iota$ = we, as in q*uee*n

(b) An *improper diphthong* comprises the vowels α, η, and ω, written with an unpronounced ι beneath (= ι subscript): $\alphą$, $\etą$, and $\omegą$. The ι subscript is always written on the line ("adscript") when capital letters are used:

(EG 1) $o\tilde{\iota}\kappa\omegą$ = $OIK\Omega I$

(2) Length

Diphthongs are always considered long, with one major exception relating to $\alpha\iota$ and $o\iota$. See D 3 below.

2. Consonants

a. Consonants may be classified in several ways (see Goodwin, para. 16–26). The most convenient is to distinguish among *gutturals* (formed at the back of the throat), *labials* (formed with the lips), and *dentals* (formed by pressing the tongue to the teeth). Several others are called *liquids* because of their smooth sound.

The following chart is useful and must be learned.

Voiceless	Voiced	Aspirated	(= w/air)
κ	γ	χ	= gutturals
π	β	ϕ	= labials
τ	δ	θ	= dentals

Liquids = λ μ ν ρ

b. ξ and ψ are called *double consonants*. They are late developments in the Greek alphabet (Goodwin, para. 27) and are a combination of a guttural (κ, γ, or χ) + σ and a labial (π, β, or ϕ) + σ respectively.

c. The consonants are pronounced as written, except that γ before any guttural is pronounced *ng*.

(EG 2) $\check{\alpha}\gamma\gamma\epsilon\lambda o\varsigma$ = a*n*gelos (not a*gg*elos)

3. Breathing Marks

A word that begins with a vowel or diphthong carries a *breathing mark,* either *rough* or *smooth.* A smooth breathing mark (') has no effect on pronunciation; a rough mark (') shows that the initial vowel or diphthong is *aspirated,* i.e., preceded by the sound *h.* (Originally, the rough breathing was marked by H, but this came to be used for Eta.) See also William W. Goodwin, *Greek Grammar,* London: MacMillian, 1963, para. 11–13.

Note: The breathing mark of a word beginning with a diphthong will appear over the *second* letter of the diphthong.

(EG 3) $\alpha\dot{\upsilon}\tau\acute{o}\varsigma$

D. Syllables

1. Vowels and Diphthongs

Greek words are divided by syllable, as are English words. The same basic principles apply:

a. *Only* one vowel or diphthong is allowed per syllable.

b. Every syllable *must have one* (and only one) vowel or diphthong.

We may, therefore, divide the following words thus:

(EG 4)　ἀ / γα / θός

(EG 5)　δοῦ / λος

(EG 6)　ἱ / ε / ρόν

2. Consonants

a. A consonant may begin or end a syllable.

b. A consonant surrounded by vowels normally begins a new syllable.

c. Several consonants together in the middle of a word begin a syllable together if they could stand at the beginning of a Greek word. (This point is somewhat difficult, because Greek begins words with many combinations with which English does not. See EG 10.)

(EG　7)　ἀ / γα / θός　　(cf. 2 a, 2 b)

(EG　8)　ἀ / πό / στο / λος　(cf. 2 a, 2 b, 2 c)

(EG　9)　πέμ / πω　　(cf. 2 c)

(EG 10)　ἤ / χθην　　(cf. 2 c)

3. Length

A syllable is long or short depending on its vowel or diphthong. If it contains a long vowel or a diphthong, it is long; if it contains a short vowel, it is short. The only exception concerns *final* αι and οι, i.e., syllables at the end of a word that have the αι and οι diphthong as the *last two letters*. These are considered *short* for accenting purposes (this will be important in chapter 2).

E. Transition between Words

Greek was highly conscious of *hiatus,* i.e., the open clash of vowels. As a result, two modifications often take place at the end of words.

1. If the final vowel of a word is a short *a*, *ι*, or *o*, it often *elides* (drops out) when the following word begins with a vowel. An apostrophe indicates the elision.

(EG 11)　παρὰ οἴκῳ → παρ᾽ οἴκῳ

(EG 12)　ἐπὶ ἀληθείας → ἐπ᾽ ἀληθείας

(EG 13)　ἀπὸ οἰκίας → ἀπ᾽ οἰκίας

2. A short ι at the end of some verb and noun forms (usually after σ) adds a ν to prevent hiatus.

(EG 14)   βλέπουσι αὐτόν → βλέπουσιν αὐτόν

(EG 15)   ἡγεμόσι ἀποστόλων → ἡγεμόσιν ἀποστόλων

Note the similarity to English:

(EG 16)   "an apple" (not "a apple")

F. Exercises

1. Which letter comes after each of the following in the alphabet?

   β   φ   π   ζ   ν   ι   τ   ε

2. Which are the short vowels? the variable vowels?

3. Classify the following consonants:

   a. κ =   d. τ =

   b. β =   e. χ =

   c. θ =   f. π =

4. Divide the following words into syllables:

   a. ἀληθής   d. εὑρίσκω   g. καταστήσονται

   b. καινός   e. οἶκος   h. ἐπιστρέφω

   c. δουλεύω   f. ἔλαιον   i. φευξόμεθα

G. Reading

Read John 1:1–5, pronouncing each word carefully.

Note

1. The pronunciation of these letter combinations follows American tradition. Continental scholars pronounce ει as *ei* (cf. h*ei*ght) and ευ as *oi* (cf. *oi*l). The latter system is superior for memorization of verb forms. On ancient pronunciation, see William W. Goodwin, *Greek Grammar*, London: MacMillian, 1963, para. 18.

2

The Rudiments of Greek
Part 2: Accenting
and Punctuation

A. Accenting

1. Introduction

Greek accent was orginally *musical,* i.e., indicating pitch, not stress. The accent marks were invented by Aristophanes of Byzantium, an Alexandrian, around 200 B.C. to aid foreigners in their pronunciation of Greek. (See William W. Goodwin, *Greek Grammar,* London: MacMillian, 1963, para. 107.)

2. Types of Accent

Greek has three basic accents, the *acute* (´), the *circumflex* (ˆ), and the *grave* (`). Originally, they indicated the rise and fall of the voice; *now they simply indicate which syllable of a word is to be stressed.*

3. Placement of Accent

a. Syllables to Be Accented

The last three syllables of a word are called the *ultima* (the last syllable), the *penult* (the second-last syllable), and the *antepenult* (before the second-last, i.e., third-last).

antepenult   penult   ultima

(EG 1)   πα / ρε / κά / λε / σα

Only one of these three syllables may a carry a word's accent.

b. Letters to Be Accented

An accent is placed on the vowel or (second letter of the) diphthong of the syllable to be accented. See EG 1.

17

4. Rules of Accenting

a. General

(1) Position

(a) A *grave* accent may stand only on the *ultima*.

(b) A *circumflex* accent may stand *only on the ultima* or *penult*.

(c) An *acute* accent may stand on the *ultima, penult,* or *antepenult*.

	(a)	(c)	(b)	(c)	(a)
(EG 2)	υἱοὶ	ἄγουσιν	μαθητῇ	παρθένον	καὶ

	(b)	(a)	(c)
	δοῦλον	καὶ	ἀδελφόν

(2) Syllable Length

(a) A *grave* accent may stand on a *long* or *short* syllable.

(b) A *circumflex* accent may stand on a *long* syllable only.

(c) An *acute* accent may stand on a *long* or *short* syllable.

	(a)	(a)	(b)	(c)	(a)
(EG 3)	υἱὸς	καὶ	δοῦλος	ἤγαγον	ἀδελφοὺς

	(a)	(c)
	καὶ	παρθένους

b. Major Modifications

(1) Ultima and Words Following

If the ultima carries an acute accent, this changes to a grave if a word follows directly, without intervening punctuation.

(EG 4)   εἶ ἀδελφός, but ἀδελφὸς εἶ

Note: A grave accent is simply an acute accent on the ultima that has been changed because a word follows.

(2) Length of Ultima and Accent

(a) *If the ultima is* long (i.e., long vowel or diphthong),

(i) *an acute accent cannot stand on the antepenult.*

(EG 5)   ἄγγελος but not ἄγγελου
(ου is long)

Note: This rule means that a long ultima prohibits *any* accent on the antepenult.

(ii) *a circumflex accent cannot stand on the penult.*

(EG 6)   δοῦλος but not δοῦλῳ (ῳ is long)

(b) If the ultima is short (short vowel or final αι or οι) and the penult is long *and the penult is to be accented,* it must carry the circumflex.

(EG 7)   δοῦλος not δούλος (ου is long and o is short)

c. Specific Applications

(1) Verb Accent

Verb accent is recessive. This means that

(a) if the *last syllable* is *short,* the verb's accent will recede to the left (from the end, i.e., "back") *three syllables* to the antepenult. This accent can only be acute; cf. A 4 a (1) (c).

(EG 8)   λείπετε

(EG 9)   παρακαλέσητε

Note: Intervening syllable length is irrelevant (cf. EG 9).

(b) if the last syllable is long, the verb's accent will recede only two syllables back (to the penult); cf. A 4 b (2) (a) (i). This accent must be acute; cf. A 4 b (2) (a) (ii).

(EG 10)   παιδεύεις not παίδευεις (ει is long)

(EG 11)   παιδεύεις not παιδεῦεις (ει is long)

Note: Because of these two rules, virtually all verb accents are acute, and on the second- or third-last syllable.

(2) Noun Accent

Noun accent is persistent. This means that a noun's accent will stay as it is on the same syllable on which it begins *unless the ultima turns long* in another form. In this case,

(a) if it began as an acute on the antepenult, it must *move* (it cannot change to a circumflex or grave, because these cannot stand on the antepenult).

(EG 12)   ἄγγελος → ἀγγέλου (ου is long)
Cf. A 4 b (2) (a) (i)

(b) if it began as a circumflex on the penult, it changes to an acute (a grave cannot stand on the penult). It need not move.

(EG 13)   δοῦλος → δούλῳ   (ῳ is long)
Cf. A 4 b (2) (a) (ii)

Note: In both cases, an acute accent on the penult results.

An acute accent on the penult will generally remain as it is throughout all forms.

Note: A noun whose accent begins on the ultima follows a special pattern of accenting (see chapter 4, D 3 b), but the accent will remain on the ultima.

d. Overall Summary

(1) Accent can always be determined for any given verb form. The verb's accent always seeks to recede as far left (i.e., back from the end) as possible. If the ultima is short, it goes back three; if the ultima is long, it recedes only two.

(2) A noun's accent is persistent, but the initial location of that accent must be learned; it cannot be deduced from general rules. It is worth remembering that, if the ultima turns long, the accent

(a) is forced to *move* only if it began on the antepenult;

(b) is forced to change *type* only if it began as a circumflex on the penult.

(3) In general a word with a long ultima will have an acute accent on the penult.

B. Punctuation

The following punctuation is common in the Greek texts printed by modern editors:

1. . (period) = . (period)

2. , (comma) = , (comma)

3. ; (semicolon) = ? (question mark)

4. ˙ (raised period) = : (colon) or ; (semicolon)

C. Exercises

1. Accent the following verb forms:

   a. βλεπομεν   g. παρακαλεσεται

   b. γραφεσθε   h. ὑπομιμνησκομεν

   c. γραφεσθω   i. λυετε

   d. λειπεσθωσαν   j. λαμβανη

   e. ἀναγινωσκω   k. ἐπιγινωσκεις

   f. ἐπιτελησατε   l. λειπει

2. The following words are nouns. The accent of the first form is given. Accent the remaining forms:

   a. <u>λόγος</u> b. <u>δοῦλος</u> c. <u>ἄνθρωπος</u> d. <u>ἀλήθεια</u> e. <u>δῶρον</u>

λογῳ	δουλου	ἀνθρωπου	ἀληθειᾱς	δωρου
λογοις	δουλον	ἀνθρωποι	ἀληθειᾳ	δωρῳ
λογοι	δουλων	ἀνθρωπους	ἀληθειαι	δωρα
λογους	δουλοι	ἀνθρωπον	ἀληθειαν	δωροις
λογων	δουλους	ἀνθρωπων	ἀληθειαις	δωρων

D. Reading

Read John 1:9–13, pronouncing each word carefully.

3

The Verb, Part 1: Present Indicative Active and Middle

A. Introduction

The Greek verb basically consists of three parts: a *stem*, a *connecting vowel*, and an *ending:*

	Stem	Connecting Vowel	Ending
(EG 1)	$\lambda\upsilon$	o	~~μαι~~ μεν
(EG 2)	$\lambda\epsilon\iota\pi$	ϵ	$\sigma\theta\epsilon$

Each part has a distinctive function (or functions).

1. The *stem* conveys two things:

   a. The *basic meaning* of the word. Thus, $\lambda\upsilon$- concerns "loosing" (i.e., "setting free"), while $\lambda\epsilon\iota\pi$- conveys "leaving" (in the sense of "deserting," not "departing").

   b. The *tense* of the verb form. In most verb forms, the time frame of the action can be determined simply by looking at the stem:

      (EG 3) $\lambda\acute{\upsilon}$ o $\mu\epsilon\nu$ is present tense.

      (EG 4) $\lambda\acute{\upsilon}\sigma$ o $\mu\epsilon\nu$ is future tense.

      (EG 5) $\lambda\epsilon\acute{\iota}\pi$ ϵ $\sigma\theta\epsilon$ is present tense.

      (EG 6) $\lambda\epsilon\acute{\iota}\psi$ ϵ $\sigma\theta\epsilon$ is future tense ($\psi = \pi + \sigma$).

      (EG 7) $\acute{\epsilon}$ $\lambda\acute{\iota}\pi$ ϵ $\sigma\theta\epsilon$ is aorist (simple past) tense.

      Note: An $\acute{\epsilon}$ is added to the front of the verb form to indicate past time. This is discussed in detail in chapter 8.

2. The *connecting vowel* (sometimes called the "thematic vowel") indicates the *mood*, e.g., indicative or subjunctive. (Mood deals with the conception the speaker or writer has of the action, e.g., whether it deals with reality [indicative] or, in the Greek, with futurity and uncertainly [subjunctive].)

22

(EG 8)   λύ o̲ μεν is indicative mood.

(EG 9)   λύ ω̲ μεν is subjunctive mood.

(EG 10)   λείπ ε̲ σθε is indicative mood.

(EG 11)   λείπ η̲ σθε is subjunctive mood.

3. The *ending* indicates two things:

   a. The verb's person and number:

      (EG 12)   λειπ ό μ̲ε̲θ̲α̲ is first person plural ("we").

      (EG 13)   λείπ o ν̲τ̲α̲ι̲ is third person plural ("they").

      (EG 14)   λυ ό μ̲ε̲θ̲α̲ is first person plural ("we").

      (EG 15)   λύ o μ̲α̲ι̲ is first person singular ("I").

   b. The verb form's *voice,* i.e., whether the subject is doing the acting (active), acting for himself (middle), or being acted on (passive). (See also G, below.)

      (EG 16)   λύ o μ̲ε̲ν̲ is active voice.

      (EG 17)   λυ ό μ̲ε̲θ̲α̲ is middle voice.

      (EG 18)   λείπ ε τ̲ε̲ is active voice.

      (EG 19)   λείπ ε σ̲θ̲ε̲ is passive voice.

B. Paradigm Forms

1. Present Indicative Active

   a. λύω = I loose

	Singular			Plural	
1	λύω (λύομι)	I loose		λύομεν	We loose
2	λύεις (λύεσι)	You loose		λύετε	You loose
3	λύει (λύετι)	He (she, it) looses		λύουσι(ν) (λύονται)	They loose

   Note: "Original" versions of several forms are given in parentheses.

   b. λείπω = I leave

	Singular			Plural	
1	λείπω (λείπομι)	I leave		λείπομεν	We leave
2	λείπεις (λείπεσι)	You leave		λείπετε	You leave
3	λείπει (λείπετι)	He (she, it) leaves		λείπουσι(ν) (λείπονται)	They leave

2. Present Indicative Middle

 a. λύω

	Singular			Plural	
1	λύομαι	I loose for myself		λυόμεθα	We loose for ourselves
2	λύῃ (λύεσαι)	You loose for yourself		λύεσθε	You loose for yourselves
3	λύεται	He (she, it) looses for himself		λύονται	They loose for themselves

 b. λείπω

	Singular			Plural	
1	λείπομαι	I leave for myself		λειπόμεθα	We leave for ourselves
2	λείπῃ (λείπεσαι)	You leave for yourself		λείπεσθε	You leave for yourselves
3	λείπεται	He (she, it) leaves for himself		λείπονται	They leave for themselves

C. Morphology

1. Stem

All forms are present tense. Therefore, the stems of both the active and the middle forms of each verb are identical. The stem of λύω ends with an υ, making it a vowel stem verb. The stem of λείπω ends with a π, making it a consonantal stem verb.

2. Connecting Vowel

a. For most Greek verbs, the connecting vowel, joining stem and ending, is either an o-vowel or and e-vowel—on the one hand, either a short o (= o) or a long o (= ω) or, on the other hand, either a short e (= ε) or a long e (= η).

b. *Indicative mood* verb forms, such as those introduced in this chapter, use *short* vowels (ε and o) for their connecting vowels.

c. The pattern of these connecting vowels is as follows:

	Singular	Plural
1	o	o
2	ε	ε
3	ε	o

Note how apparent this pattern is in most of the middle voice forms of each paradigm. In the second person singular of the middle voice and in the first, second, and third person singular and third person plural of the active voice, it is also present *in principle* (i.e., in the original forms).

3. Endings

a. General Observations

(1) There is one set of endings for present active forms, another for present middle forms.

(a) Active Endings

	Singular	Plural
1	(ω)	‑$\mu\epsilon\nu$
2	$(\epsilon\iota\varsigma)$	‑$\tau\epsilon$
3	$(\epsilon\iota)$	$(o\upsilon[\sigma\iota])$

(b) Middle Endings

	Singular	Plural
1	‑$\mu\alpha\iota$	‑$\mu\epsilon\theta\alpha$
2	‑$\eta[\sigma\alpha\iota]$	‑$\sigma\theta\epsilon$
3	‑$\tau\alpha\iota$	‑$\nu\tau\alpha\iota$

(2) There exists no small similarity between active and middle forms, especially if the "original" forms are compared (cf. B 1 and B 2 above).

(3) These are the endings not only for the present tense but also for the other two *primary tenses,* future and perfect, and as such they are called "primary endings." *Primary tenses are those that are not essentially concerned with the past.*

b. Specific Observations

(1) The singular active endings (in parentheses under General Observations above) are not the true endings but are composites, since contraction has taken place between connecting vowel and ending. ‑$\mu\iota$ in the original first person singular (cf. B 1 a and b above) still occurs in some very old verbs (see chapters 12 and 33–35).

(2) The $\nu\tau$ of the third plural active has elided and the o has lengthened into the diphthong $o\upsilon$ (compensatory lengthening).

(3) The second person singular ending in the middle has dropped its σ; the ϵ connecting vowel has combined with the α to produce η; and the ι has gone subscript. Note: σ normally drops out when situated between two vowels.

(4) The ι of the active third person plural is short, as is the α of the middle first person plural.

(5) Remember that for accenting purposes, final $\alpha\iota$ (cf. first and third singular and third plural in the middle voice) is always short. See chapter 1, D 3.

D. Accent

The accent of the verb is recessive (see chapter 2, A 4 c (1)). It will therefore recede to the left three syllables if the last syllable is short, two syllables if the last syllable is long.

(EG 20)   λείπετε

(EG 21)   λυόμεθα

(EG 22)   λείπῃ

(EG 23)   λείπονται

E. Tense

All of the forms of chapter 3 are present tense and thus deal with action in present time. Further categories of analysis related to tense will be discussed in depth in chapter 9. For the time being, a simple translation will be acceptable.

(EG 24)   λύω = "I loose."

(EG 25)   λείπω = "I leave."

F. Mood

The forms presented in this and the next 13 chapters will be indicative mood. This means that they deal with fact or reality in the sense that they make assertions or ask questions.

G. Voice

In *active* voice forms, the subject is the "agent" of the activity; he does it and is responsible for it. In the *middle* voice, the subject is also the agent of the activity. However, the verb form conveys the *additional nuance* that the *subject is acting in some way in relation to himself*, e.g., in his own interest, for his own benefit, or, rarely, even on himself (reflexively). Reflexive activity is most common in verbs concerning personal care and grooming.

(EG 26)	κλέπτω = "I steal";	κλέπτομαι	= "I steal *for myself.*"
(EG 27)	λύω = "I loose";	λύομαι	= "I loose *for myself*" (i.e., "I ransom").
(EG 28)	νίπτω = "I wash (someone or something)";	νίπτομαι	= "I wash *myself*" (i.e., "I bathe").

Greek verbs may also be put into the passive voice, so that the subject is being acted on or receiving the action. These forms will be met in chapter 11.

H. Vocabulary[1]

ἄγω: I lead; drive   κλέπτω (r): I steal

ἀκούω (r): I hear   λείπω: I leave (behind); abandon

βλέπω (R): I see   λύω (R): I loose; break

γράφω (r): I write   νίπτω (R): I wash

θεραπεύω (R): I heal   πέμπω (r): I send

κηρύσσω (R): I proclaim   σῴζω (r): I save, *rescue*

I. Exercises

1. Divide the following forms of λύω and λείπω by stem, connecting vowel, and ending (this is not the same as dividing by syllable):

   a. λύομεν   e. λύετε   i. λύουσιν

   b. λείπεσθε   f. λείπῃ   j. λείπεται

   c. λυόμεθα   g. λύω   k. λύομαι

   d. λείπονται   h. λείπεις   l. λείπει

2. Write the primary middle endings:

	Singular	Plural
1		
2		
3		

J. Practice Sentences

1. Greek to English

   a. ἄγεις   h. σῴζομεν

   b. πέμπετε   i. λείπῃ

   c. ἀκούει   j. βλέπετε

   d. λύω   k. κλέπτεται

   e. νίπτομαι   l. πεμπόμεθα

   f. κηρύσσεσθε   m. θεραπεύομεν

   g. γράφονται

2. English to Greek

a.   We steal.

b.   You (pl.)[2] loose for yourselves

c.   He washes.

d.   He washes himself.

e.   She saves.

f.   We proclaim.

g.   It hears.

h.   I lead.

i.   They write.

j.   She leaves for herself.

k.   You see.

l.   They heal.

m.   I break.

K. Bible Passage

John 9:19b πῶς . . .

Notes

1. For verbs marked with (R), all basic forms or *principal parts,* i.e., all those forms needed to make all other forms of the Greek verb, can be formed predictably from the present indicative active. All verbs marked with (r) are basically regular (predictable) but contain some irregularity (unpredictability) in forms introduced, occasionally in chapters 11 and 23, more frequently in chapters 24 and 25 (the fourth, fifth, and sixth principal parts). The first person singular present indicative active form is normally the first principal part of a verb.

2. "You" will be assumed to be singular (cf. k) unless marked (pl.).

4

Nouns, Part 1:
The O or Second
Declension

A. Introduction

1. Greek is an *inflected* language. This means that the *forms* of nouns, pronouns, and adjectives *determine* their *function*. Separate forms will be used, e.g., for the subject of a verb and for the object.

   (EG 1)   The slave ($\delta o \hat{\upsilon} \lambda o \varsigma$) sees the apostle.

   (EG 2)   The apostle sees the slave ($\delta o \hat{\upsilon} \lambda o \nu$).

   In English, which uses *word order,* not form, to determine function, such inflected differentiation rarely occurs. (The same form, "slave," is used for the subject in EG 1 and for the object in EG 2 above), though we do show possession by using forms with an " 's": "the tree's leaves, the apostle's word." Inflection does occur regularly in the pronouns of English, however. Here we do use separate forms to express different functions:

   (EG 3)   "*He* sees the apostle." = subject

   (EG 4)   "*His* servant sees the apostle." = possession

   (EG 5)   "The apostle gave (to) *him* the book." = indirect object

   (EG 6)   "The apostle saw *him*." = direct object

   Note that the identical form is used for both indirect and direct object in English. Greek inflects all of its nouns, pronouns, and adjectives to convey various functions in the sentence.

2. Declension

   a. While Greek nouns, pronouns, and adjectives have different forms, the number of forms is not countless. In fact, the forms follow set patterns. A pattern of forms is called a *declension.* Since English is not a highly inflected language, it is difficult to illustrate this concept, but we may say that English nouns could be put into five different declensions (or follow five different patterns), depending on how their plurals are formed. Some nouns add "s" to form plurals (let us call this the "s" or "first" declension), e.g., tree, plural: trees; mother, plural: mothers. Others add "en" (the so-called "en" or "second" declension"), e.g., ox, plural: *oxen*. Others change internally for the plural (the "strong" or "third declension"), e.g., mouse, plural: *mice; goose*, plural: *geese*. Still others make no change at all (the "fourth declension"), e.g., moose, plural: moose; sheep, plural: sheep. And some follow the pattern of usage of foreign languages (the "foreign" or "fifth declension"), e.g., stimulus, plural: stimul*i*; antenna, plural: antenn*ae;* cherub, plural: cherub*im*. Note that subclassifications or variants of these categories can be found. Some "s" types add "es," e.g., watch, plural: watch*es*. Odd letters sometimes come in, e.g., knife, plural: kni*v*es; child, plural: chil*d*ren. And variants occur, e.g., octopus, plural: octopus*es or* octop*i*.

b. Greek, too, has set patterns, but the different endings for its nouns (pronouns) and adjectives) are more numerous since they indicate not only singular and plural but also especially, as we saw above (A 1), usage of words in a sentence.

B. Paradigm Forms: The O or Second Declension

1. Basic Pattern for Masculine and Feminine Nouns

	Singular	Plural
N	λόγος	λόγοι
G	λόγου	λόγων
D	λόγῳ	λόγοις
A	λόγον	λόγους

2. Slightly Varied Pattern for Neuter Nouns

	Singular	Plural
N	τέκνον	τέκνα
G	τέκνου	τέκνων
D	τέκνῳ	τέκνοις
A	τέκνον	τέκνα

C. Morphology

1. Categories of Form

Each noun form may be classified by *gender, number, and case.*

a. A noun, and therefore all of its forms, is masculine, feminine, or neuter (only one), and this is its *gender.*

b. A given form is either singular or plural, which is its *number.*

c. A given form has the endings of one of the four *cases* (nominative, genitive, dative, or accusative), depending on its function in the sentence, since form determines function (see A 1 above).

2. General Observations

a. Pertaining to *all* nouns (including those of the O declension)

(1) Every noun form contains a stem and an ending. For λόγος, e.g., λόγ- is the basic stem, while the letter combinations -ος, -ου, -ῳ, etc., provide the endings. In like manner, τέκν- is the stem for τέκνον.

(2) The genitive plural form of every noun ends with -ων.

(3) The dative form of every noun contains a ι somewhere, either subscript or adscript.

(4) Neuter nominative and accusative singular forms are always identical, as are neuter nominative and accusative plurals.

b. Pertaining specifically to O declension nouns

(1) The O or second declension comprises nouns that follow a pattern of forms characterized by an O vowel near the end of every word (i.e., in the ending).

(2) These are the O or second declension endings:

(a) Masculine and Feminine

	Singular	Plural
N	-ος	-οι
G	-ου	-ων
D	-ῳ	-οις
A	-ον	-ους

(b) Neuter

	Singular	Plural
N	-ον	-α
G	-ου	-ων
D	-ῳ	-οις
A	-ον	-α

3. Specific Observations

a. Masculine and feminine forms share the same pattern of endings in the O declension.

b. Neuter forms are identical to masculine and feminine forms in the genitive and dative, both singular and plural.

c. The only non-O vowel ending in the paradigms of this chapter is that for the neuter nominative and accusative plural, -α.

D. Accent

1. A second or O declension noun's accent conforms to the general rule for accenting. See chapter 2, A 4 a and b.

2. A noun of this declension does *not*, as does a verb, possess a *recessive* accent. Its accent stays on the same syllable as the nomina-

tive unless it is forced by the general rules of accenting to move. See chapter 2, A 4 b (2) (a) (i).

(EG 7)   ἄνθρωπος → ἀνθρώπου (ου in ultima is long)

(EG 8)   ἀργύριον → ἀργυρίῳ (ῳ in ultima is long)

Note that the accent changes syllable only when it begins on the antepenult (with a short ultima) and the ultima turns long. Then it moves one syllable to the right and stays acute. See chapter 2, A 4 c (2) (a).

3. O or second declension nouns may change type of accent but only under one of three cases.

   a. The accent begins on the penult as a circumflex. When the ultima turns long, the circumflex changes to an acute. See chapter 2, A 4 c (2) (b).

      (EG 9)   δοῦλος → δούλους (long ultima)

      (EG 10)   σημεῖον → σημείοις (long ultima)

   b. The accent begins on the ultima. *In such a case only,* a special pattern is followed:

	Singular	Plural
N	ἀδελφός	ἀδελφοί
G	ἀδελφοῦ	ἀδελφῶν
D	ἀδελφῷ	ἀδελφοῖς
A	ἀδελφόν	ἀδελφούς

      Note that an "inside-outside" pattern is established. The two "outside" forms, i.e., the nominative and accusative, carry the acute (in both singular and plural), while the two "inside" forms, i.e., the genitive and dative, carry the circumflex.

   c. If a word carries an acute on the ultima (i.e., an "outside" form of 3 b above), that accent will become a grave accent when a word follows.

      (EG 11)   ἀδελφὸς γράφει.

      Such a change does not occur at the end of a clause or when an acute is on another syllable.

      (EG 12)   ἀπόστολος βλέπει ἀδελφόν.

E. Syntax

1. Case Usage (Usage of Forms)

   a. The basic case usages are as follows:

      (1) Nominative is used for the *subject:*

(EG 13)   ἀδελφοὶ γράφουσιν.
          Brothers write.

(2) Genitive is used to show *possession:*

(EG 14)   ἀδελφοὶ δούλων γράφουσιν.
          Brothers *of slaves* write.

related to another noun

(3) Dative expresses *indirect object:*

(EG 15)   ἀδελφοὶ δούλων γράφουσιν
          ἀποστόλοις.
          Brothers of slaves write *to apostles.*

related to verb

(4) Accusative expresses *direct object:*

(EG 16)   ἀδελφοὶ δούλων γράφουσιν
          ἀποστόλοις νόμους.
          Brothers of slaves write (to) apostles *laws.*

related to verb

Another example using all four cases:

(EG 17)   ἄγγελος πέμπει ἀποστόλῳ λόγον
          ἀδελφοῦ.
          A messenger sends (to) an apostle a word of a
          brother.

b. Note that the *form* of each word *determines* its *function. Word order does not determine function,* as it does in English.

EG 17 above, e.g., might have been written as follows and still carry the same meaning.

(EG 18)   ἀποστόλῳ πέμπει ἄγγελος λόγον
          ἀδελφοῦ.

It carries the same meaning because ἀποστόλῳ, being dative, functions as the indirect object, not as the subject, even though it stands first in the sentence. Likewise, ἄγγελος is still the subject, even though it follows the verb, because its "ending" is nominative. Note that if we simply attach an equivalent basic English meaning to each word, ignoring case, the sentence as a whole changes in meaning. The sentence in EG 18, if translated woodenly, in interlinear fashion, would read:"An apostle sends a messenger a word of a brother"—totally the wrong meaning!

Principle: FORM DETERMINES FUNCTION.

2. Word Order

Greek word order is *not totally flexible,* though it is a good deal looser than that of English. The following *general* principles may be observed.

a. Whatever comes first in a sentence is the most emphatic. Thus EG 18, which reads

ἀποστόλῳ πέμπει ἄγγελος λόγον ἀδελφοῦ

would emphasize to *whom* a messenger sends a word, while

(EG 19)   λόγον ἀδελφοῦ πέμπει ἄγγελος ἀποστόλῳ

would emphasize *what* a messenger sends.

b. A genitive normally follows the thing it possesses (cf. EG 19).

c. Most Hellenistic Greek sentences have a fairly natural word order, i.e., the subject generally comes first.

d. Works influenced by Semitic (i.e., Hebrew or Aramaic) speech often begin sentences with the verb.

(EG 20)   πέμπει ἄγγελος ἀποστόλῳ λόγον ἀδελφοῦ.

3. The Subject of the Verb

a. The subject of a verb is in the nominative case. It agrees with the verb in number: singular verbs take singular subjects; plural verbs take plural subjects.

(EG 21)   ἀδελφὸς γράφει νόμον. (singular)

(EG 22)   ἀδελφοὶ γράφουσι νόμον. (plural)

b. When a subject is expressed (as in EGs 21 and 22), the third person verb form is used. When, then, does γράφει, e.g., mean "*he* writes," as we learned in chapter 3 (or, γράφουσι = "they write")? Only *when no subject is specifically expressed*.

F. Translation

At this point we have not had the definite article in Greek, so "the" should not be used in English translations in this chapter. Greek has no indefinite article, but English does *in the singular* ("a/an"), and it is usually best to use it in translation. Thus, EG 21 above is best translated "*A* brother writes *a* law," not "Brother writes law." By contrast, EG 22 is rendered simply "Brothers write laws," with no "a" or "an." (Compare also EGs 16 and 17).

G. Vocabulary

ἄγγελος ‐ου, m.: angel; messenger

ἀδελφός ‐οῦ, m.: brother

ἄνθρωπος ‐ου, m.: person, man (generic)

ἀπόστολος -ου, m.: apostle, ambassador

ἀργύριον -ου, n.: silver, money

ἄρτος -ου, m.: bread (pl. loaves of bread)

δαιμόνιον -ου, n.: demon

δοῦλος -ου, m.: slave, servant

εὐαγγέλιον -ου, n.: Gospel, good news

θεός -οῦ, m.: God, god

ἱμάτιον -ου, n.: cloak, piece of clothing (pl. clothing)

καί (conj.): and, also, even

λόγος -ου, m.: word; account; *reason*

νόμος -ου, m.: law

νόσος -ου, f.: disease

παρθένος -ου, f.: virgin, maiden

πλοῖον -ου, n.: boat

σημεῖον -ου, n.: sign

τέκνον -ου, n.: child

H. Exercise

Give the dative singular and accusative plural of each noun in the vocabulary.

I. Practice Sentences

1. Greek to English

a. θεραπεύω νόσους.

b. λόγοι ἀγγέλου σῴζουσιν ἀνθρώπους.

c. δαιμόνιον λείπει τέκνον.

d. πέμπει ἄρτους ἀνθρώποις.

e. σημεῖα βλέπομεν.

f. δοῦλος κλέπτεται ἀργύρια καὶ ἱμάτια.

g. ἀδελφῷ ἀπόστολοι γράφουσιν εὐαγγέλιον.

h. παρθένος νίπτεται καὶ ἀκούει λόγους θεοῦ.

2. English to Greek

   a. She heals diseases.

   b. An apostle writes words of God to a virgin.

   c. Children send clothing of a brother.

   d. Demons lead children for their own advantage.

J. Bible Passage

   1 Corinthians 1:23a . . . Χριστόν (omit ἡμεῖς δέ)

5

Nouns, Part 2, and Elementary Prepositions

A. Nouns, Part 2: The A or First Declension

1. Introduction

In chapter 4 we described the use of nouns in Greek, saying that they are inflected, i.e., have different endings to indicate their function in the sentence, and that their endings follow a set pattern, which pattern is called a declension. We now come to a new declension. Nouns of this declension will again have different forms for the various sentence functions, but the *pattern* of their endings will differ from that of the O declension.

2. Paradigm Forms

a. Basic Pattern

(1)   Singular   Plural   (2)   Singular   Plural

	Singular	Plural		Singular	Plural
N	ἡμέρα	ἡμέραι		ἀγάπη	ἀγάπαι
G	ἡμέρας	ἡμερῶν		ἀγάπης	ἀγαπῶν
D	ἡμέρᾳ	ἡμέραις		ἀγάπῃ	ἀγάπαις
A	ἡμέραν	ἡμέρας		ἀγάπην	ἀγάπας

(3)

	Singular	Plural
N	δόξα	δόξαι
G	δόξης	δοξῶν
D	δόξῃ	δόξαις
A	δόξαν	δόξας

b. Slightly Varied Masculine Pattern

	Singular	Plural
N	προφήτης	προφῆται
G	προφήτου	προφητῶν
D	προφήτῃ	προφήταις
A	προφήτην	προφήτας

ὁ picas

↓ ≤ιρικα

3. Morphology

a. General Observations

(1) The A or first declension comprises nouns that follow a pattern of forms characterized by an "a" or long "e" (η) vowel near the end of the word.

(2) All A or first declension nouns follow the same pattern of endings in the plural:

> Plural
> N   -αι
> G   -ων
> D   -αις
> A   -ας

(3) There are *no neuter* nouns in the A or first declension.

b. Specific Observations

(1) The singular forms of the A declension follow one of three basic patterns:

(a) The a pattern, with an a as its characteristic vowel:

> Singular (cf. ἡμέρα)
> N   -α
> G   -ας
> D   -ᾳ
> A   -αν

(b) The η pattern, with an η as its characteristic vowel:

> Singular (cf. ἀγάπη)
> N   -η
> G   -ης
> D   -ῃ
> A   -ην

(c) The "hybrid" pattern, which combines characteristics of each:

> Singular (cf. δόξα)
> N   -α
> G   -ης
> D   -ῃ
> A   -αν

(2) The following rules are followed to determine the pattern for the singular forms of A or first declension nouns:

(a) If a noun has an η as the last letter of its first form (i.e, nominative singular), it will be η pattern (cf. ἀγάπη).

(b) If a noun has an a as the last letter of its first form, then

    (i) if the last letter of the stem (i.e., the letter before the a) is a vowel or ρ, it will be a pattern throughout (cf. *ἡμέρα*).

    (ii) if the last letter of the stem is a consonant other than ρ, the "hybrid" pattern will be followed (a in nominative and accusative, η in genitive and dative) (cf. *δόξα*).

(c) It may also be observed that nouns whose stems end in ϵ, ι, or ρ are always a pattern.

(3) Masculines of the A declension basically follow the η pattern (cf. A 2 b) in the singular. Note that the first two forms are slightly different; indeed the genitive singular exhibits O declension characteristics. Only a few a pattern[1] and no "hybrid" pattern masculines are found.

(4) Syllable length

(a) Nouns that begin with a short a have a short a in the accusative singular:

    (EG 1)   N *θάλασσα*

                   A *θάλασσαν*

(b) The genitive and dative singular a (if it appears) is always long:

    (EG 2)   G *ἀληθείας*

                   D *ἀληθείᾳ*

(c) The accusative plural $a\varsigma$ is always long:

    (EG 3)   *ἀληθείας*

    (EG 4)   *θαλάσσας*

4. Accent

a. Nouns of the A or first declension follow the same rules for accenting as those of the O or second declension (see chapter 4, D).

(1) Note again the movement to the right of the accent of words originally accented on the antepenult.

                    Singular

    (EG 5)   N *θάλασσα*

                   G *θαλάσσης* (long ultima)

                   D *θαλάσσῃ*   (long ultima)

                   A *θάλασσαν*

(2) Note also the "inside outside" pattern of those nouns accented on the ultima:

	Singular	Plural
(EG 6)	N ἐντολή	ἐντολαί
	G ἐντολῆς	ἐντολῶν
	D ἐντολῇ	ἐντολαῖς
	A ἐντολήν	ἐντολάς

b. All first declension nouns (including masculines) have an unusual *genitive* plural accent: ῶν (regardless of the original syllable of accent).

(EG 7)   θάλασσα → θαλασσῶν

(EG 8)   ἡμέρα → ἡμερῶν

(EG 9)   ἐντολή → ἐντολῶν

(EG 10)   προφήτης → προφητῶν

5. Syntax

No new syntax need be learned for the A or first declension nouns. As in the O declension, nominatives are used for the subject of a sentence, genitives to show possession, datives to express indirect object, and accusatives to express direct object (see chapter 4, E 1 a).

B. Elementary Prepositions

1. Introduction

a. Prepositions express the relationship between two things in a sentence. Usually, the two things related are a verb and a noun (or pronoun):

(EG 11)   "The boy ran through the forest."

In this sentence, "through" tells the relationship between "ran" and "forest." (Other relationships are possible besides the one expressed, e.g., "The boy ran *around* the forest.") When a preposition so relates a verb and noun (or pronoun), its usage is *adverbial* (it tells something more about the verbal action, e.g., where, when, etc.). All examples in these early chapters (until chapter 12) are adverbial.

b. A preposition "governs" the noun (or pronoun) that it relates to a verb (see EG 11). In English, this "governed" noun (or pronoun), the so-called "object" of the preposition, is in the accusative, or direct object, case.

(EG 12)   "I am in the *tree*." (accusative)

(EG 13)   "He is with *her*." (accusative: not "He is with *she*.")

(EG 14)   "She is before *him*." (accusative: not "She is before *he*.")

2. Greek Prepositions

a. Basic Theory

Prepositions in Greek function the same as do those in English, i.e., they (usually) link a noun (or pronoun) with a verb. Their chief difference lies in the case of the noun (or pronoun) governed. Unlike English, in which all "objects" of prepositions are in the accusative case, the object of a given preposition in Greek may be in the genitive, the dative, or the accusative case (the "oblique" cases). (Some prepositions "govern" several cases, each case expressing a separate meaning with that preposition. See chapter 13.) So, e.g.,

(EG 15)   εἰς θάλασσαν = "into a sea"

(EG 16)   ἐν θαλάσσῃ = "in a sea"

(EG 17)   ἀπὸ θαλάσσης = "from a sea"

(EG 18)   πρὸς θάλασσαν = "to(ward) a sea"

(EG 19)   σὺν θαλάσσῃ = "with a sea"

(EG 20)   ἐκ θαλάσσης = "out of a sea"

In the phrases above, "sea" is technically in the accusative case in English, yet only θάλασσαν in EGs 15 and 18 is accusative in Greek. The reason for this is that the object of the prepositions εἰς and πρός is expressed in the accusative, but the object of ἐν and σύν is expressed in the dative, and the object of ἀπό and ἐκ is expressed in the genitive. In common grammatical parlance, εἰς and πρός "take the accusative," ἐν and σύν "take the dative," and ἀπό and ἐκ "take the genitive."

b. Case Selection

While the cases governed by individual prepositions are not always predictable, a *basic pattern* is followed. Generally speaking, the *genitive* is used when expressing ideas of *source* (ἐκ) or *movement away from* (ἀπό), the *dative* for *location* (ἐν) or *association* (σύν), and the *accusative* for motion toward (πρός) or *into* (εἰς). Note the following chart:

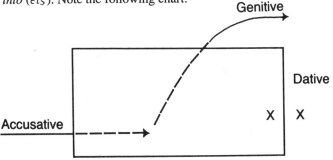

c. Syntax

The object of a preposition normally follows the preposition directly. Verbs, indirect objects, etc., do not intervene.

d. Accent

Prepositions such as εἰς, ἐκ, and ἐν (as well as other words) are *proclitic,* i.e., they "lean forward" (πρό + κλίνω = "I lean forward") onto the word following for accenting purposes.

C. Vocabulary

ἀγάπη ⁻ης, f.: love

ἀλήθεια ⁻ας, f.: truth

ἀπό (prep.+ gen.): from

δικαιοσύνη ⁻ης, f.: righteousness, justice

δόξα ⁻ης, f.: glory

    δοξάζω (R): I glorify

εἰς (prep.+ acc.): into; for (purpose, result)

ἐκ (prep. + gen.): out of (ἐξ before a vowel following)

ἐκκλησία ⁻ας, f.: church; assembly

ἐν (prep. + dat.): in; on (temporal, not local); among (group of people)

ἐντολή ⁻ῆς, f.: commandment

ἡμέρα ⁻ας, f.: day

θάλασσα ⁻ης, f.: sea, lake

κώμη ⁻ης, f.: village

μαθητής ⁻οῦ, m.: disciple

περισσεύω (R): I abound

πρός (prep. + acc.): to, toward

προφήτης ⁻ου, m.: prophet

σύν (prep. + dat.): with (in the company of)

D. Exercises

1. Give gender, number, and case:

   a. *ἐκκλησίαις*   f. *ἀγάπῃ*

   b. *ἐντολῆς*   g. *προφήτης*

   c. *θαλάσσαις*   h. *μαθητῇ*

   d. *κώμας*   i. *ἡμέρας*

   e. *δόξαι*

2. Give the genitive singular, dative singular, and accusative plural:

   a. *προφήτης*   c. *δόξα*

   b. *ἐντολή*   d. *ἀλήθεια*

E. Practice Sentences

1. Greek to English

   a. *παρθένοι πέμπουσιν ἄρτους εἰς κώμας.*

   b. *σὺν μαθηταῖς δοξάζομεν ἐντολὰς θεοῦ.*

   c. *δοῦλος ἄγει τέκνα ἐκ κώμης πρὸς θάλασσαν.*

   d. *σώζετε ἀνθρώπους ἀπὸ δαιμονίων.*

   e. *ἡμέραι ἀποστόλων περισσεύουσιν ἐν ἀγάπῃ καὶ δόξῃ.*

   f. *προφῆται γράφουσιν ἀληθείας ἀγγέλῳ.*

   g. *θεὸς πέμπεται ἀλήθειαν καὶ διδαιοσύνην ἀνθρώποις.*

2. English to Greek

   a. Prophets see boats in villages.

   b. Virgins abound in love and truth.

   c. Apostles send bread to churches.

F. Bible Passage

   1 Corinthians 13:13a . . . *ἀγάπη* (omit *δέ*, *πίστις*, and *ἐλπίς*)

Note

1. The only common first declension masculine of the *α* pattern in the New Testament is the word for "young man": *νεανίας, νεανίου, νεανίᾳ, νεανίαν*. The plural is normal.

6
Basic Adjectives and the Article

A. Introduction

Thus far, we have used nouns without modifying adjectives. We have said:

(EG 1)   "I see a slave" $(\beta\lambda\acute{\epsilon}\pi\omega \ \delta o\hat{v}\lambda ov)$.

but we have not said:

(EG 2)   "I see a *good* slave."

Also, we have only used nouns alone, without the definite article ("the"). We have said "I see a slave" (EG 1) or

(EG 3)   "I see slaves" $(\beta\lambda\acute{\epsilon}\pi\omega \ \delta o\acute{v}\lambda ov\varsigma)$.

but we have not said:

(EG 4)   "I see *the* slave(s)."

In this chapter, we will be introduced to both the adjective and the definite article, each a "modifier" of the noun.

B. The Adjective

1. Paradigm Forms

a. Basic Adjective with Feminine Singular Following η Pattern

Singular

	M	F	N
N	ἀγαθός	ἀγαθή	ἀγαθόν
G	ἀγαθοῦ	ἀγαθῆς	ἀγαθοῦ
D	ἀγαθῷ	ἀγαθῇ	ἀγαθῷ
A	ἀγαθόν	ἀγαθήν	ἀγαθόν

Plural

	M	F	N
N	ἀγαθοί	ἀγαθαί	ἀγαθά
G	ἀγαθῶν	ἀγαθῶν	ἀγαθῶν
D	ἀγαθοῖς	ἀγαθαῖς	ἀγαθοῖς
A	ἀγαθούς	ἀγαθάς	ἀγαθά

b. Basic Adjective with Feminine Singular Following a Pattern

Singular

	M	F	N
N	δίκαιος	δικαία	δίκαιον
G	δικαίου	δικαίας	δικαίου
D	δικαίῳ	δικαίᾳ	δικαίῳ
A	δίκαιον	δικαίαν	δίκαιον

Plural

	M	F	N
N	δίκαιοι	δίκαιαι	δίκαια
G	δικαίων	δικαίων	δικαίων
D	δικαίοις	δικαίαις	δικαίοις
A	δικαίους	δικαίας	δίκαια

2. Morphology

a. *Each adjective has three sets of forms,* one for each gender. It is apparent that the masculine and neuter forms of the basic adjective follow an O or second declension pattern, while the feminine forms follow an A or first declension pattern. (For this reason, these adjectives are often called "second declension," or "first and second declension" adjectives.) The logic of this patterning is sound. There are no neuters in the A or first declension, so the O pattern is the only one available for neuter adjective forms. Most other nouns in the O or second declension are masculine (perhaps four or five to one—note the vocabulary for chapter 4). It is, therefore, reasonable that this declension provide the endings for masculine forms of the adjectives. Likewise, most A or first declension nouns are feminine (note the vocabulary in chapter 5). It is, therefore, reasonable that this declension provide the endings for the feminine forms of the adjective.

b. The feminine forms of the basic adjectives follow either an η or an a pattern (cf. A declension). No "hybrid" patterns are found. The rule is this:

> If the stem of the adjective ends with a vowel or ρ, the feminine singular endings contain an a (long). If it ends in a consonant other than ρ, the endings contain an η.

Note: The stem is determined by removing the ⁻ος from the masculine, nominative, singular form.

3. Accent

a. Adjectives are accented as are nouns. Thus, an accent stays on its "nominative" syllable (the masculine singular is the key), unless the general rules force it to change.

b. The genitive plural of all feminine forms is *not* accented on the ultima ($\omega\nu$) as are A or first declension nouns.

4. Syntax

a. Basics of Usage

(1) In our largely uninflected English language, an adjective is put next to the word it modifies, and it does not change form to conform to the noun's gender, number, and case.

> (EG 5) "I see a *good* slave" ("good" and "slave" are each masc., acc., sing.).
>
> (EG 6) "I see a *good* virgin" ("good" and "virgin" are each fem., acc., sing.).
>
> (EG 7) "I see a *good* boat" ("good" and "boat" are each neut., acc., sing.).
>
> (EG 8) "I see *good* boats" ("good" and "boats" are each neut., acc., pl.).

Note that the same basic form, "good," is used in each case.

(2) In Greek, such simplicity is not possible. In Greek, each adjective "agrees" with the noun it "modifies" (i.e., tells something more about) in gender, number, and case.

> (EG 9) "I see a *good* slave" = $\beta\lambda\acute{\epsilon}\pi\omega$ $\mathring{a}\gamma a\theta\grave{\underline{o}\nu}$ $\delta o\hat{u}\lambda o\nu,$

but

> (EG 10) "I see *good* boats" = $\beta\lambda\acute{\epsilon}\pi\omega$ $\mathring{a}\gamma a\theta\underline{\grave{a}}$ $\pi\lambda o\hat{i}a.$

(3) Does this mean that adjectives carry the same endings as the nouns they modify? Unfortunately, *no*. While in a significant number of cases they do (see EGs 9 and 10), most frequently they do not. The reason for this is that adjectives have a specific set of forms, one for each gender, number, and case, and they use those forms, *and only those forms,* to modify the various noun forms. Thus,

(a) $\mathring{a}\gamma a\theta\acute{o}\varsigma$ is the masculine, nominative, singular form of the adjective "good." This form is used to modify *any* masculine nouns in the nominative singular.

> (EG 11) $\mathring{a}\gamma a\theta\grave{o}\varsigma$ $\lambda\acute{o}\gamma o\varsigma$ = "a good word."
>
> (EG 12) $\mathring{a}\gamma a\theta\grave{o}\varsigma$ $\pi\rho o\phi\acute{\eta}\tau\eta\varsigma$ = "a good prophet."
>
> (EG 13) $\mathring{a}\gamma a\theta\grave{o}\varsigma$ $\beta a\sigma\iota\lambda\epsilon\acute{u}\varsigma$ = "a good king" (third declension noun).

(b) ἀγαθή is the feminine, nominative, singular form of the adjective "good." This form is used to modify *any* feminine noun in the nominative singular.

(EG 14)   ἀγαθὴ ἀγάπη = "a good love."

(EG 15)   ἀγαθὴ ἡμέρα = "a good day."

(EG 16)   ἀγαθὴ δόξα = "a good glory."

(EG 17)   ἀγαθὴ παρθένος = "a good virgin."

(EG 18)   ἀγαθὴ νύξ = "a good night"
                              (third declension noun).

(c) ἀγαθόν is the neuter, nominative, singular form of the adjective "good." This form is used to modify *any* neuter noun in the nominative singular.

(EG 19)   ἀγαθὸν τέκνον = "a good child."

(EG 20)   ἀγαθὸν σῶμα = "a good body"
                              (third declension noun).

b. Examples

It is important to realize that an adjective "matches" its noun in *gender, number,* and *case* only, not necessarily in ending. Each word has its own set of endings. Note the following examples (all are in the singular):

(EG 21)   N ἔσχατος λόγος
          G ἐσχάτου λόγου
          D ἐσχάτῳ λόγῳ
          A ἔσχατον λόγον

(EG 22)   N ἔσχατος προφήτης
          G ἐσχάτου προφήτου
          D ἐσχάτῳ προφήτῃ
          A ἔσχατον προφήτην

(EG 23)   N ἐσχάτη κώμη
          G ἐσχάτης κώμης
          D ἐσχάτῃ κώμῃ
          A ἐσχάτην κώμην

(EG 24)   N ἐσχάτη ἡμέρα
          G ἐσχάτης ἡμέρας
          D ἐσχάτῃ ἡμέρᾳ
          A ἐσχάτην ἡμέραν

(EG 25)   N ἐσχάτη παρθένος
          G ἐσχάτης παρθένου
          D ἐσχάτῃ παρθένῳ
          A ἐσχάτην παρθένον

(EG 26)   N δικαία κώμη
          G δικαίας κώμης
          D δικαίᾳ κώμῃ
          A δικαίαν κώμην

(EG 27)   N δικαία ἡμέρα
          G δικαίας ἡμέρας
          D δικαίᾳ ἡμέρᾳ
          A δικαίαν ἡμέραν

(EG 28)   N δικαία παρθένος
          G δικαίας παρθένου
          D δικαίᾳ παρθένῳ
          A δικαίαν παρθένον

C. The Article

1. The Forms of the Article

Singular

	M	F	N
N	ὁ	ἡ	τό
G	τοῦ	τῆς	τοῦ
D	τῷ	τῇ	τῷ
A	τόν	τήν	τό

Plural

	M	F	N
N	οἱ	αἱ	τά
G	τῶν	τῶν	τῶν
D	τοῖς	ταῖς	τοῖς
A	τούς	τάς	τά

2. Morphology

Note the similarity between the article and the adjective.

a. The masculine forms are like regular adjective forms of the masculine, with τ in place of the stem:

		Singular	Plural
(EG 29)	D	ἀγαθῷ	ἀγαθοῖς
	D	τῷ	τοῖς

The only exception is the nominative plural, which has no τ, and the nominative singular, which has no τ or ς (ὁ instead of τός).

b. The feminine forms are the regular adjective forms of the feminine, again with the τ in place of the stem. Only the η pattern is followed.

		Singular	Plural
(EG 30)	D	ἀγαθῇ	ἀγαθαῖς
	D	τῇ	ταῖς

Note that for this gender, both the nominative singular and plural lack the τ.

c. The neuter forms are like the regular adjective forms for the neuter, again with τ in place of the stem.

		Plural
(EG 31)	N	ἀγαθά
	N	τά

Note that the only irregularity is τό instead of a theoretical τόν in the nominative and accusative singular.

3. Accent

Several forms of the article contain no accent. These are "proclitics." (See chapter 5, B 2 c).

4. Syntax

a. Basics of Usage

(1) it is important to realize that the article is, technically, an adjective, and as such functions as one. It also, therefore, agrees with the noun it modifies in gender, number, and case. In English, its forms do not change:

(EG 32)   "I see *the* slave" ("the" and "slave" are each masc., acc., sing.).

(EG 33)   "I see *the* virgin"("the" and "virgin" are each fem., acc., sing.).

(EG 34)   "I see *the* boat" ("the" and "boat" are each neut., acc., sing.).

(EG 35)   "I see *the* boats" ("the" and "boats" are each neut., acc., pl.).

Note that the same basic form, "the," is used in each case.

(2) In Greek, such simplicity is not possible. As with other adjectives, each article agrees with the noun it modifies in *gender, number,* and *case.* Thus

(EG 36)   "I see *the* slave" = βλέπω <u>τὸν</u> δοῦλον, but

(EG 37)   "I see *the* boats" = βλέπω <u>τὰ</u> πλοῖα.

(3) Again, the same endings are not always used for the article as are used for the noun it modifies. Rather, a set pattern of forms is used for the masculine article, another set pattern for the feminine article, and another set pattern for the neuter.

b. Examples

As with the regular adjective, the article "matches" the noun it modifies in *gender, number,* and *case* only, not necessarily in ending. Note the following examples in the singular:

(EG 38)   N ὁ λόγος   (EG 39)   N ὁ προφήτης
           G τοῦ λόγου   G τοῦ προφήτου
           D τῷ λόγῳ   D τῷ προφήτῃ
           A τὸν λόγον   A τὸν προφήτην

(EG 40)   N ἡ κώμη   (EG 41)   N ἡ ἡμέρα
           G τῆς κώμης   G τῆς ἡμέρας
           D τῇ κώμῃ   D τῇ ἡμερᾳ
           A τὴν κώμην   A τὴν ἡμέραν

(EG 42)   N ἡ παρθένος   (EG 43)   N τὸ τέκνον
          G τῆς παρθένου   G τοῦ τέκνου
          D τῇ παρθένῳ   D τῷ τέκνῳ
          A τὴν παρθένον   A τὸ τέκνον

c. The use of the article and adjective together.

(1) When a noun is modified by an article, the article normally appears directly before it.

(EG 44)   <u>ὁ δοῦλος</u> βλέπει <u>τὸν ἀπόστολον</u>.
          The slave sees *the apostle*.

When a noun is modified by an article and an adjective *together*, the *adjective* normally stands *directly after* the *article*.

(EG 45)   <u>ὁ ἀγαθὸς</u> δοῦλος βλέπει <u>τὸν
          ἔσχατον</u> ἀπόστολον.
          The good slave sees *the last* apostle.

The two adjectives in EG 45 are attributes of the nouns they modify and are said to be in "attributive position."

(2) The adjectives in EG 45 are in the more normal attributive position, i.e., between article and noun (as meat in a sandwich!). Another type of attributive position is also possible:

(EG 46)   ὁ δοῦλος <u>ὁ ἀγαθὸς</u> βλέπει τὸν
          ἀπόστολον <u>τὸν ἔσχατον</u>.
          The good slave sees *the last* apostle.

Note that in EG 46 each adjective is still *directly after the article,* but now the article must be repeated, since the adjective is placed after the noun it modifies. (If the article were not repeated, e.g., ὁ δοῦλος ἀγαθὸς . . . τὸν ἀπόστολον ἔσχατον, the two adjectives would no longer be in attributive position. This matter will be discussed in chapter 12.)

(3) Is there a difference in meaning between the two types of attributive positions? In our literature, there is not. The "sandwich" position (EG 45) is more normal in classical Greek, which means that the "repeat" position (EG 46) may be used for emphasis. There is some evidence, however, that the "repeat" position was favored by authors who were either Semites by birth or influenced by Semitic linguistic structure, which means that, in the New Testament, no significant difference is evident.

Note: It is not necessary to have an article with an adjective to put it into attributive position if the noun it modifies has no article. See B 4 a above.

D. Vocabulary

ἀγαθός -ή -όν: good

ἅγιος -α -ον: holy

ἄξιος -α -ον: worthy

δίκαιος -α -ον: just, righteous

ἔσχατος -η -ον: last

'Ιησοῦς -οῦ, m.: Jesus[1]

κακός -ή -όν: bad

καλός -ή -όν: beautiful; noble

καρδία -ας, f.: heart

κόσμος -ου, m.: world

μικρός -ά -όν: small

οἶκος -ου, m.: house; household

οὐκ (adv): not (οὐ before consonant, οὐχ before aspirated vowel)

πείθω (r): I persuade

πλούσιος -α -ον: rich

πονηρός -ά -όν: evil, wicked

πρῶτος -η -ον: first

υἱός -οῦ, m.: son[2]

E. Exercise

Decline the following phrases through each case in singular and plural:

1. ἡ πρώτη κώμη

2. ὁ καλὸς προφήτης

3. ἡ ἁγία παρθένος

F. Practice Sentences

1. Greek to English

a. οἱ πρῶτοι ἀπόστολοι καὶ οἱ ἔσχατοι προφῆται κηρύσσουσι τὸ εὐαγγέλιον τῷ κόσμῳ.

b. θεραπεύει ὁ 'Ιησοῦς τὰς νόσους τὰς κακὰς τῶν ἀξίων τέκνων.

    c. τὰ πονηρὰ δαιμόνια λείπονται τὰς καλὰς παρ-
θένους ἐν τῇ μικρᾷ κώμῃ.

    d. ὁ ἄγγελος ὁ ἅγιος οὐ πείθει τὰς καρδίας τῶν
πλουσίων ἀνθρώπων.

    e. ἄγει ὁ υἱὸς τοῦ ἀνθρώπου τὸ δίκαιον καὶ ἀγαθὸν
τέκνον ἐξ οἴκου εἰς τὴν ἐκκλησίαν.

2. English to Greek

    a. The prophet persuades the heart of the holy disciple.

    b. Jesus preaches the Gospel to evil people.

    c. The good son sees the bread of Jesus and sends money to a small
village.

G. Bible Passages

John 18:28a . . . πραιτώριον (omit οὖν)

Luke 5:33a οἱ μαθηταὶ . . . νηστεύουσιν

Use 1   *Use 2*

Substantive

articular   (a) particular   (c) categorical
              1 Cor 13:13; ἡ ἀγάπη   Lk 10:7; ὁ ἐργάτης
                                           1 Tim 3:2; τὸν ἐπίσκ

anarthrous   (b) nonparticular   (d) individual
               (qualitative)   Jn. 4:27; μετὰ γυνα
               Jn 1:14; χάριτος
               καὶ ἀληθείας

a + d are similar; b + c are similar
Conclusion: matters of particularity + individuality
are established not the basis of presence of the
article, but on wider context.   Stanley Porter, Idioms
                                 Notes   of the Greek New Testam

---

1. "Jesus" is declined slightly irregularly: Ἰησοῦς, Ἰησοῦ, Ἰησοῦ, Ἰησοῦν. This
noun is normally used with the article, as is the word for God (θεός).

2. The common New Testament phrase "the son of man" is ὁ υἱὸς τοῦ ἀνθρώπου.

7

The Verb, Part 2, and Deponent Verbs

A. The Verb, Part 2: Future Indicative Active and Middle

1. Introduction

In chapter 3 (A 1 b), we said that the *stem* of the verb *determines* (in addition to a verb's basic meaning) its *tense*. We now come to a new tense, so the stem of the verb will be changed. It should be noted that we have *not* changed mood (indicative) or voice (active or middle) for these forms.

2. Paradigm Forms

a. Future Indicative Active

(1) λύω

	Singular		Plural	
1	λύσω (λύσομι)	I will loose	λύσομεν	We will loose
2	λύσεις (λύσεσι)	You will loose	λύσετε	You will loose
3	λύσει (λύσετι)	He (she, it) will loose	λύσουσι(ν) (λύσονται)	They will loose

(2) λείπω

	Singular		Plural	
1	λείψω (λείψομι)	I will leave	λείψομεν	We will leave
2	λείψεις (λείψεσι)	You will leave	λείψετε	You will leave
3	λείψει (λείψετι)	He (she, it) will leave	λείψουσι(ν) (λείψονται)	They will leave

b. Future Indicative Middle

(1) λύω

	Singular			Plural
1	λύσομαι	I will loose for myself	λυσόμεθα	We will loose for ourselves
2	λύσῃ (λύσεσαι)	You will loose for yourself	λύσεσθε	You will loose for yourselves
3	λύσεται	He (she, it) will loose for himself	λύσονται	They will loose for themselves

(2) λείπω

	Singular			Plural
1	λείψομαι	I will leave for myself	λειψόμεθα	We will leave for ourselves
2	λείψῃ (λείψεσαι)	You will leave for yourself	λείψεσθε	You will leave for yourselves
3	λείψεται	He (she, it) will leave for himself	λείψονται	They will leave for themselves

3. Morphology

a. Stem

All forms are future tense; therefore, the stems of both the active and the middle forms of each verb are identical. The stem is characterized by a final σ (sigma). The general principle (i.e., that which characterizes regular or predictable verbs) is that present tense verb stems that end in a vowel (e.g., λύω) simply add the σ directly to the basic stem. Consonantal stem verbs (e.g., λείπω), by contrast, add the σ to the last consonant. Then the following results obtain:

Stems ending in:

Guttural = κ, γ, χ, or σσ[1] add σ to produce ξ
Labial = π, β, φ, or ππ add σ to produce ψ
Dental = τ, δ, θ, or ζ add σ to produce σ

Note that in the first two cases (guttural and labial or equivalents), a compound consonant results (ξ and ψ respectively), while with dentals (or ζ), the dental consonant is driven out by the σ.

(EG 1) διώκω → διώξω   (EG 7) διώκομαι → διώξομαι

(EG 2) ἄγω → ἄξω   (EG 8) ἄγομαι → ἄξομαι

(EG 3) πέμπω → πέμψω   (EG 9) πέμπομαι → πέμψομαι

(EG 4) γράφω → γράψω   (EG 10) γράφομαι → γράψομαι

(EG 5) $\pi\epsilon i\theta\omega \rightarrow \pi\epsilon i\sigma\omega$ (EG 11) $\pi\epsilon i\theta o\mu\alpha\iota \rightarrow \pi\epsilon i\sigma o\mu\alpha\iota$

(EG 6) $\dot{\alpha}\gamma o\rho\dot{\alpha}\zeta\omega \rightarrow \dot{\alpha}\gamma o\rho\dot{\alpha}\sigma\omega$ (EG 12) $\dot{\alpha}\gamma o\rho\dot{\alpha}\zeta o\mu\alpha\iota \rightarrow \dot{\alpha}\gamma o\rho\dot{\alpha}\sigma o\mu\alpha\iota$

A verb may, however, be *irregular* in its formation of the future stem. Then the form produced is not predictable, i.e., formed along the lines of the general principles enunciated above, but must simply be learned by observation. In such cases, a σ is normally present, but the rest of the stem is, to some degree, different from that of the present tense.

(EG 13) $\alpha\dot{\upsilon}\xi\dot{\alpha}\nu\omega \rightarrow \alpha\dot{\upsilon}\xi\dot{\eta}\sigma\omega$

b. Connecting Vowel

The standard connecting vowel pattern is retained for future forms (see chapter 3, C 2 c), since all forms are still indicative mood.

c. Endings

The future is a *primary* tense, i.e., not essentially concerned with the past (see chapter 3, C 3 a (3)). As a result, it uses the normal primary endings, as did the present tense. Note that the active endings are used for active forms, the middle endings for middle forms. Note also that the same contraction between connecting vowels and endings, observed in the present tense (see chapter 3, C 3 b (1)), takes place in the active singular forms of the future, and in the second person singular of the middle.

d. Accent

The accent for future tense verb forms is, as normal, recessive.

B. Deponent Verbs

1. Definition

Deponent verbs are verbs that have "laid aside" (Latin: *depono* = "I lay aside") their active forms and now use only forms of (normally) the middle voice in all tenses. (A few passive deponents will be encountered later; these use only passive forms.)

2. Interpretation

Deponent verbs have *middle forms* but a purely *active* meaning.

(EG 14) $\delta\dot{\epsilon}\chi o\mu\alpha\iota$ = "I receive," not "I receive for myself." (There is no form $\delta\dot{\epsilon}\chi\omega$.)

(EG 15) $\dot{\epsilon}\rho\gamma\dot{\alpha}\zeta o\mu\alpha\iota$ = "I work," not "I work for myself." (There is no form $\dot{\epsilon}\rho\gamma\dot{\alpha}\zeta\omega$.)

3. Then how does one say, "I receive for myself"? *Another vocable must be used.*

(EG 16)   λαμβάνομαι = "I receive (get) for myself."

4. It may be noted that most deponent verbs seem to carry the idea of self-interest or advantage almost inherently. This may be seen with a verb such as δέχομαι (= "I receive").

5. Future Deponents

A number of verbs are *deponent in the future tense only* (usually called "future deponents").

(EG 17)   λαμβάνω → λήμψομαι

(EG 18)   πίνω → πίομαι

(EG 19)   φεύγω → φεύξομαι

Sometimes such future deponents are "regular" in their stem formation (cf. EG 19), but usually they are irregular in stem as well (cf. EGs 17 and 18).

C. Principal Part

As we have seen above (cf. A 3 a and B 5), a number of verbs have *irregular* basic future forms (i.e., the basic future form cannot be produced predictably), sometimes because no σ is present in the stem (cf. EG 18), but usually because the stem (less σ) is not identical to the present stem (cf. EGs 13 and 17). In addition, some verbs with regular (predictable) future stems are deponent (cf. EG 19). Therefore, the basic future form of a Greek verb must be noted, and if it is unpredictable for any reason (i.e., it has an irregular stem and/or is deponent), it must be learned. The basic future form, then, is the second *principal part* of a Greek verb.

D. Vocabulary

ἀγοράζω (R): I buy

αὐξάνω, αὐξήσω (R)[2]: I increase (transitive and intransitive)

βαίνω, βήσομαι[3]: I go, step, walk

γάρ (conj.—postpositive[4]): because, for

γινώσκω, γνώσομαι[3]: I know

δέχομαι (M) (R): I receive

διδάσκω, διδάξω (r)[2]: I teach

διώκω (r): I pursue; persecute

δῶρον -ου, n.: gift

ἐργάζομαι (M) (R): I work

    ἐργάτης ‑ου, m.: workman

    ἔργον ‑ου, n.: work

ἱερόν ‑οῦ, n.: temple

λαμβάνω, λήμψομαι: I get; take

οἶνος ‑ου, m.: wine

πίνω, πίομαι: I drink

προσ‑εύχομαι (M) (R): I pray

φεύγω, φεύξομαι: I flee

φυλάσσω (r): I guard; keep

E. Exercises

1. Give the second person singular future indicative active and the third person singular future indicative middle of the following:

    a. ἀκούω

    b. κηρύσσω

    c. ἀγοράζω

2. Give the proper third person plural (indicative) form of the second principal part of the following:

    a. βαίνω

    b. φεύγω

    c. πίνω

    d. λαμβάνω

    e. δέχομαι

    f. γινώσκω

    g. προσ‑εύχομαι

F. Practice Sentences

1. Greek to English

    a. ἡ ἀγάπη τῶν ἐκκλησιῶν αὐξάνει καὶ αὐξήσει.

    b. βήσεται εἰς τὴν πρώτην κώμην καὶ ἀγοράσει ἄρτους.

    c. προσ‑εύξομαι τῷ ᾽Ιησοῦ καὶ ἀκούσει.

d. πιόμεθα οἶνον σὺν τοῖς ἀγαθοῖς ἐργάταις καὶ φυλά-
   ξομεν τοὺς λόγους τοὺς ἐσχάτους τῶν προφητῶν.

e. γινώσκετε τὴν ἀλήθειαν τοῦ θεοῦ; γνώσεσθε ἐν τῇ
   ἡμέρᾳ τοῦ υἱοῦ τοῦ ἀνθρώπου.

f. αἱ ἅγιαι παρθένοι ἐργάζονται ἐν τῇ μικρᾷ κώμῃ καὶ
   βαίνουσιν ἐν ταῖς ἐντολαῖς τοῦ θεοῦ.

g. τοῖς τέκνοις διδάξω τὰς ἀληθείας τοῦ εὐαγγελίου.

h. οἱ μαθηταὶ τοῦ Ἰησοῦ φεύξονται εἰς τὸ ἱερόν, οἱ
   γὰρ πονηροὶ προφῆται διώκουσιν ἁγίους ἀνθρώπους.

i. δέξονται τὰ κακὰ τέκνα δῶρα καλά; οὐ λήμψονται
   δῶρα.

2. English to Greek

a. The works of the Law will not save people; the gift of God saves
   from demons.

b. The children will take break out of the temple and (will) flee
   into the last house.

G. Bible Passages

John 8:32a . . . ἀλήθειαν

Acts 9:11b ἰδού . . . (C)[5]

1 Corinthians 3:8b ἕκαστος . . . λήμψεται (omit δέ)

Notes

1. Double sigma (σσ) conceals a guttural.

2. These verbs display the indicated regularity *after* the first principal part.

3. These are two very old but common verbs with unusual aorists, which will be introduced,
   not in chapter 8, but in chapter 27. For the next 20 chapters, therefore, only the present and
   future stems will be used.

4. A postpositive is a word that cannot stand first in a clause but is normally placed immediately after (Latin *postpositivus* = "placed after") the first word of the clause.

5. (C) means that a compound verb, unhyphenated, occurs in the passage. (Cs) means more
   than one compound.

8

The Verb, Part 3: Aorist Indicative Active and Middle

A. Introduction

As in chapter 7, we are introduced in this chapter to another new tense. Again, because it is a new tense, the stem will be changed. The aorist is, however, concerned with the past, and it is, therefore, a *secondary* tense. As a result, new endings will be encountered. The aorist is the basic past tense.

B. Paradigm Forms

1. Strong (Second) Aorist (λείπω)

a. Aorist Indicative Active

	Singular			Plural	
1	ἔλιπον	I left	ἐλίπομεν	We left
2	ἔλιπες	You left	ἐλίπετε	You left
3	ἔλιπε(ν)	He (she, it) left	ἔλιπον	They left

b. Aorist Indicative Middle

	Singular		Plural	
1	ἐλιπόμην	I left for myself	ἐλιπόμεθα	We left for ourselves
2	ἐλίπου (ἐλίπεσο)	You left for yourself	ἐλίπεσθε	You left for yourselves
3	ἐλίπετο	He (she, it) left for himself	ἐλίποντο	They left for themselves

2. Weak (First) Aorist (λύω)

a. Aorist Indicative Active

	Singular		Plural	
1	ἔλυσα	I loosed	ἐλύσαμεν	We loosed
2	ἔλυσας	You loosed	ἐλύσατε	You loosed
3	ἔλυσε(ν)	He (she, it) loosed	ἔλυσαν	They loosed

b.   Aorist Indicative Middle

Singular		Plural	
1 ἐλυσάμην	I loosed for myself	ἐλυσάμεθα	We loosed for ourselves
2 ἐλύσω (ἐλύσασο)	You loosed for yourself	ἐλύσασθε	You loosed for yourselves
3 ἐλύσατο	He (she, it) loosed for himself	ἐλύσαντο	They loosed for themselves

C. Morphology

1. Strong (Second) Aorist

It is important to realize that the strong (or, second) aorist is the "typical" form for the aorist tense. It is not necessarily the more numerous, but the way it is formed conforms to the basic rules of Greek verb structure, and as such, is much more revealing and informative. We will, therefore, deal with it first.

a. Stem

The stem of the strong aorist is different from either present or future forms, thereby reflecting a different tense. While a few strong aorist stems are longer than the present stem, the vast majority are one or several letters shorter (cf. λείπ ω → ἔ λιπ ον). Note: STRONG AORIST STEMS ARE UNPRE-DICTABLE.

b. Augment

To show action in the historical past, Greek augments its verbs.

(1) Generally, this is done by *adding an ἐ to the front to the appropriate stem.*

	Present	Aorist
(EG 1)	λείπω	ἔλιπον
(EG 2)	πίνω	ἔπιον

(2) Verbs beginning with vowels do not add an ἐ (which would create terrible hiatus!); rather, they lengthen the initial letter as a substitute for the augment, with the ι of a diphthong going subscript and the υ of a diphthong remaining as is. The following pattern is followed:

Single Vowels	Diphthongs with ι	Diphthongs with υ
ἐ → η	οι → ῳ	αυ → ηυ
ο → ω	αι → ῃ	ευ → ηυ
α → η		
ι → ῑ		
υ → ῡ		

Note: $\epsilon\iota$ remains $\epsilon\iota$. $\epsilon\upsilon$ may remain $\epsilon\upsilon$.

	Present	Aorist
(EG 3)	ἄγω	ἤγαγον
(EG 4)	οἰκοδομέω	ᾠκοδόμησα[1]
(EG 5)	αἰτέω	ᾔτησα[1]
(EG 6)	αὐξάνω	ηὔξησα[1]
(EG 7)	προσ-εύχομαι	προσ-ηυξάμην[1]
(EG 8)	εὑρίσκω	εὗρον

Note: The *stem* of a compound is augmented (cf. EG 7).

c. Connecting Vowel

The connecting vowels for the strong aorist are normal (see chapter 3, C 2 c).

d. Endings

The aorist is a tense concerned with the past—a *secondary tense*—and for this reason it uses secondary, rather than primary, endings. (All of the verb endings we have had thus far have been primary.) The strong (second) aorist illustrates these well:

(1) Active Voice

	Singular	Plural
1	-ν	-μεν
2	-ς	-τε
3	-	-ν

(2) Middle Voice

	Singular	Plural
1	-μην	-μεθα
2	-ου [σο]	-σθε
3	-το	-ντο

In the second person singular of the middle voice, the σ between the ϵ connecting vowel and the final o elides, producing ov.

(Note that the first singular and third plural of the active voice have identical endings.)

e. Accent

The accent, as normal, is recessive. Note that these forms illustrate well that the accent does not always fall on the verbal stem, as it tends to do in the present and future forms.

2. **Weak (First) Aorist**

a. Stem

The form of this type of aorist, while easy to identify with its characteristic a connecting vowel (see c below), is deceiving, because it does not conform to the basic rules of Greek verb structure. Note that the stem (not considering the augment) ends in σ and *is the same as the future stem!* The only distinguishing characteristics between the two tenses are the augment and the α following the σ. Here, strictly speaking, a different stem is not used to distinguish tense. Note: WEAK AORIST STEMS ARE GENERALLY PREDICTABLE.

b. Augment

Weak or first aorist forms augment according to the same rules as do strong aorists. (See EGs 4–7 above.)

c. Connecting Vowel

This is the distinguishing mark of the weak or first aorist. Note that in the active, the third person singular changes α to ϵ, no doubt in conformity with the more normal secondary pattern. Note also the ω contraction in the second singular middle form.

d. Endings

The endings for weak or first aorists basically follow the normal secondary pattern, especially in the middle voice. Note that the active forms, while normal in the plural, are abnormal in the singular, where we *would expect:*

1   ἔλυσα<u>ν</u>
2   ἔλυσα<u>ς</u>
3   ἔλυσα<u> </u>

The actual first singular form, ἔλυσα (i.e., without the ν ending), is easily distinguishable from the third plural form, and this, no doubt, influenced the change of the third singular from ἔλυσ<u>α</u> to ἔλυσ<u>ε</u>.

e. Accent

Accent is recessive as normal. (Because recessive accent is standard, we will not, generally, comment on it for remaining verb forms.)

D. Meaning and Form

1. The difference between a strong (second) and weak (first) aorist is purely morphological. Each simply produces its form in a different manner. *The strong aorist changes letters internally.* We do the same in English:

(EG 9)   λείπω → ἔλιπον, cf. "leave" → "left"

A weak aorist adds a characteristic letter to produce its form, in this case α (after σ). Again, we do the same in English:

(EG 10)   λύω → ἔλυσα, cf. "loose" → "loosed"

There is no difference in meaning or expression (i.e., each is the simple past tense of its verb).

2. A verb has, with very rare exceptions, *either* a strong (second) *or* a weak (first) aorist, *not both*.

E. Principal Part

Because the basic aorist form of Greek verbs is not always predictable (it may be either weak or strong), the following general observations will be helpful:

1. If the basic aorist form of a verb is *predictable*, its formation is *weak*, which means that its stem will be identical to the future stem, ending with a σ, and it will use an a connecting vowel following the σ.

2. If a verb's basic aorist form is *not predictable*, its formation is *strong*, which means that its stem will be different from the future stem and will not normally end with a σ. Its connecting vowels will follow the normal o/ϵ pattern.

The aorist indicative active (or middle, if it is deponent) form of a Greek verb is, then, its *third principal part*.

F. Vocabulary

ἀλλά (conj.): but (~~strong~~) *emphatic*

δέ (conj.—postpositive): and; but (~~weak~~) *unemphatic*

ἐκεῖ (adv.): there

ἐπαγγελία -ας, f.: promise

κύριος -ου, m.: lord, the Lord

νῦν (adv.): now

πρόβατον -ου, n.: sheep

Here following are the strong (second) aorists of *the* several irregular verbs that we have already met:

1	2	3
ἄγω	ἄξω	ἤγαγον
λαμβάνω	λήμψομαι	ἔλαβον
λείπω	λείψω	ἔλιπον
πίνω	πίομαι	ἔπιον
φεύγω	φεύξομαι	ἔφυγον

In addition to the vocables above, learn the common verbs in the chart below, all of which have strong (second) aorists. Note that all also have some irregularity in the second principal part (which is often deponent).

1	2	3	
ἁμαρτάνω	ἁμαρτήσω	ἥμαρτον	I sin
ἔρχομαι	ἐλεύσομαι	ἦλθον	I come, go
ἐσθίω	φάγομαι	ἔφαγον	I eat
εὑρίσκω	εὑρήσω	εὗρον	I find
λέγω	ἐρῶ[2]	εἶπον[3]	I say
πάσχω	πείσομαι	ἔπαθον	I suffer
πίπτω	πεσοῦμαι[2]	ἔπεσον	I fall
τίκτω	τέξομαι	ἔτεκον	I bear (a child)
φέρω	οἴσω	ἤνεγκον	I bear, carry, take along

G. Exercise

Give the third person singular present, future, and aorist indicative active and middle of the verbs in the chart above (omit ἔρχομαι, λέγω, and πίπτω) and of σώζω and ἀκούω.

H. Practice Sentences

1. Greek to English

a. ἡ παρθένος ἔτεκε τὸν Ἰησοῦν, ὁ δὲ Ἰωσὴφ[4] ἤνεγκε τὸ τέκνον εἰς Αἴγυπτον.

b. οἱ μαθηταὶ ἔφυγον ἀπὸ τῶν πλουσίων ἐργατῶν, ἔπεσον δὲ εἰς τὴν θάλασσαν.

c. ἥμαρτον, ἀλλὰ δέξομαι δικαιοσύνην ἀπὸ τοῦ κυρίου.

d. ὁ νόμος οὐ σώζει, ἡ δὲ ἐπαγγελία τοῦ εὐαγγελίου πείσει πονηρὰς καρδίας.

e. ἠγοράσαμεν ἄρτους καὶ οἶνον, καὶ σὺν ταῖς παρ-θένοις ἤλθομεν εἰς τὸ ἱερόν, ἐκεῖ δὲ ἐφάγομεν καὶ ἐπίομεν.

f. προσ-ηύξατο καὶ ἐθεράπευσεν τὴν νόσον τοῦ δούλου τοῦ ἀγαθοῦ καὶ εἶπεν· ἔπαθες, νῦν δὲ περισσεύσεις ἐν τοῖς τοῦ κυρίου ἔργοις.

[margin note: Transposed word order in classical common in high GK. + in Koine like style Luke]

g. τοὺς δούλους ἔλιπον ἐν τῷ οἴκῳ, τὰ δὲ πρόβατα ἤγαγον εἰς τὴν κώμην.

h. οἱ δοῦλοι εὗρον τὸ καλὸν ἱμάτιον τῆς παρθένου καὶ τὸ ἀργύριον, τὸ δὲ ἀργύριον ἐλάβοντο.

2. English to Greek

a. The last prophet proclaimed the promise to men.

b. You led the virgins into the church and they found the Lord.

I. Bible Passages

Rom. 4:11a . . . περιτομῆς

Acts 9:9b καὶ οὐκ . . .

Mark 1:9b ἦλθεν . . . Γαλιλαίας

Apocalypse 8:10a . . . ἀστήρ

Notes

1. For the terminations of these examples, see section 2 d below (weak aorist).

2. These forms will be met later and thus will not appear in the next several chapters.

3. The ϵι of this form is not an augment but part of the stem proper. See C 1 b (2) above.

4. Words underlined in the practice sentences should be decipherable, even though they have not been encountered previously.

9

Aspect and the Verb, Part 4

A. Aspect (Focus Relative to Action)

1. In both English and Greek, two factors are part of any verbal action. On the one hand, there is *time,* usually called "tense," and with this we are familiar. Less familiar but equally important, especially in Greek, is "aspect." Aspect is concerned with the *focus the speaker/writer has when considering an activity*—specifically, whether that speaker's/writer's focus is upon the act itself or upon a perceived relationship between the activity and the doer of the activity, particularly a close relationship or connection. "Focus on the action" emphasizes the action itself, while "focus upon connection" emphasizes the "bond" or "linkage" between the doer and the activity. The following are examples in English of these two types of action:

Focus on the Action:

(EG 1)   "I *see* you."

(EG 2)   "I *went* away."

Focus upon Connection:

(EG 3)   "I *am tending* the sheep now."

(EG 4)   "I *was going* home when I fell down."

(EG 5)   "I *used to go* dancing."

(EG 6)   "I *arise daily* at seven A.M."

Notice that in the "focus on the action" sentences (EGs 1–2), *what* is happening is uppermost, while the "focus upon connection" examples (EGs 3–6) emphasize that there is a close union between the subject and the act expressed. In these latter four cases, the subject either is or was *engaged in the activity* (EGs 3–4), or he engaged in or engages in the activity *habitually* (EGs 5–6), almost as if it were part of him. (There are other types of "connection" [cf. B 4 b below], but these are the two most common.)

2. Aspect and Morphology

a. In English, aspectual differences are reflected by the way in which the verb is constructed and modified. The basic verb form is used to focus on the action (EGs 1–2), while an auxiliary verb (EGs 3–5) or an adverb (EG 6) conveys a focus upon connection.

b. In Greek, such differentiation takes place via the *verb stem*. One stem is used to focus on the action, another to focus upon a perceived connection between the action and the doer of that action. To be specific, the use of the so-called "aorist" stem allows the speaker to focus—from his own point of view—upon *what* someone did, does, is to do, etc. (cf. simple expression of past act, chapter 8), while the so-called "present" stem allows that same speaker to focus upon the *relationship* between the activity and the doer and to depict it as part of him or to depict him as intimately involved in and concerned with it.[1]

It is for this reason that, while we have, heretofore, translated λύω as "I loose" and λείπω as "I leave," it is also possible, and indeed, *preferable,* to translate them as "I *am loosing*" and "I *am leaving.*" Such a translation (properly) portrays the action as closely connected to the actor—he is thoroughly involved in it or continuously doing it. What, then, about λύω = "I *loose*" or λείπω = "I *leave*" (cf. also EG 1)? Do these statements focus upon the action? Actually, it may be observed that *even this use of the "present tense,"* whether in English or in Greek, *really focuses upon connection,* though its simple form may seem to focus upon the action. Consider the following statements.

(EG   7)   "I leave the check."

(EG   8)   "I go to the store."

(EG   9)   "We come."

(EG 10)   "He visits us."

Most, if not all, of the time such statements, which seem to focus on the action, are *used in contexts* which, in fact, focus upon a connection between the action and its doer.

(EG 11)   "I leave the check *on the first of the month.*"

(EG 12)   "I go to the store *every Friday.*"

(EG 13)   *"Don't refuse us!* We come *bearing gifts!"*

(EG 14)   *"Whenever he can get away,* he visits us."

It is proper to say, then, that when Greek uses the so-called "present" stem, it focuses upon a perceived connection between an action and the doer of that action.

c. How, then, does Greek focus upon connection *in past time*? As we have seen in chapter 8, the so-called "aorist tense" (indicative mood) conveys past action; now we may add "with a focus on the action involved": ($ἔλιπον$ = I left; $ἔλυσα$ = I loosed). *Focus upon connection in the past,* logically enough, is conveyed by a "past time" form of the so-called "present" stem, what we are now describing as the "focus upon connection" stem. This is regularly called the "imperfect tense."

B. The Verb, Part 4: Imperfect Indicative Active and Middle

1. Introduction

Focus upon connection between actor and action in past time is conveyed by the so-called *"imperfect tense."* The imperfect is built off of the "present"—actually the "focus upon connection"—stem, and to show that it deals with the past, it is augmented and carries secondary endings. Note: So-called "present tense" forms are actually primary forms of the "focus upon connection" stem, which forms convey action not in past time.

2. Paradigm Forms

a. $λείπω$

(1) Imperfect Indicative Active

	Singular			Plural	
1	$ἔλειπον$	I was leaving	$ἐλείπομεν$	We were leaving
2	$ἔλειπες$	You were leaving	$ἐλείπετε$	You were leaving
3	$ἔλειπε(ν)$	He (she, it) was leaving	$ἔλειπον$	They were leaving

(2) Imperfect Indicative Middle

	Singular			Plural	
1	$ἐλειπόμην$	I was leaving for myself	$ἐλειπόμεθα$	We were leaving for ourselves
2	$ἐλείπου$ ($ἐλείπεσο$)	You were leaving for yourself	$ἐλείπεσθε$	You were leaving for yourselves
3	$ἐλείπετο$	He (she, it) was leaving for himself	$ἐλείποντο$	They were leaving for themselves

b. λύω

    (1) Imperfect Indicative Active

	Singular		Plural	
1	ἔλυον	I was loosing	ἐλύομεν	We were loosing
2	ἔλυες	You were loosing	ἐλύετε	You were loosing
3	ἔλυε(ν)	He (she, it) was loosing	ἔλυον	They were loosing

    (2) Imperfect Indicative Middle

	Singular		Plural	
1	ἐλυόμην	I was loosing for myself	ἐλυόμεθα	We were loosing for ourselves
2	ἐλύου (ἐλύεσο)	You were loosing for yourself	ἐλύεσθε	You were loosing for yourselves
3	ἐλύετο	He (she, it) was loosing for himself	ἐλύοντο	They were loosing for themselves

3. Morphology

a. Stem

We have noted (B 1 above) that the stem of the imperfect is the "present," i.e., the "focus upon connection" stem. This is most appropriate for what is conveyed. Note the difference in stem between the imperfect and the aorist of a strong verb such as λείπω (see chapter 8, B 1 a–b). *The stem is all that distinguishes these two sets of forms.*

b. Augment

The imperfect, concerned as it is with the past, is augmented, as is the aorist. The principles of augmentation are identical (see chapter 8, C 1 b).

c. Connecting Vowel

The normal ε/ο connecting vowel system is used for the imperfect forms. Note the similarity to the strong aorist (cf. λείπω). Verbs with a weak or first aorist are quite different here.

    (EG 15)   ἐλύομεν vs. ἐλύσαμεν

d. Endings

Normal secondary endings are used, again illustrating the "normality" of the strong (second) aorist vs. the weak (first) aorist.

4. Meaning

a. It must be stressed that *the imperfect is not "less past" than the aorist.* The only difference between the two "tenses" is *aspect,* i.e., focus relative to action.

b. The imperfect may focus upon the following kinds of (perceived) "connection" between doer and activity:

(1) Continuous

(EG 16)   ἔλυον = "I *was* loosing."

(2) Habitual

(EG 17)   ἔλυον = "I *used* to loose."

(3) Inceptive (beginning)

(EG 18)   ἔλυον = "I *began* to loose" (a connection was established).

(4) Conative (attempting)

(EG 19)   ἔλυον = "I *tried* to loose" (I put myself into making a connection).

(5) Repetitive

(EG 20)   ἔλυον = "I *repeatedly* loosed."

(6) Emphatic

(EG 21)   ἔλυον = "I *did* loose."

Only *context* will determine which of the six possibilities is most appropriate in a given case.

C. Vocabulary

ἀγρός ⁻οῦ, m.: field; countryside

ἀπ-άγω, etc.[2]: I drive, lead away

ἀπ-έρχομαι, etc.[2]: I go (come) away

ἀπο-θνῄσκω, ἀπο-θανοῦμαι,[3] *ἀπ-έθανον*[2]: I die

βασιλεία ⁻ας, f.: kingdom

βιβλίον ⁻ου, n.: book

ἔρημος ⁻ου, f.:desert

καθαρίζω (R): I purify

λῃστής ⁻οῦ, m.: robber, bandit

ὁράω,[3] *ὄψομαι, εἶδον*: I see (Note the augment of εἶδον. ἰδ- is the basic stem of the third principal part.)

ὄχλος ⁻ου, m.: crowd

παραβολή ⁻ῆς, f.: parable

D. Exercise

Make the corresponding *imperfect* for each verb form in the translation section of chapter 8 (H 1 a–h).

E. Practice Sentences

1. Greek to English

(Be sure to determine a type of connection for each imperfect form.)

a. αἱ παρθένοι ἐνίπτοντο ἐν τῷ ἀγρῷ.

b. οἱ μαθηταὶ εἶδον τὸν κύριον σὺν τοῖς δούλοις.

c. ὁ λόγος τῆς βασιλείας ἐκαθάριζε πονηρὰς καρδίας.

d. οἱ λησταὶ ηὕρισκον ἀργύρια ἐν τῇ ἐκκλησίᾳ, οἶνον δὲ εὗρον.

e. ὁ Ἰησοῦς ἀπ‑ῆλθεν εἰς Γαλιλαῖαν, καὶ ἐκεῖ ἐκήρυσσε τὸ εὐαγγέλιον καὶ ἐθεράπευε νόσους.

f. ὁ Ἰησοῦς ἔλεγε καλὰς παραβολάς, οἱ δὲ ὄχλοι οὐκ ἤκουον.

g. οἱ ἀπόστολοι ἔγραφον ἅγια βιβλία καὶ ἔπεμπον ταῖς ἐκκλησίαις.

h. τὰ πρόβατα λῃστὴς ἀπ‑ήγαγεν ἀπὸ τῆς κώμης εἰς τὴν ἔρημον, ἐκεῖ δὲ ἀπ‑έθανον.

2. English to Greek

a. You (pl.) were healing children.

b. The robbers used to steal the money out of the temple.

c. We went away and began to hear the words of God.

F. Bible Passages

Acts 12:24a . . . ηὔξανεν

Mark 14:53a . . . Ἰησοῦν (C)

Luke 20:31b οἱ . . . (Cs)

Acts 9:20a . . . Ἰησοῦν

G. Afterword

It can now be observed that the term "tense" is quite misleading and almost useless. The word itself means "time," but verb forms in the indicative mood convey both a focus relative to action/"aspect" *and* time. Thus, present "tense" = focus upon connection + present time; imperfect "tense" = focus upon connection + past time; aorist "tense" = focus on the action + past time, etc.

For future reference, *verb forms outside the indicative mood* (such as infinitives, participles, subjunctives, etc.) *will not convey time at all, only focus relative to action/"aspect,"* so that for them, any talk of "tense" will be unrelated to time and, therefore, strictly speaking, inappropriate. Indeed, from this point onward, *when the names of the so-called "tenses" occur in quotation marks* (e.g., "present," "aorist"), *it means that no factor of time is to be attached to the forms in question.*[4]

Notes

1. Two further possibilities must be noted. The so-called "perfect" stem focuses upon an action's result, the state that follows the completion of an activity. Forms built off of it are introduced in chapters 25 and 26. The "future" stem is more difficult to analyze. It may be said to focus upon intention relative to action not as yet performed, but its heavy temporal component—virtually all forms convey action actually in the future—makes this explanation less than fully satisfactory.

   For discussions of aspect from slightly different points of view, see Buist M. Fanning, *Verbal Aspect in New Testament Greek,* Oxford: University Press, 1990 and Stanley E. Porter, *Verbal Aspect in the Greek of the New Testament: With Reference to Tense and Mood,* New York: Peter Lang, 1989.

2. When a preposition is connected to a verbal stem to form a compound verb (cf. προσ-εύχομαι, chapter 7), it will elide its last letter, when that letter is a short vowel (see chapter 1, E 1), if the stem proper (a) begins with a vowel (cf. ἀπ-άγω, ἀπ-έρχομαι) or (b) is augmented to form an aorist or imperfect (cf. ἀπ-έθανον).

   Compound verbs may convey (a) a logical compound meaning (cf. ἀπ-άγω, ἀπ-έρχομαι, or προσ-εύχομαι) or (b) no special or extra nuance (cf. ἀπο-θνήσκω). Some convey quite different and unusual meanings or an intensified meaning, and these will be met in succeeding chapters.

   In Koine Greek, the preposition is often *repeated* in the syntax of the sentence.

   Note: The accent of a compound verb does not generally recede back into the preposition: ἀπ-ῆγον (not ἄπ-ηγον).

3. These forms will be met later.

4. When "tense" words occur in a discussion of various stems (e.g., "present" stem, "aorist" stem), they will be in quotation marks because any given stem possesses no notion of time in and of itself, only "aspect" or focus (cf. sections A 2 c, B 1, and B 3 a above). It must be recognized, however, that such a "timeless" stem will often be used to produce indicative mood forms (such as the imperfect), which do, by definition, carry a notion of time.

10

Personal Pronouns

A. Introduction

1. A pronoun is a word that "stands for" (pro) or in place of a noun.

   (EG 1) "The virgin is coming and I see *her*."

   "Her" in this example stands in place of "virgin" in the second clause.

2. The noun whose place the pronoun takes is the "antecedent." In EG 1, "virgin" is the antecedent of "her."

3. A pronoun agrees with its antecedent in *gender* and *number,* but not necessarily in case. Thus, in EG 1, "her" is feminine and singular, as is "virgin," but "virgin," as the subject of its clause, is nominative, while "her" is accusative, functioning as the object of the verb "see."

B. Personal Pronoun Forms

1. First Person

	Singular			Plural	
N	ἐγώ	(I)		ἡμεῖς	(we)
G	ἐμοῦ / μου	(my)		ἡμῶν	(our)
D	ἐμοί / μοι	([to] me)		ἡμῖν	([to] us)
A	ἐμέ / με	(me)		ἡμᾶς	(us)

2. Second Person

	Singular			Plural	
N	σύ	(you)		ὑμεῖς	(you)
G	σοῦ / σου	(your)		ὑμῶν	(your)
D	σοί / σοι	([to] you)		ὑμῖν	([to] you)
A	σέ / σε	(you)		ὑμᾶς	(you)

3. Third Person

Singular

M		F		N	
N	[αὐτός]	[αὐτή]		[αὐτό]	
G	αὐτοῦ (his)	αὐτῆς (her)		αὐτοῦ (its)	
D	αὐτῷ ([to] him)	αὐτῇ ([to] her)		αὐτῷ ([to] it)	
A	αὐτόν (him)	αὐτήν (her)		αὐτό (it)	

Plural

M		F		N	
N	[αὐτοί]	[αὐταί]		[αὐτά]	
G	αὐτῶν (their)	αὐτῶν (their)		αὐτῶν (their)	
D	αὐτοῖς ([to] them)	αὐταῖς ([to] them)		αὐτοῖς ([to] them)	
A	αὐτούς (them)	αὐτάς (them)		αὐτά (them)	

C. Morphology

1. The two forms of the first and second person singular personal pronouns in the oblique cases are the emphatic (accented) and unemphatic (unaccented) forms. (See D 1 a below.)

2. The difference between the first and second person plural forms is only the initial letter: ἡ vs. ὑ.

3. αὐτός, -ή, -ό is declined like the regular adjective (see chapter 6, B 1 a). It is the only person of the personal pronoun with separate forms for each gender. Note the neuter, which is not αὐτόν (as is the adjective, e.g., ἀγαθό*ν*) but αὐτό, with no final ν. This is similar to the neuter article, τό, and is *the pattern for all pronouns.*

D. Syntax

1. Preliminary Considerations

a. The first and second person singular personal pronouns use the accented forms in the oblique cases only if emphasis is desired or in prepositional phrases. Note the following examples:

(EG 2)   ὁ Ἰησοῦς ἔσωσεν ἐμέ.
Jesus saved *me.*

(EG 3)   ἦλθε πρὸς ἐμέ (not πρός με).
He came *to me.*

b. The nominative forms of these same pronouns are also used only for emphasis:

(EG 4)   ἐγὼ βλέπω σε.
I see you.

c. All of the nominative forms of αὐτός are bracketed because in the nominative this word is not simply a personal pronoun (e.g., "he," "she," "it," "they"). Rather, in the nominative it has other uses (see chapter 40).

2. Basic Usage

a. A personal pronoun in Greek, as in English, *agrees with its antecedent in gender and number, but not necessarily in case.* (See A 3 above.)

(EG 5) ἡ <u>παρθένος</u> ἔρχεται καὶ βλέπω <u>αὐτήν</u>.
The *virgin* is coming and I see *her.* (Cf. EG 1.)

(EG 6) ὁ <u>δοῦλος</u> ἦλθεν, καὶ πέμψω ἀργύριον <u>αὐτῷ</u>.
The *slave* came, and I will send money *to him.*

(EG 7) εἶδον τὰ <u>πλοῖα,</u> καὶ ἠγόρασα <u>αὐτά</u>.
I saw the *boats* and I bought *them.*

In EG 5, αὐτήν is feminine and singular, as is παρθένος, but it is accusative, as the object of βλέπω, while παρθένος is nominative, since it is the subject of ἔρχεται. In EG 6, αὐτῷ functioning as the indirect object, must be in the dative case, though its antecedent, δοῦλος, is a nominative subject. In EG 7, πλοῖα is neuter, plural, accusative, as is the pronoun αὐτά. Note that a plural antecedent demands a plural pronoun. They are the same case only incidentally.

b. A personal pronoun *matches gender with its antecedent in its own language.*

(EG 8) εἶδον τὸν καλὸν <u>οἶκον</u> καὶ ἠγόρασα <u>αὐτόν</u>.
I saw the beautiful *house* and I bought *it.*

In Greek, "house," the antecedent of the pronoun, is masculine. For this reason, αὐτόν—masculine—must be used. In English, "house" is neuter. As a result, in a translation, we use the pronoun "it," not "him." Another example:

(EG 9) γινώσκω τὴν <u>ἀλήθειαν,</u> καὶ κηρύσσω <u>αὐτήν</u>.
I know the *truth* and I proclaim *it.*

c. A *translation* of a personal pronoun in a prepositional phrase *must consider the case usage of each language after that preposition.*

(EG 10) οἱ <u>λῃσταὶ</u> διώκουσιν ἡμᾶς, καὶ φεύγομεν ἀπ' <u>αὐτῶν</u>.
The *robbers* are pursuing us, and we are fleeing from *them.*

In Greek, ἀπό, meaning "from," takes the genitive. In English, "from" *and every other preposition* "takes the accusative." Therefore, in our translation, we must use the accusative of the third person personal pronoun, "them." It would be wrong to translate the last clause: "and we are fleeing from *their*." αὐτῶν does not show possession, even though it is genitive. *It is genitive because* ἀπό *requires the genitive.* Another example:

(EG 11)   βλέπω πρόβατα ἐν τῷ <u>ἀγρῷ</u>, καὶ ἄξω
          αὐτὰ ἐξ <u>αὐτοῦ</u>.
          I see sheep in the field, and I will lead them out
          of *it*.

Note that here αὐτοῦ cannot be translated "its" (or "his").

E. Accent

The unaccented forms of the first and second person singular pronouns are "enclitics." This means that they "lean on" (ἐν + κλίνω = "I lean on") the word preceding. One-syllable enclitics never carry an accent, but they may cause a preceding word to add an accent or to change a grave to an acute. The instructor will provide further material on this subject. See also Donald A. Carson, *A Student's Manual of New Testament Greek Accents.* Grand Rapids, MI, Baker, 1985, 47–52.

F. Vocabulary

ἀπο-καλύπτω (R): I reveal

ἀπο-λύω (R): I release; dismiss

διάβολος -ου, m.: devil

διδάσκαλος -ου, m.: teacher

    διδαχή -ῆς, f.: teaching

μυστήριον -ου, n.: mystery

ὅτι (conj.): because

οὐδέ (adv.): and not; neither, nor

οὐρανός -οῦ, m.: heaven; sky

πότε (adv.): When?

ποῦ (adv.): Where?

πρό (prep. + gen.): before (of time and space)

πῶς (adv.): How?

συνέδριον ⁻ου, n.: Sanhedrin

τελώνης ⁻ου, m.: tax collector

Note: Do not forget the personal pronouns as vocabulary.

G. Exercise

Translate the following short sentences:

1. βλέπω σε.
2. βλέπω ὑμᾶς.
3. βλέπεις με.
4. βλέπεις ἡμᾶς.
5. γινώσκω τὸν ἀδελφόν σου.
6. γινώσκεις τὸν ἀδελφόν μου.
7. βλέπω προφήτην καὶ γινώσκω αὐτόν.
8. γινώσκω τὸν νόμον καὶ φυλάσσω αὐτόν.
9. βλέπω αὐτόν.
10. βλέπω αὐτήν.
11. βλέπω αὐτό.
12. πέμπω τὸ ἱμάτιον αὐτῷ.
13. πέμπω τὸ ἱμάτιον αὐτῇ.
14. πέμπω τὸ ἱμάτιον αὐτῆς.
15. πέμπω τὸ ἱμάτιον αὐτοῖς.
16. ἔρχομαι σὺν ὑμῖν.
17. ἔρχομαι πρὸς ὑμᾶς.
18. φεύγω ἀπὸ σοῦ.

H. Practice Sentences

1. Greek to English

a. πότε οἱ διδάσκαλοι εὗρον τὸν τελώνην καὶ ἀπ⁻έλυσαν αὐτόν;

b. ποῦ ὁ διάβολος ἀπ⁻εκάλυπτε τὸ μυστήριον τῆς βασιλείας αὐτοῦ;

c. πῶς εἰς τοὺς οὐρανοὺς ὁ ᾽Ιησοῦς ἀπ⁻ῆλθεν;

d. αἱ διδαχαὶ αἱ πονηραὶ τοῦ συνεδρίου οὐ πείσουσί με.

e. οἱ ἔσχατοι ἀπόστολοι ἀπ-έθανον πρὸ τῆς ἡμέρας
   τοῦ κυρίου.

f. οἱ λῃσταὶ ἔφευγον ἀπ᾽¹ἐμοῦ εἰς τὴν ἔρημον, ἀλλ᾽¹
   ἐγὼ ἤγαγον αὐτοὺς ἐξ αὐτῆς πρὸς ὑμᾶς.

g. ἀπ-έθνῃσκεν ὁ πλούσιος τελώνης, ὅτι οὐκ ἤσθιεν,
   οὐδὲ ἔπινεν.

h. ἐν τῷ ἱερῷ οἱ μαθηταὶ εἶδον παρθένον καὶ ἔπεμψαν
   αὐτῇ δῶρον.

i. ὑμεῖς οὐ γινώσκετε ἡμᾶς, ἡμεῖς δὲ γινώσκομεν
   ὑμᾶς.

2. English to Greek

a. We heard the teachings of the evil prophets, but we do not accept
   (receive) them.

b. The robbers release the slave, but the Lord pursued them.

I. Bible Passages

Matthew 22:16a . . . αὐτῶν (C)

Galatians 4:14b ἀλλὰ . . .

Mark 2:13b ὁ ὄχλος . . .

John 15:16a . . . ὑμᾶς (Cs)

Note

1. Note the elision of a short vowel before a vowel following (see chapter 1, E 1).

11

The Verb, Part 5:
The Passive Voice

A. Introduction

Passive voice verbs are verbs whose subject is not the doer of the action, or perhaps better, not the *agent of* the action described; rather, that subject is acted on by someone or something else. In English, the agent of the activity of such a verb form, i.e., the one responsible for the action, is expressed by a prepositional phrase with the preposition "by."

B. Paradigm Forms

1. "Focus upon Connection"/"Present" Stem

a. Present Indicative Passive

(1) λύω

	Singular			Plural	
1	λύομαι	I am being loosed	λυόμεθα	We are being loosed
2	λύῃ (λύεσαι)	You are being loosed	λύεσθε	You are being loosed
3	λύεται	He (she, it) is being loosed	λύονται	They are being loosed

(2) λείπω

	Singular			Plural	
1	λείπομαι	I am being left	λειπόμεθα	We are being left
2	λείπῃ (λείπεσαι)	You are being left	λείπεσθε	You are being left
3	λείπεται	He (she, it) is being left	λείπονται	They are being left

b. Imperfect Indicative Passive

(1) λύω

	Singular		Plural	
1	ἐλυόμην	I was being loosed	ἐλυόμεθα	We were being loosed
2	ἐλύου (ἐλύεσο)	You were being loosed	ἐλύεσθε	You were being loosed
3	ἐλύετο	He (she, it) was being loosed	ἐλύοντο	They were being loosed

(2) λείπω

	Singular		Plural	
1	ἐλειπόμην	I was being left	ἐλειπόμεθα	We were being left
2	ἐλείπου (ἐλείπεσο)	You were being left	ἐλείπεσθε	You were being left
3	ἐλείπετο	He (she, it) was being left	ἐλείποντο	They were being left

2. "Focus on the Action"/"Aorist" Stem: Aorist Indicative Passive

a. λύω

	Singular		Plural	
1	ἐλύθην	I was loosed	ἐλύθημεν	We were loosed
2	ἐλύθης	You were loosed	ἐλύθητε	You were loosed
3	ἐλύθη	He (she, it) was loosed	ἐλύθησαν	They were loosed

b. λείπω

	Singular		Plural	
1	ἐλείφθην	I was left	ἐλείφθημεν	We were left
2	ἐλείφθης	You were left	ἐλείφθητε	You were left
3	ἐλείφθη	He (she, it) was left	ἐλείφθησαν	They were left

3. "Future" Stem: Future Indicative Passive

a. λύω

	Singular		Plural	
1	λυθήσομαι	I will be loosed	λυθησόμεθα	We will be loosed
2	λυθήσῃ (λυθήσεσαι)	You will be loosed	λυθήσεσθε	You will be loosed
3	λυθήσεται	He (she, it) will be loosed	λυθήσονται	They will be loosed

b. λείπω

	Singular			Plural	
1	λειφθήσομαι	I will be left	λειφθησόμεθα	We will be left
2	λειφθήσῃ	You will be	λειφθήσεσθε	You will be
	(λειφθήσεσαι)	left		left
3	λειφθήσεται	He (she, it)	λειφθήσονται	They will be
		will be left		left

C. Morphology

1. Basic Observations

a. Forms conforming to the overall Greek verbal system: present and imperfect. The passive forms of the present and imperfect indicative exhibit characteristics in conformity with basic Greek verb formation:

(1) The appropriate stem is used to indicate aspect ("present" stem for "focus upon connection").

(2) Regular connecting vowels are used (ϵ/o pattern).

(3) Endings are identical to the middle; thus these endings are properly called *middle/passive endings*. Note that the primary "tense" (present) has primary endings, the secondary "tense" (imperfect) has secondary endings.

b. Forms with exceptional morphology: aorist and future. The passive forms of these two "tenses" are exceptional in some way.

(1) Both aorist and future passive forms use a *special stem* that ends with $\theta\eta$.[1]

(2) Future indicative passive forms are normal, with the exception of the stem (adding a σ, the normal connecting vowels, and the middle/passive endings).

(3) Aorist indicative passive forms augment normally, but they use

(a) secondary *active endings*, not secondary middle/passive endings;

(b) *no connecting vowels*.

(4) The future indicative passive is, technically, built off of the aorist indicative passive. In its formation, the augment and secondary ending are dropped, and a σ plus the appropriate connecting vowels and endings are added.

REMEMBER: AORIST *PASSIVE* FORMS USE *ACTIVE* ENDINGS.[2]

2. Formation of the Special "Focus on the Action"/"Aorist" Passive Stem

a. The general rule (i.e., applicable to verbs with *predictable* formations) is that the "focus on the action"/"aorist" passive stem is formed by adding $\theta\eta$ to the stem of the *first* (not third) principal part.

   (1) When the stem of the first principal part ends in a vowel, the $\theta\eta$ is added directly:

   (EG 1) $\lambda\acute{\upsilon}\omega \rightarrow \acute{\epsilon}\lambda\acute{\upsilon}\theta\eta\nu$

   (EG 2) $\phi o\nu\epsilon\acute{\upsilon}\omega \rightarrow \acute{\epsilon}\phi o\nu\epsilon\acute{\upsilon}\theta\eta\nu$

   (2) When the stem of the first principal part ends with a consonant, the $\theta\eta$ is added directly *and* the final consonant is "assimilated" or adjusted to the aspiration of the θ in the $\theta\eta$. The following pattern may be observed.

   Stems ending in the following:

   Guttural = κ, γ, χ, or $\sigma\sigma$ before $\theta(\eta) \rightarrow \chi$

   Labial = π, β, ϕ, or $\pi\tau$ before $\theta(\eta) \rightarrow \phi$

   Dental = τ, δ, θ, or ζ before $\theta(\eta) \rightarrow \sigma$

   Note that in the first two cases (gutturals and labials) the aspirated form of the consonant is used (χ and ϕ respectively), while dentals or ζ become σ before the aspirated θ. (See chapter 7, A 3 a for comparison.)

   (EG 3) $\check{\alpha}\gamma\omega \rightarrow \mathring{\eta}\chi\theta\eta\nu$

   (EG 4) $\pi\acute{\epsilon}\mu\pi\omega \rightarrow \acute{\epsilon}\pi\acute{\epsilon}\mu\phi\theta\eta\nu$

   (EG 5) $\pi\epsilon\acute{\iota}\theta\omega \rightarrow \acute{\epsilon}\pi\epsilon\acute{\iota}\sigma\theta\eta\nu$

   (EG 6) $\kappa\eta\rho\acute{\upsilon}\sigma\sigma\omega \rightarrow \acute{\epsilon}\kappa\eta\rho\acute{\upsilon}\chi\theta\eta\nu$

   (EG 7) $\acute{\alpha}\gamma o\rho\acute{\alpha}\zeta\omega \rightarrow \mathring{\eta}\gamma o\rho\acute{\alpha}\sigma\theta\eta\nu$

b. A number of verbs do not form their "aorist" passive stem predictably; i.e., they are *irregular*. Several types of irregularity are possible, but in this chapter we will encounter only forms that contain the characteristic $\theta\eta$ but do *not* attach the $\theta\eta$ to the stem of the first principal part.

   (EG 8) $\sigma\acute{\omega}\zeta\omega \rightarrow \acute{\epsilon}\sigma\acute{\omega}\theta\eta\nu$

   (EG 9) $\pi\acute{\iota}\nu\omega \rightarrow \acute{\epsilon}\pi\acute{o}\theta\eta\nu$

   Note: In no case does irregularity in the Greek aorist indicative passive concern connecting vowels or endings (cf. the difference between strong and weak aorists of the third principal part). Irregularities in the aorist indicative passive concern the *stem only*.[2]

D. Syntax

In Greek, as in English, the subject of the passive verb suffers treatment or is acted on. In English, however, we often do not distinguish between the *personal agent* of the activity and *instrument* or means employed:

(EG 10)   The sheep are being driven *by* the robbers.

(EG 11)   The slave was slaughtered *by* the sword of the robber.

In Greek, however, the *personal agent* of the activity is expressed by the preposition ὑπό + the genitive (= "by," agent), while the *instrument* or means is expressed simply by *putting it in the dative case* (traditionally called the dative of instrument or means):

(EG 12)   τὰ πρόβατα ἄγονται <u>ὑπὸ τῶν λῃστῶν</u>.
            The sheep are being driven *by the robbers.*

(EG 13)   ὁ δοῦλος ἐφονεύθη <u>τῇ μαχαίρῃ</u> τοῦ λῃστοῦ.
            The slave was slaughtered *by the sword* of the robber.

E. Meaning

1. It is usually best to translate present indicative passive verb forms with a *progressive* wording.

   (EG 14)   τὰ ἱμάτια κλέπτονται. = "The clothes are being stolen" (not, "The clothes are stolen").

   The translation "The clothes are stolen" is possible only if the action is *habitual*.

   (EG 15)   "The clothes are stolen *every evening.*"

   Note: Either conception of the activity (currently happening or habitual) has a *connective* focus.

2. It is important to remember that the translation "The clothes are stolen" is wholly inappropriate if the meaning is "The clothes have been taken and are now gone" or possibly, "The clothes now before us are 'hot.' "

   (EG 16)   "The clothes are stolen and are being sought by the police."

   This is the expression of the so-called "perfect tense" in Greek, namely, *the present enduring results of a past action*. This will be met in chapter 25.[3]

3. How are present and imperfect passives distinguished from middle voice forms of the same "tense"? Forms are only very occasionally ambiguous; the context is usually clear. Three things may be observed:

a. A passive normally has no object expressed (and thus there are no nouns in the accusative case [except after prepositions]).

b. A passive normally has an agent or means expressed.

c. Many middle forms are from deponent verbs.

F. Principal Part

The first person singular aorist indicative passive form is the *sixth principal part* of the Greek verb.

G. Vocabulary

ἀνα-βαίνω, etc.: I go up

ἀνα-βλέπω, etc. (R): I look up; regain sight

ἀσπάζομαι (M) (R): I greet

βαπτίζω (R): I baptize; wash (ritual)

λίθος -ου, m.: stone

μάχαιρα -ης, f.: sword

οὖν (conj.—postpositive): therefore; then

ποταμός -οῦ, m.: river

σάββατον -ου, n.: Sabbath; week

σήμερον (adv.): today

στρατιώτης -ου, m.: soldier

φονεύω (R): I slay, murder

ὡς (conj.): as (time, manner)

Here are the sixth principal parts of verbs we have already met that have irregular aorist passives:

1	2	3		6
ἀκούω	ἀκούσω	ἤκουσα	. . .	ἠκούσθην
εὑρίσκω	εὑρήσω	εὗρον	. . .	εὑρέθην
λαμβάνω	λήμψομαι	ἔλαβον	. . .	ἐλήμφθην
λέγω	ἐρῶ	εἶπον	. . .	ἐρρήθην /
				ἐρρέθην
ὁράω	ὄψομαι	εἶδον	. . .	ὤφθην
πίνω	πίομαι	ἔπιον	. . .	ἐπόθην
σῴζω	σώσω	ἔσωσα	. . .	ἐσώθην
τίκτω	τέξομαι	ἔτεκον	. . .	ἐτέχθην
φέρω	οἴσω	ἤνεγκον	. . .	ἠνέχθην

Note: The aorist passive of γράφω is very unusual and will be introduced in chapter 23.

H. Exercises

1. What "tense" and voice would you use to translate the following sentences?

a. I was taken.	k. You were glorifying.
b. It was being said.	l. You were glorified.
c. I was saying.	m. You (pl.) were being heard.
d. I will see.	n. You (pl.) heard.
e. You will be saved.	o. I will be healed.
f. I baptized.	p. I was healing.
g. I was being baptized.	q. He discovers.
h. He slew.	r. He was discovered.
i. He was slain.	s. We released.
j. She was being carried.	t. We were released.

2. Put the above sentences into Greek.

I. Practice Sentences

1. Greek to English

a. ὁ Ἰησοῦς ἐβαπτίσθη ὑπὸ τοῦ Ἰωάννου ἐν τῷ ποταμῷ.

b. οἱ λῃσταὶ ἐφονεύθησαν ὑπὸ τῶν στρατιωτῶν μαχαίραις.

c. σήμερον ἀνα-βήσομαι εἰς τὴν ἐκκλησίαν, καὶ ἐκεῖ ἀσπάσομαι τοὺς ἁγίους ἀποστόλους καὶ προφήτας.

d. τὸ εὐαγγέλιον τῆς βασιλείας ἀκουσθήσεται ἐν ταῖς κώμαις, οἱ γὰρ μαθηταὶ εἰσ-ελεύσονται εἰς αὐτὰς καὶ κηρύξουσιν αὐτό.

e. ὁ Ἰησοῦς ὤφθη ὑπὸ τῶν μαθητῶν αὐτοῦ, ὡς ἐφέρετο εἰς οὐρανόν.

f. οἱ ἐργάται τοῦ ἱεροῦ ἐφονεύοντο ὑπὸ πονηρῶν ἀνθρώπων λίθοις.

g. οἱ διδάσκαλοι τῆς κώμης ἐθεραπεύθησαν ὑπο τοῦ Ἰησοῦ καὶ ἀν-έβλεψαν. οἱ οὖν ὄχλοι ἤρχοντο πρὸς αὐτὸν καὶ ἔλεγον· πότε θεραπεύσεις καὶ τοὺς δούλους ἡμῶν;

h. ὡς οἱ στρατιῶται ἐφυλάσσοντο τὰ πλοῖα, οἱ λῃσταὶ ἔκλεψαν τὰ ἀργύρια καὶ τὰς μαχαίρας αὐτῶν.

2. English to Greek

    a. You (pl.) will know the truth of God and (will) reveal it.

    b. The slaves were released and (were) found in the field.

J. Bible Passages

Matthew 4:1a . . . ἔρημον (C)

Matthew 8:3b καὶ εὐθέως . . .

Colossians 4:14a . . . ἀγαπητός

1 Corinthians 1:13b εἰς . . .

K. Afterword

The sixth principal part does not represent a new focus/aspect, even though it is a new stem. It is simply a (special) way to make forms that convey the focus of the aorist and the future "tenses" in the passive voice.

Notes

1. Technically, the stem addition is θε, with the ε lengthening to η. The importance of this will appear later.

2. This principle is true, not only for indicative mood forms, but for all other forms as well (including infinitives and participles).

3. See also footnote 1, chapter 9.

12

The Verb "To Be"
and Further Uses
of the Article

A. The Verb "To Be"

1. Introduction

a. The verb that expresses being is, in virtually all languages, the most common and therefore the most irregular in its forms. Note the singular of the present tense in English:

(EG 1) "I *am*," "You *are*," "He *is*."

It is important to realize that clauses with "to be" do not have an object expressed in the accusative but have a noun or pronoun in the predicate of the sentence that is expressed in the same case as the subject. That case is normally the nominative, hence the name "predicate nominative."

(EG 2) "It is *I*" (not "me").

(EG 3) "The leaders are you and *I*" (not "you and me").

b. In English, the verb "to be" has all available tenses. In Greek, only three "tenses" are used: present, imperfect, and future.

2. The Forms of the Verb

a. Present Indicative Active

	Singular			Plural	
1	εἰμί	I am		ἐσμέν	We are
2	εἶ	You are		ἐστέ	You are
3	ἐστί(ν)	He (she, it) is		εἰσί(ν)	They are

b. Imperfect Indicative Active

	Singular			Plural	
1	ἤμην	I was		ἦμεν	We were
2	ἦς	You were		ἦτε	You were
3	ἦν	He (she, it) was		ἦσαν	They were

c. Future Indicative Middle

Singular		Plural	
1 ἔσομαι	I will be	ἐσόμεθα	We will be
2 ἔση (ἔσεσαι)	You will be	ἔσεσθε	You will be
3 ἔσται (ἔσεται)	He (she, it) will be	ἔσονται	They will be

3. Morphology

a. Present Indicative Forms

(1) Most forms of the present indicative are very ancient. Note especially εἰμί. -μι was the old, original first person singular ending for Greek verbs. We will consider several old verbs in chapters 33–35.

(2) In the present indicative, all forms except the second person singular are *enclitic,* i.e., normally the previous word carries the accent. (Cf. chapter 10, E, the unaccented personal pronoun forms of the first and second person singular.) Review Donald A. Carson, *A Student's Manual of New Testament Greek Accents.* Grand Rapids, MI, Baker, 1985, 47–52.

b. Imperfect Indicative Forms

(1) The endings of the imperfect are secondary, especially in the plural (cf. aorist passive endings).

(2) The first singular form is deponent (classical form: ἦν).

c. Future Indicative Forms

(1) All future forms are deponent.

(2) The third personal singular form is slightly irregular in that it has no connecting vowel. No doubt this developed from frequent usage.

4. Syntax

a. As in English, Greek clauses with the verb "to be" use a nominative in the predicate (cf. A 1 a above).

(EG 4) ὁ ἀπόστολός ἐστι δοῦλος (not δοῦλον).
The apostle is a slave.

(EG 5) διδάσκαλός εἰμι (not διδάσκαλον).
I am a teacher.

(EG 6) ἡ παρθένος ἐστὶ καλή (not καλήν).
The virgin is beautiful.

Note that the adjective in all examples matches its noun in *gender, number,* and *case.*

b. Greek does not need to express the verb "to be." EG 6 might well have been written:

(EG 7)   ἡ παρθένος καλή.

This means the same thing as EG 6. (In such cases, the verb "tense" assumed is normally present, though some exceptions do occur.) Note that here the adjective is not in attributive position, i.e., directly after the article (cf. chapter 6, C 4 c). Any position *not directly after the article* is called *predicate position.*

B. Further Uses of the Article

1. With Adjectives

The article is often used to make a noun out of an adjective. When this is done, the adjective is put into *attributive* position and an appropriate *noun is assumed.* The article indicates gender.

(EG 8)   οἱ νεκροὶ (ἄνθρωποι) ἐν τοῖς μνημείοις εἰσίν.
The dead (people or men) are in the tombs.

Note how similar our English translation is. In both languages, "people" or "men" is assumed. Greek does, however, use this structure to a much greater degree than does English.

(EG 9)   οἱ πονηροὶ ἐφόνευσαν τὰς ἀγαθάς.
The evil [men] slew *the good [women].*

In English we must add the words "men" and "women." Neuters in these constructions indicate things:

(EG 10)   ἀπόστολοι πράσσουσι τὰ καλά.
Apostles do *the [things]* (i.e., deeds, works) *that are noble.*

2. With Prepositional Phrases

a. Sometimes a prepositional phrase relates a noun (or pronoun) not to a verb but to *another noun (or pronoun).*

(EG 11)   "The horse in the village is small."

Here a relationship is established between village and horse, not between village and the verb "is." (The sentence does not say, e.g., that the horse is small when it is in the village, but outside its confines it becomes large!) When this occurs, the prepositional phrase is said to modify the noun, just as an adjective does. As a result, we may say that it *functions adjectivally.* How do we know when a prepositional phrase functions adjectivally? In English, word order is crucial. Context is also critical. (Is the propositional phrase in the sentence: "She hit the man with the big stick" adjectival [telling which man], or adverbial [telling how]? Only context will tell!) *Greek indicates adjectival functions by treating the prepositional phrase as an adjective and putting it into attributive position, using the article.* Thus the sentence in EG 11 would be written:

(EG 12)   ὁ ἵππος ὁ ἐν τῇ κώμῃ ἐστὶ μικρός.
           The horse (that is) in the village is small.
           (Literally: "The horse, the one in the village, is small.")

The article ties "in the village" to "horse" to make it an attribute and function adjectivally, so that the phrase cannot be treated adverbially and modify the verb, ἐστί. Note the following examples:

(EG 13)   ὁ δοῦλος ὁ ἐν τῇ κώμῃ ἐστὶ
           διδάσκαλος.
           The slave (who is) in the village is a teacher.
           (Literally: "The slave, the one in the village, . . .")

(EG 14)   ὁ δοῦλος ἐν τῇ κώμῃ ἐστὶ διδάσκαλος.
           The slave is a teacher in the village.

This sentence tells where he performs his teaching function.

The presence or absence of the article determines if the prepositional phrase modifies the noun or the verb (i.e., functions adjectivally or adverbially).

b. Just as the article may be used to make adjectives into nouns, so the article can make prepositional phrases into nouns. Again, an appropriate noun is assumed.

(EG 15)   <u>οἱ ἐν</u> τῇ κώμῃ εἶδον με.
           The [people] in the village saw me.

(EG 16)   εἶδον <u>τὰς ἐν</u> τῇ κώμῃ.
           I saw *the [women] in* the village.

(EG 17)   εἶδον <u>τὰ ἐν</u> τῷ πλοίῳ.
           I saw *the [things] in* the boat.

In each case, we must add the bracketed words in our English translation to indicate gender.

C. Vocabulary

ἁμαρτωλός ‾ή ‾όν: sinful

γίνομαι, γενήσομαι, ἐγενόμην, . . . ἐγενήθην (M):
    I become; am

εἰμί, ἔσομαι: I am

ἐχθρός -ά -όν: hostile, enemy

'Ιουδαῖος -α -ον: Jewish

ἵππος -ου: m.: horse

κωφός -ή -όν: deaf, mute (dumb)

μακάριος -α -ον: blessed

μνημεῖον -ου, n.: tomb

νεκρός -ά -όν: dead

πιστός -ή -όν: faithful

πράσσω (r): I do, act

πτωχός -ή -όν: poor

σοφός -ή -όν: wise

τυφλός -ή -όν: blind

χωλός -ή -όν: lame

Note: All of the adjectives in this list are regularly used with the article to make nouns.

D. Exercises

1. Tell in which position the following underlined words are (attributive or predicate) and translate the sentences.

   a. ὁ <u>σοφὸς</u> δοῦλός ἐστι <u>τυφλός</u>.

   b. ὁ δοῦλός ἐστι <u>σοφός</u>.

   c. ὁ δοῦλος ὁ <u>σοφός</u> ἐστι <u>τυφλός</u>.

   d. ὁ δοῦλος <u>σοφός</u>.

   e. <u>σοφὸς</u> ὁ δοῦλος.

   f. δοῦλος ὁ <u>σοφός</u> ἐστι ἅγιος.

2. Translate the following:

   a. βλέπω τοὺς ἀγαθούς.

   b. βλέπω τὰς ἀγαθάς.

   c. βλέπω τοὺς ἐν τῇ ἐρήμῳ.

   d. βλέπω τὰ ἐν τῷ ἀγρῷ.

E. Practice Sentences

1. Greek to English

a. οἱ 'Ιουδαῖοι ἦσαν ἁμαρτωλοί, ἀλλ᾽ ἦλθον πρὸς τὸν σοφὸν ἀπόστολον.

b. ὁ 'Ιησοῦς ἐθεράπευε τοὺς χωλοὺς καὶ τοὺς κωφοὺς καὶ τοὺς τυφλούς.

c. μακάριοι οἱ πτωχοί, ὅτι δέξονται τὴν βασιλείαν τοῦ θεοῦ.

d. ἐν τῇ ἐσχάτῃ ἡμέρᾳ, οἱ νεκροὶ ἐξ-ελεύσονται ἐκ τῶν μνημείων. οἱ πιστοὶ ἔσονται σὺν τῷ κυρίῳ, οἱ δὲ ἄπιστοι ἀπ-ελεύσονται σὺν τῷ διαβόλῳ.

e. ἠγόρασα τὸν ἵππον ἐν τῇ κώμῃ.

f. ἠγόρασα τὸν ἵππον τὸν ἐν τῇ κώμῃ.

g. ἐπράξατε τὸ πονηρόν. πείσεσθε οὖν σὺν τοῖς ἐν τῇ ἐρήμῳ.

h. οἱ πλούσιοι εἶδον τὰς πτωχὰς ἐν τοῖς ἀγροῖς, καὶ αὐταῖς οἶνον καὶ ἄρτον ἐπέμψαντο.

i. οἱ ἐργάται οἱ ἐν τοῖς ἀγροῖς εὗρον τὸ ἀργύριον καὶ ἤνεγκον αὐτὸ πρὸς τὰς ἐν τῷ ἱερῷ παρθένους.

j. οἱ ἐχθροὶ στρατιῶται γενήσονται μαθηταὶ 'Ιησοῦ Χριστοῦ.

2. English to Greek

The blind were suffering, but the rich women in the village led them to Jesus.

F. Bible Passages

James 5:6a ἐφονεύσατε . . . δίκαιον

Apocalypse 1:8a . . . θεός

James 4:1a . . . ὑμῖν

Matthew 11:5a . . . ἐγείρονται (C) (omit καὶ χωλοὶ περιπατοῦσιν)

13

Miscellanea 1

A. Introduction

A number of features of Greek are minor adjustments to the overall system: exceptions, extensions, small points, etc. We will deal with a number of these in special chapters such as this one.

B. Demonstrative Pronouns

1. The Forms

a. οὗτος = "This"; Plural = "These"

Singular

	M	F	N
N	οὗτος	αὕτη	τοῦτο
G	τούτου	ταύτης	τούτου
D	τούτῳ	ταύτῃ	τούτῳ
A	τοῦτον	ταύτην	τοῦτο

Plural

	M	F	N
N	οὗτοι	αὗται	ταῦτα
G	τούτων	τούτων	τούτων
D	τούτοις	ταύταις	τούτοις
A	τούτους	ταύτας	ταῦτα

b. ἐκεῖνος = "That"; Plural = "Those"

Singular

	M	F	N
N	ἐκεῖνος	ἐκείνη	ἐκεῖνο
G	ἐκείνου	ἐκείνης	ἐκείνου
D	ἐκείνῳ	ἐκείνη	ἐκείνῳ
A	ἐκεῖνον	ἐκείνην	ἐκεῖνο

Plural

	M	F	N
N	ἐκεῖνοι	ἐκεῖναι	ἐκεῖνα
G	ἐκείνων	ἐκείνων	ἐκείνων
D	ἐκείνοις	ἐκείναις	ἐκείνοις
A	ἐκείνους	ἐκείνας	ἐκεῖνα

2. Morphology

a. The forms of both demonstrative pronouns are similar to regular adjectives. Note that the neuter singular ending is ‾*o*, not ‾*ον* (cf. the article *τό*). Note also that masculine and feminine nominatives, both singular and plural, of *οὗτος* lack the initial *τ*, as does the definite article.

b. The forms of *οὗτος* have the following internal peculiarity:

   (1) If the ending contains an O vowel (cf. the masculines), the internal diphthong is *ου*.

   (2) If the ending contains *η* or *α* (cf. most feminines and the neuter nominative and accusative plural), the internal diphthong is *αυ*.

3. Syntax

a. The demonstratives, when used to modify a noun, always occur in *predicate position to the noun and its article.*

   (EG 1)   *οὗτος ὁ δοῦλος ἀγαθός ἐστιν.*
            This slave is good.

   (EG 2)   *εἶδεν ἐκεῖνα τὰ τέκνα.*
            He saw *those children.*

   Note that the article is always present with the noun.

b. Each demonstrative may be used alone to convey a noun of the appropriate gender.

   (EG 3)   *οὗτος ἠγόρασε πλοῖον.*
            This [man] bought a boat.

   (EG 4)   *εἴδομεν ταύτας.*
            We saw *these [women].*

   (EG 5)   *οὐ πράξομεν ἐκεῖνα.*
            We shall not do *those [things].*

   In English, the bracketed words are necessary.

C. Prepositions with Two Cases

1. Introduction

Some prepositions govern two cases. In these instances

a. the meaning of the preposition is revealed by the case of the word it governs;

b. the basic meaning of the cases revealed by the elementary prepositions is generally *not* adhered to (cf. chapter 5, B 2 b). Often the genitive is abstract and the accusative local and/or temporal.

2. Examples

(EG 6) εἴπομεν περὶ τῆς ἐκκλησίας.
We spoke *concerning* the church.

(EG 7) ἤλθομεν περὶ τὴν ἐκκλησίαν.
We went *around* the church.

(EG 8) οἱ ἅγιοι διώκονται ὑπὸ τῶν πονηρῶν.
The saints are being persecuted *by* the wicked.

(EG 9) τὸ ἀργύριον ὑπὸ τὴν ἐκκλησίαν ἐστίν.
The money is *under* the church.

D. Making Adverbs

Often adverbs can be made from adjectives. English does this by adding "-ly":

(EG 10)   "swift" → "swiftly"

Greek makes adverbs by changing the final ν of the genitive masculine plural form of the adjective to ς:

(EG 11)   τυφλῶν (τυφλός) → τυφλῶς

(EG 12)   δικαίων (δίκαιος) → δικαίως

Note that the accent remains the same.

E. Neuter Plural Subjects

It was normal in classical Greek to use a *singular* verb with a *neuter plural* subject. This is sometimes retained in Koine Greek.

(EG 13)   τὰ πλοῖα ἐν τῇ κώμῃ ἐστίν (instead of εἰσίν).
The boats *are* in the village.

(EG 14)   τὰ ἀργύρια ἐν τῇ ἐκκλησίᾳ ἦν (instead of ἦσαν).
The money *was* in the church.

It is true, however, that often the New Testament does use plural verbs with neuter plural subjects.

F. The Article with Abstractions or Concepts

The article is often used with abstract ideas such as "truth," "righteousness," "grace," etc., and even with concepts such as "life" and "death." In English, we normally omit the article in such cases.

(EG 15)   ἡ ἀγάπη σῴζει ἡμᾶς.
Love (not, *The* love) saves us.

(EG 16)   οἱ ἄνθρωποι θέλουσι τὴν ζωήν.
          Men/people desire *life* (not *The* men/people desire *the*
          life).

G. Lack of Article in Prepositional Phrases

Often Koine Greek omits the definite article with a definite noun in a
prepositional phrase.

(EG 17)   ἐν ἀρχῇ οἱ πονηροὶ μαθηταὶ ἔπραξαν καλά.
          In *the* beginning the evil disciples did noble things.

H. Uses of the Dative Case

1. Often the dative case is used to express the person(s) for whom
   (i.e., for whose benefit) something is done. "For" is usually a good
   translation here. (This is often called *dative of advantage*.)

   (EG 18)   οἱ δοῦλοι ἠγόρασαν δῶρον τῷ δεσπότῃ
             αὐτῶν.
             The slaves bought a gift *for* their master (i.e., for his
             benefit.)

   Sometimes the "benefit" is negative:

   (EG 19)   ὁ θάνατος ἡτοιμάσθη τοῖς λῃσταῖς.
             Death was prepared *for* the robbers.

2. The dative of *means* is often used not only with passive formations
   but also with active or middle forms.

   (EG 20)   οἱ λῃσταὶ ἐφόνευσαν αὐτοὺς μαχαίραις.
             The robbers slew them *with* (i.e., by means of)
             swords.

I. μέν and δέ

When two balanced things are contrasted, μέν and δέ are usually used,
each postpositively (i.e., after the first word) in its own clause.

(EG 21)   ἐγὼ μέν εἰμι ἀπόστολος, σὺ δὲ εἶ ὁ κύριος.
          I am an apostle, but *You* are the Lord.

If the contrasted clauses have some length, "on the one hand" and "on
the other hand" often provides a good translation in English.

J. Verbs with Unpredictable Imperfect Indicative Formations

The vast majority of verbs form their imperfect forms predictably
from their first principal part. (This is why the imperfect is not a

separate principal part.) A small number of verbs, however, do not form their imperfects predictably, usually because the augment is irregular.

(EG 22) $\check{\epsilon}\chi\omega$ → $\epsilon\hat{\iota}\chi o\nu$

(EG 23) $\theta\acute{\epsilon}\lambda\omega$ → $\mathring{\eta}\theta\epsilon\lambda o\nu$

K. Vocabulary

$\check{\alpha}\lambda\lambda o\varsigma$ ⁻η ⁻o: other (cf. $\alpha\mathring{\upsilon}\tau\acute{o}\varsigma$ for neuter ending)

$\mathring{\alpha}\mu\alpha\rho\tau\acute{\iota}\alpha$ ⁻$\alpha\varsigma$, f.: sin

$\mathring{\alpha}\rho\chi\acute{\eta}$ ⁻$\hat{\eta}\varsigma$, f.: beginning

$\delta\epsilon\sigma\pi\acute{o}\tau\eta\varsigma$ ⁻$o\upsilon$, m.: master

$\delta\iota\acute{\alpha}$ (prep.)   + gen.: through (local and means)
                    + acc.: on account of

$\epsilon\mathring{\iota}\rho\acute{\eta}\nu\eta$ ⁻$\eta\varsigma$, f.: peace

$\mathring{\epsilon}\kappa\epsilon\hat{\iota}\nu o\varsigma$ ⁻η ⁻o: that (pl. those)

$\mathring{\epsilon}\tau o\iota\mu\acute{\alpha}\zeta\omega$ (R): I prepare

$\check{\epsilon}\chi\omega$, $\check{\epsilon}\xi\omega$, $\check{\epsilon}\sigma\chi o\nu$: I have (Note the aspirated future form. The imperfect is $\epsilon\hat{\iota}\chi o\nu$; note the unusual augment.)

$\zeta\omega\acute{\eta}$ ⁻$\hat{\eta}\varsigma$, f.: life

$\theta\acute{\alpha}\nu\alpha\tau o\varsigma$ ⁻$o\upsilon$, m.: death

$\theta\acute{\epsilon}\lambda\omega$, $\theta\epsilon\lambda\acute{\eta}\sigma\omega$, $\mathring{\eta}\theta\acute{\epsilon}\lambda\eta\sigma\alpha$: I desire (The imperfect is $\mathring{\eta}\theta\epsilon\lambda o\nu$. Its augment and that of the aorist betrays the classical form of this verb: $\underline{\acute{\epsilon}}\theta\acute{\epsilon}\lambda\omega$.)

$\kappa\alpha\theta\acute{\omega}\varsigma$ (adv.): just as

$\kappa\alpha\tau\acute{\alpha}$ (prep.)   + gen.: against; down
                     + acc.: according to

  $\kappa\alpha\tau\alpha$⁻$\beta\alpha\acute{\iota}\nu\omega$, etc.: I go down

$\mu\acute{\epsilon}\nu$ (particle—postpositive): (on the one hand)

$\mu\epsilon\tau\acute{\alpha}$ (prep.)   + gen.: with
                     + acc.: after

$o\mathring{\upsilon}\tau o\varsigma$, $\alpha\mathring{\upsilon}\tau\eta$, $\tau o\hat{\upsilon}\tau o$: this (pl. these)

$o\mathring{\upsilon}\tau\omega\varsigma$ (adv.): in this way; so

$\pi\epsilon\rho\acute{\iota}$ (prep.)   + gen.: concerning
                     + acc.: around

$\mathring{\upsilon}\pi\acute{\epsilon}\rho$ (prep.)   + gen.: on behalf of
                     + acc.: beyond

ὑπό (prep.)   + gen.: by (agent)
              + acc.: under

L. Exercises

1. Translate the following short sentences:

a. ἤλθετε ὑπὲρ τὸν ποταμόν.

b. ἤλθετε ὑπὸ τὸ ἱερόν.

c. ἤλθετε περὶ τὴν ἐκκλησίαν.

d. ἤλθετε μετὰ τὸ σάββατον.

e. ἤλθετε διὰ τοῦ ἀγροῦ.

f. ἤλθετε μετὰ τῶν δούλων.

g. εἴπετε ὑπὲρ τῶν πτωχῶν.

h. εἴπετε περὶ τῆς ἀληθείας.

i. εἴπετε κατὰ τοῦ κυρίου.

2. Make the following adverbs in Greek: blindly, wisely, lamely.

M. Practice Sentences

1. Greek to English

a. ἡ εἰρήνη καὶ ἡ ἀγάπη αὐξήσουσιν ἐν ἐκκλησίᾳ.

b. ἐν ἀρχῇ ὁ ᾽Ιησοῦς ἐδίδασκε τοὺς ὄχλους παραβολαῖς.

c. εἴχομεν πρόβατα ἐν τῇ κώμῃ ἡμῶν, οἱ δὲ λησταὶ
ἀπ-ήγαγον αὐτὰ διὰ τοῦ ἀγροῦ περὶ τὰς θαλάσσας.

d. οὗτος ὁ διδάσκαλος γινώσκει ταύτας, καὶ σοφῶς
φυλάξεται αὐτὰς ἀπ᾽ ἐκείνου τοῦ δεσπότου.

e. διὰ νόμον οἱ ᾽Ιουδαῖοι οὐκ ἠργάζοντο ἐν σαββάτῳ.

f. καθὼς ἐκεῖνος ἀπ-έθανε δι᾽ ἁμαρτίαν, οὕτως αὕτη
σωθήσεται διὰ δικαιοσύνην.

g. ὁ ᾽Ιησοῦς εἶπεν· ἄλλα πρόβατα ἔχω. αὐτὰ μὲν γινώσκω, ἐμὲ δὲ γινώσκουσιν.

h. οἱ μετὰ τῶν τελωνῶν ἔλεγον κατὰ τοῦ εὐαγγελίου.
τὰς οὖν ἐπαγγελίας τοῦ θεοῦ οὐκ ἐδέξαντο.

i. ἐν τῇ ἐσχάτῃ ἡμέρᾳ ὁ ᾽Ιησοῦς κατα-βήσεται ἐξ
οὐρανοῦ καὶ ἑτοιμάσει τὴν μὲν ζωὴν τοῖς ἁγίοις,
τὸν δὲ θάνατον τοῖς πονηροῖς.

j. οἱ ἅγιοι ἠθέλησαν τὰ τοῦ θεοῦ οὐδὲ τὰ τοῦ πονηροῦ.

2. English to Greek

Jesus died on behalf of the sinners of the world.

N. Bible Passages

John 1:19a . . . Ἰωάννου

Matthew 9:37

John 1:1

James 1:12b λήμψεται . . . ζωῆς

14

Contracted (Contract)
Verbs in $-\acute{\epsilon}\omega$

A. Introduction

The verbs we have encountered thus far have had stems ending in either a long vowel (cf. $\lambda\acute{v}\omega$) or a consonant (cf. $\lambda\epsilon\acute{\iota}\pi\omega$). A small but very significant number of verbs have stems that end in a short vowel: ϵ, a, or o. In this chapter we will consider the first type of these verbs, verbs whose stem ends in ϵ. Of the three types, these are by far the most numerous.

B. "Focus upon Connection"/"Present" Stem

1. Paradigm Forms ($\phi\iota\lambda\acute{\epsilon}\omega$)

a. Present Indicative Active

	Singular			Plural	
1	$\phi\iota\lambda\hat{\omega}$	$(\phi\iota\lambda\acute{\epsilon}\omega)$	$\phi\iota\lambda o\hat{v}\mu\epsilon\nu$	$(\phi\iota\lambda\acute{\epsilon}o\mu\epsilon\nu)$
2	$\phi\iota\lambda\epsilon\hat{\iota}\varsigma$	$(\phi\iota\lambda\acute{\epsilon}\epsilon\iota\varsigma)$	$\phi\iota\lambda\epsilon\hat{\iota}\tau\epsilon$	$(\phi\iota\lambda\acute{\epsilon}\epsilon\tau\epsilon)$
3	$\phi\iota\lambda\epsilon\hat{\iota}$	$(\phi\iota\lambda\acute{\epsilon}\epsilon\iota)$	$\phi\iota\lambda o\hat{v}\sigma\iota(\nu)$	$(\phi\iota\lambda\acute{\epsilon}o\nu\sigma\iota[\nu])$

b. Present Indicative Middle/Passive

	Singular			Plural	
1	$\phi\iota\lambda o\hat{v}\mu\alpha\iota$	$(\phi\iota\lambda\acute{\epsilon}o\mu\alpha\iota)$	$\phi\iota\lambda o\acute{v}\mu\epsilon\theta\alpha$	$(\phi\iota\lambda\epsilon\acute{o}\mu\epsilon\theta\alpha)$
2	$\phi\iota\lambda\hat{\eta}$	$(\phi\iota\lambda\acute{\epsilon}\eta)$	$\phi\iota\lambda\epsilon\hat{\iota}\sigma\theta\epsilon$	$(\phi\iota\lambda\acute{\epsilon}\epsilon\sigma\theta\epsilon)$
3	$\phi\iota\lambda\epsilon\hat{\iota}\tau\alpha\iota$	$(\phi\iota\lambda\acute{\epsilon}\epsilon\tau\alpha\iota)$	$\phi\iota\lambda o\hat{v}\nu\tau\alpha\iota$	$(\phi\iota\lambda\acute{\epsilon}o\nu\tau\alpha\iota)$

c. Imperfect Indicative Active

	Singular			Plural	
1	$\acute{\epsilon}\phi\acute{\iota}\lambda o\nu\nu$	$(\acute{\epsilon}\phi\acute{\iota}\lambda\epsilon o\nu)$	$\acute{\epsilon}\phi\iota\lambda o\hat{v}\mu\epsilon\nu$	$(\acute{\epsilon}\phi\iota\lambda\acute{\epsilon}o\mu\epsilon\nu)$
2	$\acute{\epsilon}\phi\acute{\iota}\lambda\epsilon\iota\varsigma$	$(\acute{\epsilon}\phi\acute{\iota}\lambda\epsilon\epsilon\varsigma)$	$\acute{\epsilon}\phi\iota\lambda\epsilon\hat{\iota}\tau\epsilon$	$(\acute{\epsilon}\phi\iota\lambda\acute{\epsilon}\epsilon\tau\epsilon)$
3	$\acute{\epsilon}\phi\acute{\iota}\lambda\epsilon\iota$	$(\acute{\epsilon}\phi\acute{\iota}\lambda\epsilon\epsilon)$	$\acute{\epsilon}\phi\acute{\iota}\lambda o\nu\nu$	$(\acute{\epsilon}\phi\acute{\iota}\lambda\epsilon o\nu)$

d. Imperfect Indicative Middle/Passive

	Singular			Plural	
1	$\acute{\epsilon}\phi\iota\lambda o\acute{v}\mu\eta\nu$	$(\acute{\epsilon}\phi\iota\lambda\epsilon\acute{o}\mu\eta\nu)$	$\acute{\epsilon}\phi\iota\lambda o\acute{v}\mu\epsilon\theta\alpha$	$(\acute{\epsilon}\phi\iota\lambda\epsilon\acute{o}\mu\epsilon\theta\alpha)$
2	$\acute{\epsilon}\phi\iota\lambda o\hat{v}$	$(\acute{\epsilon}\phi\iota\lambda\acute{\epsilon}o\nu)$	$\acute{\epsilon}\phi\iota\lambda\epsilon\hat{\iota}\sigma\theta\epsilon$	$(\acute{\epsilon}\phi\iota\lambda\acute{\epsilon}\epsilon\sigma\theta\epsilon)$
3	$\acute{\epsilon}\phi\iota\lambda\epsilon\hat{\iota}\tau o$	$(\acute{\epsilon}\phi\iota\lambda\acute{\epsilon}\epsilon\tau o)$	$\acute{\epsilon}\phi\iota\lambda o\hat{v}\nu\tau o$	$(\acute{\epsilon}\phi\iota\lambda\acute{\epsilon}o\nu\tau o)$

2. Morphology

a. Stem

(1) The most important thing to note about ⁻έω contract verbs is that *the ε at the end of the "focus upon connection" / "present" stem contracts with the connecting vowel that follows to produce one amalgamated syllable.* (See uncontracted forms in parentheses.) You will not see uncontracted forms in the New Testament or the LXX.

(2) The rules for contraction are as follows:

(a) The ε at the end of the stem combines with a following ε to produce ει:

$$\epsilon + \epsilon \rightarrow \epsilon\iota$$

(EG 1) φιλέ/ετε → φιλεῖτε

(b) The ε at the end of the stem combines with a following o to produce ου:

$$\epsilon + o \rightarrow ου$$

(EG 2) φιλέ/ομεν → φιλοῦμεν

(c) The ε at the end of the stem combines with a long vowel or diphthong following and *is absorbed* by the vowel or diphtong:

$$\epsilon + \text{long syllable} \rightarrow \epsilon \text{ absorbed}$$

(EG 3) φιλέ/ω → φιλῶ

(EG 4) φιλέ/ουσι → φιλοῦσι

b. Connecting Vowel

The normal connecting vowels are used for all forms. It is these that contract with the end of the stem.

c. Endings

Normal endings are used for all forms.

d. Dictionary Listing

The verb's first form is listed in a dictionary with the έω *uncontracted:*

(EG 5) φιλέω in the dictionary, not φιλῶ.

3. Accenting

The *uncontracted* forms must be accented first. Then

a. if the accent falls on the ε at the end of the stem, it will become a circumflex on the contracted syllable:

(EG 6)   φιλέ|εσθε → φιλεῖσθε

b. in all other cases, the accent remains where and as it is.

(EG 7)   ἐφίλε|ον → ἐφίλουν

(EG 8)   ἐφιλε|όμεθα → ἐφιλούμεθα

C. "Future" and "Focus on the Action"/"Aorist" Stems

1. Paradigm Forms (φιλέω)

a. Future Indicative Active

	Singular	Plural
1	φιλήσω	φιλήσομεν
2	φιλήσεις	φιλήσετε
3	φιλήσει	φιλήσουσι(ν)

b. Aorist Indicative Active

	Singular	Plural
1	ἐφίλησα	ἐφιλήσαμεν
2	ἐφίλησας	ἐφιλήσατε
3	ἐφίλησε	ἐφίλησαν

c. Future Indicative Middle

	Singular	Plural
1	φιλήσομαι	φιλησόμεθα
2	φιλήσῃ	φιλήσεσθε
3	φιλήσεται	φιλήσονται

d. Aorist Indicative Middle

	Singular	Plural
1	ἐφιλησάμην	ἐφιλησάμεθα
2	ἐφιλήσω	ἐφιλήσασθε
3	ἐφιλήσατο	ἐφιλήσαντο

e. Future Indicative Passive

	Singular	Plural
1	φιληθήσομαι	φιληθησόμεθα
2	φιληθήσῃ	φιληθήσεσθε
3	φιληθήσεται	φιληθήσονται

f. Aorist Indicative Passive

	Singular	Plural
1	ἐφιλήθην	ἐφιλήθημεν
2	ἐφιλήθης	ἐφιλήθητε
3	ἐφιλήθη	ἐφιλήθησαν

2. Morphology

a. Stem

(1) The most important thing to note about all forms of contract verbs is that *the ε at the end of the "focus upon connection"/"present" stem lengthens to η in the forms of all other stems.* For this reason, only the present and imperfect forms contract.[1]

	Present Indicative	Future Indicative	Aorist Indicative
(EG 9)	φιλέω	φιλήσω	ἐφίλησα

(2) The σ for the future and aorist indicative active and middle forms and the θη of the aorist and future indicative passive are added directly after the η.

(3) For this reason, generally speaking, all forms of -έω contract verbs are normal after the "present" stem. Aorists are weak (first).

b. Connecting Vowel

Normal connecting vowels are used for all forms after the "present" stem. An a is used for the weak (first) aorist forms, as normal.

c. Endings

The normal endings are used for all future, aorist, and other forms.

D. Syntax

The use of contract verbs is exactly the same as it is for regular verbs. The only difference is morphological—in the first principal part.

E. Vocabulary

αἰτέω (R): I request

γῆ, γῆς, f.: earth; land

ζητέω (R): I seek

κληρονομέω (R): I inherit

λαλέω (R): I speak (openly)

μετα⁻νοέω (R): I repent

οἰκοδομέω (R): I build

ποιέω (R): I make; do

στέφανος ⁻ου, m.: crown

τηρέω (R): I keep, observe (laws)

φιλέω (R): I love

φωνέω (R): I call[2]

    φωνή ⁻ῆς, f.: voice; call

F. Exercises

1. Parse (i.e., give person, number, "tense," mood, and voice) and translate the following:

a. κληρονομεῖτε

b. λαλοῦσιν

c. φωνεῖται

d. φιλεῖ

e. ᾠκοδομήσατε

f. ἐποίεις

g. ἐζήτουν

h. μετ⁻ενόησας

i. ᾔτησαν

j. τηρούμεθα

2. Put each form in column one above (F 1) into the (corresponding) imperfect "tense" form.

G. Practice Sentences

1. Greek to English

a. φωνῇ μικρᾷ ὁ θεὸς ἐφώνησε τὸν προφήτην.

b. οἱ κακοὶ μετ‑ενόησαν ἀπὸ τῶν ἁμαρτιῶν αὐτῶν καὶ ἐτήρουν τὰς ἐντολὰς τοῦ νόμου.

c. οἱ πτωχοὶ αἰτοῦσιν ἄρτους καὶ δέξονται αὐτούς.

d. τὴν παρθένον ὁ δοῦλος ἐφίλησεν καὶ περὶ αὐτῆς προσ‑ηύχετο τῷ θεῷ.

e. ὡς ὁ Ἰησοῦς ἐλάλει τοῖς ὄχλοις, οἱ μαθηταὶ ἐζή‑τουν οἶνον ἐν τῇ κώμῃ.

f. οἱ Ἰουδαῖοι ἀπ‑ῆλθον εἰς τὴν γῆν τὴν ὑπὲρ τὴν θάλασσαν καὶ ἐκεῖ τῷ θεῷ ᾠκοδόμησαν ἱερόν.

g. ὁ μὲν τελώνης ἐποίησε πονηρά, ἡμεῖς δὲ φιλοῦμεν τὴν ἀλήθειαν τοῦ θεοῦ.

h. ὁ δοῦλος ἐποίησε στέφανον καλὸν τῷ δεσπότῃ αὐτοῦ, ὁ δὲ υἱὸς τούτου ἐκληρονόμησεν αὐτόν.

2. English to Greek

We love God and will inherit life in heaven.

H. Bible Passages

Matthew 23:1

James 4:3a . . . αἰτεῖσθε

John 17:16

Notes

1. This principle is true, not only for indicative mood forms, but for all other forms as well (including infinitives and participles).

2. With animals = "I make a sound."

15

Relative Pronouns and Three-Case Prepositions

A. Relative Pronouns

1. Introduction

Relative pronouns *relate* or connect a clause to a noun or pronoun elsewhere in the sentence.

(EG 1)   The man whom I saw is a teacher.

In this example, "whom" is the relative pronoun, and it *relates* my seeing to the man. It may be diagramed thus:

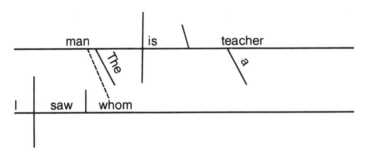

As with the personal pronoun (see chapter 10, A 3), the relative pronoun agrees with its antecedent in gender and in number, but not necessarily in case. Its case is determined by its usage in its own clause.

2. Forms

	Singular					Plural		
	M	F	N			M	F	N
N	ὅς	ἥ	ὅ		N	οἵ	αἵ	ἅ
G	οὗ	ἧς	οὗ		G	ὧν	ὧν	ὧν
D	ᾧ	ᾗ	ᾧ		D	οἷς	αἷς	οἷς
A	ὅν	ἥν	ὅ		A	οὕς	ἅς	ἅ

105

Approximate English equivalents are as follows:

Singular and Plural

	when antecedent is *personal*	when antecedent is *impersonal*
N	who, that	that, which
G	whose	whose
D	(to) whom	(to) which
A	whom, that	that, which

3. Morphology

The morphology of the relative pronouns is familiar. Except for ὅ in the nominative and accusative neuter singular (instead of ὅν; cf. τό, αὐτό, τοῦτο, ἐκεῖνο), the relative pronoun is like the ending of the regular adjective (feminine = η pattern).

4. Accent

The "inside outside" pattern of accenting is followed. (See chapter 4, D 3 b).

5. Syntax

The syntax for relative pronouns in Greek is the same as for English:

(EG 2)   ὁ ἄνθρωπος, ὅν εἶδον, διδάσκαλός ἐστιν.
The man *whom* I saw is a teacher.

Note that ὅν agrees with ἄνθρωπος in gender and number but not in case. Its case is determined by its usage in its own clause (in this sentence it is the object of εἶδον).

(EG 3)   ὁ ἄνθρωπος, ᾧ ἔπεμψα δῶρα, ἔρχεται.
The man *to whom* I sent gifts is coming.

In this example the relative pronoun is dative because it functions as indirect object.

(EG 4)   ἡ παρθένος, ᾗ ἔπεμψα δῶρα, ἔρχεται.
The virgin *to whom* I sent gifts is coming.

Here ᾗ must be feminine to agree with the gender of παρθένος.

(EG 5)   ἡ παρθένος, ἧς τὸ ἱμάτιον ἔλαβον, ἔρχεται.
The virgin *whose* cloak I took is coming.

ἧς τὸ ἱμάτιον could be rendered, "The cloak of whom," but "whose" is better English, showing possession.

(EG 6)   ὁ οἶκος, ὅν ἠγόρασα, μικρός ἐστιν.
The house *that* I bought is small.

Note here that the gender of each language must be considered. Greek says literally, "The house *whom* I bought . . .," for "house" is masculine. In English, "house" is neuter; therefore "that" is used.

(EG 7)   ἡ παρθένος ἐξ ἧς ὁ Ἰησοῦς ἐτέχθη ἦν
τέκνον τοῦ θεοῦ.

The virgin from *whom* Jesus was born was a child
of God.

In Greek, ἐκ (ἐξ) "takes" the genitive; therefore ἧς is used with it.
In English, "from" (and all other prepositions) "takes" the accusa-
tive. For this reason, we must say "from *whom*," not "from *whose*."
Each language's usage must be respected.

Note: Frequently Greek, like English, omits the antecedent of a
relative pronoun if that antecedent is a *thing* (~~abstract~~), *a man*, or a
woman. *in the abstract/*

(EG 8)   βλέπω ὃ εἶδες.   (= βλέπω τοῦτο ὃ εἶδες.)
I see *what* you saw.   (= I see *this thing that* you saw.)

(EG 9)   ὃς βλέπει με   (= ὁ ἄνθρωπος ὃς βλέπει
σωθήσεται.   με σωθήσεται.)
(He) *who* sees me will   (= *The man/person who* sees me
be saved.   will be saved.)

B. Three-Case Prepositions

There are several common prepositions that govern all three oblique
cases. In general, they conform to the basic usage of prepositions outlined in chapter 5. Note, however the special meaning for ἐπί +
genitive.

1. παρά

   a. παρά + genitive = away from (the side of)

      (EG 10)   ὁ Ἰησοῦς ἦλθε παρὰ τῆς θαλάσσης.
      Jesus went away from (beside) the sea.

      (EG 11)   ἐδεξάμην ἄρτον παρὰ τοῦ ἀδελφοῦ μου.
      I received bread from my brother.

   b. παρά + dative = at (the side of)

      (EG 12)   ὁ Ἰησοῦς ἦν παρὰ τῷ οἴκῳ.
      Jesus was beside the house.

   c. παρά + accusative = to (the side of)

      (EG 13)   ὁ Ἰησοῦς ἦλθε παρὰ τὸν οἴκῳ.
      Jesus went to the side of the house.

2. ἐπί

    a. ἐπί + genitive =

        (1) on

            (EG 14)   ὁ ἄνθρωπος ἐκάθιζεν ἐπὶ τοῦ ἵππου.
                      The man was sitting on the horse.

        (2) in the time of

            (EG 15)   ὁ Ἰωάννης ἐκήρυξεν ἐπὶ τοῦ Ἰησοῦ.
                      John preached in the time of Jesus.

        (3) in the presence of

            (EG 16)   ὁ Στέφανος ἐδιώχθη ἐπὶ τοῦ Σαύλου.
                      Stephen was persecuted in the presence of Saul.

    b. ἐπί + dative = at

        (EG 17)   ὁ δοῦλος ἦν ἐπὶ τῇ θύρᾳ.
                  The slave was at the door.

        (EG 18)   ὁ ὄχλος ἐθαύμαζεν ἐπὶ τῷ εὐαγγελίῳ.
                  The crowd was amazed at the Gospel.

    c. ἐπί + accusative=on (with motion onto) or over (=moving along over)

        (EG 19)   ὁ ἵππος ἔπεσεν ἐπὶ τὴν γῆν.
                  The horse fell on(to) the ground.

        (EG 20)   ὁ ἄγγελος τοῦ θανατοῦ ἦλθεν ἐπὶ τὴν γῆν.
                  The angel of death went over the land.

Note: All three cases can be used to mean "over" in the sense of "having authority over" or "ruling over."

(EG 21)   ἔχει ἐξουσίαν ἐπὶ τῆς ἐκκλησίας.

(EG 22)   ἔχει ἐξουσίαν ἐπὶ τῇ ἐκκλησίᾳ.

(EG 23)   ἔχει ἐξουσίαν ἐπὶ τὴν ἐκκλησίαν.

All three say: He has authority over the church.

C. Vocabulary

βασιλεύω (R): I rule

γαμέω (R): I marry

ἐξουσία ⁻ας, f.: power, authority

ἐπι‐θυμέω (R): I desire earnestly, crave

θαυμάζω (R): (intrans.) I wonder at, marvel

θύρα ⁻ας, f.: door

καθίζω (R): I sit; sit down

κλαίω, κλαύσω (R): I weep

νύμφη ⁻ης, f.: bride

νυμφίος ⁻ου, m.: groom

ὁδός ⁻οῦ, f.: road, way

παρα‐γίνομαι, etc.: I am present; appear

παρα‐λαμβάνω, etc.: I take along; receive

τόπος ⁻ου, m.: place

Be sure to include ἐπί, παρά, and the relative pronoun as vocabulary.

D. Exercise

Fill in the proper form of the relative pronoun:

1. λέγω τῷ ἀποστόλῳ _____ ἐδίωξας.
   I am speaking to the apostle *whom* you persecuted.

2. λέγω τῷ ἀποστόλῳ _____ ἀργύριον ἔπεμψας.
   I am speaking to the apostle *to whom* you sent money.

3. λέγω τῷ ἀποστόλῳ _____ τὰ ἱμάτια ἔλαβες.
   I am speaking to the apostle *whose* clothes you took.

E. Practice Sentences

1. Greek to English

a. ὁ δὲ Ἰησοῦς παρ‐έλαβε τὸν Πέτρον καὶ τὸν Ἰωάννην καὶ ἀπ‐ῆλθεν εἰς ἅγιον τόπον.

b. σήμερον ὁ νυμφίος ἐγάμησεν τὴν νύμφην αὐτοῦ ἐν τῇ ἐκκλησίᾳ ἣ ἐν τῇ κώμῃ ἐστίν.

c. οἱ ὄχλοι ἐθαύμασαν ἐπὶ ταῖς διδαχαῖς ἃς ἤκουον παρὰ τοῦ Ἰησοῦ.

d. ὁ πονηρὸς προφήτης ἐπ‐εθύμησεν ἐξουσίαν ἐπὶ τῶν ἁγίων οἳ ἐτήρουν τὰς ἐντολὰς τοῦ κυρίου.

e. ἐκάθιζεν ὁ χωλὸς ἐπὶ τῇ θύρᾳ τοῦ οἴκου τοῦ παρὰ τῇ ὁδῷ, καὶ ᾔτει ἀργύρια.

f. ἐν τῇ βασιλείᾳ τῶν οὐρανῶν, οἱ κακοὶ οὐ βασι-
λεύσουσιν ἐπὶ τοὺς ἀγαθούς.

g. ὁ *βαπτιστὴς* παρ-εγένετο παρὰ τῷ ποταμῷ καὶ
ἐκήρυσσεν ἐφ '[1] ἁμαρτωλῶν.

h. αἱ πτωχαὶ κλαίουσιν ἐφ '[1] ἃ ἐκλέφθη ὑπὸ τῶν
κακῶν τελωνῶν.

2. English to Greek

The slave whom you love wept in the presence of his master.

F. Bible Passages

Luke 1:12b καὶ   φόβος . . . (C)

1 Corinthians 15:1 (ἑστήκατε = στήκετε) (Cs) (omit ἀδελφοί)

James 1:12a . . . πειρασμόν (C)

Luke 9:50b ὅς . . .

Romans 7:15b οὐ γὰρ . . .

Note

1. ἐφ ' = ἐπ ' before rough breathing

16
The Infinitive, Part 1

A. Introduction

The infinitive is best understood as pure action, the pure verbal idea. Thus, "to come" = "the act of coming." As a result, the infinitive is a *verbal,* a combination verb and noun. As a verb it conveys action or state, may take an object, is modified by adverbs, etc. As a noun, it may be the subject of a verb, the object of a verb, etc.

(EG 1)   *To love* God faithfully is noble.

(EG 2)   I desire *to love.*

The forms of an infinitive do not convey person or number, though they do have tense in English. Greek is different (see D below).

(EG 3)   *To love* is good (present infinitive).

(EG 4)   'Tis better *to have loved* . . . (perfect infinitive).

Overall, Greek use of the infinitive is very similar to that of English, though it is somewhat expanded. Since Greek does not use gerunds, the infinitive must do double duty.

(EG 5)   *Loving* is fun.

Here "loving" is a gerund in English; Greek would use the infinitive.

B. Forms

1. λείπω

	Active	Middle	Passive
"Focus upon Connection"/ "Present"	λείπειν	λείπεσθαι	λείπεσθαι
"Future"	λείψειν	λείψεσθαι	λειφθήσεσθαι
"Focus on the Action"/ "Aorist"	λιπεῖν	λιπέσθαι	λειφθῆναι

2. εἰμί

	Active
"Focus upon Connection"/ "Present"	εἶναι

111

3. λύω

	Active	Middle	Passive
"Focus upon Connection"/			
"Present"	λύειν	λύεσθαι	λύεσθαι
"Future"	λύσειν	λύσεσθαι	λυθήσεσθαι
"Focus on the Action"/			
"Aorist"	λῦσαι	λύσασθαι	λυθῆναι

C. Morphology

Generally speaking, infinitive forms have stem, connecting vowel, and ending.

1. The basic endings are as follows:

Active Endings	Middle/Passive Ending
⁻ειν	
⁻ναι	⁻σθαι
⁻αι	

2. Normally, ϵ is the connecting vowel (contracted in $\epsilon\iota\nu$), with a, as usual, in the weak "aorist."

3. Note the unusual accent of the strong "aorist" active and middle. This accent helps to distinguish it from "present" forms. Note, however, that the "present" infinitive of ⁻έω contract verbs is accented identically in the active:

   φιλέἰειν → φιλεῖν (Middle/passive is φιλεῖσθαι.)

4. The weak "aorist" ending, $a\iota$, is unusual, but it does have the characteristic a.

5. $\nu a\iota$, the "aorist" passive infinitive ending is, technically, active and is used in many very old verbs (cf. εἰμί, B 2 above). But as we have noted (chapter 11, C 1 b (3)(a)), "aorist" passives use *active* forms. Note that there is no connecting vowel.

6. No infinitive form carries an augment. Thus all "aorist" infinitives will either drop the ϵ or shorten their initial letter, compared to the indicative forms. ONLY INDICATIVE FORMS ARE AUGMENTED.

D. "Tense"

In forms of the verb other than the indicative mood—such as the infinitive—"tense" indicates focus relative to action only, *not time*. Compare and contrast chapter 9, A 2, B 1, and G. As a result, the so-called "present" infinitive focuses upon the connection between the action and the doer of the action, and the so-called "aorist" infinitive focuses on the action *only*. It would, therefore, really be much more accurate to call the "present" infinitive the "focus upon connection" infinitive and the "aorist" infinitive the "focus on the action" infinitive, for each of these conveys the "focus"/"aspect" of the stem it represents, not time.

Put another way, the infinitive represents the focus of a given stem, not the time which is associated with any indicative mood form of that stem. Therefore, there is only one infinitive per "focus" and only one infinitive per stem. For this reason, there is no "imperfect infinitive," for the only difference between present and imperfect indicative forms is time (not focus): the imperfect indicative conveys a focus upon connection between doer and activity in the past, the present indicative a focus upon such a connection in the present.

Note: The "future" infinitive is given only for completeness. It is not used in the constructions described in this and in the succeeding chapter. It is simply used in indirect discourse, a function described in chapter 42.

E. Syntax

1. There are five major uses of the infinitive without the article:

a. Purpose

(EG 6)   ἔρχεται *ἰδεῖν* τὸν ἀπόστολον.
He is coming *to see* the apostle.

The infinitive tells *why* he came.

b. Object

(EG 7)   θέλει *ἰδεῖν* τὸν ἀπόστολον.
He desires *to see* the apostle.

The infinitive tells *what* he desires.

c. Epexegetical

(EG 8)   ἄξιός ἐστιν *ἰδεῖν* τὸν ἀπόστολον.
He is worthy *to see* the apostle.

The infinitive tells *in what respect* he is worthy.

d. Appositional

(EG 9)   τοῦτό ἐστιν ἀγαθόν, *φιλῆσαι* τὸν θεόν.
This is good, *to love* God.

The infinitive tells *what "this"* is.

e. Subject (normally of an impersonal verb)

(EG 10)   ἔξεστι *φιλῆσαι* τὸν θεόν.
It is proper *to love* God.

The infinitive tells *what is proper*. ("It" is a "dummy subject.")

2. The infinitive without the article is also used to convey *result*. In such cases, however, the clause in which the infinitive stands begins with ὥστε.

   (EG 11)   ὁ ἐχθρὸς εἰσ-ῆλθεν εἰς τὸ ἱερόν, <u>ὥστε</u>
             ἰδεῖν τὸ ἀργύριον ἐν αὐτῷ.
             The enemy entered the temple, *with the result that* he
             saw the money in it.

3. The subject of the infinitive, if identical to the subject of the main verb, is normally not expressed (see EGs 6–11 above). If it is not identical to the main subject, it is expressed in the *accusative* case.

   (EG 12)   ὁ ἐχθρὸς ἀπ-ῆλθεν, ὥστε <u>τὸν λαὸν</u>
             δοξάσαι τὸν θεόν.
             The enemy went away, *with the result that the people*
             glorified God.

   Note: This principle applies to all uses of the infinitive, not only to those with ὥστε.

4. The negative for the infinitive, as for all forms of the verb outside the indicative (generally speaking), is μή, not οὐκ.

F. Vocabulary

ἄρχω (R): I rule; (mid.) I begin

δεῖ: It is necessary

ἐλπίζω (R): I hope

ἔξεστι(ν): It is possible; lawful

ἱκανός -ή -όν: suitable, adequate, able

καιρός -οῦ, m.: due time, season

κελεύω (R): I order

λαός -οῦ, m.: people

μέλλω, μελλήσω: I am going (to), about (to) (imperfect = ἤμελλον)

μή (adv.): not (with verb forms other than the indicative)

ὀφείλω: I owe (only present and imperfect); I ought (+ infinitive)

χρεία -ας, f.: need

ὥρα -ας, f.: hour

ὥστε (conj.): so that (result)

G. Exercise

Give the "focus upon connection"/"present" and "focus on the action"/ "aorist" active, middle, and passive infinitives of the following:

1. πέμπω

2. λαμβάνω

3. σώζω

4. αἰτέω

5. φέρω

6. ἄγω

H. Practice Sentences

1. Greek to English

(Watch infinitive stem and aspect!)

a. ὁ προφήτης ἦλθεν ἰδεῖν τὸν λαὸν καὶ λαλῆσαι τὴν ἀλήθειαν.

b. ἐγὼ μὲν χρείαν ἔχω βαπτισθῆναι ὑπὸ σοῦ, σὺ δὲ αἰτεῖς βαπτισθῆναι ὑπ᾽ ἐμοῦ;

c. τοῦτό ἐστιν ἀγαθόν, ἡμᾶς φιλεῖν τὸν θεὸν καὶ τηρεῖν τὰς ἐντολὰς αὐτοῦ.

d. ἐν τῇ βασιλείᾳ, δεῖ ὑμᾶς γενέσθαι τέκνα.

e. οὐχ ἱκανός εἰμι διδάξαι τὸν μαθητὴν ὃν ἔπεμψας.

f. οὐκ εἶπεν λόγον ὁ Χριστός, ὥστε τὸν <u>Πιλᾶτον</u> θαυμάζειν.

g. οἱ μαθηταὶ ἤρξαντο κηρύσσειν[1] τὸ εὐαγγέλιον, ἀλλ᾽ οἱ Ἰουδαῖοι ἐκέλευσαν αὐτοὺς ἀχθῆναι ἐκ τοῦ ἱεροῦ.

h. ἔξεστιν εἰπεῖν περὶ Ἰησοῦ, καὶ μέλλομεν ποιεῖν[1] τοῦτο.

i. ὀφείλομεν φιλεῖν τοὺς ἐχθροὺς ἡμῶν, ὁ γὰρ Ἰησοῦς ἀπ-έθανεν σῶσαι καὶ αὐτούς.

j. ὁ <u>Παῦλος</u> ἤλπισεν καὶ ἐλθεῖν πρὸς τοὺς ἁγίους ἐν Ῥώμῃ.

k. αὕτη ἐστὶν ἡ ὥρα τοῦ θανάτου. ὁ οὖν καιρὸς μετα-νοῆσαι.

2. English to Greek

Jesus commanded the disciples to go into the world and to preach the Gospel to men/people.

I. Bible Passages

Luke 15:15b καὶ ἔπεμψεν . . .

John 12:21b θέλομεν . . .

Apocalypse 4:11a . . . τιμήν

Matthew 15:30b–31a καὶ ἐθεράπευσεν . . . θαυμάσαι.

Note

1. **Note:** ἄρχομαι and μέλλω normally take the "present" infinitive.

17

The Infinitive, Part 2

A. Introduction

The infinitive is often used with the article. In such cases, it may be used both as the subject of a verb and (especially) with prepositions. No new morphology need be learned for these uses.

B. Syntax

1. Basic Theory

Often the infinitive is used with the *neuter* article (because it is an abstract concept). This emphasizes the noun aspect of the infinitive. In terms of English, it is perhaps better to think of it in these cases as "the act of . . ." rather than as "to . . ."

(EG 1)   τὸ ἐλθεῖν = "the act of going"

2. Uses

a. The articular infinitive is often used as the subject of the verb "to be" (the infinitive without the article is more common with impersonal verbs such as ἔξεστιν and δεῖ).

(EG 2)   τὸ φιλῆσαι καλόν ἐστιν.
To love (the very act of loving) is noble.

(EG 3)   τὸ κηρῦξαι τὸ εὐαγγέλιόν ἐστιν ἀγαθὸν ἔργον.
To preach (the very act of preaching) the Gospel is a good work.

b. Perhaps even more commonly, the articular infinitive is used after prepositions. In such constructions, the infinitive is governed by the preposition. This is reflected by the article taking the case required by the preposition. (The infinitive itself never changes form.) Such constructions derive their meaning from the meaning of the preposition, and any *time* relationship to the main verb must be obtained from the logic and the overall meaning of the sentence.

117

(EG 4)   μετὰ τὸ ἐλθεῖν τὸν Ἰησοῦν εἰς τὸν
         οἶκον, οἱ μαθηταὶ ἐκηρύσσον.
         After Jesus had come into the house, the disciples
         began to preach. (Literally: After the act of coming
         into the house—Jesus is the doer—the disciples
         began to preach.)

Note in EG 4:

(1) The preposition governs the articular infinitive just as it
     governs a noun. Because the infinitive has noun character-
     istics, this is possible. Thus, τό in this sentence is *accusa-
     tive,* since μετά is followed by the accusative when it
     means "after."

(2) The infinitive is unaffected morphologically by the prepo-
     sition.

(3) The infinitive can be modified by a prepositional phrase.

(4) The subject of the infinitive is in the accusative.

(5) The translation of the "aorist" infinitive as *pluperfect* ("had
     come") is necessitated by the logic of the sentence and En-
     glish usage. Jesus' coming was a past act prior to another
     past act—in English, pluperfect. The so-called *"tense"* of
     the infinitive is *irrelevant;* it expresses focus relative to ac-
     tion only.

(EG 5)   μετὰ τὸ κηρῦξαι τὸν δοῦλον τὸ εὐαγγέλιον,
         ἐλευσόμεθα εἰς τὸ ἱερόν.
         After the slave preaches the Gospel, we will go
         into the temple. (Literally: After the act of
         preaching the Gospel—the slave is the doer—we
         will go into the temple.)

Note in EG 5:

(6) Both the subject of the infinitive and its object are in the ac-
     cusative case. Normally, the one nearer the infinitive is the
     subject. Sometimes the subject will stand in the "sandwich"
     position:

     (EG 6)   μετὰ <u>τὸ</u> τὸν δοῦλον <u>κηρῦξαι</u> τὸ
              εὐαγγέλιον . . .

(7) The infinitive need not be translated as in the past at all,
     even though it is "aorist," if the logic of the sentence action
     is not in the past. Here (in EG 5) it is future. After a future
     preaching, a future going will occur. REMEMBER:
     "TENSE" OF THE INFINITIVE CONVEYS ASPECT/
     FOCUS RELATIVE TO ACTION ONLY.

c. The following prepositions are common with infinitives and are easily understood:

(1) μετά (+ τό + infinitive)

See EGs 4 and 5 above.

(2) πρό (+ τοῦ + infinitive)

(EG 7) πρὸ τοῦ ἐλθεῖν τὸν 'Ιησοῦν εἰς τὸν οἶκον, οἱ μαθηταὶ ἐκήρυσσον.
Before Jesus came into the house, the disciples began to preach. (Literally: Before the act of coming into the house—Jesus is the doer—. . .)

Note that the article is genitive, because πρό "takes" the genitive.

(3) διά (+ τό + infinitive)

(EG 8) διὰ τὸ ἐλθεῖν τὸν 'Ιησοῦν εἰς τὸν οἶκον, οἱ μαθηταὶ ἐκήρυσσον.
Because Jesus had come into the house, the disciples began to preach. (Literally: Because of the act of coming into the house—Jesus is the doer—. . .)

Note that when διά "takes" the accusative it means "because."

d. The following three uses of prepositions with the articular infinitive are not as immediately obvious as the three uses above, but they are logical.

(1) πρός (+ τό + infinitive)

(EG 9) ὁ 'Ιησοῦς ἦλθε πρὸς τὸ ἰδεῖν τοὺς μαθητάς.
Jesus came in order to see the disciples.
(Literally: Jesus came toward this end: the act of seeing the disciples.)

(2) εἰς (+ τό + infinitive)

(EG 10) ὁ 'Ιησοῦς ἦλθεν εἰς τὸ ἰδεῖν τοὺς μαθητάς.
Jesus came in order to see the disciples.
(Literally: Jesus came for this end: the act of seeing the disciples.)

Both πρός and εἰς are used interchangeably in this construction, with εἰς the more common.

(3) $\dot{\epsilon}\nu$ (+ $\tau\hat{\omega}$ + infinitive)

    (EG 11)   ὁ 'Ιησοῦς ἦλθεν ἐν τῷ τοὺς
                   μαθητὰς κηρύσσειν τὸ εὐαγγέλιον.
                   Jesus came while the disciples were preaching
                   the Gospel. (Literally: Jesus came in the act of
                   the disciples preaching the Gospel.)

Note in EG 11 that $\tau\hat{\omega}$ (dative) is necessary because $\dot{\epsilon}\nu$ "takes" the dative. Note also that the "focus upon connection"/"present" infinitive is usually used with $\dot{\epsilon}\nu$ because its focus is appropriate to the thought. (Note here that the so-called "present tense" infinitive is used for a past act!)

C. Vocabulary

δένδρον ⁻ου, n.: tree

δεύτερος ⁻α ⁻ον: second

καρπός ⁻οῦ, m.: fruit

νηστεύω (R): I fast

ὀργή ⁻ῆς, f.: wrath

οὔπω (adv.): not yet

ὀφθαλμός ⁻οῦ, m.: eye

πάλιν (adv.): again; back

πορνεία ⁻ας, f.: unchastity, immorality

πρόσωπον ⁻ου, n.: face

ὠφελέω (R): I help

D. Exercise

Give the "tense" and voice of the following infinitives:

1. λυθῆναι

2. ἰδεῖν

3. γίνεσθαι

4. φιλῆσαι

5. γενέσθαι

6. λαλεῖσθαι

7. αἰτεῖν

8. λαβεῖν

9. κληρονομήσασθαι

10. ἐλθεῖν

11. πραχθῆναι

12. ἀπο-λύσειν

E. Practice Sentences

1. Greek to English

a. ὁ 'Ιησοῦς εἰσ-ῆλθε τὸν κόσμον πρὸς τὸ ὠφελῆσαι ἁμαρτωλούς.

b. εἶπον· νῦν κατα-βήσομαι εἰς τὴν ἔρημον εἰς τὸ νηστεύειν.

c. διὰ τὸ θεραπεῦσαι τὸν 'Ιησοῦν τοὺς ὀφθαλμοὺς αὐτῶν, οἱ τυφλοὶ ἀν-έβλεψαν.

d. τὴν ὀργὴν αὐτοῦ ὁ θεὸς πέμψει ἐπὶ πορνείαν ἐν γῇ.

e. ἀγαθὸς μὲν ὁ καρπὸς τοῦ πρώτου δένδρου, κακὸς δὲ ὁ καρπὸς τοῦ δευτέρου.

f. μετὰ τὸ τὸν στρατιώτην φονευθῆναι μαχαίρῃ, ἔπεσεν ἐπὶ τὸ πρόσωπον αὐτοῦ.

g. ἐν τῷ πάλιν εἰσ-έρχεσθαι αὐτὸν εἰς τὸν οἶκον ἐν ᾧ ἔλιπε τὸ ἅγιον βιβλίον, εἶδεν ἄλλους μαθητάς.

h. τὸ μὴ γινώσκειν τὴν ἀλήθειαν κακόν ἐστιν.

i. πρὸ τοῦ ἄρξασθαι τὸν 'Ιωάννην κηρύσσειν παρὰ τῷ ποταμῷ, οὔπω ὁ 'Ιησοῦς παρ-εγένετο ἐπὶ τοῦ λαοῦ.

2. English to Greek

After the disciple had left his slave in the village, he went into the field.

F. Bible Passages

1 Thessalonians 3:2a . . . ὑμᾶς (στηρίξαι is from στηρίζω)

Acts 19:21b μετὰ τὸ . . .

James 4:2b μάχεσθε . . .

18

Nouns, Part 3:
The Third Declension

A. Introduction

In chapters 3 and 4 we introduced O (second) and A (first) declension nouns. There we saw that

1. a declension is essentially a pattern of endings;

2. gender, number, and case are not tied to any one ending or set of letters but vary by declension:

    (EG 1) $\pi\alpha\rho\theta\acute{\epsilon}\nu o\varsigma$ = feminine, nominative, singular
    $\dot{\eta}\mu\acute{\epsilon}\rho\alpha$ = feminine, nominative, singular

3. function is independent of specific form; function depends only on gender, number, and case, whatever the form:

    (EG 2) $\beta\lambda\acute{\epsilon}\pi\omega\ \tau\grave{o}\nu\ \upsilon\acute{\iota}\acute{o}\nu.$
    I see the son.

    $\beta\lambda\acute{\epsilon}\pi\omega\ \tau\grave{\eta}\nu\ \kappa\acute{\omega}\mu\eta\nu.$
    I see the village.

Both nouns in EG 2 function as direct object, though their endings (because they are different declensions) are dissimilar.

In this chapter we will encounter the third (and final) declension—and specifically consonantal stem nouns. Their pattern, while it does have many subvariations, is fairly standard.

B. Paradigm Forms

1. Basic Pattern for Masculine and Feminine Nouns

	Singular	Plural	Singular	Plural
N	$\sigma\omega\tau\acute{\eta}\rho$	$\sigma\omega\tau\hat{\eta}\rho\epsilon\varsigma$	$\sigma\acute{\alpha}\rho\xi$	$\sigma\acute{\alpha}\rho\kappa\epsilon\varsigma$
G	$\sigma\omega\tau\hat{\eta}\rho o\varsigma$	$\sigma\omega\tau\acute{\eta}\rho\omega\nu$	$\sigma\alpha\rho\kappa\acute{o}\varsigma$	$\sigma\alpha\rho\kappa\hat{\omega}\nu$
D	$\sigma\omega\tau\hat{\eta}\rho\iota$	$\sigma\omega\tau\hat{\eta}\rho\sigma\iota(\nu)$	$\sigma\alpha\rho\kappa\acute{\iota}$	$\sigma\alpha\rho\xi\acute{\iota}(\nu)$
A	$\sigma\omega\tau\hat{\eta}\rho\alpha$	$\sigma\omega\tau\hat{\eta}\rho\alpha\varsigma$	$\sigma\acute{\alpha}\rho\kappa\alpha$	$\sigma\acute{\alpha}\rho\kappa\alpha\varsigma$

2. Basic Pattern for Neuter Nouns

	Singular	Plural
N	πνεῦμα	πνεύματα
G	πνεύματος	πνευμάτων
D	πνεύματι	πνεύμασι(ν)
A	πνεῦμα	πνεύματα

C. Morphology

1. The endings for the masculine and feminine nouns are as follows:

	Singular	Plural
N	(nothing) or ˉς	ˉες
G	ˉος	ˉων
D	ˉι	ˉσι
A	ˉα	ˉας

The nominative singular, if it has no ending (i.e., without ˉς), is often lengthened:

(EG 3) N ἡγεμών
        G ἡγεμόνος

Note that the *true stem* of a third declension noun can only be obtained from the *genitive singular* form (minus ος). See EG 3.

2. The neuter pattern uses a shortened stem in the nominative and accusative singular. All neuters of this type have μα at the end of the short stem (cf. πνεῦμα) and a τ at the end of the stem proper, after the μα (cf. πνεύματος).

3. Generally, all alphas in third declension endings are *short*.

4. Forms with Sigma

    a. The σ of the dative plural ending combines with the final consonant of the stem in the same ways in which the futures of consonantal stem verbs are formed (see chapter 7, A 3 a). Note: The same principle is applied to the nominative singular if a ς appears (cf. σάρξ).

    b. In the dative plural

        (1) a ρ at the end of the stem remains before the σ (cf. σωτήρ);

        (2) a ν drops out before σ:

        (EG 4)   Nominative singular: ἡγεμών
                         Genitive singular: ἡγεμόνος
                         Dative plural: ἡγεμόσι

(3) a ντ elides before σ, but the previous vowel compensates by lengthening into a diphthong:

(EG 5)   Nominative singular: ἄρχων
          Genitive singular: ἄρχοντος
          Dative plural: ἄρχουσι

5. It is more important than ever to learn the genitive singular of every noun, since it cannot be deduced from the nominative singular form. Note the following:

		Singular	
(EG 6)	N	αἰών	
	G	αἰῶνος	(cf. EGs 3 and 4 above)
(EG 7)	N	νύξ	
	G	νυκτός	(cf. σάρξ, σαρκός)
(EG 8)	N	ποιμήν	
	G	ποιμένος	(cf. σωτήρ, σωτῆρος)
(EG 9)	N	πούς	
	G	ποδός	

It must also be noted that gender must be learned and cannot be deduced (see vocabulary in E below).

D. Accent

The accent of all nouns is constant (see chapter 2, A 4 c (2)). This rule also applies in the third declension, with the exception of nouns that are monosyllabic in the nominative singular. Note the accent of σάρξ, B 1 above. Its accent moves from the stem in the nominative to the ending in the genitive and dative and returns to the stem in the accusative. (See also EG 7.)

E. Vocabulary

αἷμα ˗ατος, n.: blood

αἰών ˗ῶνος, m.: age, aeon[1]

ἄρχων ˗οντος, m.: ruler

εἰκών ˗όνος, f.: image

Ἕλλην ˗ηνος, m.: Greek

ἐλπίς ˗ίδος, f.: hope

ἡγεμών ˗όνος, m.: leader

νύξ, νυκτός, f.: night

πνεῦμα ˗ατος, n.: spirit; breath

ποιμήν -ένος, m.: shepherd

πούς, ποδός, m.: foot

σάρξ, σαρκός, f.: flesh

σῶμα -ατος, n.: body

σωτήρ -ῆρος, m.: savior

F. Exercise

Give the dative singular, accusative singular, and dative plural of the following:

1. αἷμα

2. ἄρχων

3. εἰκών

4. ἐλπίς

5. πούς

G. Practice Sentences

1. Greek to English

a. ὁ ᾽Ιησοῦς ἔνιψε τοὺς πόδας τῶν μαθητῶν.

b. ἡ νὺξ ἐγένετο καὶ οἱ ποιμένες ἐκάθιζον ἐπὶ τῆς γῆς.

c. πονηρὰ πνεύματα οὐκ εἶχον ἐξουσίαν βασιλεῦσαι ἐν τῷ αἰῶνι ἐκείνῳ.

d. ὁ σωτὴρ ἐπέμφθη εἰς τὸν κόσμον ἡμῶν πρὸς τὸ κηρῦξαι τὴν ἀγάπην τοῦ θεοῦ ἡγεμόσι καὶ ἄρχουσιν.

e. ἡ σάρξ καὶ τὸ αἷμα οὐ κληρονομήσει τὴν βασιλείαν τῶν οὐρανῶν.

f. οἱ ῞Ελληνες ᾠκοδόμουν ἱερὰ ταῖς εἰκόσι τῶν θεῶν αὐτῶν, ἡ δὲ ἐλπὶς ἡμῶν εἰς[2] τὸν <u>ἀληθινὸν</u> θεόν ἐστιν.

g. τὸ μὲν αἷμα τῶν ἐχθρῶν εὗρον οἱ στρατιῶται, τὰ δὲ σώματα οὐκ εἶδον.

2. English to Greek

This is the body and blood of our Savior, Jesus Christ.

H. Bible Passages

John 1:14a . . . $\dot{\epsilon}\gamma\acute{\epsilon}\nu\epsilon\tau o$

John 10:14a . . . $\kappa\alpha\lambda\acute{o}\varsigma$

Luke 2:8a . . . $\chi\acute{\omega}\rho\alpha$

1 Corinthians 2:6 (omit last two words)

Notes

1. $\epsilon\dot{\iota}\varsigma$ $\tau\grave{o}\nu$ $\alpha\dot{\iota}\hat{\omega}\nu\alpha$ and $\epsilon\dot{\iota}\varsigma$ $\tau o\grave{\upsilon}\varsigma$ $\alpha\dot{\iota}\hat{\omega}\nu\alpha\varsigma$ are often rendered "forever."

2. This is idiomatic for hope *in*.

19

Nouns, Part 4, and Third Declension Adjectives

A. Third Declension Vowel and Sigma Stem Nouns

1. Introduction

A number of nouns following the third declension pattern are built off of a vowel or sigma stem. (The nouns of chapter 18 were consonantal stem nouns.) The same basic pattern of endings is employed with several peculiarities.

2. Paradigm Nouns

a. πόλις

	Singular	Plural
N	πόλις	πόλεις (πόλε|ες)
G	πόλεως	πόλεων
D	πόλει (πόλε|ι)	πόλεσι(ν)
A	πόλιν	πόλεις (πόλε|ες)

b. βασιλεύς

	Singular	Plural
N	βασιλεύς	βασιλεῖς (βασιλέ|ες)
G	βασιλέως	βασιλέων
D	βασιλεῖ (βασιλέ|ι)	βασιλεῦσι(ν)
A	βασιλέα	βασιλεῖς / βασιλέας

c. ἔθνος

	Singular	Plural
N	ἔθνος	ἔθνη (ἔθνε|α)
G	ἔθνους (ἔθνε|ος)	ἐθνῶν (ἐθνέ|ων)
D	ἔθνει (ἔθνε|ι)	ἔθνεσι(ν) (ἔθνε|σι)
A	ἔθνος	ἔθνη (ἔθνε|α)

3. Morphology

a. πόλις pattern

(1) Nouns in this pattern have a stem that ends technically in ι, practically in ε. The nominative and accusative singular

preserve the ι; the other forms have ϵ.

   (2) The accusative singular ending is ν, not α.

   (3) The accusative plural has the same form as the nominative plural.

   (4) All nouns of this pattern are feminine.

b. βασιλεύς pattern

   (1) This pattern is similar to that of πόλις, though the accusative singular is normal third declension, as is one option for the accusative plural. (This "normal" ending is classical.)

   (2) All nouns of this pattern are masculine.

c. ἔθνος pattern

   (1) The stem of these nouns is ἔθνεσ- and contraction of the ϵ with the vowel following is normal (σ drops out).

   (2) All nouns of this pattern are neuter.

B. Third Declension Adjectives

1. Introduction

All adjectives met thus far we have called "basic" or "regular." These have had O or second declension endings in the masculine and neuter, A or first declension endings in the feminine. (These are, indeed, often called O or second declension adjectives.) We now encounter adjectives that follow a third declension pattern, with vowel, sigma, or consonantal stems.

2. Adjective Paradigms

a. Consonantal Stem

	Singular		Plural	
	M/F	N	M/F	N
N	ἄφρων	ἄφρον	ἄφρονες	ἄφρονα
G	ἄφρονος	ἄφρονος	ἀφρόνων	ἀφρόνων
D	ἄφρονι	ἄφρονι	ἄφροσι(ν)	ἄφροσι(ν)
A	ἄφρονα	ἄφρον	ἄφρονας	ἄφρονα

b. Sigma Stem

	Singular	
	M/F	N
N	ἀληθής	ἀληθές
G	ἀληθοῦς (ἀληθέσ|ος)	ἀληθοῦς (ἀληθέσ|ος)
D	ἀληθεῖ (ἀληθέσ|ι)	ἀληθεῖ (ἀληθέσ|ι)
A	ἀληθῆ (ἀληθέσ|α)	ἀληθές

Plural

	M/F	N
N	ἀληθεῖς (ἀληθέσ|ες'')	ἀληθῆ (ἀληθέσ|α)
G	ἀληθῶν (ἀληθέσ|ων)	ἀληθῶν (ἀληθέσ|ων)
D	ἀληθέσι(ν) (ἀληθέσ|σι)	ἀληθέσι(ν) (ἀληθέσ|σι)
A	ἀληθεῖς (ἀληθέσ|ες)	ἀληθῆ (ἀληθέσ|α)

c. Vowel Stem

Singular

	M	F	N
N	εὐθύς	εὐθεῖα	εὐθύ
G	εὐθέος	εὐθείας	εὐθέος
D	εὐθεῖ (εὐθέ|ϊ)	εὐθείᾳ	εὐθεῖ (εὐθέ|ϊ)
A	εὐθύν	εὐθεῖαν	εὐθύ

Plural

	M	F	N
N	εὐθεῖς (εὐθέ|ες)	εὐθεῖαι	εὐθέα
G	εὐθέων	εὐθειῶν	εὐθέων
D	εὐθέσι(ν)	εὐθείαις	εὐθέσι(ν)
A	εὐθεῖς	εὐθείας	εὐθέα

3. Morphology

a. Note the identity of pattern between the consonantal stem *ἄφρων* and *ἡγεμών*.

b. *ἀληθής* is similar to *ἔθνος* with *εσ* ending the stem proper. The *ε* contracts with the vowel following, *σ* eliding. (Note especially the identity of the neuter forms.)

c. *εὐθύς* in its masculine forms is similar to *πόλις* with a close vowel in the nominative and accusative singular and an *ε* at the end of the stem in the other forms. The feminine is A declension *α* pattern.

C. Vocabulary

ἀληθής ⁻*ές*: true

ἀνάστασις ⁻*εως*, f.: resurrection

ἀσθενής ⁻*ές*: weak, sick

ἄφρων ⁻*ον*: foolish

βασιλεύς ⁻*έως*, m.: king

γραμματεύς ⁻*έως*, m.: scribe

ἔθνος ⁻*ους*, n.: nation (pl. Gentiles)

εὐθύς -εῖα -ύ: straight

εὐθέως (adv.): straightway, immediately

ἱερεύς -έως, m.: priest

ὄρος -ους, n.: mountain

πίστις -εως, f.: faith

πόλις -εως, f.: city

ταχύς -εῖα -ύ: swift

D. Exercise

Give the dative singular, accusative singular, and dative plural of the following:

1. ἀνάστασις

2. ἀσθενής

3. γραμματεύς

4. ὄρος

5. ταχύς

E. Practice Sentences

1. Greek to English

a. ὁ σωτὴρ ἐλεύσεται εἰς τὸ σῶσαι καὶ τὰ ἔθνη.

b. μετὰ τὴν ἀνάστασιν τῶν νεκρῶν, οἱ ἅγιοι βασι-
λεύσουσιν ἐπὶ τῆς βασιλείας τοῦ διαβόλου.

c. μετὰ τὸ κλέψαι τὸν τελώνην ταχὺν ἵππον, εὐθέως
ἀπ-ῆλθεν.

d. ἐν τῷ θεραπεύειν τὸν ᾽Ιησοῦν τοὺς ἀσθενεῖς, οἱ
μαθηταὶ αὐτοῦ ἐκήρυσσον τὸ εὐαγγέλιον τοῖς
ἱερεῦσι καὶ Φαρισαίοις.

e. οὐκ ἐστιν ἀληθὴς εἰκὼν τοῦ θεοῦ, πίστει γὰρ
βλέπομεν αὐτὸν οὐδὲ τοῖς ὀφθαλμοῖς ἡμῶν.

f. οἱ ἄφρονες γραμματεῖς ἔφυγον ἐκ τῆς πόλεως, εἰς
δὲ τὰ ὄρη ἀν-έβαινον, ὅτι ὁ βασιλεὺς ἐκέλευσεν
αὐτοὺς φονευθῆναι ἐπὶ τοῦ συνεδρίου.

2. English to Greek

Jesus came to heal the diseases of the sick and to preach to kings and rulers.

F. Bible Passages

3 John 14

Mark 9:2a . . . ὄρος (Cs)

Mark 14:55 (omit εἰς τὸ θανατῶσαι αὐτόν)

Acts 9:36b αὕτη . . . ἀγαθῶν

20

Participles, Part 1: "Focus upon Connection"/ "Present Tense" Forms

A. Introduction

The participle is a verbal; it is part verb and part adjective. Because it is part adjective, it has gender, number, and case. Because it is part verb, it has a focus relative to action and voice, may take an object, may be modified by adverbs, etc.

B. Paradigm Forms

1. Active Voice

a. λείπω (εἰμί)

Singular

	M	F	N
N	λείπων (ὤν)	λείπουσα (οὖσα)	λεῖπον (ὄν)
G	λείποντος (ὄντος)	λειπούσης (οὔσης)	λείποντος (ὄντος)
D	λείποντι (ὄντι)	λειπούσῃ (οὔσῃ)	λείποντι (ὄντι)
A	λείποντα (ὄντα)	λείπουσαν (οὖσαν)	λεῖπον (ὄν)

Plural

	M	F	N
N	λείποντες (ὄντες)	λείπουσαι (οὖσαι)	λείποντα (ὄντα)
G	λειπόντων (ὄντων)	λειπουσῶν (οὐσῶν)	λειπόντων (ὄντων)
D	λείπουσι(ν) (οὖσι[ν])	λειπούσαις (οὔσαις)	λείπουσι(ν) (οὖσι[ν])
A	λείποντας (ὄντας)	λειπούσας (οὔσας)	λείποντα (ὄντα)

b. λύω

Singular

	M	F	N
N	λύων	λύουσα	λῦον
G	λύοντος	λυούσης	λύοντος
D	λύοντι	λυούσῃ	λύοντι
A	λύοντα	λύουσαν	λῦον

Plural

	M	F	N
N	λύοντες	λύουσαι	λύοντα
G	λυόντων	λυουσῶν	λυόντων
D	λύουσι(ν)	λυούσαις	λύουσι(ν)
A	λύοντας	λυούσας	λύοντα

2. Middle/Passive Voice

a. λείπω

Singular

	M	F	N
N	λειπόμενος	λειπομένη	λειπόμενον
G	λειπομένου	λειπομένης	λειπομένου
D	λειπομένῳ	λειπομένη	λειπομένῳ
A	λειπόμενον	λειπομένην	λειπόμενον

Plural

	M	F	N
N	λειπόμενοι	λειπόμεναι	λειπόμενα
G	λειπομένων	λειπομένων	λειπομένων
D	λειπομένοις	λειπομέναις	λειπομένοις
A	λειπομένους	λειπομένας	λειπόμενα

b. λύω

Singular

	M	F	N
N	λυόμενος	λυομένη	λυόμενον
G	λυομένου	λυομένης	λυομένου
D	λυομένῳ	λυομένη	λυομένῳ
A	λυόμενον	λυομένην	λυόμενον

Plural

	M	F	N
N	λυόμενοι	λυόμεναι	λυόμενα
G	λυομένων	λυομένων	λυομένων
D	λυομένοις	λυομέναις	λυομένοις
A	λυομένους	λυομένας	λυόμενα

C. Morphology

1. Basic Pattern

a. Active Voice

(1) Masculine and neuter forms follow a third declension pattern.

(2) Feminine forms follow an A declension "hybrid" pattern.

b. Middle/Passive Voice

  (1) Masculine and neuter forms follow an O declension pattern.

  (2) Feminine forms follow an A declension η pattern.

Note: For $-\acute{\epsilon}\omega$ contract verb morphology, see the paradigm charts in the back of the book.

2. Relationship of Basic Pattern to Forms of $\epsilon\dot{\iota}\mu\acute{\iota}$ ("To Be")

The *active* forms of the "focus upon connection"/"present" participle may be described as the participle of the verb "to be" preceded by the verbal stem. Thus, $\lambda\epsilon\acute{\iota}\pi\omega\nu$ may be seen as $\lambda\epsilon\acute{\iota}\pi + \omega\nu$.

D. Meaning

A *literalistic* translation of the "focus upon connection"/"present" participle, taking into account its nature as part adjective, would be with "-ing" at the end of the basic word.

(EG 1) $\lambda\epsilon\acute{\iota}\pi\omega\nu$ = "leaving"

E. Syntax

1. As part adjective, the participle may stand in either attributive or predicate position. IN INTERPRETING ANY PARTICIPLE, IT IS CRUCIAL TO DETERMINE ITS POSITION.

2. If the participle is in *attributive* position, it is an attribute of the noun or pronoun it modifies, as is any adjective (cf. EG 2) or prepositional phrase (cf. EG 3) in attributive position.

   (EG 2) $\dot{o}$ *$\dot{a}\gamma a\theta\dot{o}\varsigma$* $\mu a\theta\eta\tau\dot{\eta}\varsigma$ $\kappa\eta\rho\dot{\upsilon}\sigma\sigma\epsilon\iota$ $\tau\dot{o}$ $\epsilon\dot{\upsilon}a\gamma\gamma\dot{\epsilon}\lambda\iota o\nu.$
   The *good* disciple is preaching the Gospel.

   (EG 3) $\dot{o}$ *$\dot{a}\pi\dot{o}$ $\tau\hat{\eta}\varsigma$ $\dot{a}\gamma\acute{\iota}a\varsigma$ $\pi\acute{o}\lambda\epsilon\omega\varsigma$* $\mu a\theta\eta\tau\dot{\eta}\varsigma$ $\kappa\eta\rho\dot{\upsilon}\sigma\sigma\epsilon\iota$
   $\epsilon\dot{\upsilon}a\gamma\gamma\dot{\epsilon}\lambda\iota o\nu.$
   The disciple *(who is) from the holy city* is preaching the Gospel.

   (EG 4) $\dot{o}$ *$\theta\epsilon\rho a\pi\epsilon\acute{\upsilon}\omega\nu$ $\tau o\dot{\upsilon}\varsigma$ $\dot{a}\sigma\theta\epsilon\nu\epsilon\hat{\iota}\varsigma$* $\mu a\theta\eta\tau\dot{\eta}\varsigma$
   $\kappa\eta\rho\dot{\upsilon}\sigma\sigma\epsilon\iota$ $\tau\dot{o}$ $\epsilon\dot{\upsilon}a\gamma\gamma\dot{\epsilon}\lambda\iota o\nu.$
   The disciple *who is healing the sick* is preaching the Gospel. (Literally: The healing-the-sick disciple is preaching . . .) (A translation conveying *habitual* action would be: The disciple who heals the sick preaches the Gospel.)

It may be noted that the second, non-"sandwich" type of attributive position is more common with participles:

(EG 5)   ὁ μαθητὴς ὁ θεραπεύων τοὺς ἀσθενεῖς
κηρύσσει τὸ εὐαγγέλιον.

3. If the participle is in *predicate* position, it becomes more closely attached to the main verb of the sentence.

a. Force of the Participle

In predicate position, the participle still refers to a person (or thing) in the sentence, but now it tells more about the main verb, i.e., the *circumstances under which that verbal action takes place*. In other words, it still has a noun or pronoun as a referent, but now it also modifies the verb of its clause, as does an adverb. Note EG 6 in contrast to EG 4:

(EG 6)   θεραπεύων τοὺς ἀσθενεῖς, ὁ μαθητὴς
κηρύσσει τὸ εὐαγγέλιον.
Literally: *Healing* the sick, the disciple is preaching the Gospel.

What does this mean? Simply this: under the circumstances of healing the sick, the disciple is preaching the Gospel. And how is that to be understood? Usually, it is best to take such structures *temporally*, i.e., as denoting time. Thus the translation is as follows:

"*While* he is healing the sick, the disciple is preaching the Gospel."

Such a temporal force may also be understood *habitually:*

"(*Customarily*) while he heals the sick, the disciple preaches the Gospel."

It must be recognized, however, that the relationship between a predicate position participle and its verb need not be temporal. Other relationships are possible. *Causal* is frequent.

(EG 7)   λέγων τὴν ἀλήθειαν, ὁ μαθητὴς διώκεται.
Because he is speaking the truth, the disciple is being persecuted.

Concessive is also possible.

(EG 8)   λέγων τὴν ἀλήθειαν, ὁ μαθητὴς οὐ
πείθει τοὺς ὄχλους.
Even though he is speaking the truth, the disciple is not persuading the crowds.

Especially in the gospels, a participle may express *circumstances attendant* on the action of the main verb.

(EG 9)   ὁ μαθητὴς ἔρχεται διὰ τῆς γῆς
         <u>κηρύσσων</u> καὶ <u>θεραπεύων</u>.
         The disciple is going through the land *preaching*
         and *healing*.

Context alone will determine which force of the participle is
preferable.[1]

b. Referent

  (1) In EGs 6–8, who is doing the healing or the speaking? The
      answer, of course, is the disciple; he is the only one acting
      in the sentence. But *grammatically* how may this be deter-
      mined? Here morphology is the key. *A participle in predi-
      cate position agrees with its referent in gender, number,
      and case.* Thus, in EG 6 θεραπεύων and in EGs 7 and 8
      λέγων are both masculine, nominative, singular. Therefore,
      the person doing the healing or speaking is masculine,
      nominative, and singular in the sentence. And that can only
      be μαθητής.

  (2) Note these examples in other cases:

      (EG 10)   οἱ ἐχθροὶ φονεύουσι <u>τοὺς δούλους</u>
                <u>κηρύσσοντας</u>.
                The enemies are slaying *the slaves* while *they*
                are preaching. (Literally: The enemies are
                slaying the slaves preaching.)

      In EG 10 the people preaching are the slaves, not the en-
      emies, because κηρύσσοντας is masculine, *accusative*,
      plural, which means that a masculine, accusative, plural in
      the sentence is doing the activity of the participle. If it were
      the enemies who are preaching, the sentence would be
      written thus:

      (EG 11)   <u>οἱ ἐχθροὶ</u> φονεύουσι τοὺς δούλους
                κηρύσσοντ<u>ες</u>.
                The enemies are slaying the slaves while *they*
                (the enemies) are preaching.

      More normally this is written with this word order:

      (EG 12)   κηρύσσοντες οἱ ἐχθροὶ φονεύουσι
                τοὺς δούλους.

      Usage in the dative is also common.

      (EG 13)   οἱ μαθηταὶ λέγουσι <u>τῷ κυρίῳ</u>
                <u>κηρύσσοντι</u>.
                The disciples are speaking *to the Lord* while
                He is preaching.

Note that if the disciples were preaching, the structure would be like this:

(EG 14)   οἱ μαθηταὶ λέγουσι τῷ κυρίῳ κηρύσσοντες.
The disciples are speaking to the Lord while *they* are preaching.

More normally, this would be written as follows:

(EG 15)   κηρύσσοντες οἱ μαθηταὶ λέγουσι τῷ κυρίῳ.

4. The negative of the participle is basically μή, not οὐκ (cf. chapter 16, E 4).

F. "Tense" and Time

1. Basic Principles

a. As a non-indicative mood form of the verb, the participle's "tense" conveys focus relative to action/aspect *only* [2] (cf. chapter 16, D). This is true of all participles. The time frame of the main verb provides the time frame for the participle.

b. Generally, in translation, the time of the participle is understood *relative to the time of the main verb.* As a result, the "focus upon connection"/"present" participle normally conveys *action at the same time as the main verb,* whatever that time may be. This is so, because the action of the "present" participle is seen as connected to someone (or something) in the sentence, and where that person (or thing) is in time is generally determined by the time frame of the main verb in the sentence. Thus, if the main verb conveys action in the past, the action of the participle will be translated as in the past (normally, the imperfect). If that verb conveys future time, the action of the participle is future.[3] (Attendant circumstance participles may be translated "literally," regardless of the main verb's time frame.)

c. These basic principles hold true for both attributive and predicate position participles.

2. Examples

a. Note the following examples with a main verb in past time. These are simply EGs 4, 6, 7, 8, 9, 10, and 13, with the main verb put back into the past.

(EG 16)   ὁ θεραπεύων τοὺς ἀσθενεῖς μαθητὴς ἐκήρυσσε τὸ εὐαγγέλιον.
The disciple *who was healing* the sick *was preaching* the Gospel (cf. EG 4).

(EG 17)   θεραπεύων τοὺς ἀσθενεῖς, ὁ μαθητὴς
ἐκήρυσσε τὸ εὐαγγέλιον.
While he *was healing* the sick, the disciple *was
preaching* the Gospel (cf. EG 6).

(EG 18)   λέγων τὴν ἀλήθειαν, ὁ μαθητὴς
ἐδιώκετο.
Because he *was speaking* the truth, the disciple
was being persecuted (cf. EG 7).

(EG 19)   λέγων τὴν ἀλήθειαν, ὁ μαθητὴς οὐκ
ἔπειθε τοὺς ὄχλους.
Even though he *was speaking* the truth, the
disciple *was* not *persuading* the crowds (cf. EG 8).

(EG 20)   ὁ μαθητὴς ἤρχετο διὰ τῆς γῆς
κηρύσσων καὶ θεραπεύων.
The disciple *was going* through the land *preaching*
and *healing* (cf. EG 9).

(EG 21)   οἱ ἐχθροὶ ἐφόνευσαν τοὺς δούλους
κηρύσσοντας.
The enemies *slew* the slaves while they *were
preaching* (cf. EG 10).

(EG 22)   οἱ μαθηταὶ εἶπον τῷ κυρίῳ κηρύσσοντι.
The disciples *spoke* to the Lord while He *was
preaching* (cf. EG 13).

b. Note the following examples with a main verb in the future.
Note the English translation (cf. F 1 b above).

(EG 23)   θεραπεύων τοὺς ἀσθενεῖς, ὁ μαθητὴς
κηρύξει τὸ εὐαγγέλιον.
While he *is healing* the sick, the disciple *will
preach* the Gospel. (Literally: While he will be
healing the sick, . . .)

(EG 24)   φονεύσουσι τοὺς κηρύσσοντας.
They *will slay* the people who *preach*. (Literally:
They *will slay* the people who *will be preaching*.)

G. Another View

Another way to view the participle is as *shorthand for a subordinate
clause*. Consider the following sentence with participle (+ object):

(EG 25)   *Pursuing* the slave, the soldier saw the bandit.

This is "shorthand" for a fuller expression which contains a complete
subordinate clause:

(EG 26)   *As/while he was pursuing* the slave, the soldier saw the bandit.

Note that the words "As/while he was" are assumed.

The following sentence also contains a participle (+ object):

(EG 27)   The soldier *pursuing* the slave saw the bandit.

This is "shorthand" for a fuller expression which, again, contains a complete subordinate clause:

(EG 28)   The soldier *who was pursuing* the slave saw the bandit.

Note that the words "who was" are assumed.

The same principle holds in Greek, though it is not as simple as omitting words, as one can do in English. Consider the next four examples. The first two (EGs 29 and 30) are translations and equivalents of EGs 25 and 26 and of each other, while the second two (EGs 31 and 32) parallel EGs 27 and 28 and each other.

(EG 29)   <u>διώκων</u> τὸν δοῦλον, ὁ στρατιώτης εἶδε τὸν ληστήν.

(EG 30)   <u>ὡς ἐδίωκε</u> τὸν δοῦλον, ὁ στρατιώτης εἶδε τὸν ληστήν.

(EG 31)   ὁ στρατιώτης <u>ὁ διώκων</u> τὸν δοῦλον εἶδε τὸν ληστήν.

(EG 32)   ὁ στρατιώτης <u>ὃς ἐδίωκε</u> τὸν δοῦλον εἶδε τὸν ληστήν.

Several important points can be seen from this analysis:

1. A predicate position participle (EG 29) is the equivalent of a subordinate clause introduced by a subordinating conjunction (EG 30). *To determine the force of a predicate position participle is*, essentially, *to determine which conjunction is assumed* to introduce the equivalent subordinate clause.

2. An attributive position participle (EG 31) is the equivalent of a subordinate clause introduced by a relative pronoun (EG 32). Thus, when interpreting such participles, one tends to use a relative pronoun in English translation (cf. "who" in EG 28).

H. Vocabulary

δέκα: ten

δώδεκα: twelve

ἐπιστολή ⁻ῆς, f.: epistle

ἕπτα: seven

ἔτι (adv.): still, yet

μηκέτι ⎫
          ⎬   (adv.): no longer
οὐκέτι ⎭

πέντε: five

τέσσαρες ‑α: four (third declension)

τρεῖς, τρία: three (third declension)[4]

ὧδε (adv): here

I. Exercises

1. Parse the following participles by gender, number, case, "tense,"
    and voice:

    a. λύοντες   e. τίκτουσα   i. γινόμενον

    b. φονευομένη   f. πίνοντες   j. ἀνα‑βαίνοντας

    c. φιλοῦντος   g. γινόμενα   k. αἰτουμένου

    d. ἐσθιομένῳ   h. ζητοῦντα   l. ποιῶν

2. Rewrite Greek-to-English sentence E 1 g in chapter 17, using a
    "present" participle in place of the infinitive clause.

J. Practice Sentences

1. Greek to English

a. ἀνα‑βαίνων πρὸς Ἱεροσόλυμα, ὁ Ἰησοῦς ἐδίδασκε
   τοὺς δώδεκα.

b. ὧδε ἐφόνευσαν οἱ πέντε στρατιῶται τοὺς τρεῖς
   γραμματεῖς τοὺς ὠφελοῦντας τὰς πτωχάς.

c. διωκόμενοι ὑπὸ τοῦ ἡγεμόνος, οἱ πλούσιοι τελῶναι
   ἤνεγκον τὰ ἀργύρια αὐτῶν εἰς τὴν ἔρημον.

d. ὄντες ἐν Ἐφέσῳ γράψομεν ἐπιστολὰς ταῖς ἑπτὰ
   πόλεσιν.

e. οἱ λαοὶ ἐθαύμασαν ἐπὶ ταῖς ἀληθείαις ταῖς ἀπο‑
   καλυπτομέναις ἐν ταῖς δέκα παραβολαῖς.

f. ὁ Ἰησοῦς δι‑ῆλθεν διὰ ταύτης τῆς γῆς θεραπεύων
   τὰς νόσους τῶν ἀσθενῶν.

g. μηκέτι κηρυσσομένους τὸ εὐαγγέλιον, τὸ συνέδριον
   ἐκέλευσε τοὺς τέσσαρας μαθητὰς ἀπο‑λυθῆναι.

h. ὁ θεὸς ἔτι φυλάσσεται τὰ ἐπὶ τῆς γῆς τέκνα αὐτοῦ
   τὰ τηροῦντα τὰς ἐντολάς, ἐν οὐρανῷ ὤν.

2. English to Greek

While they were writing epistles, the disciples saw the Lord.

K. Bible Passages

Mark 1:14 b $\hat{\eta}\lambda\theta\epsilon\nu$ . . .

John 10:2 (C)

Matthew 4:18 (C)

1 Thessalonians 3:1 (C)

Notes

1. A number of other forces for predicate position participles are fairly common. The instructor will provide further information.

2. Note that as with the infinitive, there is only one set of participle forms per focus and, therefore, only one set of forms per stem.

3. Often such a participle is best translated with the present tense in English.

   (EG 15a)   While we *are* in Madrid, we will contact your relatives.

4. M/F—N: $\tau\rho\epsilon\hat{\imath}s$, G: $\tau\rho\iota\hat{\omega}\nu$, D: $\tau\rho\iota\sigma\acute{\iota}$, A: $\tau\rho\epsilon\hat{\imath}s$

   Neut.—N: $\tau\rho\acute{\iota}a$, G: $\tau\rho\iota\hat{\omega}\nu$, D: $\tau\rho\iota\sigma\acute{\iota}$, A: $\tau\rho\acute{\iota}a$

21

Participles, Part 2:
"Focus on the Action"/
"Aorist" Active and Middle

A Introduction

In this chapter we meet the "focus on the action"/"aorist" participle.
What is to be learned is not greatly unlike what was learned in chapter
20. The morphology of this participle is similar to that of the "focus
upon connection"/"present" participle. Its usage is the same. The basic
difference is the relative time that is conveys.

it/

B. Paradigm Forms

1. Active Voice

a. λείπω

	Singular		
	M	F	N
N	λιπών	λιποῦσα	λιπόν
G	λιπόντος	λιπούσης	λιπόντος
D	λιπόντι	λιπούσῃ	λιπόντι
A	λιπόντα	λιποῦσαν	λιπόν

	Plural		
	M	F	N
N	λιπόντες	λιποῦσαι	λιπόντα
G	λιπόντων	λιπουσῶν	λιπόντων
D	λιποῦσι(ν)	λιπούσαις	λιποῦσι(ν)
A	λιπόντας	λιπούσας	λιπόντα

b. λύω

	Singular		
	M	F	N
N	λύσας	λύσασα	λῦσαν
G	λύσαντος	λυσάσης	λύσαντος
D	λύσαντι	λυσάσῃ	λύσαντι
A	λύσαντα	λύσασαν	λῦσαν

Plural

	M	F	N
N	λύσαντες	λύσασαι	λύσαντα
G	λυσάντων	λυσασῶν	λυσάντων
D	λύσασι(ν)	λυσάσαις	λύσασι(ν)
A	λύσαντας	λυσάσας	λύσαντα

2. Middle Voice

a. λείπω

Singular

	M	F	N
N	λιπόμενος	λιπομένη	λιπόμενον
G	λιπομένου	λιπομένης	λιπομένου
D	λιπομένῳ	λιπομένῃ	λιπομένῳ
A	λιπόμενον	λιπομένην	λιπόμενον

Plural

	M	F	N
N	λιπόμενοι	λιπόμεναι	λιπόμενα
G	λιπομένων	λιπομένων	λιπομένων
D	λιπομένοις	λιπομέναις	λιπομένοις
A	λιπομένους	λιπομένας	λιπόμενα

b. λύω

Singular

	M	F	N
N	λυσάμενος	λυσαμένη	λυσάμενον
G	λυσαμένου	λυσαμένης	λυσαμένου
D	λυσαμένῳ	λυσαμένῃ	λυσαμένῳ
A	λυσάμενον	λυσαμένην	λυσάμενον

Plural

	M	F	N
N	λυσάμενοι	λυσάμεναι	λυσάμενα
G	λυσαμένων	λυσαμένων	λυσαμένων
D	λυσαμένοις	λυσαμέναις	λυσαμένοις
A	λυσαμένους	λυσαμένας	λυσάμενα

C. Morphology

1. The "focus on the action"/"aorist" participle is similar to its "focus upon connection"/"present" counterpart in that it uses third declension endings for the masculine and neuter forms, and A declension "hybrid" endings for the feminine forms in the active; in the middle it uses O declension forms for the masculine and neuter, A declension pattern for the feminine.

2. As is true with the infinitive, the "aorist" participle carries *no augment.*[1]

3. Strong "aorist" participles are almost identical to "present" participles, except, of course, for stem and also for accent (cf. the infinitive).

4. Weak "aorist" participles have the characteristic a connecting vowel and the same basic pattern of endings. (**Note:** In the nominative, masculine, singular, the a is long.)

D. Meaning

As we shall see below, the "focus on the action"/"aorist" participle generally conveys action *prior* in time to the action of the main verb. Therefore, a literal translation would begin with "having":

(EG 1) $\lambda\iota\pi\dot{\omega}\nu$ = "having left"

E. Syntax

The usage of the "aorist" participle is the same as that of the "present."

1. The "aorist" participle may be used in attributive or predicate position.

2. When the "aorist" participle is used in the predicate position, the same principles for determining force and referent are operative, although attendant circumstance usage is *not* now possible.

3. The negative is also basically $\mu\dot{\eta}$, not $o\dot{\upsilon}\kappa$.

F. "Tense" and Time

1. Like the "focus upon connection"/"present" participle, the time of the "focus on the action"/"aorist" participle is understood *relative to the time of the main verb*. Unlike the "present" participle, however, the action of the "aorist" is not contemporaneous with the action of the main verb but *precedes* it in time. Thus

   a. an "aorist" participle dependent upon a verb whose action is in the *past* will be translated as pluperfect;

   b. an "aorist" participle dependent upon a verb whose action is in the *present* will be translated as simple past;

   c. an "aorist" participle dependent upon a verb whose action is in the *future* will be translated as present tense.

Note the following basic examples:

(EG 2)   ὁ θεραπεύσας τοὺς ἀσθενεῖς μαθητὴς ἦλθεν
εἰς τὸν οὐρανόν.
The disciple *who had healed* the sick *went* into
heaven.

(EG 3)   ὁ θεραπεύσας τοὺς ἀσθενεῖς μαθητὴς
ἔρχεται εἰς, τὸν οὐρανόν.
The disciples *who healed* the sick *is going* into
heaven.

(EG 4)   ὁ θεραπεύσας τοὺς ἀσθενεῖς μαθητὴς
ἐλεύσεται εἰς τὸν οὐρανόν.
The disciple *who heals* the sick *will go* into heaven.

2. The following examples are modifications of sentences with a
present time main verb from the previous chapter.

(EG 5)   εἰπὼν τὴν ἀλήθειαν, ὁ μαθητὴς διώκεται.
Because he *spoke* the truth, the disciple *is being
persuaded* (cf. EG 7, chapter 20).

(EG 6)   εἰπὼν τὴν ἀλήθειαν, ὁ μαθητὴς οὐ πείθει
τοὺς ὄχλους.
Even though he *spoke* the truth, the disciple *is* not
persuading the crowds (cf. EG 8, chapter 20).

It may be noted that with a main verb in the present, it is awkward
to translate an "aorist" participle temporally in English. We simply
do not say:

(EG 7)   "*After* he spoke the truth, the disciple *is being
persecuted*" (cf. EG 5 above and EG 7, chapter 20).

We normally render these constructions causally (cf. EG 5) or con-
cessively.[2]

3. The following examples are modifications of sentences from the
previous chapter that contained main verbs in past time.

(EG 8)   ὁ θεραπεύσας τοὺς ἀσθενεῖς μαθητὴς
ἐκήρυσσε τὸ εὐαγγέλιον.
The disciple *who had healed* the sick *was preaching*
the Gospel (cf. EG 16, chapter 20).

(EG 9)   θεραπεύσας τοὺς ἀσθενεῖς, ὁ μαθητὴς
ἐκήρυσσε τὸ εὐαγγέλιον.
After he *had healed* the sick, the disciple *was
preaching* the Gospel (cf. EG 17, chapter 20).

(EG 10)   *εἰπὼν τὴν ἀλήθειαν, ὁ μαθητὴς οὐκ ἔπειθε τοὺς ὄχλους.*
            Even though he *had spoken* the truth, the disciple *was not persuading* the crowds (cf. EG 19, chapter 20).

(EG 11)   *οἱ ἐχθροὶ ἐφόνευσαν τοὺς δούλους κηρύξαντας.*
            The enemies slew the slaves after they *had preached* (cf. EG 21, chapter 20).

4. If the verb on which the participle depends is future, the "aorist" participle is often best rendered with the English present tense (though the present perfect will also work):

(EG 12)   *θεραπεύσας τοὺς ἀσθενεῖς, ὁ μαθητὴς κηρύξει τὸ εὐαγγέλιον.*
            After he *heals* (or, *has healed*) the sick, the disciple *will preach* the Gospel (cf. EG 23, chapter 20).

G. Aspect and Relative Time

We have said that the "aorist" participle conveys action preceding the action of the main verb in time (cf. F 1 above). This does not vitiate what has been said previously concerning aspect/focus and the verbal stem (cf. chapter 20, F 1 a). It will be remembered that the "present" participle focuses upon connection (i.e., the action it describes is seen as connected to a person/thing discussed in the sentence) and that, therefore, logically, the time of the activity of such a participle coincides with the time frame of that person/thing (cf. chapter 20, F 1 b). By contrast, the "aorist" participle focuses on the action itself. Now, if the action of the participle is itself the focus, *it is but a small step* to say that its action is not seen as connected *anymore*, i.e., that it has already happened and now some other activity is occupying the people or things in the sentence. Therefore, it is logical to use the "aorist" participle to convey action prior to the action of the controlling verb.[3]

H. Vocabulary

ἐγγίζω (R): I draw near, approach

ἐκλεκτός -ή -όν: elect

ἐλεέω (R): I pity, have mercy on

εὐχαριστέω (R): I give thanks

μισέω (R): I hate

περι- πατέω[4] (R): I walk; conduct my life

ὕδωρ, ὕδατος, n.: water

φῶς, φωτός, n.: light

χαρίζομαι (M) (R): I grant; forgive

I. Exercises

1. Parse the following participles by gender, number, case, "tense," and voice:

a. πιόντες	e. φαγούσης	i. τεκοῦσαν
b. φονευσαμένου	f. ἰδόντα	j. λύοντι
c. αἰτήσαντος	g. γενόμενος	k. ἀκούσας
d. πεσόντι	h. εἰπόντες	l. ἐνεγκόντων

2. Change the participles in I 1 a–d of chapter 20 into the corresponding "aorist" form.

J. Practice Sentences

1. Greek to English

a. οἱ λησταὶ ἐφόνευσαν τὸν ἱερέα εὑρόντα τὰ ἀργύρια αὐτῶν.

b. περι-πατῶν παρὰ τὴν θάλασσαν, ὁ Ἰησοῦς εἶδεν τοὺς ὄχλους καὶ ἠλέησεν αὐτούς.

c. εὐχαριστήσαντες, οἱ ποιμένες ἔφαγον ἄρτον καὶ ἔπιον ὕδωρ ἐπὶ τοῦ ὄρους.

d. οἱ ἱερεῖς οἱ δεξάμενοι τὸ βιβλίον τοῦ νόμου ἔπεμψαν αὐτὸ τῷ καλῷ γραμματεῖ.

e. τὸ ἀληθὲς φῶς τοῦ κόσμου οὐκ ἐμίσησε τοὺς μισοῦντας αὐτόν.

f. ἀκούσαντες τὰς ἐπαγγελίας τοῦ θεοῦ, οἱ μαθηταὶ ἐκήρυξαν αὐτὰς τοῖς ἔθνεσιν, ὥστε τὰς ἐκκλησίας τῆς Ἰουδαίας θαυμάσαι.

g. οἱ κακῶς παθόντες ἐξ-ῆλθον πρὸς τὸν Ἰησοῦν ἐγγίσαντα ἐπὶ τῇ πόλει αὐτῶν.

h. ὁ κύριος χαρίσεται εἰρήνην τοῖς αἰτουμένοις αὐτήν.

i. ἐκλεκτὸς υἱὸς θεοῦ ἐστιν ὁ Χριστός.

2. English to Greek

After they had seen the child, they had mercy on the people in the village.

K. Bible Passages

Luke 9:16a . . . αὐτούς (C)

John 11:28a . . . αὐτῆς

Matthew 21:15

Notes

1. Note that the participle of εἶπον (cf. εἰπών) technically is not augmented (cf. chapter 8, C 1 b (2)).

2. If a "present tense" verb is understood to convey *habitual* action, then a temporal translation is feasible, but normally we translate the participle with a present or present perfect tense verb in English under these circumstances:

   (EG 7a)   εἰπὼν τὴν ἀλήθειαν, ὁ πιστὸς μαθητὴς διώκεται.
             After he speaks the truth (or, after he has spoken the truth), the faithful disciple is persecuted.

3. See also chapter 41, where uses of the "aorist" participle are introduced that do not convey action prior to the action of the main verb.

4. The ι of περί in compounds does *not* elide before the vowel of a stem or augment.

22

Participles, Part 3: The Genitive Absolute and "Aorist" Passive

A. The Genitive Absolute

1. Introduction

We come now to the last major use of participles syntactically, a use that requires no new morphology. This use is limited to participles in the *predicate* position.

2. Basic Principles

a. Referent

In chapter 20, E 3 b (1), we said that it was fairly obvious what the referent of the participle in the following sentence was:

(EG 1)   θεραπεύων τοὺς ἀσθενεῖς, ὁ μαθητὴς κηρύσσει τὸ εὐαγγέλιον.
While *he is healing* the sick, *the disciple* is preaching the Gospel.

No one else is acting; therefore the person healing has to be the disciple. But what if we want to say:

(EG 2)   While *Jesus* is healing the sick, the *disciple* is preaching the Gospel?

In what case should the participle be in Greek? There is no reference to Jesus in the main clause. Jesus is not the disciple, so we cannot put the participle into the nominative (for then it would refer to disciple). Likewise, we cannot put "Jesus" into the nominative case, for he is not the subject of the main verb ("is preaching").

The solution is to make the participal phrase "absolute," i.e., to separate it from the rest of the sentence, because both its subject and its action are, in fact, *grammatically* unrelated to the rest of the sentence. This is done by putting the participle into the *genitive* case and expressing its referent (the doer of the action)

149

also in the genitive case. Therefore, in order to express the thought of EG 2 above in Greek, we would say:

(EG 3)   *θεραπεύοντος τοῦ 'Ιησοῦ τοὺς ἀσθενεῖς,*
          ὁ μαθητὴς κηρύσσει τὸ εὐαγγέλιον.
          While *Jesus is healing* the sick, the disciple is
          preaching the Gospel.

b. Time

The genitive absolute structure has no effect on the time relationship between the participle and the main verb. It is only a special syntactical construction used when a participle has as its referent someone or something outside the main clause. Thus, if EG 3 took place in the past we would say:

(EG 4)   *θεραπεύοντος τοῦ 'Ιησοῦ τοὺς ἀσθενεῖς,*
          ὁ μαθητὴς ἐκήρυσσε τὸ εὐαγγέλιον.
          While *Jesus was healing* the sick, the disciple was
          preaching the Gospel.

Note that the participle's "tense" in the Greek has not changed.

If the participle is "aorist," it still denotes action prior to the main verb.

(EG 5)   *θεραπεύσαντος τοῦ 'Ιησοῦ τοὺς*
          ἀσθενεῖς, ὁ μαθητὴς κηρύσσει τὸ
          εὐαγγέλιον.
          Because *Jesus healed* the sick, the disciple is
          preaching the Gospel.

(EG 6)   *θεραπεύσαντος τοῦ 'Ιησοῦ τοὺς*
          ἀσθενεῖς, ὁ μαθητὴς ἐκήρυσσε τὸ
          εὐαγγέλιον.
          After *Jesus had healed* the sick, the disciple was
          preaching the Gospel.

B. "Focus on the Action"/"Aorist" Passive Participles

1. Introduction

As we have seen (chapter 11, B 2 and C 1 b (1)), the "aorist" passive forms are not built off of the normal "aorist" stem but use a special stem lengthened by the addition of θε. The "focus on the action"/"aorist" passive participle will use this stem.

2. Paradigm Forms

a. λύω

Singular

	M	F	N
N	λυθείς	λυθεῖσα	λυθέν
G	λυθέντος	λυθείσης	λυθέντος
D	λυθέντι	λυθείσῃ	λυθέντι
A	λυθέντα	λυθεῖσαν	λυθέν

Plural

	M	F	N
N	λυθέντες	λυθεῖσαι	λυθέντα
G	λυθέντων	λυθεισῶν	λυθέντων
D	λυθεῖσι(ν)	λυθείσαις	λυθεῖσι(ν)
A	λυθέντας	λυθείσας	λυθέντα

b. λείπω

Singular

	M	F	N
N	λειφθείς	λειφθεῖσα	λειφθέν
G	λειφθέντος	λειφθείσης	λειφθέντος
D	λειφθέντι	λειφθείσῃ	λειφθέντι
A	λειφθέντα	λειφθεῖσαν	λειφθέν

Plural

	M	F	N
N	λειφθέντες	λειφθεῖσαι	λειφθέντα
G	λειφθέντων	λειφθεισῶν	λειφθέντων
D	λειφθεῖσι(ν)	λειφθείσαις	λειφθεῖσι(ν)
A	λειφθέντας	λειφθείσας	λειφθέντα

3. Morphology

a. The forms of the "focus on the action"/"aorist" passive participle are third declension for the masculine and neuter, first declension "hybrid" for the feminine. Note that these follow the pattern for the active participles. Again, the "aorist" passive uses *active* forms.

b. The stem for the participle is lengthened by θε, not θη. (This is the "real" suffix of the basic stem; in the indicative and infinitive the ε is, technically, lengthened to an η.) Do not forget to remove the augment.

4. Syntax

The usage of the "aorist" passive participle is the same as for the "aorist" active and middle participles, except that the subject is not the agent of the action.

(EG 7) εἶδον τὸν μαθητὴν <u>διδαχθέντα</u> ὑπὸ τοῦ
        κυρίου.
        I saw the disciple, after he had *been* taught by the Lord.

(EG 8) <u>διδαχθεὶς</u> ὑπὸ τοῦ κυρίου, ὁ μαθητὴς
        ἐδίδαξε τὰ τέκνα.
        After he had *been* taught by the Lord, the disciple
        taught the children.

(EG 9) <u>διδαχθέντος</u> τοῦ μαθητοῦ ὑπὸ τοῦ κυρίου,
        οἱ ἄγγελοι ἐδόξασαν τὸν θεόν.
        After the disciple had *been* taught by the Lord, the
        angels glorified God.

C. Vocabulary

γνωρίζω (R): I make known

δύο[1]: two

θρίξ, τριχός, f.: hair (strand) (pl. = head of hair) (dat. pl. = θριξί)

ἰχθύς -ύος, m.: fish (acc. sing. = ἰχθύν)

κεφαλή -ῆς, f.: head

μέλος -ους, n.: member

οὔτε . . . οὔτε; neither . . . nor[2]

πειράζω (R): I tempt, try; attempt

σκότος -ους, n.: darkness

χάρις -ιτος, f.: grace (acc. sing. = χάριν)

χείρ, χειρός, f.: hand (dat. pl. = χερσί)

D. Exercises

1. Which of the following sentences would be translated with a genitive absolute in Greek?

   a. After half of them had come, we started to leave.

   b. While we were watching, the ball sailed over the fence.

   c. While he was preaching, Jesus retied his sandal.

   d. I saw the brothers, even though the soldier was present.

   e. I was looking at Jesus, even though he had told me not to do so.

   f. Because the course is crowded, we will not be able to golf.

   g. After he had finished preaching, Jesus got into a boat.

h. While the disciples were inspecting their new oars, Jesus made another bench.

2. Make the "aorist" passive participle of the following verbs in the genitive singular and accusative plural of the masculine and feminine.

   a. *φονεύω*

   b. *ἐτοιμάζω*

   c. *πράσσω*

   d. *πέμπω*

E. Practice Sentences

1. Greek to English

a. γενομένων σημείων ἐν τῷ σκότει, οἱ ποιμένες ἐδόξασαν τὸν θεόν.

b. πειρασθεὶς ὑπὸ τοῦ διαβόλου, ὁ Ἰησοῦς ἐνήστευεν ἐν ἐρήμῳ.

c. οἱ ἄφρονες εἶπον· αἱ τρίχες εἰσὶ μέλος τοῦ σώματος.

d. ἀπο-λυθέντος τοῦ κλέπτου ὑπὸ τοῦ βασιλέως, δύο ἰχθύες ἐκλέφθησαν ἐκ τοῦ ἱεροῦ.

e. ὁ δὲ χωλὸς ἀπ-ῆλθεν εἰς τὰς κώμας πρὸς τὸ γνωρίσαι τὴν χάριν τοῦ θεοῦ θεραπευθεὶς ὑπὸ τῶν μαθητῶν.

f. θεραπευθεισῶν τῶν χειρῶν τοῦ τελώνου, οὔτε οἱ ἱερεῖς οὔτε οἱ γραμματεῖς ἠθέλησαν ἀκοῦσαι ἃ ὁ Ἰησοῦς ἔλεγεν αὐτοῖς.

g. τεκούσης τῆς Μαρίας τὸ ἅγιον τέκνον, ὁ Ἰωσὴφ ἡτοίμασεν ἀπ-ελθεῖν εἰς Γαλιλαῖαν, ἀλλ᾽ ἄγγελος εἶπεν αὐτῷ· δεῖ φυγεῖν εἰς Αἴγυπτον, μέλλει γὰρ Ἡρῴδης ζητεῖν τὸν υἱόν σου εἰς τὸ φονεῦσαι αὐτόν. ἀπο-θανόντος δὲ τοῦ βασιλέως, παρα-λαβὼν τὸ τέκνον καὶ Μαρίαν, ἀνα-βήσῃ εἰς τὴν γῆν Ἰσραήλ.

2. English to Greek

After the disciple had been sent into the villages, Jesus spoke to the priests.

F. Bible Passages

Acts 16:6 (C)

Matthew 26:47

Acts 4:23a . . . *ἰδίους* (C)

Acts 12:18a . . . *στρατιώταις*

1. While *δύο* is indeclinable in three cases, dative plural is *δυσί*.

2. *καί* . . . *καί* also appears as "both . . . and."

23

Miscellanea 2

A. Introduction

This is the second chapter of adjustments, extensions, and exceptions to the overall system of Greek.

B. The Article with δέ to Change Subjects

Sometimes in a conversation or narrative section describing interaction between two people (or parties), a change of speaker or actor in the next clause will be indicated simply with ὁ δέ (for a man, ἡ δέ for a woman).

(EG 1) ὁ Ἰησοῦς ἐζήτησε τὸν πλούσιον τελώνην, <u>ὁ δὲ</u> οὐκ ἤθελησεν ἰδεῖν αὐτόν.
Jesus sought the rich tax collector, but he (the tax collector) did not desire to see Him.

(EG 2) ὁ Ἰησοῦς ἐφίλησεν ἁμαρτωλούς, <u>οἱ δὲ</u> εἶπον· οὐ φιλοῦμέν σε.
Jesus loved sinners, but they said, "We do not love you."

C. Weak Aorist Terminations on Strong "Aorist" Stems (Indicative Mood)

Already in the centuries before Christ a tendency arose to affix weak aorist connecting vowels and endings to strong "aorist" stems (third principal part) in the indicative mood. This development had the merit of avoiding confusion between first singular and third plural forms of the strong aorist active, and at the same time, such terminations marked the form as aorist, thus avoiding any possible confusion with "imperfect tense" formations. ἤνεγκον, εἶπον, ἦλθον, and εἶδον were especially prone to this modification.

(EG 3) ἤνεγκα = ἤνεγκον (first singular)

(EG 4) εἶπαν = εἶπον (third plural)

(EG 5) ἤλθαμεν = ἦλθομεν (first plural)

D. Strong (Second) "Focus on the Action"/ "Aorist" Passive Forms

The vast majority of "focus on the action"/"aorist" passives contain the familiar $\theta\eta$ at the end of the stem (cf. $\dot{\epsilon}\lambda\dot{\upsilon}\theta\eta\nu$). A few such passives, however, do not contain the θ, but the stem ends simply with η. Sometimes this stem is simply the stem of the first principal part plus η (EG 6), but usually such an exact relationship is not exhibited (EG 7).

	Present Indicative Active	Aorist Indicative Passive	
(EG 6)	$\gamma\rho\acute{a}\phi\omega$	$\dot{\epsilon}\gamma\rho\acute{a}\phi\eta\nu$	(not $\dot{\epsilon}\gamma\rho\acute{a}\phi\theta\eta\nu$)
(EG 7)	$\kappa\rho\acute{\upsilon}\pi\tau\omega$	$\dot{\epsilon}\kappa\rho\acute{\upsilon}\beta\eta\nu$	(not $\dot{\epsilon}\kappa\rho\acute{\upsilon}\phi\theta\eta\nu$)

Note that there is no difference in connecting vowels and endings between weak and strong aorist indicative passives, as there is between weak and strong aorist indicative active and middle forms. (Of course, the aorist indicative passive contains no connecting vowel at all.) Which verbs have a strong "aorist" passive stem must be memorized. A verb with a strong aorist indicative active (third principal part) normally does *not* have a strong aorist indicative passive (sixth principal part).

E. Verbs Taking Cases Other Than the Accusative for Direct Object

Some transitive verbs do not have their direct object expressed in the accusative case. Which verbs do so must be memorized, though it can be said that verbs of sense, except verbs of sight, normally take the genitive.

$\dot{a}\kappa o\acute{\upsilon}\omega$ (+ genitive)

(EG   8) $o\acute{\iota}\ \sigma\tau\rho a\tau\iota\hat{\omega}\tau a\iota\ \mathring{\eta}\kappa o\upsilon\sigma a\nu\ \underline{\tau\mathring{\eta}\varsigma\ \phi\omega\nu\mathring{\eta}\varsigma}.$
              The soldiers heard the voice.

$\mathring{a}\pi\tau o\mu a\iota$ (+ genitive)

(EG   9) $a\mathring{\upsilon}\tau\eta\ \mathring{\eta}\psi a\tau o\ \underline{\tau o\hat{\upsilon}\ \mathring{\prime}I\eta\sigma o\hat{\upsilon}}.$
              This woman touched Jesus.

$\mu a\rho\tau\upsilon\rho\acute{\epsilon}\omega$ (+ dative)

(EG   10) $\mathring{o}\ \mathring{a}\pi\acute{o}\sigma\tau o\lambda o\varsigma\ \dot{\epsilon}\mu a\rho\tau\acute{\upsilon}\rho\eta\sigma\epsilon\ \underline{\tau\hat{\eta}\ \mathring{a}\lambda\eta\theta\epsilon\acute{\iota}\underset{\cdot}{a}}.$
              The apostle bore witness to the truth.

$\dot{a}\kappa o\lambda o\upsilon\theta\acute{\epsilon}\omega$ (+ dative)

(EG   11) $\mathring{o}\ \Pi\acute{\epsilon}\tau\rho o\varsigma\ \mathring{\eta}\kappa o\lambda o\acute{\upsilon}\theta\eta\sigma\epsilon\ \underline{\tau\hat{\omega}\ \mathring{\iota}\epsilon\rho\epsilon\hat{\iota}}.$
              Peter followed the priest.

πιστεύω (+ dative)

(EG 12)   ὁ δεσπότης ἐπίστευσε <u>τῷ δούλῳ</u>.
The master believed the slave.

F. Constructions with ἐγένετο

The gospels and Acts frequently use a Semitic construction reminiscent of the LXX. Many paragraphs begin with καὶ ἐγένετο or ἐγένετο δέ = "And it came to pass . . ." (literally, "And it happened . . ."). Three different constructions are possible after the ἐγένετο phrase:

1. καὶ ἐγένετο + καί

(EG 13)   <u>καὶ ἐγένετο καὶ</u> ὁ ᾽Ιησοῦς ἐδίδασκε τοὺς ὄχλους.

2. καὶ ἐγένετο in asyndeton (i.e. with no connection to the main clause):

(EG 14)   <u>καὶ ἐγένετο</u> ὁ ᾽Ιησοῦς ἐδίδασκε τοὺς ὄχλους.

3. καὶ ἐγένετο + infinitive:

(EG 15)   <u>καὶ ἐγένετο</u> τὸν ᾽Ιησοῦν <u>διδάσκειν</u> τοὺς ὄχλους.

All three examples may be translated: "And it came to pass *that* Jesus began to teach the crowds."

G. Syncopated Third Declension Nouns

1. Introduction

Several important third declension nouns have slightly irregular forms and a "moving" accent (cf. σάρξ, chapter 18, B 1 a). These must be learned.

2. Forms

a. γυνή = Woman

	Singular	Plural
N	γυνή	γυναῖκες
G	γυναικός	γυναικῶν
D	γυναικί	γυναιξί(ν)
A	γυναῖκα	γυναῖκας

b. ἀνήρ = Man

	Singular	Plural
N	ἀνήρ	ἄνδρες
G	ἀνδρός	ἀνδρῶν
D	ἀνδρί	ἀνδράσι(ν)
A	ἄνδρα	ἄνδρας

c. πατήρ = Father

	Singular	Plural
N	πατήρ	πατέρες
G	πατρός	πατέρων
D	πατρί	πατράσι(ν)
A	πατέρα	πατέρας

H. Vocabulary

ἀκολουθέω (R) + dat.: I follow

ἀνήρ, ἀνδρός, m.: man (male); husband

ἅπτομαι (M)(R) + gen.: I touch

γυνή, γυναικός, f.: woman; wife

μαρτυρέω (R) + dat.: I bear witness to

μήτηρ, μητρός, f.: mother

πατήρ, πατρός, m.: father

πιστεύω (R) + dat.: I believe; with εἰς + acc. = I believe *in*

προσ-έρχομαι, etc., + dat.: I come (go) to

προσ-κυνέω (R) + dat.: I worship; prostrate myself before

προσ-φέρω, etc., (+ dat.): I bear (carry) to

τάσσω (r): I arrange; command

    δια-τάσσω, etc.,

    ἐπι-τάσσω, etc.,   } (+ dat.): I command, direct

    προσ-τάσσω, etc.,

ὑπ-ακούω, etc., + dat.: I obey

I. Exercise

Translate the following into proper Greek morphology and syntax.

1. I follow him.

2. I believe her.

3. I believe in him.

4. He commanded them to come.

5. She obeyed him.

6. I touched her.

7. They came to God.

J. Practice Sentences

1. Greek to English

a. οἱ κακοὶ εἶπαν· τὰ βιβλία ἐγράφη ὑπὸ τοῦ ἐν τῇ ἐρήμῳ προφήτου.

b. καὶ ἐγένετο καὶ ὁ Ἰησοῦς ἐθεράπευσεν τὸν ἄνδρα τῆς γυναικός, ὁ δὲ ἐπίστευσεν εἰς αὐτόν.

c. καὶ ἐγένετο ὁ Ἰησοῦς ἥψατο τῆς χειρὸς τῆς μητρὸς καὶ δι-έταξεν αὐτῇ μαρτυρῆσαι τῷ σημείῳ ὃ ἔπραξεν, ἡ δὲ ὑπ-ήκουσεν αὐτῷ.

d. προσ-ελθὼν τῷ Ἰησοῦ, ὁ ἀνὴρ προσ-εκύνησεν αὐτῷ καὶ ἠκολούθησεν αὐτῷ εἰς τὸ ἱερόν.

e. μετὰ τὸ τὸν πατέρα προσ-ενεγκεῖν τὸν υἱὸν αὐτοῦ τῷ κυρίῳ, οὗτος ἐπ-έταξεν αὐτῷ πιστεῦσαι τῷ λόγῳ αὐτοῦ.

2. English to Greek

The woman who (had) touched Jesus' cloak bore witness to the truth.

K. Bible Passages

Mark 1:9

John 18:15 (C)

Matthew 2:11 (Cs)

Matthew 4:11b καί . . . (Cs)

Matthew 15:34

24

Miscellanea 3

A. Introduction

This third miscellanea chapter presents only three new items, but all are of great importance because of their frequency.

B. The Adjective "One"

1. Introduction

The third declension adjective "one" exhibits characteristics similar to the syncopated nouns of chapter 23. These forms must be learned. Note that there are three genders.

2. Forms

	M	F	N
N	εἷς	μία	ἕν
G	ἑνός	μιᾶς	ἑνός
D	ἑνί	μιᾷ	ἑνί
A	ἕνα	μίαν	ἕν

3. Compound Formations

Often οὐ is compounded to these forms (or μή if they are used with infinitives or participles [or subjunctives, etc.]), along with δ or δε in between, to produce "no one" (masculine and feminine) or "nothing" (neuter).

(EG 1) οὐδεὶς βλέπει με.
  No one sees me.

(EG 2) βλέπω οὐδέν.
  I see *nothing*.

C. Interrogative and Indefinite Pronouns

1. Introduction

We have thus far met personal, demonstrative, and relative pronouns. We now encounter pronouns that ask a question. Such interrogative pronouns follow a strict third declension pattern, with

$\tau\iota\nu$- as the basic stem. The same morphology is also used for in-definite pronouns ("someone," "something").

2. Interrogative and Indefinite Pronoun Forms

	Singular		Plural	
	M/F	N	M/F	N
N	τίς	τί	τίνες	τίνα
G	τίνος	τίνος	τίνων	τίνων
D	τίνι	τίνι	τίσι(ν)	τίσι(ν)
A	τίνα	τί	τίνας	τίνα

3. Usage

a. All forms of this pronoun *with an acute accent* ask a question and are called *interrogative*.

(EG 3)   <u>τίς</u> εἶδε τοῦτον;
Who saw this man?

b. An *unaccented* (and enclitic) form of this pronoun is *indefinite*.

(EG 4)   εἶδέ <u>τις</u> ἡμᾶς.
Someone saw us.

(EG 5)   εἶδόν <u>τινα</u>.
I saw *someone*.

c. At times, the *neuter* interrogative form τί asks *why*.

(EG 6)   <u>τί</u> ἐποίησας τοῦτο;
Why did you do this?

Note that an interrogative pronoun *never* changes its acute accent to a grave (cf. EGs 3 and 6).

D. The Use of the Passive Voice in Active Senses

1. In Greek as in English, some verbs have both a transitive and an intransitive sense of their basic meaning. Occasionally verbs use the same forms for each (cf. αὐξάνω = "I increase"), but frequently a distinction is made. The full range of forms is used for the transitive sense, which may be used actively, with middle force, or passively, while the *passive* forms are *also* used for the *intransitive* sense, which is active. This latter sense or meaning is a logical extension of the transitive sense used passively.

(EG 7)   <u>συν-ήγαγον</u> τοὺς δούλους.
They *gathered* the slaves *together* (transitive active).

(EG 8)   <u>συν-ηγάγοντο</u> τοὺς δούλους.
They *gathered* the slaves *together for themselves*
(transitive middle).

(EG 9)   οἱ δοῦλοι <u>συν-ήχθησαν</u> ὑπ' αὐτῶν.
          The slaves *were gathered together* by them (transitive
          passive).

and

(EG 10)   οἱ δοῦλοι <u>συν-ήχθησαν</u>.
          The slaves *gathered,* i.e., assembled (intransitive
          active).

In EG 10 the intransitive active sense can easily be seen as EG 9
(transitive sense used passively) viewed from another perspective.

2. Other verbs that display this phenomenon carry related but, at least
   in English, not identical meanings as vocabulary when used transi-
   tively and intransitively. Often such verbs have a *causative* meaning when *transitive* but express an *active state of being* when *intransitive.*

(EG 11)   <u>ἐφόβησαν</u> τοὺς δούλους.
          They *caused* the slaves *to be afraid* (transitive
          active).

(EG 12)   οἱ δοῦλοι <u>ἐφοβήθησαν</u> ὑπ' αὐτῶν.
          The slaves *were caused to be afraid* by them
          (transitive passive).

(EG 13)   οἱ δοῦλοι <u>ἐφοβήθησαν</u>.
          The slaves *were afraid* (intransitive active).

Again, the meaning of EG 13, "were afraid," can be seen as EG 12
viewed from a different perspective.

3. Subsequently, some of these verbs developed *transitive active* usages in the passive (as an extension of their intransitive active
   meaning,) so that φοβέω in the passive, e.g., can mean not only "to
   be caused to fear" or "to be afraid" but also "to fear" someone or
   "to be afraid of" someone.

(EG 14)   οἱ δοῦλοι <u>ἐφοβήθησαν αὐτούς</u>.
          The slaves *feared them* (transitive active).

Here a passive form carries not an active intransitive meaning, as in
EGs 10 and 13, but an active, fully transitive meaning, which may
take a direct object.

4. As a further extension of D 1 and 2 above, some verbs have become *passive deponents* in that their active (and middle) forms
   have disappeared. Now only passive forms are common. The voice
   of these forms is *active in translation,* and they convey, sometimes
   their own basic meaning, with no relation to any previously exist-
   ing active forms (EG 15), but usually either a transitive or intransitive thought related to the verb's basic or original (transitive active)
   meaning (EG 16).

(EG 15) βούλομαι ="I want" (no "original" active forms)

(EG 16) πορεύομαι = "I travel, journey"
(πορεύω = I convey, make to go)

E. Vocabulary

ἀπο-κρίνομαι . . . ἀπ-εκρίθην (P): I answer

βούλομαι . . . ἐβουλήθην (P): I want

κρύπτω (r) . . . ἐκρύβην: I hide (something); pass.: I hide (intrans.)

λυπέω (R): I grieve, cause to mourn; pass.: I mourn

πορεύομαι (P) (R): I journey[1]

στρέφω (r) . . . ἐστράφην: I turn (trans.); pass.: I turn (intrans.)

ἐπι-στρέφω, etc.: I turn toward, turn around (trans.);
pass.: I turn toward, turn around (intrans.)

συν-άγω, etc.: I gather (trans.); pass.: I gather, assemble (intrans.)

φοβέω (R): I frighten, cause to fear; pass.: I am frightened; fear

Note: Do not forget εἷς and τίς as vocabulary.

F. Exercise

Translate the following into proper Greek morphology or syntax.

1. Who did these things?

2. I wanted to see him.

3. I turn around.

4. I turn the boat.

5. He journeyed.

6. We assembled.

7. I feared the woman.

G. Practice Sentences

1. Greek to English

a. ἐγένετο δέ τινα φωνῆσαι τὸν προφήτην. οὗτος ἤκουσε τῆς φωνῆς καὶ εἶπεν· τίς ὧδέ ἐστιν; οὐδεὶς δὲ εἶπε λόγον.

b. οἱ Φαρισαῖοι ἐβουλήθησαν ἀπ-αγαγεῖν τὸν Ἰησοῦν λαλήσαντα κατ' αὐτῶν.

c. αἱ γυναῖκες ἐπορεύθησαν πρὸς τὸ μνημεῖον καὶ ἐκεῖ ἐλυποῦντο.

d. συν-αγαγόντες τὰ πρόβατα αὐτῶν, καὶ οἱ ποιμένες ἐν τῷ ἀγρῷ συν-ήχθησαν.

e. ἁψαμένη τοῦ ἱματίου τοῦ Ἰησοῦ, ἡ μήτηρ ἐφο-βεῖτο καὶ ἐκρύπτετο ἐν τῷ ὄχλῳ.

f. αἰτήσαντός τινος ἄρτους, στραφεὶς ὁ Ἰησοῦς ἀπ-εκρίθη καὶ εἶπεν· τί οὐκ ἐπι-θυμεῖς τὸν ἄρτον τοῦ πατρός μου;

g. ὁ ἀνὴρ ἐπ-εστράφη καὶ οὐκ ἠκολούθει τῷ κυρίῳ.

2. English to Greek

After he had journeyed to the village, the father brought his son to the Savior.

H. Bible Passages

Ephesians 4:5

Mark 5:30 (omit ἐπιγνοὺς . . . ἐξελθοῦσαν) (C)

John 9:27a . . . ἀκούειν (C)

John 4:50b ἐπίστευσεν . . .

Mark 16:8 (C) (omit οὐδενὶ)

Note

1. A middle form from a second principal part may be encountered to convey the future: πορεύσομαι.

25

The Verb, Part 6: "Focus upon Result"/ "Perfect Tense" Forms

A. Introduction

We now come to the last set of stems of the Greek verb. These convey another aspect, namely, *focus upon result, the state following the completion of an activity.* As with the other stems, forms of the indicative mood from these stems convey both aspect and time, while forms outside the indicative mood convey aspect only. Indicative forms conveying a focus upon result or state in the present time are called, traditionally, "perfect tense" forms and are the basis for non-indicative mood forms. These are covered in this chapter. Indicative mood forms conveying a focus upon result or state in past time are called "pluperfect tense" forms and are covered in chapter 26.

B. Active Voice

1. Paradigm Forms

a. λύω

	Singular			Plural	
1	λέλυκα	I have loosed		λελύκαμεν	We have loosed
2	λέλυκας	You have loosed		λελύκατε	You have loosed
3	λέλυκε(ν)	He (she, it) has loosed		λελύκασι(ν)	They have loosed

Infinitive: λελυκέναι

Participle:

	Singular		
	M	F	N
N	λελυκώς	λελυκυῖα	λελυκός
G	λελυκότος	λελυκυίας	λελυκότος
D	λελυκότι	λελυκυίᾳ	λελυκότι
A	λελυκότα	λελυκυῖαν	λελυκός

165

Plural

	M	F	N
N	λελυκότες	λελυκυῖαι	λελυκότα
G	λελυκότων	λελυκυιῶν	λελυκότων
D	λελυκόσι(ν)	λελυκυίαις	λελυκόσι(ν)
A	λελυκότας	λελυκυίας	λελυκότα

b. λείπω

	Singular			Plural	
1	λέλοιπα	I have left	λελοίπαμεν	We have left
2	λέλοιπας	You have left	λελοίπατε	You have left
3	λέλοιπε(ν)	He (she, it) has left	λελοίπασι(ν)	They have left

Infinitive: λελοιπέναι

Participle:

Singular

	M	F	N
N	λελοιπώς	λελοιπυῖα	λελοιπός
G	λελοιπότος	λελοιπυίας	λελοιπότος
D	λελοιπότι	λελοιπυίᾳ	λελοιπότι
A	λελοιπότα	λελοιπυῖαν	λελοιπός

Plural

	M	F	N
N	λελοιπότες	λελοιπυῖαι	λελοιπότα
G	λελοιπότων	λελοιπυιῶν	λελοιπότων
D	λελοιπόσι(ν)	λελοιπυίαις	λελοιπόσι(ν)
A	λελοιπότας	λελοιπυίας	λελοιπότα

2. Morphology

a. Stem

(1) "Focus upon result"/"perfect tense" forms are characterized by the duplication of the initial letter (often called "reduplication"). The major exception to this rule is that verbs beginning with a vowel "duplicate" the initial letter not by repeating it with an ε in between—which would occasion terrible hiatus!—but by "augmenting" it, as is done in the imperfect or aorist indicative. Such an "augment" is not actually an augment. The lengthened letter is actually an integral part of the verbal stem and does *not* disappear in the forms of the infinitive and participle.

	Present Indicative	Perfect Indicative	"Perfect" Infinitive	"Perfect" Participle
(EG 1)	αἰτέω	ᾔτηκα	ᾐτηκέναι	ᾐτηκώς

Note: Verbs beginning with an aspirated consonant use the corresponding voiceless consonant form in reduplicating.

(EG 2) $\phi\iota\lambda\acute{\epsilon}\omega$ → $\underline{\pi\epsilon}\phi\acute{\iota}\lambda\eta\kappa\alpha$

Note: Verbs beginning with three consonants generally "augment" to reduplicate.

(EG 3) $\sigma\tau\rho\acute{\epsilon}\phi\omega$ → $\underline{\acute{\epsilon}}\sigma\tau\rho o\phi\alpha$

(2) Weak verbs (cf. $\lambda\acute{\upsilon}\omega$) add κ to the basic stem.

     Note: Dentals are usually weak and drop the dental before κ.

     (EG 4) $\acute{\epsilon}\lambda\pi\acute{\iota}\zeta\omega$ → $\acute{\eta}\lambda\pi\iota\underline{\kappa}\alpha$

(3) Strong verbs (cf. $\lambda\epsilon\acute{\iota}\pi\omega$) do not add κ but usually change the last letter of the basic stem by aspirating it.

     (EG 5) $\acute{\alpha}\gamma\omega$ → $\hat{\eta}\chi\alpha$

     (EG 6) $\pi\rho\acute{\alpha}\sigma\sigma\omega$ → $\pi\acute{\epsilon}\pi\rho\alpha\chi\alpha$

     (EG 7) $\kappa\lambda\acute{\epsilon}\pi\tau\omega$ → $\kappa\acute{\epsilon}\kappa\lambda o\underline{\phi}\alpha$

Note that internal modification of the stem may also occur.

b. Connecting Vowel

The connecting vowel is α in the perfect indicative active for both weak and strong forms. Note the ϵ in the third singular.

c. Endings

(1) Indicative

The endings for the indicative forms are slightly peculiar: secondary in the singular (cf. normal weak aorist endings) and primary in the plural. The reason for this will perhaps be seen when we consider the meaning of this "tense" below (B 4).

(2) Infinitive

The infinitive uses the old $-\nu\alpha\iota$ active ending (cf. "aorist" passive infinitive).

(3) Participle

The participle follows a normal active pattern: third declension in the masculine and neuter, A declension in the feminine (here, α pattern). Note that strong and weak participles are identical except for the κ (unlike, e.g., strong and weak "aorist" active participles).

d. Accent

The accent of "focus upon result"/"perfect" forms is recessive, as normal, but note the accent of the infinitive and participle, which is near to the end of the word.

3. Aspect

In terms of aspect, the "perfect tense" expresses a *focus upon result, the state which follows upon past activity.* An action has ceased. Now a resultant state of affairs or condition is in force.

4. Time and Meaning

In the indicative mood, "focus upon result"—so-called "perfect tense"—forms, while dealing with the past to some extent, are not essentially concerned with the past. Their focus is on a *current* condition, the *present* result of a past action. It is important to note that *the forms of the "perfect" do not say that a past action is still happening.*

(EG 8)   ἐλήλυθα = "I have come," i.e., "*I am here.*"

(EG 9)   ἀκήκοα = "I have heard," i.e., "*I understand.*"

5. Principal Part

The basic perfect indicative active form of a verb is its fourth principal part. It may be noted that, with the exception of γίνομαι (see D below), deponent verbs do not have a fourth principal part, since *all* their active forms have been "laid aside."

C. Middle/Passive Voice

1. Paradigm Forms

a. λύω

	Singular	Plural
1	λέλυμαι	λελύμεθα
2	λέλυσαι	λέλυσθε
3	λέλυται	λέλυνται

(For meaning, see section 3 below.)

Infinitive: λελῦσθαι

Participles:

Singular

	M	F	N
N	λελυμένος	λελυμένη	λελυμένον
G	λελυμένου	λελυμένης	λελυμένου
D	λελυμένῳ	λελυμένῃ	λελυμένῳ
A	λελυμένον	λελυμένην	λελυμένον

Plural

	M	F	N
N	λελυμένοι	λελυμέναι	λελυμένα
G	λελυμένων	λελυμένων	λελυμένων
D	λελυμένοις	λελυμέναις	λελυμένοις
A	λελυμένους	λελυμένας	λελυμένα

b. λείπω

	Singular	Plural
1	λέλειμμαι	λελείμμεθα
2	λέλειψαι	λέλειφθε
3	λέλειπται	λελειμμένοι ἐισί(ν)

(For meaning, see section 3 below.)

Infinitive: λελεῖφθαι

Participles:

Singular

		M	F	N
	N	λελειμμένος	λελειμμένη	λελειμμένον
	G	λελειμμένου	λελειμμένης	λελειμμένου
▷	N	λελειμμένῳ	λελειμμένη	λελειμμένῳ
	A	λελειμμένον	λελειμμένην	λελειμμένον

Plural

		M	F	N
	N	λελειμμένοι	λελειμμέναι	λελειμμένα
	G	λελειμμένων	λελειμμένων	λελειμμένων
▷	N	λελειμμένοις	λελειμμέναις	λελειμμένοις
	A	λελειμμένους	λελειμμένας	λελειμμένα

2. Morphology

a. Stem

  (1) The "perfect" middle/passive forms exhibit the same type of "reduplication" as do the active forms.

  (2) The middle/passive forms of the "perfect" are built off of a slightly different stem than the "perfect" active. One of three stem formations will be apparent.

    (a) Most frequently, a reduplicated form of the verb's first principal part—normally, the basic stem or root—is used (this is *regular* and is followed by all verbs classified as (R) in the vocabulary.)

	Perfect Indicative Middle/Passive	Present Indicative Active	Perfect Indicative Active
(EG 10)	ἦγμαι	ἄγω	ἦχα

    (b) Often the κ is simply dropped from the "perfect" active stem and the proper terminations are added.

	Perfect Indicative Middle/Passive	Present Indicative Active	Perfect Indicative Active
(EG 11)	εἴρημαι	λέγω	εἴρηκα

Note: Often formation of the "perfect" middle/passive by simply dropping the κ of the "perfect" active stem reveals that the first principal part does not contain the true stem or root of a given verb. We observed in chapter 7 (D) that $\delta\iota\delta\acute{\alpha}\sigma\kappa\omega$ is regular after the first principal part, which means that the basic future form (second principal part), $\delta\iota\delta\acute{\alpha}\xi\omega$, reveals the true verbal stem: $\delta\iota\delta\alpha\kappa$-. The same may be said for $\acute{\alpha}\mu\alpha\rho\tau\acute{\alpha}\nu\omega$, $\epsilon\acute{\upsilon}\rho\acute{\iota}\sigma\kappa\omega$, $\lambda\acute{\epsilon}\gamma\omega$, and actually, $\lambda\alpha\mu\beta\acute{\alpha}\nu\omega$. (See also D below.)

    (c) Sometimes a totally new stem, different from the stems of the first or fourth principal parts, is used.

	Perfect Indicative Middle/Passive	Present Indicative Active	Perfect Indicative Active
(EG 12)	$\acute{\epsilon}\sigma\tau\rho\alpha\mu\mu\alpha\iota$	$\sigma\tau\rho\acute{\epsilon}\phi\omega$	$\acute{\epsilon}\sigma\tau\rho\phi\alpha$

b. Connecting Vowels

The middle/passive forms of the "perfect tense" employ *no connecting vowel*. This is, in fact, one of the chief, if not *the* chief, means of recognizing any "perfect" middle/passive form.

c. Endings

    (1) Type

The "perfect" indicative middle/passive uses *normal* primary middle/passive endings. Note that $\sigma\alpha\iota$ is used for the second singular, the *original* primary second singular ending (cf. chapter 3, C 3 a (1) (b)).

    (2) Placement

The endings of the "perfect" middle/passive are added *directly* to *the verbal stem*. (In the participle, they are preceded by the normal - $\mu\epsilon\nu$ - addition.) There is no connecting vowel (see b above). If the stem ends with a vowel (cf. $\lambda\acute{\upsilon}\omega$), this occasions no difficulty. If the verb is a consonantal stem verb, however (cf. $\lambda\epsilon\acute{\iota}\pi\omega$), problems arise. The consonant at the end of the verb stem must assimilate to the consonant that begins the ending proper. Three patterns may be observed in indicative formations:

Guttural ($\pi\rho\acute{\alpha}\sigma\sigma\omega$)

	Singular	Plural
1	$\pi\acute{\epsilon}\pi\rho\alpha\gamma\mu\alpha\iota$	$\pi\epsilon\pi\rho\acute{\alpha}\gamma\mu\epsilon\theta\alpha$
2	$\pi\acute{\epsilon}\pi\rho\alpha\xi\alpha\iota$	$\pi\acute{\epsilon}\pi\rho\alpha\chi\theta\epsilon$
3	$\pi\acute{\epsilon}\pi\rho\alpha\kappa\tau\alpha\iota$	$\pi\epsilon\pi\rho\alpha\gamma\mu\acute{\epsilon}\nu\omega\iota\ \epsilon\acute{\iota}\sigma\acute{\iota}(\nu)$

Labial (στρέφω)

	Singular	Plural
1	ἔστραμμαι	ἐστράμμεθα
2	ἔστραψαι	ἔστραφθε
3	ἔστραπται	ἐστραμμένοι εἰσί(ν)

Dental (πείθω)

	Singular	Plural
1	πέπεισμαι	πεπείσμεθα
2	πέπεισαι	πέπεισθε
3	πέπεισται	πεπεισμένοι εἰσί(ν)

Note in these examples:

(a) Dental-stemmed verbs change their dental to σ before each ending. (The second person forms do not preserve two sigmas.)

(b) The voiceless dental (τ) of the third singular ending attracts the voiceless guttural (κ) or labial (π) for verbs of these stems.

(c) The σ of the second singular ending produces ξ and ψ in guttural and labial stemmed verbs, respectively.

(d) The second plural ending lacks the σ, because σ elides, not only between two vowels, but also between two consonants. The consonant at the end of the stem then aspirates, assimilating to the aspiration of the θ following.

(e) Because of the μ beginning the first singular, first plural, and third plural ending (also the participle), the final letter of a guttural stem softens to γ, while the final letter of a labial becomes μ also.

(f) Because of the awkward form produced by the string of consonants, the third plural of consonantal stem verbs uses εἰσί(ν) + the "perfect" passive participle (of the appropriate gender) in the plural (a *periphrastic* form).

> (EG 13)   Not λέλειπνται but λελειμμένοι
> εἰσί(ν) = "They are left (abandoned)."

Note: It is possible to encounter periphrastic formations also in other persons and numbers of the perfect indicative passive.

> (EG 14)   λελειμμένοι ἐσμέν = "We are left."

> (EG 15)   λελειμμένος ἐστίν = "He is left."

The ending of the participle must be adjusted if it is used to refer to a singular subject (cf. EG 15).

d. Accent

The accent for "perfect" middle/passive forms is normal, but note again the slightly unusual accent placement in the infinitive, and especially in the participle.

3. Meaning

a. The meaning for the "perfect" middle/passive is the same as for the active, except that in the passive the subject is not the agent of the action.

(EG 16)   *τὰ ἱμάτια κεκλεμμένα εἰσίν.*
The clothes have been stolen (i.e., "they are no longer here," or in another context, "they are 'hot' ").

b. Normally what looks like a present time translation is to be recommended for the perfect indicative passive. The thought is that something has happened to someone (or something) and the *present resultant condition* is now described. Thus, EG 16 is best translated:

(EG 17)   "The clothes *are* stolen."

Note: See chapter 11, E 1 and 2 to compare and contrast the use of "present tense" forms in the passive voice.

c. It may be noted that the *"perfect" passive participle* is especially *frequent*. It is often used in attributive position to describe the state of a person or thing.

(EG 18)   *φιλῶ τὸν γεγραμμένον λόγον.*
I love the *written* word (i.e., the word that has been and *now stands* written).

Note that the participle is translated essentially as an adjective in this construction.

4. Principal Part

The basic perfect indicative middle/passive form of a verb is its *fifth* principal part.

D. Vocabulary

ἁγιάζω (R): I make holy, sanctify

δοκιμάζω (R): I test for approval; approve

κατ-αρτίζω (R): I fashion, create

κρατέω (R) + gen.: I seize; arrest

λατρεύω (R) + dat.: I worship

σφραγίζω (R): I seal

Here following are irregular fourth and fifth principal parts of verbs already met (some of which will be used in this lesson):

Chapter	Verb		4	5
3	ἄγω	. . .	ἦχα	reg.
	ἀκούω	. . .	ἀκήκοα	ἤκουσμαι
	γράφω	. . .	γέγραφα	reg.
	κλέπτω	. . .	κέκλοφα	(reg.)[1]
	λείπω	. . .	λέλοιπα	(reg.)
	πέμπω	. . .	πέπομφα	(reg.)
6	πείθω	. . .	πέποιθα	(reg.)
7	διδάσκω	. . .	δεδίδαχα	reg.
	διώκω	. . .	δεδίωχα	reg.
	λαμβάνω	. . .	εἴληφα	εἴλημμαι
	πίνω	. . .	πέπωκα	_____
	φεύγω	. . .	πέφευγα	_____
	φυλάσσω	. . .	πεφύλαχα	reg.
8	ἁμαρτάνω	. . .	ἡμάρτηκα	ἡμάρτημαι
	ἔρχομαι	. . .	ἐλήλυθα	_____
	εὑρίσκω	. . .	εὕρηκα	εὕρημαι
	λέγω	. . .	εἴρηκα	εἴρημαι
	πάσχω	. . .	πέπονθα	_____
	πίπτω	. . .	πέπτωκα	_____
	φέρω	. . .	ἐνήνοχα	ἐνήνεγμαι
9	ἀπο-θνήσκω	. . .	τέθνηκα	_____
	ὁράω	. . .	ἑώρακα	(ἑώραμμαι)
12	γίνομαι	. . .	γέγονα(!)	γεγένημαι
	πράσσω	. . .	πέπραχα	reg.
13	ἔχω	. . .	ἔσχηκα	_____
23	τάσσω	. . .	τέταχα	reg.
24	στρέφω	. . .	ἔστροφα	ἔστραμμαι

E. Exercises

1. Form the regular fifth principal part of the verbs indicated as regular in the chart above according to principles given in the text.

2. Parse the following "perfect" forms and give the first principal part.

   a. δεδίδακται   h. γέγραπται

   b. ἠκούσμεθα   i. πέπωκας

   c. πέπεμψαι   j. εἰρήκαμεν

   d. λέλοιπε   k. ἐστραμμένοι εἰσίν

   e. ἤγμεθα   l. τεθνηκότα

   f. ἐληλύθατε   m. πεφυλαχώς

   g. κέκλεφθε   n. τεταγμένον

F. Practice Sentences

1. Greek to English

a. ὁ θεὸς σώσει τοὺς ἐσφραγισμένους τῷ αἵματι τοῦ σωτῆρος.

b. ἐλήλυθας ἰδεῖν τὰ γεγραμμένα ἐπὶ τῇ θύρᾳ τοῦ ἱεροῦ;

c. ἀκήκοα τὸ εὐαγγέλιον καὶ ἑώρακα τὰ πραχθέντα ὑπὸ τοῦ Ἰησοῦ.

d. οἱ δεδοκιμασμένοι ἐργάται ἐν τῇ βασιλείᾳ σωθή- σονται, οἱ δὲ μὴ ἡγιασμένοι καὶ μὴ λατρεύοντες τῷ ἀληθεῖ θεῷ ἀπο-πεμφθήσονται.

e. ὁ λῃστὴς ἐκράτησε τοῦ στεφάνου τοῦ κατ-ηρτισ- μένου τῷ βασιλεῖ, ἀλλὰ φυγὼν εὑρέθη ὑπὸ τῶν στρατιωτῶν.

f. τίς οὐκ ἐπι-θυμεῖ τὸν ἀγαθὸν οἶνον τὸν ἡτοιμασ- μένον τῷ δεσπότῃ;

g. αἱ λελειμμέναι ἐν τῇ ἐρήμῳ ἀπο-θνήσκουσιν, μὴ ἔχουσαι ἄρτον καὶ ὕδωρ.

2. English to Greek

Those who are sanctified love even those who hate them.

G. Bible Passages

John 19:22 (C)

John 9:37

Matthew 4:7b πάλιν . . . (C)

Apocalypse 7:4a . . . ἐσφραγισμένων

1 Corinthians 2:7 (Cs)

Note

1. Entries in parentheses occur, but not in the books of the NT.

26

The Verb, Part 7
Principal Parts
and Indirect Discourse

A. The Verb, Part 7: Pluperfect Indicative Active, Middle, and Passive

1. Introduction

a. In English, the pluperfect (which uses "had" as an auxiliary verb: "after I *had come* . . .") is relatively frequent. In Greek, however, it is rare except in one -μι verb (cf. chapter 35). For the sake of this verb, and for the sake of completeness, the pluperfect indicative forms are now presented.

b. The Greek pluperfect is, as it were, the "past tense of the perfect," or a *secondary* version of the "focus upon result" stem (just as the imperfect is a secondary version of the "focus upon connection"/"present" stem).

2. Paradigm Forms

a. Active

(1) λύω

	Singular			Plural	
1	ἐλελύκειν	I had loosed		ἐλελύκειμεν	We had loosed
2	ἐλελύκεις	You had loosed		ἐλελύκειτε	You had loosed
3	ἐλελύκει	He (she, it) had loosed		ἐλελύκεισαν	They had loosed

(2) λείπω

	Singular			Plural	
1	ἐλελοίπειν	I had left		ἐλελοίπειμεν	We had left
2	ἐλελοίπεις	You had left		ἐλελοίπειτε	You had left
3	ἐλελοίπει	He (she, it) had left		ἐλελοίπεισαν	They had left

175

b. Middle/Passive

   (1) λύω

Singular		Plural	
1 ἐλελύμην	I was loosed	ἐλελύμεθα	We were loosed
2 ἐλέλυσο	You were loosed	ἐλέλυσθε	You were loosed
3 ἐλέλυτο	He (she, it) was loosed	ἐλέλυντο	They were loosed

   (2) λείπω

Singular		Plural	
1 ἐλελείμμην	I was left	ἐλελείμμεθα	We were left
2 ἐλέλειψο	You were left	ἐλέλειφθε	You were left
3 ἐλέλειπτο	He (she, it) was left	λελειμμένοι ἦσαν	They were left

3. Morphology

a. Stem

The pluperfect indicative is built off of the appropriate "perfect" stem, the active off of the "perfect" active stem, the middle/passive off of the "perfect" middle/passive.

b. Augment

The pluperfect is a secondary "tense." Therefore, it is augmented. Two points must be noted, however.

   (1) Verbs whose initial letters have been lengthened as a substitute for reduplication cannot add an augment. Again, the secondary endings must be the key to "tense."

    (EG 1)   ᾔτημαι is ᾐτήμην in the pluperfect.

   Note: Verbs that reduplicate their stems in the "perfect" by "augmenting" with an ἐ (cf. ἔστροφα) do *not* lengthen that ἐ to ἠ for the pluperfect.

   (2) At times, no augment is added. In these cases, only the secondary endings reveal that the form is pluperfect, not perfect.

    (EG 2)   ἐλελύκειν may appear as λελύκειν.

c. Connecting Vowel

   (1) In the active, the pluperfect connecting vowel is ει in Koine Greek, (In classical Greek, it was η in the singular, ε in the plural.)

   (2) There is no connecting vowel for pluperfect middle/passive forms.

d. Endings

The pluperfect, being a secondary "tense,' uses secondary endings ($^-\sigma\alpha\nu$ in third plural active and $^-\sigma o$ in second singular middle/passive). Note that for the third person plural of consonantal stem verbs, the compound or periphrastic form is made secondary by changing the "tense" of the verb "to be" ($\epsilon i\sigma i[\nu]$ becomes $\mathring{\eta}\sigma\alpha\nu$).

4. Meaning

The pluperfect, as the secondary form of the "focus upon result"/ "perfect" stem, conveys a focus upon *completed action in past time whose results endured in the past* (and may not be enduring now). As is apparent, such a thought is expressed only infrequently.

(EG 3)   ἡ ἐπαγγελία τοῦ θεοῦ <u>ἐγέγραπτο</u> ἐπὶ τοῦ Ἰησοῦ.

The promise of God *was written* (i.e., stood written) at the time of Jesus. (It had been written down many years before.)

B. Principal Parts of Greek Verbs

With the pluperfect we are now able to identify all of the *principal parts,* i.e., key stems, of the Greek verb and delineate which forms are made from which stems. (See following page.)

C. Indirect Discourse (Reported Speech)

1. Introduction

Indirect discourse occurs when a statement or question is *reported,* not actually quoted. EG 4 is an example of *direct* discourse.

(EG 4)   He said, "*I am teaching you.*"

EG 5 is *indirect* discourse.

(EG 5)   He said *that he was teaching you.*

There is a special difficulty in translating indirect discourse from Greek to English, because Greek usage is unlike English usage.

2. Principles of Indirect Discourse Formation

a. *Greek retains the "tense" and the mood of the statement actually spoken, when that statement is reported.*

(EG 6)   λέγει ὅτι διδάσκει σε.

(EG 7)   εἶπεν ὅτι διδάσκει σε.

Principal Parts

λύω

		1	2	3	4	5	6
PRIMARY TENSE FORMS	Active	λύω	λύσω		λέλυκα	λέλυμαι	
	Middle	λύομαι	λύσομαι			λέλυμαι	
	Passive	λύομαι	λύσομαι			λέλυμαι	λυθήσομαι
SECONDARY TENSE FORMS	Active			ἔλυσα	ἐλελύκειν	ἐλελύμην	ἐλύθην
	Middle	ἐλυόμην		ἐλυσάμην		ἐλελύμην	
	Passive	ἐλυόμην		ἐλυσάμην		ἐλελύμην	ἐλύθην

λείπω

		1	2	3	4	5	6
PRIMARY TENSE FORMS	Active	λείπω	λείψω		λέλοιπα	λέλειμμαι	
	Middle	λείπομαι	λείψομαι			λέλειμμαι	
	Passive	λείπομαι	λείψομαι			λέλειμμαι	λειφθήσομαι
SECONDARY TENSE FORMS	Active			ἔλιπον	ἐλελοίπειν	ἐλελείμμην	ἐλείφθην
	Middle	ἐλειπόμην		ἐλιπόμην		ἐλελείμμην	
	Passive	ἐλειπόμην		ἐλιπόμην		ἐλελείμμην	ἐλείφθην

Note: Verbs in any one column are built off of the form (principal part) underlined.

The direct statement is this: διδάσκω σε = "I teach (or, am teaching) you." Because the teacher is no longer speaking but his words are being reported, the person of the verb must be changed from first ("I") to third ("he"), as is natural, but the "present tense" of the original statement is retained in the Greek *regardless of the time of the main verb.* Compare the direct statement to EGs 6 and 7: all three contain a present indicative form of διδάσκω.[1]

b. English follows a different procedure. *English preserves the time relationship between the action in the reported speech and the act of speaking.* Thus, EG 6 is translated as follows:

(EG 6a) "He says that he teaches you (habitual action)," or "He says that he is teaching you,"

because both teaching and speaking are going on together and both are in the present time. But EG 7 is translated like this:

(EG 7a) "He said that he *taught* you (habitual action)," or "He said that he *was teaching* you."

because the speaking took place in the past, and, therefore, the teaching, which occurred *at the same time,* also must be translated as past. Note the next example.

(EG 8) εἶπεν ὅτι ἐποίησεν τοῦτο.

Here the actual statement was this: ἐποίησα τοῦτο = "I did this," and an aorist indicative form is preserved in Greek indirect discourse structure. In English indirect discourse, however, ἐποίησεν must be translated with the *pluperfect,* because the doing took place before the speaking, and the speaking is now in the past: "He said that he *had done* this."

3. Principles for Translation

The basic pattern for translating indirect discourse is as follows:

a. If the main verb is a *primary* "tense," translate the reported (indirect) discourse verbs, i.e., the verbs in the ὅτι clause, *normally,* preserving the normal time frame of these verbs.

b. If the main verb is a *secondary* "tense," translate the verbs of the reported (indirect) discourse *one step back in time from the time that they normally convey.* It is helpful to preserve the same description of the activity (simple or progressive).

(EG 9) λέγει ὅτι διδάσκει σε.
He *says* that he *is* teaching you.

(EG 10) εἶπεν ὅτι διδάσκει σε.
He *said* that he *was* teaching you.

(EG 11)   λέγει ὅτι ἐδίδασκε σε.
He *says* that he *was* teaching you.

(EG 12)   εἶπεν ὅτι ἐδίδασκε σε.
He *said* that he *had been* teaching you.

(EG 13)   λέγει ὅτι ἐδίδαξε σε.
He *says* that he *taught* you.

(EG 14)   εἶπεν ὅτι ἐδίδαξε σε.
He *said* that he *had* taught you.

The following chart may prove helpful:

WHEN THE MAIN VERB (OF SPEAKING) IS A *SECONDARY* TENSE—

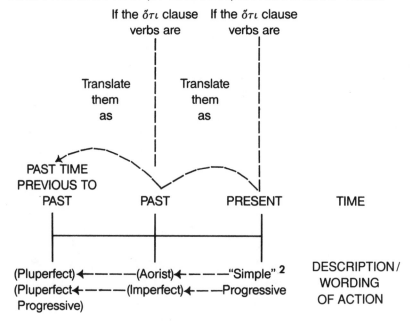

c. Future forms must be considered an exception, not when they occur as the main verb of speaking, but when they occur in the reported speech. Here, in a secondary sequence, i.e., after a secondary main verb (of speaking), the "will" (or, "shall") of the future is simply put back to "would" (it is not translated as present).

(EG 15)   λέγει ὅτι διδάξει σε.
He *says* that he *will* teach you.

(EG 16)   εἶπεν ὅτι διδάξει σε.
He *said* that he *would* teach you.

4. The same principles are used with clauses following verbs of seeing, hearing, knowing, perceiving, learning, etc.

(EG 17)   εἶδον ὅτι ὁ 'Ιησοῦς ἐστιν ἐκεῖ.
They *saw* that Jesus *was* there.

(EG 18)   ἤκουσαν ὅτι οἱ μαθηταὶ ἦλθον.
They *heard* that the disciples *had come*.

D. Vocabulary

ἀν-οίγω (Irreg.): I open

ἀρνέομαι (M)(R): I deny

δοκέω, δόξω (R): I think; third singular may be intransitive and impersonal = It seems

καλέω (Irreg.): I call

παρα-καλέω, etc.: I exhort; comfort; encourage

προσ-καλέομαι (M), etc.: I summon

λογίζομαι (M) (R): I reckon, account as

μανθάνω (Irreg.): I learn

μιμνήσκομαι . . . ἐμνήσθην (P) + gen.: I remember

οἶδα (perf.): I know (ἤδειν, pluperfect = "I knew"; stem is ειδ-)

ὁμολογέω (R): I confess

ὅτι (conj.): that (introducing indirect discourse or thought)

Be sure to start memorizing the principal parts of the irregular verbs that have been met so far, using the special chart after the paradigms in the back of the book. (The irregular fourth and fifth principal parts were introduced in chapter 25.) The following irregular verbs are not included in the chart, because they have only two or three principal parts:

ἐσθίω	Chapter 8
εἰμί	Chapter 12
θέλω	Chapter 13
μέλλω	Chapter 16
ἀπο-κρίνομαι	Chapter 24
βούλομαι	Chapter 24

From this chapter on, irregular verbs with four or more principals parts will be marked with (Irreg.) and will appear on the principal parts chart. Irregular verbs with three or fewer principal parts will have all parts given in the vocabulary.

E. Exercises

1. Make the corresponding pluperfect of verb forms a, b, c, d, h, i, j, k of exercise E 2 in chapter 25.

2. Translate the following:

   a. λέγει ὅτι ἐργάζεται ἐν τῇ βασιλείᾳ.

   b. λέγει ὅτι ἠργάσατο ἐν τῇ βασιλείᾳ.

   c. εἶπεν ὅτι ἐργάζεται ἐν τῇ βασιλείᾳ.

   d. εἶπεν ὅτι ἠργάσατο ἐν τῇ βασιλείᾳ.

   e. λέγει ὅτι ἐργάσεται ἐν τῇ βασιλείᾳ.

   f. εἶπεν ὅτι ἐργάσεται ἐν τῇ βασιλείᾳ.

   g. λέγει ὅτι ἠργάζετο ἐν τῇ βασιλείᾳ.

   h. εἶπεν ὅτι ἠργάζετο ἐν τῇ βασιλείᾳ.

F. Practice Sentences

1. Greek to English

   a. εἶπεν ὅτι εἰσ-ῆλθε διὰ τῆς ἀν-εῳγμένης θύρας.

   b. πρὸ τοῦ ἀπ-αχθῆναι τὰ πρόβατα, ὁ ποιμὴν ἠληλύθει.

   c. οἱ μὲν ἀρνούμενοι τὸν δεσπότην φονευθήσονται, οἱ δὲ ὁμολογοῦντες ὅτι ὁ Ἰησοῦς κύριός ἐστιν ἐλεύσονται εἰς τὴν βασιλείαν.

   d. ἐγὼ μὲν οἶδα ὅτι ὁ Ἰησοῦς ἐκάλεσε δώδεκα μαθητάς, σὺ δὲ μιμνήσκῃ ταύτης τῆς ἀληθείας;

   e. περι-πατοῦντος τοῦ Ἰησοῦ ἐπὶ τὰ ὕδατα, οἱ μαθηταὶ ἔδοξαν ὅτι βλέπουσι πονηρὸν πνεῦμα.

   f. μαθόντες ὅτι κλέπτης ἐν τῷ ἱερῷ ἐστιν, οἱ ἱερεῖς προσ-εκαλέσαντο τοὺς στρατιώτας, ὥστε τούτους κρατῆσαι αὐτοῦ.

   g. ἀκούσας ὅτι οἱ δοῦλοι φοβοῦνται τοὺς Ἰουδαίους, ὁ Παῦλος παρ-εκάλεσεν αὐτοὺς ταῖς ἐπαγγελίαις τοῦ εὐαγγελίου.

   h. ἡ πίστις τῆς μητρὸς ἐλογίσθη αὐτῇ εἰς δικαιοσύνην.

2. English to Greek

The prophets thought that the king had gone into the temple.

G. Bible Passages

John 11:30a . . . *κώμην*

John 9:24b *οἴδαμεν* . . .

Luke 5:32

Hebrews 11:13 (omit *πάντες*) (C)

Notes

1. Note that *ὅτι* now means "that," introducing the reported speech (cf. the vocabulary, section D).

2. Usually "habitual" (cf. EGs 6, 6a; 7, 7a).

27

Liquid Verbs and the Third Principal Part of βαίνω and γινώσκω

A. Liquid Verbs

1. Introduction

A number of verbs have stems ending in a liquid consonant (λ, μ, ν, ρ). Many of these verbs are irregular in their principal parts, and in many ways it is best simply to regard them as such, learning their six principal parts as one would learn the principal parts of any irregular verb. A few basic principles can be observed, however, and we will introduce them in this chapter.

2. Principal Parts: Paradigm Verbs

(1)	(2)	(3)	(4)	(5)	(6)
ἀγγέλλω	ἀγγελῶ	ἤγγειλα	ἤγγελκα	ἤγγελμαι	ἠγγέλην
αἴρω	ἀρῶ	ἦρα	ἦρκα	ἦρμαι	ἤρθην
βάλλω	βαλῶ	ἔβαλον	βέβληκα	βέβλημαι	ἐβλήθην
φθείρω	φθερῶ	ἔφθειρα	ἔφθαρκα	ἔφθαρμαι	ἐφθάρην

3. Basic Principles of Morphology

a. Second Principal Part

(1) The *second principal part* reveals the *verb's basic stem* or *root*.

(2) To form this principal part

    (a) one λ from a double lambda in the "present" stem is always dropped (cf. ἀγγέλλω, βάλλω);

    (b) a ι in the "present" stem is always dropped from a diphthong (cf. αἴρω, φθείρω).

(3) The second principal part is normally a *contracted* form, since originally an εσ was added to the stem before the connecting vowel and ending. The σ then elided, since it was between two vowels. Such forms are conjugated like -έω contract verbs:

	Singular	Plural
(EG 1)	βαλῶ	βαλοῦμεν
	βαλεῖς	βαλεῖτε
	βαλεῖ	βαλοῦσι(ν)

b. Third Principal Part

(1) The "aorist" stem may be strong (cf. βάλλω) but is usually weak. A weak "aorist" stem has no σ before α.

(2) A ι appears in the stem if the stem proper (second principal part) has an ε (cf. ἀγγέλλω, φθείρω).

(3) A ι does not appear if the stem proper has an α, even if a ι appeared in the first principal part (cf. βάλλω, αἴρω).

c. Fourth Principal Part

(1) The "perfect" active stem is normally weak (i.e., with a κ).

(2) A verb ending in ν usually elides the ν before the κ.

	Present Indicative	Perfect Indicative
(EG 2)	κρίνω	κέκρικα

d. Fifth Principal Part

The stem of the "perfect" middle/passive is usually the fourth principal part minus κ (cf. all paradigm verbs). This is common with verbs whose true stem is not revealed in principal part one (cf. chapter 25, C 2 a (2) (b)).

e. Sixth Principal Part

(1) The "aorist" passive stem is often strong (i.e., no θ) (cf. ἀγγέλλω, φθείρω).

(2) The sixth principal part is often slightly unusual and must be learned.

	Present Indicative Active	Aorist Indicative Passive
(EG 3)	ἀπο‑κτείνω	ἀπ‑εκτάνθην

B. The Third Principal Part of βαίνω and γινώσκω

1. Introduction

In previous chapters, we have encountered βαίνω and γινώσκω, two very old verbs, only in their first and second principal parts. We now come to their "aorist" forms, which use a very old morphology still preserved in the ancient -μι verbs (see chapters 33–35). These forms must be mastered.

2. The "Aorist" Active Forms of the Verbs

a. βαίνω

(1) Indicative

	Singular	Plural
1	ἔβην	ἔβημεν
2	ἔβης	ἔβητε
3	ἔβη	ἔβησαν

(2) Infinitive: βῆναι

(3) Participle

Singular

	M	F	N
N	βάς	βᾶσα	βάν
G	βάντος	βάσης	βάντος
D	βάντι	βάσῃ	βάντι
A	βάντα	βᾶσαν	βάν

Plural

	M	F	N
N	βάντες	βᾶσαι	βάντα
G	βάντων	βασῶν	βάντων
D	βᾶσι(ν)	βάσαις	βᾶσι(ν)
A	βάντας	βάσας	βάντα

b. γινώσκω

(1) Indicative

	Singular	Plural
1	ἔγνων	ἔγνωμεν
2	ἔγνως	ἔγνωτε
3	ἔγνω	ἔγνωσαν

(2) Infinitive: γνῶναι

(3) Participle

Singular

	M	F	N
N	γνούς	γνοῦσα	γνόν
G	γνόντος	γνούσης	γνόντος
D	γνόντι	γνούσῃ	γνόντι
A	γνόντα	γνοῦσαν	γνόν

Plural

	M	F	N
N	γνόντες	γνοῦσαι	γνόντα
G	γνόντων	γνουσῶν	γνόντων
D	γνοῦσι(ν)	γνούσαις	γνοῦσι(ν)
A	γνόντας	γνούσας	γνόντα

3. Morphology

  a. Stem

    (1) These two verbs use a shortened stem ending with a vowel. This vowel is usally lengthened:

      (a) In *βαίνω*, the *a* is lengthened to *η*.

      (b) In *γινώσκω*, the *o* is lengthened to *ω*.

    (2) The stem vowel is short in the participle in both verbs.

  b. Connecting Vowel

    No connecting vowel is used in indicative, infinitive, or participle forms of these verbs.

  c. Endings

    (1) Normal secondary endings are used in the indicative. Note that the endings in the indicative and infinitive are added directly to the stem, giving these forms a look very similar to the sixth principal part of other verbs.

    (2) Note the old *-ναι* active infinitive ending (cf. normal "aorist" passive forms).

    (3) Participle endings follow a third declension pattern in the masculine and neuter, A declension in the feminine (hybrid), as normal.

    (4) *No* middle forms occur.

Note: *βαίνω* appears only in compounds in our literature.

4. Syntax

It is important to note that construction after *γινώσκω* often function the same as indirect discourse. Thus, "He knew that . . ." should be regarded the same as "he said that . . ." for purposes of time sequencing (cf. chapter 26, C 4).

(EG 4)   *ἔγνω ὅτι ὁ δοῦλος ὧδέ ἐστιν.*
        He *knew* that the slave *was* here.

C. Vocabulary

ἀγγέλλω (Irreg.): I announce

αἴρω (Irreg.): I take up; carry away

ἀπο-κτείνω (Irreg.): I kill

ἀπο-στέλλω (Irreg.): I send out

βάλλω (Irreg.): I throw; put

περι-βάλλω, etc.: I throw around, clothe (two objects possible);
mid.: I clothe myself

ἐγείρω (Irreg.): I rouse (the dead), raise; pass.: I rise

κρίνω (Irreg.): I judge

κατα-κρίνω, etc.: I condemn

κρίσις -εως, f.: judgment

κριτής -οῦ, m.: judge

μένω (Irreg.): I remain

ὑπο-μένω, etc.: I endure

σπείρω (Irreg.): I sow

φθείρω (Irreg.): I corrupt, destroy

Note also the third principal parts of βαίνω and γινώσκω:

ἔβην   ἔγνων

Be sure to learn also the remaining principal parts of these two verbs.

D. Exercise

Determine on the basis of the principles given in A 3 above the second
and third principal parts of the following *fictitious* liquid verbs:

1. βέλλω

2. βαίλλω

3. βάρω

4. βείρω

5. βένω

E. Practice Sentences

1. Greek to English

a. ἐγερθεὶς ἐκ νεκρῶν, ὁ Ἰησοῦς ἀν-έβη εἰς τὸν
οὐρανόν.

b. ἀπ-εστάλησαν οἱ δώδεκα ἀγγεῖλαι ὅτι ἡ κρίσις
τοῦ θεοῦ μέλλει φθείρειν τὸν κόσμον.

c. ὁ δὲ κύριος εἶπεν ὅτι οἱ κρίνοντες ἄλλους κατα-
κριθήσονται.

d. οἱ μαθηταὶ ἔγνωσαν ὅτι ὁ διδάσκαλος αὐτῶν ἐστιν
ὁ θεός;

e. ὁ σπείρων ἐξ-ῆλθε σπεῖραι ἐν τῷ ἀγρῷ.

f. ἄραντες τὰς μαχαίρας αὐτῶν, οἱ μαθηταὶ ἔδοξαν ὅτι παρὰ τῷ κυρίῳ μενοῦσιν.

g. φθαρέντων τῶν οἴκων τῆς κώμης ὑπὸ τῶν πονηρῶν, οἱ ἅγιοι ὑπ-έμειναν κακά.

h. ὁ πλούσιος τελώνης περι-εβάλετο καλὰ ἱμάτια, ἀλλ' οἱ στρατιῶται ἔβαλον αὐτὸν εἰς φυλακὴν (cf. φυλάσσω) καὶ ἀπ-εκτάνθη.

2. English to Greek

Jesus came down (κατα-βαίνω) to earth to save those under the judgment of the devil.

F. Bible Passages

Acts 13:30

Matthew 22:18

Luke 1:26a . . . Γαλιλαίας (C)

1 Corinthians 16:8 (C)

Luke 9:2a . . . θεοῦ (C)

Matthew 27:6–7a . . . κεραμέως

Mark 12:12a . . . εἶπεν

The Verb, Part 8a:
The Subjunctive Mood 1

A. Introduction

The subjunctive is a second *mood,* in addition to the indicative. Mood as such concerns the way in which an action is conceived. The indicative deals with reality, the subjunctive, especially in English, with unreality. Thus English uses the subjunctive to express, e.g.,

1. *conditions contrary to fact:*

   (EG 1)   "If I *were* you, I would not go."

2. *wishes:*

   (EG 2)   "God *go* with you."

3. *reported commands:*

   (EG 3)   "I demand that he *come* here."

Greek use of the subjunctive is in some ways similar to that of English but in many respects it is quite different. The essence of the Greek subjunctive is *futurity,* i.e., it describes, generally speaking, acts that pertain to the future, and additionally, those about which there is some *uncertainty.* (In this latter respect it differs from the future indicative.) As we shall see, however, the Greek subjunctive does have many different uses, and as such it has no one simple translation.

B. Paradigm Forms

1. λείπω

a. "Present"/"Focus upon Connection"

	Active		Middle/Passive	
	Singular	Plural	Singular	Plural
1	λείπω	λείπωμεν	λείπωμαι	λειπώμεθα
2	λείπῃς	λείπητε	λείπῃ	λείπησθε
3	λείπῃ	λείπωσι(ν)	λείπηται	λείπωνται

b. "Aorist"/"Focus on the Action"

	Active			Middle	
	Singular	Plural		Singular	Plural
1	λίπω	λίπωμεν		λίπωμαι	λιπώμεθα
2	λίπῃς	λίπητε		λίπῃ	λίπησθε
3	λίπῃ	λίπωσι(ν)		λίπηται	λίπωνται

Passive

	Singular			Plural	
1	λειφθῶ	(λειφθέω)		λειφθῶμεν	(λειφθέωμεν)
2	λειφθῇς	(λειφθέῃς)		λειφθῆτε	(λειφθέητε)
3	λειφθῇ	(λειφθέῃ)		λειφθῶσι(ν)	(λειφθέωσι[ν])

2. λύω

a. "Present"/"Focus upon Connection"

	Active			Middle/Passive	
	Singular	Plural		Singular	Plural
1	λύω	λύωμεν		λύωμαι	λυώμεθα
2	λύῃς	λύητε		λύῃ	λύησθε
3	λύῃ	λύωσι(ν)		λύηται	λύωνται

b. "Aorist"/"Focus on the Action"

	Active			Middle	
	Singular	Plural		Singular	Plural
1	λύσω	λύσωμεν		λύσωμαι	λυσώμεθα
2	λύσῃς	λύσητε		λύσῃ	λύσησθε
3	λύσῃ	λύσωσι(ν)		λύσηται	λύσωνται

Passive

	Singular			Plural	
1	λυθῶ	(λυθέω)		λυθῶμεν	(λυθέωμεν)
2	λυθῇς	(λυθέῃς)		λυθῆτε	(λυθέητε)
3	λυθῇ	(λυθέῃ)		λυθῶσι(ν)	(λυθέωσι[ν])

3. εἰμί

	Singular	Plural
1	ὦ	ὦμεν
2	ᾖς	ἦτε
3	ᾖ	ὦσι(ν)

Note: There are subjunctive forms for the "focus upon result"/"perfect" but these are largely confined to the passive voice and are normally periphrastic.

(EG 4)   λελυμένος ᾖ

(EG 5)   λελυμένοι ὦσι(ν)

In such constructions, the participle functions essentially as an adjective.

C. Morphology

1. Stem

The forms of the subjunctive use the stem of the appropriate "tense." Note that, as is true with both the infinitive and the participle, the "aorist" forms carry no augment since they are not indicative mood. There is *no "future" stem* in use for the subjunctive mood.

(EG 6)   λύσωμεν is "aorist," not "future."

2. Connecting Vowel

a. The connecting vowel is the distinguishing feature of the subjunctive mood. (Cf. chapter 3, A 2: "The connecting vowel . . . indicates the mood. . . .") In the indicative mood, the connecting vowel is regularly short; in the subjunctive, it is always long.

Indicative	Subjunctive
ε	η
ο	ω

Note that a ι in a diphthong goes subscript:

ει   η

but that the ου contraction of the third plural is simply ω (cf. the original λυ|ο|ντσι form [chapter 3, B 1 a and b]).

b. The weak "aorist," being generally atypical in that it regularly uses a special connecting vowel (α) to distinguish "tense," not mood (its stem is generally the same as the "future" stem: cf. λύσω—ἔλυσα), loses its α and uses the regular η/ω pattern of connecting vowels. Note again how much more "typical" the strong "aorist" forms are.

c. The "aorist" passive forms are contracted in the connecting vowel, the ε of the θε combining with the long η or ω. Note that, as with the "aorist" passive participle, θε, not θη, is the addition to the stem (cf. chapter 22, B 3 b).

3. Endings

The endings for the forms of all three voices are primary. ("Aorist" passive employs, as usual, active endings.) Primary endings are appropriate because the subjunctive deals essentially with futurity, not with the past (cf. A above and F below).

The subjunctive may be summarized morphologically as *appropriate stem*, plus *long connecting vowel*, plus *primary endings* (of the appropriate voice).

D. "Tense"/Aspect

The "tense" of the subjunctive indicates aspect/focus relative to action, not time. Review the principles of aspect in chapter 9. Since the subjunctive deals essentially with the future (cf. A above and F below), there is *no future* in the subjunctive.

E. Meaning: Part 1

The subjunctive does not have any specific meaning that may be attached to it at every occasion. λύσωμεν, e.g., does not mean "We *might* loose" or "We *should* loose"; it means simply: "We loose (in some context of futurity)." The specific syntactical construction will determine the exact force and, therefore, the meaning of a subjunctive in any given context. See also G below.

F. Syntax

The subjunctive is used either *independently* or *dependently,* i.e., either as a main verb or as a verb in a subordinate clause. In this chapter, we will consider the *independent* uses.

1. Hortatory (Cohortative)

The first person plural (rarely, singular) subjunctive is often used when someone is exhorting a group of which he is a part.

(EG 7)   λύσωμεν τοὺς δούλους.
         Let us loose the slaves.

This is not asking for permission; it is saying: "Come, let's do it."

2. Deliberative

The first person plural is also, and more rarely, used either to deliberate or ponder a difficult decision or to ask a rhetorical question.

(EG 8)   ἀκολουθήσωμεν τῷ Ἰησοῦ;
         Shall we follow Jesus?

Here, the speaker is either "thinking out loud" or asking the question rhetorically.

3. Emphatic Denial

Any person of the subjunctive may be used in emphatic denial. In this case, the "aorist" subjunctive is used, preceded by οὐ μή.

(EG 9)   οὐ μὴ ποιήσωμεν τοῦτο τὸ πονηρόν.
         We *shall surely not* do this evil deed!

4. Negative Command

When someone prohibits another from an action, especially *when that action has not yet been begun, the "aorist"* subjunctive plus μή is used, normally in the second person (singular or plural).

(EG 10)   μὴ ποιήσητε τοῦτο τὸ πονηρόν.
            Do not (plural) do this evil deed.

(EG 11)   μὴ ποιήσῃς τοῦτο τὸ πονηρόν.
            Do not (singular) do this evil deed.

Such commands may also be given in the *third* person, to command someone who is either not present or unknown.

(EG 12)   μὴ οἱ ἅγιοι πιστεύσωσι τοῖς λόγοις τῶν
            δαιμονίων.
            Let the saints not believe the words of the demons!

(EG 13)   ὁ ἄφρων μὴ δόξῃ ὅτι σοφός ἐστιν.
            Let the foolish man not think that he is wise!

Again, these are commands, not requests for permission (cf. F 1 above).

The negative for the subjunctive, as generally for all forms outside the indicative, is μή, not οὐκ.

G. Meaning: Part 2

In reviewing the various possible uses of the subjunctive in F above, we can see that a subjunctive takes its meaning from its context. Thus λύσωμεν may mean: "Let us loose" (cf. EG 7), "Shall we loose" (cf. EG 8), or with a negative, "We shall surely not loose" (cf. EG 9). In each case, however, we may note that a future orientation is involved.

H. Appendix: "Aorist" Subjunctive Active Forms of βαίνω and γινώσκω

1. βαίνω

	Singular	Plural
1	βῶ	βῶμεν
2	βῇς	βῆτε
3	βῇ	βῶσι(ν)

2. γινώσκω

	Singular	Plural
1	γνῶ	γνῶμεν
2	γνῷς	γνῶτε
3	γνῷ	γνῶσι(ν)

I. Vocabulary

ἀνα-γινώσκω, etc.: I read

ἐμ-βαίνω, etc.: I get into (a boat), embark (ἐμ = ἐν)

ἐπι-γινώσκω, etc.: I know thoroughly

θερίζω (R): I reap, harvest

θυγάτηρ, θυγατρός, f.: daughter

μισθός ‑οῦ, m.: pay, wages

νεφέλη ‑ης, f.: cloud

παρ-έρχομαι, etc.: I pass by; pass away

τρίτος ‑η ‑ον: third

J. Exercises

1. Make the third singular and second plural "present" and "aorist" subjunctive active of each vocabulary verb (use the middle for the first principal part of παρ-έρχομαι).

2. Parse the following:

   a. λύσωμεν   e. ἐνέγκησθε   i. κηρυχθῆς

   b. φάγωνται   f. ἴδωσιν   j. ἔβαλον

   c. ἀγγείλητε   g. εἴπωμεν   k. μείνῃς

   d. λείψομεν   h. γένηται   l. λυθῇ

K. Practice Sentences

1. Greek to English

a. οἱ προφῆται εἶπον· ἀνα-γνῶμεν τῷ λαῷ τοὺς λόγους τοῦ νόμου.

b. εἰσ-έλθωμεν εἰς τὸ ἱερὸν καὶ ἐκεῖ προσ-κυνήσωμεν τῷ θεῷ.

c. ἐμ-βὰς εἰς τὸ πλοῖον, ὁ Ἰησοῦς <u>ἀπ-ήγγειλεν</u> ὅτι τὴν καρδίαν τοῦ ἀνθρώπου ἐπι-γινώσκει.

d. εἰσ-έλθωμεν εἰς τὴν κώμην εἰς τὸ δέξασθαι τοὺς μισθοὺς ἡμῶν;

e. οὐ μὴ παρ-έλθῃ ὁ νόμος πρὸ τοῦ πάλιν κατα-βῆναι τὸν Ἰησοῦν κρῖναι τὴν γῆν.

f. οἱ ἐπι-θυμοῦντες πορνείαν θερίσουσιν ἃ σπείρουσιν, κριθήσονται γὰρ ὑπὸ τοῦ σωτῆρος.

g. ἐν τῇ τρίτῃ ἡμέρᾳ ὁ 'Ιησοῦς ἠγέρθη, καὶ δια-
τάξας τοῖς μαθηταῖς πορευθῆναι εἰς τὰ ἔσχατα
τῆς γῆς, ἤρθη εἰς τὰς νεφέλας.

h. ὁ 'Ιησοῦς ἤγειρε τὴν θυγατέρα τοῦ ἡγεμόνος καὶ
εἶπεν· μὴ θαυμάσητε ὅτι αὕτη οὐκέτι τέθνηκεν.

2. English to Greek

Do not believe the evil prophets, for they shall surely not obtain
(get for themselves) true life.

L. Bible Passages

Mark 8:26 (Cs)

Luke 8:22 (omit αὐτός) (Cs)

John 13:6–8a . . . αἰῶνα (omit κύριε)

29

The Verb, Part 8b:
The Subjunctive Mood 2

A. Introduction

We move now to *dependent* uses of the subjunctive, i.e., those that occur in subordinate clauses and are not main verbs. (No new morphology is involved.) Again, it must be emphasized that context determines the meaning of the subjunctive.

B. Syntax

1. Uses with ἵνα

The subjunctive is used most frequently in subordinate clauses that begin with ἵνα. These uses directly parallel the uses of the infinitive without the article. See chapter 16, E 1 a–e. (Not included is the use of the infinitive after ὥστε to express result, chapter 16, E 2.)

a. Purpose

    (EG 1)   ἔρχεται <u>ἵνα ἴδῃ</u> τὸν ἀπόστολον.
               He is coming *in order to see* the apostle.

Cf. chapter 16, EG 6. This is the most basic use with ἵνα and is classical. Note: ὅπως may be used in place of ἵνα to introduce purpose clauses, especially in Matthew.

b. Object

    (EG 2)   θέλει <u>ἵνα ἴδῃ</u> τὸν ἀπόστολον.
               He desires *to see* the apostle.

Cf. chapter 16, EG 7.

c. Epexegetical

    (EG 3)   ἄξιός ἐστιν <u>ἵνα ἴδῃ</u> τὸν ἀπόστολον.
               He is worthy *to see* the apostle.

Cf. chapter 16, EG 8.

d. Appositional

(EG 4)   τοῦτό ἐστιν ἀγαθόν, *ἵνα φιλήσωμεν* τὸν
          θεόν.
          This is good, *that we love* God.

Cf. chapter 16, EG 9.

e. Subject

(EG 5)   ἔξεστιν *ἵνα φιλήσωμεν* τὸν θεόν.
          It is proper *that we love* God.

Cf. chapter 16, EG 10.

Note that a subject must be added in the appositional and subject uses, since the infinitive conveys pure act, while the subjunctive does not.

2. Uses with *ἄν*

The subjunctive is also used in clauses that contain an *ἄν*, either in close proximity to a relative pronoun or subordinating conjunction, or connected to such a conjunction. Such clauses make statements either about the *future* or about *general truths* and concern time, condition, person, or place.

a. One of the most frequent uses of the subjunctive with *ἄν* concerns *time*. ὅτε, meaning "when," is used alone to introduce a temporal clause in past time with the indicative. (A participial construction for such a thought is much more common.)

(EG 6)   *ὅτε* ὁ ᾽Ιησοῦς *ἦλθεν*, οἱ λαοὶ ἐδόξασαν
          τὸν θεόν.
          When Jesus *came*, the peoples glorified God.

A statement concerning *future* time, however, uses ὅτε + ἄν → ὅταν + the subjunctive.

(EG 7)   *ὅταν* ὁ ᾽Ιησοῦς *ἔλθῃ* ἐν δόξῃ,
          σωθησόμεθα.
          When Jesus *comes* in glory, we will be saved.

A *general* statement also uses ὅταν + the subjunctive.

(EG 8)   *ὅταν* ὁ ᾽Ιησοῦς *ἴδῃ* τυφλόν, θεραπεύει
          αὐτόν.
          Whenever Jesus *sees* a blind man, He heals him.

b. *ἄν* is also used with the expressions of *condition*. εἰ means "if" and is often used alone with an indicative mood verb for particular conditions in the past or present.

(EG 9)   *εἰ ἐποίησεν* τοῦτο, ἔλυσε τὸν νόμον.
          If he *did* this, he broke the law.

(EG 10)   εἰ ποιεῖς τοῦτο, λύεις τὸν νόμον.
If you *are doing* this (now), you are breaking the law.

A statement concerning a *future* condition, however, uses εἰ + ἄν → ἐάν + the subjunctive.

(EG 11)   ἐὰν ὁ μαθητὴς ἔλθῃ, σώσει ἡμᾶς.
If the disciple *comes,* he will save us.

A *general* statement also uses ἐάν + the subjunctive.

(EG 12)   ἐὰν ὁ ᾿Ιησοῦς ἴδῃ χωλόν, θεραπεύει αὐτόν.
If (ever, on any occasion) Jesus *sees* a lame man, He (always) heals him.

c. ἄν is frequently used with *relative pronouns* in future and general contexts. ὅς, ἥ, etc., are frequently used alone in past and *non*general present contexts with the indicative.

(EG 13)   εἶδον τὸν κλέπτην ὃν εἶδες.
I saw the thief *whom* you *saw.*

(EG 14)   βλέπω τὸν κλέπτην ὃν βλέπεις.
I see the thief *whom* you *see.*

A statement concerning *future* time, however, uses ὅς + ἄν, ἥ + ἄν, etc., (in various cases) + the subjunctive.

(EG 15)   ὃς ἂν ἀποκτείνῃ τὸ θηρίον λήμψεται τὸ ἀργύριον.
Whoever (= *the one who*) *kills* the wild beast will get the money.

A *general* statement also uses ὅς + ἄν, etc. + the subjunctive.

(EG 16)   ὃς ἂν ἔλθῃ πρὸς τὸν ᾿Ιησοῦν δέχεται τὴν ἄφεσιν τῶν ἁμαρτιῶν.
Whoever comes to Jesus receives forgiveness of sins.

d. ἄν is also used with adverbial conjunctions of *place* in future and general contexts. ὅπου means "where" and is used alone with the indicative mood in past and *non*general present contexts.

(EG 17)   ὁ ᾿Ιησοῦς ἦλθεν ὅπου ὁ ᾿Ιωάννης ἦν.
Jesus went *where* John *was.*

A statement concerning *future* time, however, uses ὅπου + ἄν + the subjunctive.

(EG 18)   ὁ διδάσκαλος ἔρχεται πρὸς τὸ ἱερόν, ἐλεύσομαι δὲ ὅπου ἂν ἔλθῃ.
The teacher is going to the temple, and I will go *where* he *goes.*

A *general* statement also uses ὅπου + ἄν + the subjunctive.

(EG 19)   ὅπου ἄν πορευθῇ, ὁ ᾿Ιησοῦς θεραπεύει
           τοὺς ἀσθενεῖς.
           Wherever He *goes,* Jesus heals the sick.

Note that the difference between general and future statements re-sides chiefly in the main verb. If that verb is present, the thought is general; if it is future, the thought is future (though it may also be general).

3. The "general" use of the subjunctive with ἄν does not really con-tradict the idea that the subjunctive is used in contexts of futurity, for the general statements are unlimited and stretch, by implication, into the future. The same cannot as easily be said for the use of the subjunctive with ἵνα, however, with the exception of *purpose* clauses, which are obviously future oriented. The other four uses with ἵνα are late developments in Greek—they are not classical usages—though it may perhaps be said that they are general and therefore indefinite in character.

C. Vocabulary

ἄφεσις ⁻εως, f.: forgiveness

εἰ (conj.): if

ἐλεύθερος ⁻α ⁻ον: free

ἑορτή ⁻ῆς, f.: feast

ἕως (conj.): until

θησαυρός ⁻οῦ, m.: treasure

ἵνα (conj.): (that)

κατ⁻αργέω (R): I abolish, nullify

κατ⁻οικέω (R): I inhabit; dwell in (+ ἐν)

ὅπου (conj.): where

ὅπως (conj.): (in order) that

ὅτε (conj.): when

συλ⁻λαμβάνω, etc.: I seize; conceive a child (συλ = συν)

D. Exercises

1. Redo sentences a–e in section H 1 of chapter 16, substituting ἵνα clauses for the infinitives.

2. T—F: A subordinate clause with ἄν (+ subjunctive) may refer to past time.

E. Practice Sentences

1. Greek to English

a. ἐάν τις ὁμολογῆται τὰς ἁμαρτίας αὐτοῦ, δέχεται ἄφεσιν παρὰ τοῦ πατρός.

b. ὅταν ὁ Ἰησοῦς ἀνα-βῇ ~~ἐπὶ ἑορτῇ~~ πρὸς ἑορτήν παρα-λαμβάνει τοὺς μαθητὰς αὐτοῦ.

c. ὅτε ἡ Μαρία συν-έλαβε τὸ πρῶτον τέκνον αὐτῆς, ὁ Ἰωσὴφ οὐκ ἐπίστευσεν ὅτι ἔτι ἐστὶν παρθένος.

d. ἐὰν φθείρωμεν τὰ ἱερὰ τῶν Ἑλλήνων, ποῦ κατ- οικήσουσιν οἱ θεοὶ αὐτῶν;

e. ὅπου ἂν ὁ θησαυρός σου ᾖ ἐκεῖ ἔσται ἡ καρδία σου.

f. ἦλθεν ὁ σωτὴρ ἵνα ἀπο-λύσῃ τοὺς ὑπὸ τὸν διάβο- λον δούλους καὶ ποιήσῃ αὐτοὺς ἐλευθέρους.

g. ἄξιοί ἐσμεν ἵνα κληθῶμεν υἱοὶ τοῦ θεοῦ.

h. οἱ στρατιῶται ἔμειναν ἐν τῷ τόπῳ ὅπου ὁ Ἰησοῦς ἦν, ἕως ὁ ἡγεμὼν προσ-έταξεν αὐτοῖς ἵνα ἐξ- αγάγωσιν αὐτόν, ὅπως ὑπὸ τῶν ὄχλων ὀφθῇ.

i. ἡ νύμφη τοῦ Χριστοῦ, ἥ ἐστιν ἡ ἐκκλησία, ὑπο- μενεῖ ἕως ἂν ὁ νυμφίος αὐτῆς πάλιν ἔλθῃ.

2. English to Greek

Do not go out to see the signs that have occurred (γίνομαι) in the sky.

F. Bible Passages

1 Corinthians 16:5a . . . διέλθω (C)

Mark 8:22 (C)

John 9:39

Matthew 27:20a . . . βαραββᾶν

John 12:23

Matthew 5:21

1 Peter 3:18a . . . θεῷ (C)

30
Contracted (Contract) Verbs in -άω

A. Introduction

We come now to other verbs with contracted forms in the "present" stem, the -άω contract verbs. These verbs have an α instead of an ε at the end of the "focus upon connection"/"present" stem (cf. the -έω contracts, chapter 14). In the forms built off of this stem, the short α combines with the following connecting vowel in a manner similar to the -έω contract verbs. In all other principal parts, the α normally lengthens to an η; if not, no contraction takes place. We will, therefore, concentrate on the principles of contraction for the "present" stem.

B. "Focus upon Connection"/"Present" Stem

1. Paradigm Forms (τιμάω)

a. Present Indicative Active

	Singular		Plural	
1	τιμῶ	(τιμάω)	τιμῶμεν	(τιμάομεν)
2	τιμᾷς	(τιμάεις)	τιμᾶτε	(τιμάετε)
3	τιμᾷ	(τιμάει)	τιμῶσι(ν)	(τιμάουσι)

b. Present Indicative Middle/Passive

	Singular		Plural	
1	τιμῶμαι	(τιμάομαι)	τιμώμεθα	(τιμαόμεθα)
2	τιμᾷ	(τιμάη)	τιμᾶσθε	(τιμάεσθε)
3	τιμᾶται	(τιμάεται)	τιμῶνται	(τιμάονται)

c. "Present" Subjunctive Active

	Singular		Plural	
1	τιμῶ	(τιμάω)	τιμῶμεν	(τιμάωμεν)
2	τιμᾷς	(τιμάης)	τιμᾶτε	(τιμάητε)
3	τιμᾷ	(τιμάη)	τιμῶσι(ν)	(τιμάωσι)

d. "Present" Subjunctive Middle/Passive

	Singular		Plural	
1	τιμῶμαι	(τιμάωμαι)	τιμώμεθα	(τιμαώμεθα)
2	τιμᾷ	(τιμάῃ)	τιμᾶσθε	(τιμάησθε)
3	τιμᾶται	(τιμάηται)	τιμῶνται	(τιμάωνται)

e. Imperfect Indicative Active

	Singular		Plural	
1	ἐτίμων	(ἐτίμαον)	ἐτιμῶμεν	(ἐτιμάομεν)
2	ἐτίμας	(ἐτίμαες)	ἐτιμᾶτε	(ἐτιμάετε)
3	ἐτίμα	(ἐτίμαε)	ἐτίμων	(ἐτίμαον)

f. Imperfect Indicative Middle/Passive

	Singular		Plural	
1	ἐτιμώμην	(ἐτιμαόμην)	ἐτιμώμεθα	(ἐτιμαόμεθα)
2	ἐτιμῶ	(ἐτιμάου)	ἐτιμᾶσθε	(ἐτιμάεσθε)
3	ἐτιμᾶτο	(ἐτιμάετο)	ἐτιμῶντο	(ἐτιμάοντο)

g. "Present" Infinitive

Active		Middle/Passive	
τιμᾶν	(τιμάειν)	τιμᾶσθαι	(τιμάεσθαι)

h. "Present" Participle

(See section D below.)

2. Morphology

a. Stem

(1) As in the ⁻*έω* contract verbs, the short *α* at the end of the "present" stem in the ⁻*άω* contract verbs contracts with the connecting vowel that follows to produce one amalgamated syllable. (See uncontracted forms in parentheses.) You will not see uncontracted forms in the New Testament or the LXX.

(2) The rules for contraction are as follows:

(a) The *α* at the end of the stem combines with a following *ε* or *η* to produce *α*:

$α + ε/η → α$

(EG 1)   τιμά|ετε → τιμᾶτε

(EG 2)   τιμά|ητε → τιμᾶτε

(b) The a at the end of the stem combines with a following o or ω to produce ω:

$a + o/\omega \rightarrow \omega$

(EG 3) $\tau\iota\mu\acute{a}|o\mu\epsilon\nu \rightarrow \tau\iota\mu\hat{\omega}\mu\epsilon\nu$

(EG 4) $\tau\iota\mu\acute{a}|\omega\mu\epsilon\nu \rightarrow \tau\iota\mu\hat{\omega}\mu\epsilon\nu$

(c) Any ι in a syllable following the a goes subscript.[1]

(EG 5) $\tau\iota\mu\acute{a}|\epsilon\iota\varsigma \rightarrow \tau\iota\mu\hat{q}\varsigma$

(EG 6) $\tau\iota\mu\acute{a}|\eta\varsigma \rightarrow \tau\iota\mu\hat{q}\varsigma$

b. Connecting Vowel

The normal connecting vowels are used for all forms. It is these that contract with the end of the stem.

c. Endings

Normal endings are used for all forms.

d. Dictionary Listing

The verb's first form is listed in a dictionary with the $\acute{a}\omega$ *un-contracted:*

(EG 7) $\tau\iota\mu\acute{a}\omega$ (not $\tau\iota\mu\hat{\omega}$)

3. Accenting

The uncontracted forms must be accented first.

a. If the accent falls on the a at the end of the stem, it will become a circumflex on the contracted syllable:

(EG   8) $\tau\iota\mu\acute{a}|\epsilon\sigma\theta\epsilon \rightarrow \tau\iota\mu\hat{a}\sigma\theta\epsilon$

b. In all other cases, the accent remains where and as it is.

(EG   9) $\acute{\epsilon}\tau\acute{\iota}\mu a|o\nu \rightarrow \acute{\epsilon}\tau\acute{\iota}\mu\omega\nu$

(EG 10) $\acute{\epsilon}\tau\iota\mu a|\acute{o}\mu\epsilon\theta a \rightarrow \acute{\epsilon}\tau\iota\mu\acute{\omega}\mu\epsilon\theta a$

These rules for accenting are identical to those used for the $\acute{\bar{\epsilon}}\omega$ contract verbs.

C. Principal Parts 2–6

1. Forms

(1)	(2)	(3)	(4)	(5)	(6)
$\tau\iota\mu\acute{a}\omega$	$\tau\iota\mu\acute{\eta}\sigma\omega$	$\acute{\epsilon}\tau\acute{\iota}\mu\eta\sigma a$	$\tau\epsilon\tau\acute{\iota}\mu\eta\kappa a$	$\tau\epsilon\tau\acute{\iota}\mu\eta\mu a\iota$	$\acute{\epsilon}\tau\iota\mu\acute{\eta}\theta\eta\nu$

2. Morphology

a. In the -άω contract verbs, the short α of the "present" stem (first principal part) is regularly lengthened in the other principal parts to η (even as the ε of -έω contract verbs was lengthened to η). Onto this stem with the long η the σ of the "future" and "aorist," the κ of the "perfect" active, and the θη of the "aorist" passive stems are added. Again, *no contraction takes place in principal parts 2–6.*

b. A number of -άω contract verbs do not lengthen α to η after the first principal part; the short α simply goes to long α. Normally, these are verbs whose stems have a vowel before the α.

	Present Indicative	Future Indicative	Aorist Indicative
(EG 11)	ἐάω	ἐάσω	εἴασα[2]
(EG 12)	ἀγαλλιάω	ἀγαλλιάσω	ἠγαλλίασα

Exceptions to this rule do, however, occur.

D. Appendix: "Focus upon Connection"/"Present" -άω Contract Verb Participles

Active

Singular

	M	F	N
N	τιμῶν (τιμάων)	τιμῶσα (τιμάουσα)	τιμῶν (τιμάον)
G	τιμῶντος (τιμάοντος)	τιμώσης (τιμαούσης)	τιμῶντος (τιμάοντος)
D	τιμῶντι (τιμάοντι)	τιμώσῃ (τιμαούσῃ)	τιμῶντι (τιμάοντι)
A	τιμῶντα (τιμάοντα)	τιμῶσαν (τιμάουσαν)	τιμῶν (τιμάον)

Plural

	M	F	N
N	τιμῶντες (τιμάοντες)	τιμῶσαι (τιμάουσαι)	τιμῶντα (τιμάοντα)
G	τιμώντων (τιμαόντων)	τιμωσῶν (τιμαουσῶν)	τιμώντων (τιμαόντων)
D	τιμῶσι (τιμάουσι)	τιμώσαις (τιμαούσαις)	τιμῶσι(ν) (τιμάουσι)
A	τιμῶντας (τιμάοντας)	τιμώσας (τιμαούσας)	τιμῶντα (τιμάοντα)

Middle/Passive

Singular

	M	F	N
N	τιμώμενος (τιμαόμενος)	τιμωμένη (τιμαομένη)	τιμώμενον (τιμαόμενον)
G	τιμωμένου (τιμαομένου)	τιμωμένης (τιμαομένης)	τιμωμένου (τιμαομένου)
D	τιμωμένῳ (τιμαομένῳ)	τιμωμένῃ (τιμαομένῃ)	τιμωμένῳ (τιμαομένῳ)
A	τιμώμενον (τιμαόμενον)	τιμωμένην (τιμαομένην)	τιμώμενον (τιμαόμενον)

Plural

	M	F	N
N	τιμώμενοι (τιμαόμενοι)	τιμώμεναι (τιμαόμεναι)	τιμώμενα (τιμαόμενα)
G	τιμωμένων (τιμαομένων)	τιμωμένων (τιμαομένων)	τιμωμένων (τιμαομένων)
D	τιμωμένοις (τιμαομένοις)	τιμωμέναις (τιμαομέναις)	τιμωμένοις (τιμαομένοις)
A	τιμωμένους (τιμαομένους)	τιμωμένας (τιμαομένας)	τιμώμενα (τιμαόμενα)

E. Vocabulary

ἀγαλλιάω (-άσω) (R): I rejoice, exult (usually deponent)

ἀγαπάω (R): I love

γεννάω (R): I beget

ἐάω, ἐάσω, εἴασα: I allow

ἐπι-τιμάω (R) + dat.: I rebuke

ἐρωτάω³ (R): I inquire

ζάω⁴ (R): I live

θεάομαι (-άσομαι) (M) (R): I look at

καυχάομαι (-άσομαι) (M) (R): I boast

κοπιάω (-άσω) (R): I toil, labor

μεριμνάω (R): I worry (about)

πλανάω (R): I lead astray; pass.: I err; *wander*

τιμάω (R): I honor

     τιμή -ῆς, f.: honor; price, value

Note: ὁράω, the first principal part of εἶδον (chapter 9) is an -άω contract verb.

F. Exercise

Parse the following:

1. ἐγέννησα	6. πεπλανήμεθα	11. εἴασε
2. ἀγαπᾶτε	7. μεριμνῶμεν	12. ἐπ-ετίμησα
3. ἠγαλλιασάμεθα	8. ἐτίμων	13. ἀγαπῶντος
4. ἠρώτων	9. κοπιάσετε	14. γεννηθέντες
5. ζῇ	10. καυχῶνται	15. τιμᾶν

G. Practice Sentences

1. Greek to English

a. ἀγαπῶμεν τὸν θεόν, ὅτι ἠγάπησεν ἡμᾶς ἐν Χριστῷ.

b. ἀγαλλιώμεθα καὶ καυχώμεθα ἐν τῇ χάριτι τοῦ θεοῦ.

c. κοπιάσας ἐν τῷ ἀγρῷ, ὁ δοῦλος ἐκάθισεν ἐν τῷ οἴκῳ.

d. ὁ δὲ Ἰησοῦς ἐπ-ετίμησε τῷ πονηρῷ δαιμονίῳ καὶ ἐξ-έβαλεν αὐτὸ ἐκ τοῦ ἀνδρός.

e. ἐὰν ζῆτε ἐν Χριστῷ, σὺν αὐτῷ καὶ βασιλεύσετε.

f. ἀπ-ελθόντων τῶν ὄχλων, ὁ κύριος εἴασε τοὺς μα-θητὰς αὐτοῦ θεάσασθαι τὴν δόξαν αὐτοῦ ἐπὶ τοῦ ὄρους.

g. γεννήσας τὸ τέκνον, ὁ πατὴρ ἐμερίμνησε περὶ αὐτοῦ.

h. πλανᾶσθε εἰ οὐκ οἴδατε ὅτι δεῖ ἵνα τιμῶμεν τοὺς πατέρας καὶ τὰς μητέρας ἡμῶν.

i. οἱ Ἕλληνες ἠρώτησαν εἰ[5] ὁ ἀληθὴς σωτὴρ ἐλή-λυθεν εἰς τὸν κόσμον.

j. τιμὴ καὶ δόξα κεχαρισμένοι εἰσὶν τῷ Χριστῷ ὑπὸ τοῦ πατρός.

2. English to Greek

Men love women, but God loves us in Christ.

H. Bible Passages

John 4:40a . . . αὐτοῖς

John 11:11

John 18:7–8a . . . εἰμι (C)

Apocalypse 1:5b–6 Τῷ . . . (ἐποίησεν = ποιήσαντι)

1 John 3:9 (omit πᾶς)

Notes

1. The active infinitive is an exception to this rule (cf. B 1 g above).

2. Note the irregular augment on the aorist indicative of this verb. The imperfect augments in the same manner.

3. Often ἐπ-ερωτάω is used with no difference in meaning.

4. This verb is conjugated irregularly in the present indicative: ζῶ, ζῆς, ζῇ, ζῶμεν, ζῆτε, ζῶσιν. Note the use of η instead of α.

5. Functions exactly as does indirect discourse.

31

Contracted (Contract) Verbs in -όω

A. Introduction

The final type of contract verb has a short *o* at the end of the "focus upon connection"/"present" stem. It is the rarest and most regular of the three types. We will again concentrate on the principles of contraction of the first principal part.

B. "Focus upon Connection"/"Present" Stem

1. Paradigm Forms (δηλόω)

a. Present Indicative Active

	Singular		Plural	
1	δηλῶ	(δηλόω)	δηλοῦμεν	(δηλόομεν)
2	δηλοῖς	(δηλόεις)	δηλοῦτε	(δηλόετε)
3	δηλοῖ	(δηλόει)	δηλοῦσι(ν)	(δηλόουσι)

b. Present Indicative Middle/Passive

	Singular		Plural	
1	δηλοῦμαι	(δηλόομαι)	δηλούμεθα	(δηλοόμεθα)
2	δηλοῖ	(δηλόῃ)	δηλοῦσθε	(δηλόεσθε)
3	δηλοῦται	(δηλόεται)	δηλοῦνται	(δηλόονται)

c. "Present" Subjunctive Active

	Singular		Plural	
1	δηλῶ	(δηλόω)	δηλῶμεν	(δηλόωμεν)
2	δηλοῖς	(δηλόῃς)	δηλῶτε	(δηλόητε)
3	δηλοῖ	(δηλόῃ)	δηλῶσι(ν)	(δηλόωσι)

d. "Present" Subjunctive Middle/Passive

	Singular		Plural	
1	δηλῶμαι	(δηλόωμαι)	δηλώμεθα	(δηλοώμεθα)
2	δηλοῖ	(δηλόῃ)	δηλῶσθε	(δηλόησθε)
3	δηλῶται	(δηλόηται)	δηλῶνται	(δηλόωνται)

e. Imperfect Indicative Active

	Singular		Plural	
1	ἐδήλουν	(ἐδήλοον)	ἐδηλοῦμεν	(ἐδηλόομεν)
2	ἐδήλους	(ἐδήλοες)	ἐδηλοῦτε	(ἐδηλόετε)
3	ἐδήλου	(ἐδήλοε)	ἐδήλουν	(ἐδήλοον)

f. Imperfect Indicative Middle/Passive

	Singular		Plural	
1	ἐδηλούμην	(ἐδηλοόμην)	ἐδηλούμεθα	(ἐδηλοόμεθα)
2	ἐδηλοῦ	(ἐδηλόου)	ἐδηλοῦσθε	(ἐδηλόεσθε)
3	ἐδηλοῦτο	(ἐδηλόετο)	ἐδηλοῦντο	(ἐδηλόοντο)

g. "Present" Infinitive

	Active		Middle/Passive	
	δηλοῦν	(δηλόειν)	δηλοῦσθαι	(δηλόεσθαι)

h. "Present" Participle

(See section D below.)

2. Morphology

a. Stem

(1) As in the ⁻έω and ⁻άω contract verbs, the short *o* at the end of the "present" stem in the ⁻όω contract verbs contracts with the connecting vowel that follows to produce one amalgamated syllable. (See uncontracted forms in parentheses.) You will not see uncontracted forms in the New Testament or the LXX.

(2) The rules for contraction are as follows:

(a) The *o* at the end of the stem combines with a following ε or *o* to produce ου:

o + ε/o → ου

(EG 1)   δηλό|ετε → δηλοῦτε

(EG 2)   δηλό|ομεν → δηλοῦμεν

(b) The *o* at the end of the stem combines with a following η or ω to produce ω:

o + η/ω → ω

(EG 3)   δηλό|ητε → δηλῶτε

(EG 4)   δηλό|ωμεν → δηλῶμεν

    (c) Any ι in a syllable following produces $o\iota$:[1]

        $o + \iota$ following $\rightarrow o\iota$

        (EG 5) $\delta\eta\lambda\acute{o}|\epsilon\iota\varsigma \rightarrow \delta\eta\lambda o\hat{\iota}\varsigma$

        (EG 6) $\delta\eta\lambda\acute{o}|\eta\varsigma \rightarrow \delta\eta\lambda o\hat{\iota}\varsigma$

b. **Connecting Vowel**

The normal connecting vowels are used for all forms. It is these that contract with the end of the stem.

c. **Endings**

Normal endings are used for all forms.

d. **Dictionary Listing**

The verb's first form is listed in a dictionary with the $\acute{o}\omega$ *uncontracted*:

    (EG 7) $\delta\eta\lambda\acute{o}\omega \rightarrow$ (not $\delta\eta\lambda\hat{\omega}$)

3. Accenting

The uncontracted forms must be accented first.

a. If the accent falls on the o at the end of the stem, it will become a circumflex on the contracted syllable:

    (EG 8) $\delta\eta\lambda\acute{o}|\epsilon\sigma\theta\epsilon \rightarrow \delta\eta\lambda o\hat{v}\sigma\theta\epsilon$

b. In all other cases, the accent remains where and as it is.

    (EG 9) $\dot{\epsilon}\delta\acute{\eta}\lambda o|o\nu \rightarrow \dot{\epsilon}\delta\acute{\eta}\lambda o\nu\nu$

    (EG 10) $\dot{\epsilon}\delta\eta\lambda o|\acute{o}\mu\epsilon\theta a \rightarrow \dot{\epsilon}\delta\eta\lambda o\acute{v}\mu\epsilon\theta a$

These rules of accenting are identical to those used for the $\bar{\epsilon}\omega$ and $\bar{a}\omega$ contract verbs.

C. Principal Parts 2–6

1. Forms

(1)	(2)	(3)	(4)	(5)	(6)
$\delta\eta\lambda\acute{o}\omega$	$\delta\eta\lambda\acute{\omega}\sigma\omega$	$\dot{\epsilon}\delta\acute{\eta}\lambda\omega\sigma a$	$\delta\epsilon\delta\acute{\eta}\lambda\omega\kappa a$	$\delta\epsilon\delta\acute{\eta}\lambda\omega\mu a\iota$	$\dot{\epsilon}\delta\eta\lambda\acute{\omega}\theta\eta\nu$

2. Morphology

In the $\bar{o}\omega$ contract verbs, the short o of the "present" stem (first principal part) is regularly lengthened in the other principal parts to ω, (even as the ϵ of $\bar{\epsilon}\omega$ contract verbs and the a of $\bar{a}\omega$ contract verbs was lengthened to η). Onto this stem with the long ω the σ of the "future" and "aorist," the κ of the "perfect" active, and the $\theta\eta$ of the "aorist" passive stems are added. Again, no contraction takes place in principal parts 2–6.

D. Appendix: "Focus upon Connection"/"Present" -δω Contract Verb Participles

Active

Singular

	M		F		N	
N	δηλῶν	(δηλόων)	δηλοῦσα	(δηλόουσα)	δηλοῦν	(δηλόον)
G	δηλοῦντος	(δηλόοντος)	δηλούσης	(δηλοούσης)	δηλοῦντος	(δηλόοντος)
D	δηλοῦντι	(δηλόοντι)	δηλούσῃ	(δηλοούσῃ)	δηλοῦντι	(δηλόοντι)
A	δηλοῦντα	(δηλόοντα)	δηλοῦσαν	(δηλόουσαν)	δηλοῦν	(δηλόον)

Plural

	M		F		N	
N	δηλοῦντες	(δηλόοντες)	δηλοῦσαι	(δηλόουσαι)	δηλοῦντα	(δηλόοντα)
G	δηλούντων	(δηλόοντων)	δηλουσῶν	(δηλοουσῶν)	δηλούντων	(δηλόοντων)
D	δηλοῦσι(ν)	(δηλόουσι)	δηλούσαις	(δηλοούσαις)	δηλοῦσι(ν)	(δηλόουσι)
A	δηλοῦντας	(δηλόοντας)	δηλούσας	(δηλοούσας)	δηλοῦντα	(δηλόοντα)

Middle/Passive

Singular

	M		F		N	
N	δηλούμενος	(δηλοόμενος)	δηλουμένη	(δηλοομένη)	δηλούμενον	(δηλοόμενον)
G	δηλουμένου	(δηλοομένου)	δηλουμένης	(δηλοομένης)	δηλουμένου	(δηλοομένου)
D	δηλουμένῳ	(δηλοομένῳ)	δηλουμένῃ	(δηλοομένῃ)	δηλουμένῳ	(δηλοομένῳ)
A	δηλούμενον	(δηλοόμενον)	δηλουμένην	(δηλοομένην)	δηλούμενον	(δηλοόμενον)

Plural

	M		F		N	
N	δηλούμενοι	(δηλοόμενοι)	δηλούμεναι	(δηλοόμεναι)	δηλούμενα	(δηλοόμενα)
G	δηλουμένων	(δηλοομένων)	δηλουμένων	(δηλοομένων)	δηλουμένων	(δηλοομένων)
D	δηλουμένοις	(δηλοομένοις)	δηλουμέναις	(δηλοομέναις)	δηλουμένοις	(δηλοομένοις)
A	δηλουμένους	(δηλοομένους)	δηλουμένας	(δηλοομένας)	δηλούμενα	(δηλοόμενα)

E. Vocabulary

δηλόω (R): I make plain

δικαιόω (R): I justify, make righteous legally

κοινόω (R): I make common, defile

    κοινωνία ⁻ας, f.: fellowship; participation

ὁμοιόω (R)(+ dat): I make like, liken ; *pass. : be like*

    ὅμοιος ⁻α ⁻ον + dat.: like, similar (to)

πληρόω (R): I fill (acc. = thing filled, gen. = contents)

    πλήρωμα ⁻ατος, n.: fulness

σταυρόω (R): I crucify

    σταυρός ⁻οῦ, m.: cross

τελειόω (R): I make complete, perfect

    τέλειος ⁻α ⁻ον: complete, perfect, mature

F. Exercises

1. Give the third singular indicative and subjunctive active in each "tense" for πληρόω and ὁμοιόω.

2. Parse the following:

a. δικαιοῖ	e. ἐσταύρωσαν	i. ἐδικαιώθητε
b. κοινούμεθα	f. ἐτελείου	j. ἐπλήρουν
c. ὁμοιωθῆτε	g. δηλῶμεν	k. τετελείωκε
d. πληρώσετε	h. κοινῶσθε	l. σταυροῦσθε

G. Practice Sentences

1. Greek to English

a. ὁ θεὸς ἐπ⁻εθύμησεν δικαιῶσαι ἁμαρτωλούς.

b. ἐάν τις μένῃ ἐν ταῖς ἐπαγγελίαις τοῦ θεοῦ, ἔχει κοινωνίαν μετὰ τοῦ υἱοῦ αὐτοῦ.

c. ὁμοία ἐστὶν ἡ βασιλεία τοῦ θεοῦ τῷ ποιμένι τηροῦντι τὰ πρόβατα αὐτοῦ.

d. ἐν Χριστῷ τὸ πλήρωμα τοῦ θεοῦ ἐστιν, καὶ ἐκεῖνος δηλοῖ τὰς ὁδοὺς τούτου.

e. ἐξ⁻αγαγόντες τὸν Ἰησοῦν ἐκ τῆς πόλεως, οἱ στρατιῶται ἦραν σταυρὸν καὶ ἐπ' αὐτοῦ ἐσταύρω⁻ σαν τὸν κύριον.

f. ἐπλήρωσαν οἱ μαθηταὶ τὴν πόλιν τῆς διδαχῆς αὐτῶν, ὥστε τοὺς γραμματεῖς βουληθῆναι ἀπο-κτεῖναι αὐτούς.

g. τῇ ἀναστάσει ὁ ᾽Ιησοῦς τετελείωκε τὴν <u>σωτηρίαν</u> τὴν ἡτοιμασμένην τοῖς ἁγίοις.

h. μὴ κοινώσωμεν τὰ σώματα ἡμῶν, ὁ γὰρ θεὸς θέλει ἵνα τέλειοι ὧμεν.

i. ὡμοίωσεν ὁ κύριος τὴν βασιλείαν τῶν οὐρανῶν θησαυρῷ κεκρυμμένῳ ἐν ἀγρῷ.

2. English to Greek

Jesus was crucified by the governor, even though He had spoken the truth.

H. Bible Passages

Romans 8:30

1 John 1:3a . . . ἡμῶν (C)

1 John 1:4

John 17:23 (C)

Note

1. The active infinitive is an exception to this rule (cf. B 1 g above).

32

The Verb, Part 9:
The Imperative Mood

A. Introduction

The imperative is a new mood. It is a form of a verb used to give a command, either positive or negative. (We have had the use of the subjunctive in negative commands in chapter 28; see C below.) For this reason, imperatives will occur only in *direct* discourse. The Greek imperative is very complex when compared with English, and its forms and usage should be learned carefully.

Note: "Focus upon result"/"perfect" imperatives do exist, but they are too rare to concern the beginner.

B. Paradigm Forms

1. λείπω

a. Active Voice

(1) "Focus upon Connection"/"Present" Imperative Active

	Singular		Plural	
2	λεῖπε	Leave!	λείπετε	Leave!
3	λειπέτω	Let him (her, it) leave!	λειπέτωσαν	Let them leave!

(2) "Focus on the Action"/"Aorist" Imperative Active

	Singular		Plural	
2	λίπε	Leave!	λίπετε	Leave!
3	λιπέτω	Let him (her, it) leave!	λιπέτωσαν	Let them leave!

b. Middle Voice

(1) "Focus upon Connection"/"Present" Imperative Middle

	Singular		Plural	
2	λείπου	Leave for yourself!	λείπεσθε	Leave for yourselves!
3	λειπέσθω	Let him (her, it) leave for himself!	λειπέσθωσαν	Let them leave for themselves!

(2) "Focus on the Action"/"Aorist" Imperative Middle

	Singular		Plural	
2	λιποῦ	Leave for yourself!	λίπεσθε	Leave for yourselves!
3	λιπέσθω	Let him (her, it) leave for himself!	λιπέσθωσαν	Let them leave for themselves!

c. Passive Voice

(1) "Focus upon Connection"/"Present" Imperative Passive

	Singular		Plural	
2	λείπου	Be left!	λείπεσθε	Be left!
3	λειπέσθω	Let him (her, it) be left!	λειπέσθωσαν	Let them be left!

(2) "Focus on the Action"/"Aorist" Imperative Passive

	Singular		Plural	
2	λείφθητι	Be left!	λείφθητε	Be left!
3	λειφθήτω	Let him (her, it) be left!	λειφθήτωσαν	Let them be left!

2. λύω

a. Active Voice

(1) "Focus upon Connection"/"Present" Imperative Active

	Singular		Plural	
2	λῦε	Loose!	λύετε	Loose!
3	λυέτω	Let him (her, it) loose!	λυέτωσαν	Let them loose!

(2) "Focus on the Action"/"Aorist" Imperative Active

	Singular		Plural	
2	λῦσον	Loose!	λύσατε	Loose!
3	λυσάτω	Let him (her, it) loose!	λυσάτωσαν	Let them loose!

b. Middle Voice

(1) "Focus upon Connection"/"Present" Imperative Middle

	Singular		Plural	
2	λύου	Loose for yourself!	λύεσθε	Loose for yourselves!
3	λυέσθω	Let him (her, it) loose for himself!	λυέσθωσαν	Let them loose for themselves!

      (2) "Focus on the Action"/"Aorist" Imperative Middle

	Singular		Plural	
2	λῦσαι	Loose for yourself!	λύσασθε	Loose for yourselves!
3	λυσάσθω	Let him (her, it) loose for himself!	λυσάσθωσαν	Let them loose for themselves!

    c. Passive Voice

      (1) "Focus upon Connection"/"Present" Imperative Passive

	Singular		Plural	
2	λύου	Be loosed!	λύεσθε	Be loosed!
3	λυέσθω	Let him (her, it) be loosed!	λυέσθωσαν	Let them be loosed!

      (2) "Focus on the Action"/"Aorist" Imperative Passive

	Singular		Plural	
2	λύθητι	Be loosed!	λύθητε	Be loosed!
3	λυθήτω	Let him (her, it) be loosed!	λυθήτωσαν	Let them be loosed!

Note: For the imperative forms of contract verbs in the "present," of εἰμί, and of βαίνω and γινώσκω in the "aorist," see section G below.

C. Morphology

1. Stem

The appropriate stem is used. Note that no augment appears in "aorist" forms.

2. Connecting Vowel

Imperative forms are very *atypical* in that, as a distinct mood, they should have distinctive connecting vowels but they do not. (Cf. the indicative, subjunctive, and also optative [chapter 38].) For this reason, they must be identified simply by ending and in the "aorist" by lack of augment.

    a. Normal forms use the normal ε/ο connecting vowel.

    b. Weak "aorists" use the familiar α connecting vowel, though not in the second person singular active.

    c. "Aorist" passive imperatives have, as usual, no connecting vowel.

3. Endings

    a. Endings are the key to the imperative and are unusual. The second person plural in all voices is the same as the corresponding indicative ending. The third singular and plural endings are odd but are easily recognizable: ⁻τω, ⁻τωσαν; ⁻σθω, σθωσαν. It is the second person singular ending which is odd, unpredictable, and yet so important. These must by all means be memorized by rote. (Note especially the weak "aorist" forms: λῦσον, λῦσαι.)

b. It may be noted that the second person singular imperative ending of the "aorist" passive (⁻τι) is active. It is a modification of the strong (second) "aorist" ending ⁻θι, which is a very old active ending (cf. εἰμί, βαίνω, and γινώσκω in G below).

(EG 1)   ἀποστάληθι (not ἀποστάλητι)

Note: It is important to remember that μή + the "aorist" imperative is *not* in use to convey a negative command. See chapter 28, F 4. μή + the "aorist" *subjunctive* is the proper idiom for a prohibition with the "focus on the action"/"aorist" stem.

D. Accent

The accent for the imperative is normally recessive (even on compounds!). Note, however, that the accent on the strong "aorist" second singular middle is unusual: λιποῦ. It must also be observed that several important strong "aorists" used an irregular "ultima accent" also in the active voice:

εἰπέ not εἶπε
ἐλθέ not ἔλθε

ἰδέ, λαβέ, and εὑρέ also follow this pattern, but the latter is rare, and the former two have been made normal by most editors.

E. "Tense"/Aspect

The so-called "tense" of the imperative, like the "tense" of the subjunctive and infinitive, indicates aspect/focus relative to action, not time. As we shall see below (F), the usage of the forms conveying these aspects is quite complex.

F. Syntax and Meaning

All uses of the imperative are *independent*. Observation suggests that two distinct patterns of usage may be detected, depending on context. (As with all moods other than the indicative, the negative is μή, not οὐκ.)

1. Use of imperatives in a particular situation or to confront a *specified* case.

    a. Positive Commands

        (1) *"Focus on the action"/"aorist"* forms are *normal* in this context; fully 72 percent of all New Testament specified case imperatives are "aorist."

            (EG 2)   <u>λάβετε, φάγετε</u>, τοῦτό ἐστι τὸ σῶμά μου.

                      "Take, eat; this is My body." (Matt. 26:26)

        (2) *"Present"* forms are *abnormal* in this context, usually focusing upon some special connection between the doer and the action to be done. They are used in

            (a) demands for *continual* activity:

                (EG 3)   <u>κηρυσσέτω</u> διὰ τῆς πλατείας τῆς πόλεως . . .

                          "Let him proclaim through the street of the city . . ." (Esther 6:9, LXX)

            (b) demands for *repeated* activity:

                (EG 4)   <u>ἀσπάζου</u> τοὺς φίλους κατ᾽ ὄνομα.

                          "Greet the friends by name (*each one*)." (3 John 15)

            (c) demands that are *emphatic*—frenzied or desperate or insistent:

                (EG 5)   <u>σταύρου, σταύρου</u> αὐτόν.

                          "Crucify, crucify him!" (Luke 23:21)

                (EG 6)   πιστεύω, <u>βοήθει</u> μου τῇ ἀπιστίᾳ.

                          "I believe, *help* my unbelief." (Mark 9:24; cf. the "aorist" in v. 22)

                (EG 7)   <u>ὑπόστρεφε</u> εἰς τὸν οἶκον σου.

                          "Return to your house." (Luke 8:39)

            (d) demands that *signal action to commence:*

                (EG 8)   Ἀμήν, <u>ἔρχου</u>, κύριε Ἰησοῦ.

                          "Amen; *come*, Lord Jesus." (Apoc. 22:20; Jesus has just said, ναί, ἔρχομαι ταχύ.)

            (e) demands that use certain verbs, especially ἔχω, λαλέω, φεύγω, ἐκπορεύομαι, βόσκω, προσέχω, περιπατέω, φέρω, θαρσέω.

    b. Negative Commands

        (1) μή + the *"focus upon connection"/"present"* imperative is used to prohibit an action *already engaged in:*

            (EG 9)   <u>μὴ ποίει</u> τοῦτο.

                      Stop doing this!

(2) μή + the *"focus on the action"* / *"aorist"* subjunctive is used to prohibit *the commencing of an action* (cf. C 3 above and chapter 28, F 4):

(EG 10)   μὴ ποιήσῃς τοῦτο.
           Don't (start) do(ing) this!

2. Use of imperatives to give long-standing or *policy* commands.

Most authors use either "present" or "aorist" forms *consistently* in their policy commands. Thus, both positive and negative commands tend to use the same stem, either "present" or "aorist," with *no distinction* made in prohibitions (as in F 1 b above).

a. Most authors (e.g., Paul, Luke, John) use "present" forms for policy imperatives and prohibitions:

(EG 11)   αἱ γυναῖκες, ὑποτάσσεσθε τοῖς
           ἀνδράσιν.
           "Wives, *be subject* to [your] husbands." (Col. 3:18)

(EG 12)   τὸ λαλεῖν μὴ κωλύετε γλώσσαις.
           "Never forbid [not, "stop forbidding"] speaking with tongues." (1 Cor. 14:39)

b. A few authors use *"aorist"* forms for policy imperatives and prohibitions:

(EG 13)   ἐκ καρδίας ἀλλήλους ἀγαπήσατε.
           "(Always) love one another from the heart." (1 Peter 1:22)

(EG 14)   μὴ οὖν μεριμνήσητε λέγοντες· τί
           φάγωμεν; . . .
           "Therefore, *never be anxious,* saying, 'What shall we eat?' . . ." (Matt. 6:31)

3. Both specified case and policy commands use "aorist" forms for addresses to God. (The distinction between prohibitions with "present" and "aorist" forms for specified case commands is not maintained.)

(EG 15)   κύριε, μὴ τῷ θυμῷ σου ἐλέγξῃς με. . . .
           ἴασαί με, κύριε, ὅτι ἐταράχθη τὰ ὀστᾶ
           μου.
           "Lord, *do not punish* me in Your wrath. . . . *Heal* me, Lord, because my bones are troubled." (Ps. 6:2a, 3b, LXX) (Note: David is now experiencing distress.)

(EG 16)   ἁγιασθήτω τὸ ὄνομά σου.
           "Let Your name *be hallowed."* (Matt. 6:9)

G. Appendix

1. "Focus upon Connection"/"Present" Imperative Forms for Contract Verbs

a. -έω Contract Verbs

(1) "Present" Imperative Active

	Singular		Plural	
2	φίλει	(φίλεε)	φιλεῖτε	(φιλέετε)
3	φιλείτω	(φιλεέτω)	φιλείτωσαν	(φιλεέτωσαν)

(2) "Present" Imperative Middle/Passive

	Singular		Plural	
2	φιλοῦ	(φιλέου)	φιλεῖσθε	(φιλέεσθε)
3	φιλείσθω	(φιλεέσθω)	φιλείσθωσαν	(φιλεέσθωσαν)

b. -άω Contract Verbs

(1) "Present" Imperative Active

	Singular		Plural	
2	τίμα	(τίμαε)	τιμᾶτε	(τιμάετε)
3	τιμάτω	(τιμαέτω)	τιμάτωσαν	(τιμαέτωσαν)

(2) "Present" Imperative Middle/Passive

	Singular		Plural	
2	τιμῶ	(τιμάου)	τιμᾶσθε	(τιμάεσθε)
3	τιμάσθω	(τιμαέσθω)	τιμάσθωσαν	(τιμαέσθωσαν)

c. -όω Contract Verbs

(1) "Present" Imperative Active

	Singular		Plural	
2	δήλου	(δήλοε)	δηλοῦτε	(δηλόετε)
3	δηλούτω	(δηλοέτω)	δηλούτωσαν	(δηλοέτωσαν)

(2) "Present" Imperative Middle/Passive

	Singular		Plural	
2	δηλοῦ	(δηλόου)	δηλοῦσθε	(δηλόεσθε)
3	δηλούσθω	(δηλοέσθω)	δηλούσθωσαν	(δηλοέσθωσαν)

2. Imperative Forms of the Verb "To Be" (εἰμί)

	Singular	Plural
2	ἴσθι	[ἔστε]
3	ἔστω	ἔστωσαν

3. "Focus on the Action"/"Aorist" Imperative Forms of βαίνω **and** γινώσκω

a. βαίνω: "Aorist" Imperative Active

	Singular	Plural
2	βῆθι / βά	βάτε
3	βάτω	βάτωσαν

b. γινώσκω: "Aorist" Imperative Active

	Singular	Plural
2	γνῶθι	γνῶτε
3	γνώτω	γνώτωσαν

Note: For the forms of βαίνω, the *short* vowel stem is used for three forms, and there is also an alternative second person singular form that uses a long *a* and no ending.

H. Vocabulary[1]

βοηθέω (R) + dat.: I come to the aid of, help

καταφρονέω (R) + gen.: I despise

οὖς, ὠτός, n.: ear

παῖς, παιδός, m., f.: child

προσέχω, etc. + dat.: I give heed to, pay attention to

πῦρ, πυρός, n.: fire

ὑπάγω, etc.: I depart (intrans.)

ὑπαντάω (R) + dat.: I meet

ὑποστρέφω, etc.: I return; turn back (intrans.)

χαίρω . . . ἐχάρην: I rejoice[2]

χήρα ‑ας, f.: widow

I. Exercise

Parse the following:

1. ὑποστρέψατε	6. καταφρονησάτω	11. λύου
2. ὕπαγε	7. χαρῆτε	12. φονευέτωσαν
3. βοήθησον	8. λίπετε	13. ὑπήντησαν
4. προσέχετε	9. γνῶθι	14. βάτε
5. ἐργάζου	10. θεραπεύθητι	15. ἔστω

J. Practice Sentences

1. Greek to English

(Decide if a command is a policy or specified case command.)

a. ὑπόστρεψον εἰς τὴν κώμην σου καὶ ἄγγειλον τὸ εὐαγγέλιον τοῖς πτωχοῖς.

b. ὁ δὲ τελώνης προσηύξατο τῷ θεῷ οὕτως· μὴ βάλῃς με εἰς τὸ πῦρ, ἀλλὰ σῶσον με.

c. ταχέως ὕπαγε καὶ βοήθει τῷ πατρὶ οὗ ἡ θυγάτηρ ἀποθνήσκει.

d. μὴ χαίρετε ὅτι ἐσχήκατε <u>δύναμιν</u> ἐπὶ δαιμονίων, ἀλλὰ χάρητε ὅτι τὰ <u>ὀνόματα</u> ὑμῶν γέγραπται ἐν τῷ βιβλίῳ τῆς ζωῆς.

e. ὠφελείτωσαν οἱ παῖδες τὰς χήρας καὶ μὴ καταφρο-νείτωσαν αἱ χῆραι τῶν παρθένων.

f. ὁ ἔχων ὦτα ἀκουσάτω καὶ προσεχέτω τοῖς λόγοις τοῦ υἱοῦ τοῦ θεοῦ.

g. ἀγαπήσατε τοὺς ἀδελφοὺς καὶ τὰς <u>ἀδελφὰς</u> καὶ μὴ ποιήσητε πονηρὰ τοῖς μισοῦσιν ὑμᾶς.

h. οἱ δοῦλοι ἐξῆλθον εἰς τὸ ὑπαντῆσαι τῷ δεσπότῃ αὐτῶν, ἰδόντες δὲ αὐτόν, ἐχάρησαν.

2. English to Greek

Never despise (pl.) those who have needs but (always) help them.

K. Bible Passages

2 Timothy 4:21a . . . ἐλθεῖν

2 Timothy 4:19

1 Corinthians 16:13

Matthew 6:7–8a . . . αὐτοῖς and 9–10

John 19:6–7a . . . ἀποθανεῖν

Matthew 5:16

1 Peter 5:6

Acts 21:34b ἐκέλευσεν . . .

Notes

1. Beginning with this chapter, compounds will no longer be hyphenated.

2. "Future" and "aorist" forms are passive deponents.

33

-μι Verbs, Part 1:
Active Forms
of δίδωμι and τίθημι

A. Introduction

In this and the succeeding two chapters we will encounter several very basic verbs that preserve many ancient forms. Because the first person singular ends in the old termination μι (cf. εἰμί), these are called -μι verbs. These verbs use several standard features that will be outlined here and reviewed in section C below. These features are

1. a reduplicated "focus upon connection"/"present" stem with a ι, not an ε, between the initial consonants;

2. a stem that ends in a short vowel, ο or ε, which may be lengthened to ω or η, respectively, in given forms;

3. no connecting vowels, but endings put directly onto the vowel stem in all forms but the subjunctive in the first and third principal parts;

4. a third principal part that is weak in the active indicative but strong in all other forms;

5. ~~irregularity~~ abnormality only in the first and third principal parts; parts 2, 4, 5, and 6 are normal.

B. Verb Forms

1. First Principal Part

a. Present Indicative Active

	Singular	Plural	Singular	Plural
1	δίδωμι	δίδομεν	τίθημι	τίθεμεν
2	δίδως	δίδοτε	τίθης	τίθετε
3	δίδωσι(ν)	διδόασι(ν)	τίθησι(ν)	τιθέασι(ν)

b. Imperfect Indicative Active

	Singular	Plural	Singular	Plural
1	ἐδίδουν	ἐδίδομεν	ἐτίθην	ἐτίθεμεν
2	ἐδίδους	ἐδίδοτε	ἐτίθεις	ἐτίθετε
3	ἐδίδου	ἐδίδοσαν	ἐτίθει	ἐτίθεσαν

c. "Present" Subjunctive Active

	Singular	Plural	Singular	Plural
1	διδῶ	διδῶμεν	τιθῶ	τιθῶμεν
2	διδῷς	διδῶτε	τιθῇς	τιθῆτε
3	διδῷ	διδῶσι(ν)	τιθῇ	τιθῶσι(ν)

d. "Present" Imperative Active

	Singular	Plural	Singular	Plural
2	δίδου	δίδοτε	τίθει	τίθετε
3	διδότω	διδότωσαν	τιθέτω	τιθέτωσαν

e. "Present" Infinitive Active

διδόναι   τιθέναι

f. "Present" Participle Active

(1) δίδωμι

Singular

	M	F	N
N	διδούς	διδοῦσα	διδόν
G	διδόντος	διδούσης	διδόντος
D	διδόντι	διδούσῃ	διδόντι
A	διδόντα	διδοῦσαν	διδόν

Plural

	M	F	N
N	διδόντες	διδοῦσαι	διδόντα
G	διδόντων	διδουσῶν	διδόντων
D	διδοῦσι(ν)	διδούσαις	διδοῦσι(ν)
A	διδόντας	διδούσας	διδόντα

(2) τίθημι

Singular

	M	F	N
N	τιθείς	τιθεῖσα	τιθέν
G	τιθέντος	τιθείσης	τιθέντος
D	τιθέντι	τιθείσῃ	τιθέντι
A	τιθέντα	τιθεῖσαν	τιθέν

	M	F	N
		Plural	
N	τιθέντες	τιθεῖσαι	τιθέντα
G	τιθέντων	τιθεισῶν	τιθέντων
D	τιθεῖσι(ν)	τιθείσαις	τιθεῖσι(ν)
A	τιθέντας	τιθείσας	τιθέντα

2. Second Principal Part

δώσω   θήσω

3. Third Principal Part

a. Aorist Indicative Active

	Singular	Plural	Singular	Plural
1	ἔδωκα	ἐδώκαμεν [ἔδομεν]	ἔθηκα	ἐθήκαμεν [ἔθεμεν]
2	ἔδωκας	ἐδώκατε [ἔδοτε]	ἔθηκας	ἐθήκατε [ἔθετε]
3	ἔδωκε(ν)	ἔδωκαν [ἔδοσαν]	ἔθηκε(ν)	ἔθηκαν [ἔθεσαν]

b. "Aorist" Subjunctive Active

	Singular	Plural	Singular	Plural
1	δῶ	δῶμεν	θῶ	θῶμεν
2	δῷς	δῶτε	θῇς	θῆτε
3	δῷ	δῶσι(ν)	θῇ	θῶσι(ν)

c. "Aorist" Imperative Active

	Singular	Plural	Singular	Plural
2	δός	δότε	θές	θέτε
3	δότω	δότωσαν	θέτω	θέτωσαν

d. "Aorist" Infinitive Active

δοῦναι   θεῖναι

e. "Aorist" Participle Active

(1) δίδωμι

	M	F	N
		Singular	
N	δούς	δοῦσα	δόν
G	δόντος	δούσης	δόντος
D	δόντι	δούσῃ	δόντι
A	δόντα	δοῦσαν	δόν

Plural

	M	F	N
N	δόντες	δοῦσαι	δόντα
G	δόντων	δουσῶν	δόντων
D	δοῦσι(ν)	δούσαις	δοῦσι(ν)
A	δόντας	δούσας	δόντα

(2) τίθημι

Singular

	M	F	N
N	θείς	θεῖσα	θέν
G	θέντος	θείσης	θέντος
D	θέντι	θείσῃ	θέντι
A	θέντα	θεῖσαν	θέν

Plural

	M	F	N
N	θέντες	θεῖσαι	θέντα
G	θέντων	θεισῶν	θέντων
D	θεῖσι(ν)	θείσαις	θεῖσι(ν)
A	θέντας	θείσας	θέντα

4. Fourth Principal Part

δέδωκα   τέθεικα

(Fifth and sixth principal parts are introduced in the next chapter, which deals with middle-passive forms.)

C. Morphology

1. First Principal Part

a. Stem

(1) Both verbs reduplicate the stem's initial letter with a ι in between the consonants.

(2) Both verbs used the lengthened stem vowel in the present indicative singular, the short vowel in the plural.

(3) Both verbs use a long diphthong in the imperfect indicative singular (τίθημι uses long η in the first person), with a short vowel in the plural.

(4) Both verbs use the short vowel in the infinitive.

b. Connecting Vowel

(1) Both verbs use no connecting vowel in the indicative (but cf. (3) below), imperative, infinitive, or participle. The endings are attached to the stem directly.

(2) Both verbs use connecting vowels with the subjunctive mood forms.

   (a) δίδωμι uses ω in every form as connecting vowel.

   (b) τίθημι follows the (normal) pattern of an -έω contract verb.

(3) Both verbs use an α connecting vowel in the third plural indicative.

c. Endings

(1) Both verbs use standard primary endings in the present plural indicative, but -μι and -σι in the first and third person singular, respectively. This is one of the chief -μι verb characteristics.

(2) Both verbs use standard secondary endings in the imperfect with -σαν in the third person plural.

(3) Both verbs use standard primary endings in the subjunctive.

(4) Both verbs use the old active infinitive ending -ναι.

(5) Both verbs have participles that follow a normal pattern.

   (a) δίδωμι follows λύων, except in the nominative singular. (It follows the "aorist" participle of γινώσκω exactly.)

   (b) τίθημι follows the pattern of an *"aorist" passive participle*.

2. Second Principal Part

The second principal part is *normal*. Note that the short stem vowel has been lengthened before the addition of the σ.

3. Third Principal Part

a. Both verbs use the long vowel in the stem of the indicative in the weak forms. These weak forms use κ instead of σ as their "sign." Note that a standard weak (first) aorist α connecting vowel is used, as are standard weak aorist endings.

b. Both verbs have optional strong forms in the indicative plural. *These strong forms reveal the true "focus on the action" / "aorist" stem.* They are identical to the imperfect plural, except that the initial reduplication is missing.

c. Both verbs have subjunctive forms identical to their "present" subjunctive forms, except that the initial reduplication is missing.

d. With the exception of the second person singular, both verbs have imperative forms identical to their "present" imperative forms, except that the initial reduplication is missing.

e. Both verbs have participle forms identical to their "present" participle forms, except that the initial reduplication is missing.

f. Both verbs have infinitive forms very similar to their "present" infinitive forms, except that a diphthong (ου and ει respectively) replaces the simple short vowel, and the initial reduplication is missing.

4. Fourth Principal Part

The fourth principal part is normal. Note that both verbs use a *normal "perfect" reduplication,* as well as the normal weak stem formation with κ. διδωμι uses long ω before the κ, τίθημι the ει diphthong.

D. Accent

1. The accent of the subjunctive forms follows a contract verb pattern, because the short vowel stem of each verb contracts with the long connecting vowel following.

2. Note the slightly irregular accent on the infinitive and participle.

E. Vocabulary

διδωμι (Irreg.): I give

     ἀποδιδωμι etc.: I give back; middle: I sell

     παραδιδωμι, etc.: I hand over; betray

θηρίον -ου, n.: wild beast

ἵημι[1] (Irreg.): I send

     ἀφίημι etc.: I forgive; allow; leave

     συνίημι, etc.: I understand

τίθημι (Irreg.): I place, set

     ἐπιτίθημι, etc.: I lay on, impose

F. Exercises

1. Parse the following finite verb forms:

a.	τίθησι	g.	ἐτίθει	l.	δώσετε
b.	ἔδομεν	h.	δέδωκας	m.	ἧκα
c.	τιθῇς	i.	ἔθηκε	n.	ἔθετε
d.	διδῶτε	j.	ἐδίδοσαν	o.	δῶμεν
e.	θήσω	k.	ἵησι	p.	τεθείκαμεν
f.	ἔδωκα				

2. Parse the following infinitive and participles:

a.	διδόντας	e.	θέντα	i.	διδόναι
b.	τιθέντος	f.	διδούσης	j.	τιθέναι
c.	δούς	g.	δοῦναι	k.	θεῖναι
d.	ἱείς	h.	ἱέναι	l.	δεδωκέναι

G. Practice Sentences

1. Greek to English

a. ὁ θεὸς δίδωσιν ἀγαθὰ δῶρα τοῖς αἰτοῦσιν.

b. ὁ στρατιώτης ἔθηκε τὴν μάχαιραν αὐτοῦ ἐπὶ τὴν γῆν, καὶ ἐπιστραφεὶς ἀπῆλθεν πρὸς τὴν κώμην αὐτοῦ.

c. ἐπιθεὶς τὰς χεῖρας αὐτοῦ ἐπὶ τῆς κεφαλῆς τοῦ Τιμοθέου, ὁ Παῦλος ὑπέστρεψεν πρὸς τὴν ἁγίαν πόλιν.

d. ὁ κριτὴς παρέδωκε τὸν λῃστὴν τῷ φύλακι (cf. φυλάσσω), ὃς τῷ θηρίῳ αὐτὸν ἔβαλεν.

e. ὁ Ἰησοῦς ἀφῆκεν τὰς ἁμαρτίας τοῦ τελώνου, ὁ δὲ προσήνεγκεν τῷ κυρίῳ ἄλλους, ἵνα ἐκεῖνος ἀφῇ καὶ αὐτούς.

f. συνίετε ἃ ὁ Ἰησοῦς διέταξεν; ἐάν τις συνῇ, μακάριός ἐστιν.

g. οὔτε ἐδόξασε τὸν θεὸν οὔτε ἔδωκεν ἀργύριον τοῖς πτωχοῖς ὁ κωφὸς ὃν ὁ κύριος ἐθεράπευσεν.

h. μετὰ τὸ τὸν πατέρα δοῦναι αὐτῷ πέντε ἰχθύας, ὁ υἱὸς ἀπέδωκε δύο.

i. μηδεὶς ἐπιτιθέτω πονηροὺς νόμους ὑμῖν.

2. English to Greek

The master gave a loaf of bread to his servant, who placed it into the hand of the Lord.

H. Bible Passages

John 19:19

Matthew 5:26

John 17:14–15

John 14:27 (ἐμὴν = ἐμοῦ)

Matthew 22:19b–22 (οἱ δὲ . . .)

Note

1. This verb does not occur alone in the New Testament. Its two most frequent compounds are given in this lesson. It is conjugated in virtually every case like τίθημι.

34

⁻μι Verbs, Part 2:
Middle and Passive Forms
of δίδωμι and τίθημι

A. Introduction

The middle and passive forms of the two paradigm ⁻μι verbs are even more similar and regular than their corresponding active forms. Many of the same general characteristics will be present—among the most important are the following:

1. Endings are added directly onto stems, except in the subjunctive.

2. Standard primary and secondary endings are used, similar to perfect and pluperfect indicative forms.

B. Verb Forms

1. First Principal Part

a. Present Indicative Middle/Passive

	Singular	Plural	Singular	Plural
1	δίδομαι	διδόμεθα	τίθεμαι	τιθέμεθα
2	δίδοσαι	δίδοσθε	τίθεσαι	τίθεσθε
3	δίδοται	δίδονται	τίθεται	τίθενται

b. Imperfect Indicative Middle/Passive

	Singular	Plural	Singular	Plural
1	ἐδιδόμην	ἐδιδόμεθα	ἐτιθέμην	ἐτιθέμεθα
2	ἐδίδοσο	ἐδίδοσθε	ἐτίθεσο	ἐτίθεσθε
3	ἐδίδοτο	ἐδίδοντο	ἐτίθετο	ἐτίθεντο

c. "Present" Subjunctive Middle/Passive

	Singular	Plural	Singular	Plural
1	διδῶμαι	διδώμεθα	τιθῶμαι	τιθώμεθα
2	διδῷ	διδῶσθε	τιθῇ	τιθῆσθε
3	διδῶται	διδῶνται	τιθῆται	τιθῶνται

d. "Present" Imperative Middle/Passive

	Singular	Plural	Singular	Plural
2	δίδοσο	δίδοσθε	τίθεσο	τίθεσθε
3	διδόσθω	διδόσθωσαν	τιθέσθω	τιθέσθωσαν

e. "Present" Infinitive Middle/Passive

δίδοσθαι   τίθεσθαι

f. "Present" Participle Middle/Passive

(1) δίδωμι

Singular

	M	F	N
N	διδόμενος	διδομένη	διδόμενον
G	διδομένου	διδομένης	διδομένου
D	διδομένῳ	διδομένη	διδομένῳ
A	διδόμενον	διδομένην	διδόμενον

Plural

	M	F	N
N	διδόμενοι	διδόμεναι	διδόμενα
G	διδομένων	διδομένων	διδομένων
D	διδομένοις	διδομέναις	διδομένοις
A	διδομένους	διδομένας	διδόμενα

(2) τίθημι

Singular

	M	F	N
N	τιθέμενος	τιθεμένη	τιθέμενον
G	τιθεμένου	τιθεμένης	τιθεμένου
D	τιθεμένῳ	τιθεμένη	τιθεμένῳ
A	τιθέμενον	τιθεμένην	τιθέμενον

Plural

	M	F	N
N	τιθέμενοι	τιθέμεναι	τιθέμενα
G	τιθεμένων	τιθεμένων	τιθεμένων
D	τιθεμένοις	τιθεμέναις	τιθεμένοις
A	τιθεμένους	τιθεμένας	τιθέμενα

2. Second Principal Part

The future middle is built off of the future active in a regular manner:

δώσομαι   θήσομαι

3. Third Principal Part

a. Aorist Indicative Middle

	Singular	Plural	Singular	Plural
1	ἐδόμην	ἐδόμεθα	ἐθέμην	ἐθέμεθα
2	ἔδου (ἔδοσο)	ἔδοσθε	ἔθου (ἔθεσο)	ἔθεσθε
3	ἔδοτο	ἔδοντο	ἔθετο	ἔθεντο

b. "Aorist" Subjunctive Middle

	Singular	Plural	Singular	Plural
1	δῶμαι	δώμεθα	θῶμαι	θώμεθα
2	δῷ	δῶσθε	θῇ	θῆσθε
3	δῶται	δῶνται	θῆται	θῶνται

c. "Aorist" Imperative Middle

	Singular	Plural	Singular	Plural
2	δοῦ	δόσθε	θοῦ	θέσθε
3	δόσθω	δόσθωσαν	θέσθω	θέσθωσαν

d. "Aorist" Infinitive Middle

δόσθαι   θέσθαι

e. "Aorist" Participle Middle

(1) δίδωμι

	Singular		
	M	F	N
N	δόμενος	δομένη	δόμενον
G	δομένου	δομένης	δομένου
D	δομένῳ	δομένῃ	δομένῳ
A	δόμενον	δομένην	δόμενον

	Plural		
	M	F	N
N	δόμενοι	δόμεναι	δόμενα
G	δομένων	δομένων	δομένων
D	δομένοις	δομέναις	δομένοις
A	δομένους	δομένας	δόμενα

(2) τίθημι

	Singular		
	M	F	N
N	θέμενος	θεμένη	θέμενον
G	θεμένου	θεμένης	θεμένου
D	θεμένῳ	θεμένῃ	θεμένῳ
A	θέμενον	θεμένην	θέμενον

	M	Plural F	N
N	θέμενοι	θέμεναι	θέμενα
G	θεμένων	θεμένων	θεμένων
D	θεμένοις	θεμέναις	θεμένοις
A	θεμένους	θεμένας	θέμενα

5. Fifth Principal Part

δέδομαι   τέθειμαι

6. Sixth Principal Part

ἐδόθην   ἐτέθην

C. Morphology

1. First Principal Part

a. Stem

(1) Both verbs reduplicate their stem's initial consonant with a ι in between.

(2) Both verbs use the short vowel throughout both singular and plural indicative forms.

b. Connecting Vowel

(1) Both verbs use no connecting vowel in the indicative, imperative, infinitive, or participle.

(2) Both verbs use connecting vowels with subjunctive forms.

(a) δίδωμι uses ω in every form as connecting vowel.

(b) τίθημι follows the (normal) pattern of -έω contract verbs.

c. Endings

(1) Both verbs use standard primary and secondary endings in the indicative with *no contraction in the second person singular.*

(2) Both verbs use standard primary endings in the subjunctive, with normal contraction in the second person singular.

(3) Both verbs use standard infinitive and participle endings.

2. Second Principal Part

The second principal part is normal, using the long stem vowel.

3. Third Principal Part

a. Both verbs use *strong forms* with a short vowel in the aorist middle indicative.

b. Both verbs use standard secondary endings in the indicative, but note that *contraction does take place* in the *second* person *singular* middle (unlike the imperfect indicative middle).

c. Both verbs have subjunctive forms identical to their "present" subjunctive forms, except that the initial reduplication is missing.

d. Except for the second singular, both verbs have imperative forms identical to their "present" imperative forms, except that the initial reduplication is missing.

e. Both verbs have infinitive forms identical to their "present" infinitive forms, except that the initial reduplication is missing.

f. Both verbs have participle forms identical to their "present" participle forms, except that the initial reduplication is missing.

4. Fifth Principal Part

The fifth principal part is normal. Note that $\delta i \delta \omega \mu \iota$ returns to a short stem vowel, while $\tau i \theta \eta \mu \iota$ retains the diphthong.

5. Sixth Principal Part

The sixth principal part uses normal endings, no connecting vowel in the indicative, etc. In the stem, however,

a. $\delta i \delta \omega \mu \iota$ uses a short vowel supplemented by $\theta \eta$ (normal), but

b. $\tau i \theta \eta \mu \iota$ makes a *major change,* substituting an unaspirated dental τ for the aspirated θ of the stem proper. Thus, it uses $\dot{\epsilon} \tau \dot{\epsilon} \theta \eta \nu$, *not* $\dot{\epsilon} \theta \dot{\epsilon} \theta \eta \nu$ as might be expected.

D. The Six Principal Parts of $\delta i \delta \omega \mu \iota$ and $\tau i \theta \eta \mu \iota$

(1)	(2)	(3)	(4)	(5)	(6)
$\delta i \delta \omega \mu \iota$	$\delta \omega \sigma \omega$	$\ddot{\epsilon} \delta \omega \kappa \alpha$ $[\delta o\text{-}]$	$\delta \dot{\epsilon} \delta \omega \kappa \alpha$	$\delta \dot{\epsilon} \delta o \mu \alpha \iota$	$\dot{\epsilon} \delta \acute{o} \theta \eta \nu$
$\tau i \theta \eta \mu \iota$	$\theta \acute{\eta} \sigma \omega$	$\ddot{\epsilon} \theta \eta \kappa \alpha$ $[\theta \epsilon\text{-}]$	$\tau \dot{\epsilon} \theta \epsilon \iota \kappa \alpha$	$\tau \dot{\epsilon} \theta \epsilon \iota \mu \alpha \iota$	$\dot{\epsilon} \tau \dot{\epsilon} \theta \eta \nu$

E. Vocabulary

$\dot{\alpha} \pi \acute{o} \lambda \lambda \upsilon \mu \iota$[1] (Irreg): I destroy; lose

$\dot{\alpha} \pi \acute{o} \lambda \lambda \upsilon \mu \alpha \iota$ (M) (Irreg) I perish; am being lost

$\delta \epsilon \acute{\iota} \kappa \nu \upsilon \mu \iota$,[1] $\delta \epsilon \acute{\iota} \xi \omega$ (R): I show διατίθεμαι, etc. (M): I make a covenant with (+ dat. or with πρός + acc.)

    διαθήκη -ης, f.: covenant; testament

ἐλέγχω (R): I convict; convince; reprove

καινός -ή -όν: new (different)

κεῖμαι (M): I lie, recline (conjugated as middle of -μι verb)

νέος -α -ον: new

παρατίθημι, etc.: I set before; middle: I entrust

περιτέμνω (Irreg.): I circumcise

    περιτομή -ῆς, f.: circumcision

F. Exercises

1. Parse the following finite verb forms:

a.	τιθέμεθα	g.	ἐτίθεντο	l.	ἵεσο
b.	δίδοσαι	h.	ἐδόμην	m.	ἐδόθημεν
c.	ἵεμαι	i.	τέθειμαι	n.	ἐτίθεσο
d.	διδῶσθε	j.	δοῦ	o.	ἀφέθητε
e.	θησόμεθα	k.	ἐτέθην	p.	τίθεσο
f.	δεδόμεθα				

2. Parse the following infinitive and participles:

a.	διδόμενος	e.	ἀφεθέντες	i.	δοθῆναι
b.	θεμένη	f.	δόμενος	j.	θέσθαι
c.	δοθέντος	g.	δόσθαι	k.	δίδοσθαι
d.	τεθειμένον	h.	τίθεσθαι	l.	τεθῆναι

G. Practice Sentences

1. Greek to English

a. ὁ Παῦλος διέταξεν Τιμοθέῳ παραθέσθαι τὸ εὐαγ-γέλιον πιστοῖς διδασκάλοις.

b. ὁ πτωχὸς ἀπέδοτο τὴν μάχαιραν τῷ στρατιώτῃ τῷ πλουσίῳ.

c. ὁ θεὸς διέθετο καινὴν διαθήκην πρὸς τὸν λαόν, ὅτι οὐχ ὑπήκουσαν ταῖς πρώταις ἐντολαῖς αὐτοῦ.

d. τρεῖς γραμματεῖς προσῆλθον τῷ Ἰησοῦ κειμένῳ ἐπὶ τῆς γῆς.

e. ὁ ἀπόστολος περιέτεμε Τιμόθεον, ὁ δὲ <u>Τίτος</u> οὐ περιετμήθη.

f. ὁ Ἰησοῦς παρέθηκεν ἄλλην παραβολὴν τοῖς ὄχλοις πρὸς τὸ δεῖξαι αὐτοῖς τὰς ἁμαρτίας τῶν ἡγεμόνων.

g. ἡ μὲν περιτομὴ οὐ σῴζει τὸν Ἰουδαῖον, ἡ δὲ <u>σοφία</u> οὐ τὸν Ἕλληνα.

h. τὸ ἅγιον πνεῦμα ἐλέγξει τὰς καρδίας τῶν μὴ πιστευόντων ὅτι ὁ σωτὴρ ἦλθεν εἰς τὸ σῶσαι τοὺς ἀπολωλότας.

i. τοῖς ἐν ταῖς κώμαις πτωχοῖς νέοι ἵπποι δοθήσονται.

2. English to Greek

The hands of the apostles were placed on the heads of the saints.

H. Bible Passages

John 1:17

Acts 20:32a . . . αὐτοῦ (omit τά)

Mark 15:47 (omit ἡ Ἰωσῆτος)

2 Corinthians 8:1 (omit ἀδελφοί)

Matthew 4:8–11 (omit πάσας, v. 8 and πάντα, v. 9)

Acts 19:21a . . . Ἱεροσόλυμα

Note

1. This old verb is conjugated after a -μι verb pattern in the "present" stem.

35

⁻μι **Verbs, Part 3:** *ἵστημι*

A. Introduction

1. *ἵστημι* is the third major ⁻μι verb, and it is somewhat unusual. It shares many features with the verbs of chapters 33 and 34.

   a. It uses no connecting vowels in the indicative of the first principal part.

   b. It uses a short or long vowel to terminate its basic stem.

   c. Its irregularity is chiefly confined to principal parts one and three.

   d. It has both strong and weak aorist indicative active forms.

2. The chief differences between it and *δίδωμι* and *τίθημι* are as follows:

   a. It reduplicates its stem in the first principal part, but the "focus upon connection"/"present" stem begins with ι and a rough breathing mark, not a consonant.

   b. It has two "aorist" stems with a complete weak and a complete strong system of forms.

   c. It has slightly irregular "perfect" participles.

   d. Its *uses* of the perfect and pluperfect are unusual.

B. Verb Forms

1. First Principal Part

a. Active

(1) Indicative

	Present		Imperfect	
	Singular	Plural	Singular	Plural
1	ἵστημι	ἵσταμεν	ἵστην	ἵσταμεν
2	ἵστης	ἵστατε	ἵστης	ἵστατε
3	ἵστησι(ν)	ἱστᾶσι(ν)	ἵστη	ἵστασαν

(2) "Present" Subjunctive

	Singular	Plural
1	ἱστῶ	ἱστῶμεν
2	ἱστῇς	ἱστῆτε
3	ἱστῇ	ἱστῶσι(ν)

(3) "Present" Imperative

	Singular	Plural
2	ἵστη	ἵστατε
3	ἱστάτω	ἱστάτωσαν

(4) "Present" Infinitive

ἱστάναι

(5) "Present" Participle

	Singular		
	M	F	N
N	ἱστάς	ἱστᾶσα	ἱστάν
G	ἱστάντος	ἱστάσης	ἱστάντος
D	ἱστάντι	ἱστάσῃ	ἱστάντι
A	ἱστάντα	ἱστᾶσαν	ἱστάν

	Plural		
	M	F	N
N	ἱστάντες	ἱστᾶσαι	ἱστάντα
G	ἱστάντων	ἱστασῶν	ἱστάντων
D	ἱστᾶσι(ν)	ἱστάσαις	ἱστᾶσι(ν)
A	ἱστάντας	ἱστάσας	ἱστάντα

b. Middle/Passive

(1) Indicative

	Present		Imperfect	
	Singular	Plural	Singular	Plural
1	ἵσταμαι	ἱστάμεθα	ἱστάμην	ἱστάμεθα
2	ἵστασαι	ἵστασθε	ἵστασο	ἵστασθε
3	ἵσταται	ἵστανται	ἵστατο	ἵσταντο

(2) "Present" Subjunctive

	Singular	Plural
1	ἱστῶμαι	ἱστώμεθα
2	ἱστῇ	ἱστῆσθε
3	ἱστῆται	ἱστῶνται

(3) "Present" Imperative

	Singular	Plural
2	ἵστασο	ἵστασθε
3	ἱστάσθω	ἱστάσθωσαν

(4) "Present" Infinitive

ἵστασθαι

(5) "Present" Participle

Singular

	M	F	N
N	ἱστάμενος	ἱσταμένη	ἱστάμενον
G	ἱσταμένου	ἱσταμένης	ἱσταμένου
D	ἱσταμένῳ	ἱσταμένη	ἱσταμένῳ
A	ἱστάμενον	ἱσταμένην	ἱστάμενον

Plural

	M	F	N
N	ἱστάμενοι	ἱστάμεναι	ἱστάμενα
G	ἱσταμένων	ἱσταμένων	ἱσταμένων
D	ἱσταμένοις	ἱσταμέναις	ἱσταμένοις
A	ἱσταμένους	ἱσταμένας	ἱστάμενα

2. Second Principal Part

στήσω

3. Third Principal Part

a. Weak (First) "Aorist"

ἔστησα (normal)

b. Strong (Second) "Aorist" (Active Only)

(1) Indicative

	Singular	Plural
1	ἔστην	ἔστημεν
2	ἔστης	ἔστητε
3	ἔστη	ἔστησαν

(2) Subjunctive

	Singular	Plural
1	στῶ	στῶμεν
2	στῇς	στῆτε
3	στῇ	στῶσι(ν)

(3) Imperative

	Singular	Plural
2	στῆθι / στά	στῆτε
3	στήτω	στήτωσαν

(4) Infinitive

στῆναι

(5) Participle

	Singular		
	M	F	N
N	στάς	στᾶσα	στάν
G	στάντος	στάσης	στάντος
D	στάντι	στάσῃ	στάντι
A	στάντα	στᾶσαν	στάν

	Plural		
	M	F	N
N	στάντες	στᾶσαι	στάντα
G	στάντων	στασῶν	στάντων
D	στᾶσι(ν)	στάσαις	στᾶσι(ν)
A	στάντας	στάσας	στάντα

4. Fourth Principal Part

a. Perfect Active Indicative

ἕστηκα (normal conjugation)

b. Pluperfect Active Indicative

εἱστήκειν (normal conjugation)

c. "Perfect" Active Infinitive

ἑστάναι (strong, no κ)

d. "Perfect" Active Participle

  (1) Weak

    ἑστηκώς, ἑστηκυῖα, ἑστηκός (normal)

  (2) Strong

	Singular	
M	**F**	**N**
N ἑστώς	ἑστῶσα	ἑστός
G ἑστῶτος	ἑστώσης	ἑστῶτος
D ἑστῶτι	ἑστώσῃ	ἑστῶτι
A ἑστῶτα	ἑστῶσαν	ἑστός

	Plural	
M	**F**	**N**
N ἑστῶτες	ἑστῶσαι	ἑστῶτα
G ἑστώτων	ἑστωσῶν	ἑστώτων
D ἑστῶσι(ν)	ἑστώσαις	ἑστῶσι(ν)
A ἑστῶτας	ἑστώσας	ἑστῶτα

5. Fifth Principal Part

ἕσταμαι

6. Sixth Principal Part

ἐστάθην (normal)

C. Morphology

1. First Principal Part

  a. ἵστημι does *not* reduplicate its initial σ before the ι. The rough breathing mark stands in place of the σ.

  b. As do δίδωμι and τίθημι, ἵστημι uses a short vowel in the plural of its present and imperfect indicative active, a short vowel throughout the indicative middle of these two "tenses," and a long vowel in the singular of the present indicative active. Note that it uses η, not a diphthong, in the singular of the imperfect indicative active.

  c. As do δίδωμι and τίθημι, ἵστημι uses a short vowel with both the active and middle/passive infinitive and participle. The imperatives are also very similar, with the exception of the second person singular.

  d. As do δίδωμι and τίθημι, ἵστημι uses no connecting vowel outside the subjunctive. The endings are attached directly to the stem.

e. As do $\delta\acute{\iota}\delta\omega\mu\iota$ and $\tau\acute{\iota}\theta\eta\mu\iota$, $\acute{\iota}\sigma\tau\eta\mu\iota$ uses a connecting vowel with subjunctive forms in both active and middle/passive. It uses the $^-\acute{\epsilon}\omega$ contract verb pattern, as does $\tau\acute{\iota}\theta\eta\mu\iota$.

f. *Unlike* $\delta\acute{\iota}\delta\omega\mu\iota$ or $\tau\acute{\iota}\theta\eta\mu\iota$, $\acute{\iota}\sigma\tau\eta\mu\iota$ contracts its stem vowel with the α connecting vowel of the third plural indicative ending.

2. Second Principal Part

As do $\delta\acute{\iota}\delta\omega\mu\iota$ and $\tau\acute{\iota}\theta\eta\mu\iota$, $\acute{\iota}\sigma\tau\eta\mu\iota$ lengthens its stem vowel before adding the σ of the second principal part.

3. Third Principal Part

The third principal part is the most unusual in this verb and the greatest point of difference between it and $\delta\acute{\iota}\delta\omega\mu\iota$ and $\tau\acute{\iota}\theta\eta\mu\iota$.

a. Points of Difference

(1) $\acute{\iota}\sigma\tau\eta\mu\iota$ does not use a weak aorist formation with κ in the aorist indicative active. *Its weak aorist is normal* (with σ).

(2) $\acute{\iota}\sigma\tau\eta\mu\iota$ has *two separate "aorists."* (See D below for the difference in meaning.)

(3) $\acute{\iota}\sigma\tau\eta\mu\iota$'s strong "aorist" has strong forms throughout, including the indicative. Note that the second person singular imperative has an optional form.

(4) $\acute{\iota}\sigma\tau\eta\mu\iota$'s strong "aorist" uses a long vowel in its stem (except participle).

b. Points of Similarity

(1) The strong "aorist" of $\acute{\iota}\sigma\tau\eta\mu\iota$ uses connecting vowels for the subjunctive *only*. In the subjunctive, it follows the contract verb pattern of $\tau\acute{\iota}\theta\eta\mu\iota$.

(2) The strong "aorist" participle is declined like the corresponding "present" participle, without the reduplication.

(3) The strong "aorist" participle uses the short vowel in the stem.

4. Fourth Principal Part

a. The "perfect" of $\acute{\iota}\sigma\tau\eta\mu\iota$ is unusual in that

(1) its initial σ is represented only by a rough breathing mark over the ϵ, and

(2) it has *two participles,* one strong, one weak.

b. The pluperfect of $\acute{\iota}\sigma\tau\eta\mu\iota$ has an irregular augment: $\epsilon\iota$. This may be seen to reflect an original $\acute{\epsilon}\underline{\sigma\epsilon}\sigma\tau\acute{\eta}\kappa\epsilon\iota\nu$ formation, the rough breathing mark indicating the lost σ.

5. Fifth Principal Part

This principal part is rare, but it is normal.

6. Sixth Principal Part

The final principal part is normal, using the short stem vowel and the normal θη addition.

D. Forms[1] and Meaning

1. Introduction

ἵστημι means "to stand" and carries either the transitive or intransitive meaning of this word.

(EG 1)   "I *stood the book* on end" (transitive).

(EG 2)   "I *stood* before the king" (intransitive).

2. Transitive

The *transitive* meaning (i.e., "to cause to stand up") is conveyed by the following forms (and the other active forms made from them):

Present Active: ἵστημι
Imperfect Active: ἵστην
Future Active: στήσω
Weak (First) Aorist Active: ἔστησα

(EG 3)   ὁ στρατιώτης <u>ἔστησε</u> τὸν σταυρὸν ἐπὶ τὴν γῆν.
           The soldier *stood* the cross upon the ground.

3. Intransitive

The *intransitive* meaning (i.e., "to be on one's feet") is conveyed by *all other forms.*

(EG 4)   ὁ δοῦλος <u>ἔστη</u> ἐπὶ τοῦ δεσπότου αὐτοῦ.
           The slave *stood* in the presence of his master.

a. It is also important to note that the perfect and pluperfect active forms of this verb have taken over the regular functions of the present and imperfect middle and passive, i.e., the forms of the "present" stem that carry an *intransitive* meaning. Thus

(EG 5)   ἔστηκα = "I stand" (not normally ἵσταμαι)

(EG 6)   εἱστήκειν = "I was standing" (not normally ἱστάμην)

For this reason alone, the forms of the perfect and pluperfect must be mastered (cf. chapters 25 and 26).

b. The simple past intransitive idea is conveyed by the strong aorist ἔστην.

c. The following chart details the most common forms used to convey the most basic intransitive meanings:

Present ("I stand"): Perfect Active—ἕστηκα

Imperfect ("I was standing"): Pluperfect Active—εἱστήκειν

Future ("I shall stand"): Future Middle—στήσομαι

Aorist ("I stood"): Strong Aorist—ἔστην

Note: Passive forms, especially the aorist passive, may very occasionally carry a *transitive passive* meaning, namely, "to be made to stand."

(EG 7)   ὁ σταυρὸς ἐστάθη ἐπὶ τὴν γῆν ὑπό τοῦ
στρατιώτου.
The cross *was made to stand* upon the ground by the soldier.

E. Vocabulary ⟨ ἵστημι: I stand (transitive / intransitive)

ἀνίστημι, etc.: trans.: I raise
                   intrans.: I stand up, rise

ἀφίστημι, etc.: trans.: I draw away
                   intrans.: I depart, withdraw

ἐξίστημι, etc.: trans.: I amaze
                   intrans.: I am beside myself; am amazed

καθίστημι, etc.: trans.: I establish
                    intrans.: I am established

παρίστημι, etc.: trans.: I present
                    intrans.: I am present; stand by

διάκονος ⁻ου, m.: servant; deacon

δύναμαι, δυνήσομαι . . . ἠδυνήθην: I am able (conjugated as is ἵσταμαι)

θρόνος ⁻ου, m.: throne

κάθημαι (M): I am seated, sit (conjugated as is κεῖμαι)

πρεσβύτερος ⁻ου, m.: elder

F. Exercises

1. Parse the following finite verb forms and determine whether they are transitive or intransitive.

   a. ἵσταμαι   f. ἔστησας   k. ἔστηκε

   b. ἔστην   g. στῶ   l. στήσῃς

   c. στήσεις   h. ἵστην   m. ἔστημεν

   d. ἔστηκα   i. εἱστήκειν   n. ἵσταται

   e. ἐστάθην   j. ἵστησι   o. σταθήσομαι

2. Parse the following participle and infinitive forms and determine whether they are transitive or intransitive.

   a. ἱστάς   f. στάσης   k. στῆσαι

   b. στάντος   g. ἑστώς   l. σταθῆναι

   c. σταθείς   h. ἑστηκότα   m. ἑστάναι

   d. στήσαντος   i. ἱστάναι   n. ἵστασθαι

   e. ἱστάμενος   j. στῆναι

G. Practice Sentences

1. Greek to English

a. ὁ Ἰησοῦς ἔστη ἐπὶ τοῦ ἡγεμόνος καὶ ἀπεκρίθη οὐδέν.

b. ὁ σωτὴρ ἀνέστησε καὶ τὴν θυγατέρα τοῦ ἡγεμόνος καὶ τὸν υἱὸν τῆς χήρας.

c. ὁ Παῦλος κατέστησεν διακόνους καὶ πρεσβυτέρους ἐν ταῖς ἐκκλησίαις τῆς Ἀσίας.

d. ἑστὼς μετὰ τεσσάρων μαθητῶν ἐν τῷ ἱερῷ, ὁ Ἰησοῦς παρέστησε δῶρον τοῖς ἱερεῦσιν.

e. οἱ λόγοι τοῦ Ἰησοῦ ἐξέστησαν τοὺς ὄχλους, ὥστε τούτους εἰπεῖν ὅτι ἐξίσταται.

f. ἀναστὰς ὁ διάκονος ταχέως ἀπέστη ἀπὸ τοῦ δεσπότου αὐτοῦ καὶ ἐκρύβη ἐν τοῖς δένδροις.

g. καθήμενος ἐπὶ τοῦ θρόνου ἐν οὐρανῷ, ὁ κύριος ἡμῶν δύναται καλῶς φυλάσσεσθαι τὰ τέκνα αὐτοῦ.

h. σήμερον εἱστήκειμεν πρὸ τοῦ σταυροῦ, θεώμενοι τὸ σῶμα τοῦ κυρίου ἡμῶν.

i. μὴ ἐᾶτε τὸν διάβολον ἀποστῆσαι ὑμᾶς ἀπὸ τῆς ἀληθείας.

j. ἄξιος ἀποθανεῖν ὤν, ἕστηκα ἐφ᾽ ὑμῶν ὡς βασιλεύς.

2. English to Greek

We stood before the Lord and inquired about our father.

H. Bible Passages

Matthew 4:5

2 Timothy 4:17a . . . με

Acts 1:10b–11a καὶ ἰδοὺ . . . οὐρανόν

Matthew 27:11a . . . Ἰουδαίων

John 18:5b εἱστήκει . . .

Acts 9:39 (omit πᾶσαι)

Note

1. Indicative mood forms are used throughout the discussion in this section. What is said concerning them applies also to all other forms (infinitives, participles, subjunctives, etc.).

36

Irregular Adjectives; Comparative and Superlative Adjectives and Adverbs

A. Introduction

In this chapter we will consider several irregular adjectives, as well as the use of adjectives in degrees other than positive.

B. Irregular Adjectives

Several very common adjectives are irregular:

1. For μέγας and πολύς the irregularity is that the masculine and neuter nominative and accusative singular forms follow a third declension pattern, while the rest of the forms are normal O declension. (Feminines follow a normal A declension pattern.)

   a. μέγας = "Great"

	Singular		
	M	F	N
N	μέγας	μεγάλη	μέγα
G	μεγάλου	μεγάλης	μεγάλου
D	μεγάλῳ	μεγάλη	μεγάλῳ
A	μέγαν	μεγάλην	μέγα

	Plural		
	M	F	N
N	μεγάλοι	μεγάλαι	μεγάλα
G	μεγάλων	μεγάλων	μεγάλων
D	μεγάλοις	μεγάλαις	μεγάλοις
A	μεγάλους	μεγάλας	μεγάλα

b. πολύς = "Much"; Plural: "Many"

Singular

	M	F	N
N	πολύς	πολλή	πολύ
G	πολλοῦ	πολλῆς	πολλοῦ
D	πολλῷ	πολλῇ	πολλῷ
A	πολύν	πολλήν	πολύ

Plural

	M	F	N
N	πολλοί	πολλαί	πολλά
G	πολλῶν	πολλῶν	πολλῶν
D	πολλοῖς	πολλαῖς	πολλοῖς
A	πολλούς	πολλάς	πολλά

2. πᾶς follows the pattern of the weak (first) "aorist" active participle in the masculine and neuter, not one of the three third declension patterns introduced in chapter 19. Note also the accent in the singular. The feminine forms are normal A declension "hybrid."

a. Forms of πᾶς = "All"

Singular

	M	F	N
N	πᾶς	πᾶσα	πᾶν
G	παντός	πάσης	παντός
D	παντί	πάσῃ	παντί
A	πάντα	πᾶσαν	πᾶν

Plural

	M	F	N
N	πάντες	πᾶσαι	πάντα
G	πάντων	πασῶν	πάντων
D	πᾶσι(ν)	πάσαις	πᾶσι(ν)
A	πάντας	πάσας	πάντα

b. Usage

πᾶς has slightly different meanings, depending on its position relative to the word it modifies.

(1) If it is in *predicate* position to an *arthrous* noun (one with its article), it means "all." This is its *most important* usage.

(EG 1)   πᾶσα ἡ πόλις ἐξῆλθεν ὑπαντῆσαι τῷ βασιλεῖ.
All the city went out to meet the king.

(2) If it is in *attributive* position to an *arthrous* noun, it means "whole."

(EG 2)   ἡ πᾶσα πόλις ἐξῆλθεν ὑπαντῆσαι τῷ βασιλεῖ.

The *whole* city went out to meet the king.

(3) If it is in *attributive* position to an *anarthrous* noun, it means "every" in the sense of "any."

(EG 3)   πᾶσα γυνὴ γινώσκει τὴν ἀλήθειαν περὶ ἀνδρῶν.

Every woman knows the truth concerning men.

C. Comparative Adjectives and Adverbs

1. Introduction

Comparative adjectives and adverb forms are used when an author or speaker likens or contrasts two persons, things, or actions.

2. Morphology

a. Adjectives

(1) Regular

(a) In English, comparison is usually indicated by the addition of "-er" to the end of the regular adjective:

(EG 4)   "fast," comparative: "faster"

(EG 5)   "high," comparative: "higher"

(EG 6)   "long," comparative: "longer"

(b) In Greek, ‑τερος, ‑τερα, ‑τερον, added in place of the masculine singular nominative ς ending of the normal adjective performs the same function:

(EG 7)   ἰσχυρός, comparative: ἰσχυρό<u>τερος</u>

Some adjectives lengthen the ο before the τερος (when the previous syllable is short):

(EG 8)   σοφός, comparative: σοφ<u>ώ</u>τερος

(c) Third declension adjectives use the same ‑τερος, ‑τερα, ‑τερον, endings, but these either are added directly to the stem (ἀληθέστερος, εὐθύτερος) or are preceded by εσ (ἀφρονέστερος). These are rare and in any case are easily recognized.

(2) Irregular

(a) Some adjectives are irregular in their comparative formations:

(EG   9)   "good," comparative: "better"

(EG 10)   "bad," comparative: "worse"

(EG 11)   "much," comparative: "more"

(b) In Greek, a number of irregular comparatives also occur (and as with the English examples above, they occur with common words). Here, however, a common
pattern of endings is followed. These comparatives end
in ⁻ων, ⁻ον and are declined like ἄφρων.

Singular

	M/F	N
N	κρείσσων	κρεῖσσον
G	κρείσσονος	κρείσσονος
D	κρείσσονι	κρείσσονι
A	κρείσσονα	κρεῖσσον

Plural

	M/F	N
N	κρείσσονες	κρείσσονα
G	κρεισσόνων	κρεισσόνων
D	κρείσσοσι(ν)	κρείσσοσι(ν)
A	κρείσσονας	κρείσσονα

b. Adverbs

The *neuter accusative singular* of the comparative adjective is
regularly used for the comparative adverb.

(EG 12)   ἰσχυρότερον = "more strongly"

3. Syntax of the Comparative Adjectives and Adverbs

a. Comparison is made between two nouns or pronouns by means
of *comparative adjectives* in two ways:

(1) ἤ = "than" is used to link the two items compared. Both
nouns or pronouns will be in the same case.

(EG 13)   οὗτος ἰσχυρότερός ἐστιν ἤ ἐκεῖνος.
This [man] is stronger than that [man].

(2) The thing compared may simply be put into the *genitive*
case:

(EG 14)   οὗτος ἰσχυρότερός ἐστιν ἐκείνου.
This [man] is stronger than that [man].

No difference in meaning between these two constructions
is apparent.

b. Adverbs

Verbal acts are compared by comparative adverbs using ἤ.

(EG 15)   οἱ ἅγιοι ἔπραξαν σοφώτερον ἢ οἱ υἱοὶ
τοῦ σκότους.
The saints acted more wisely than the sons of
darkness [acted].

D. Superlative Adjectives and Adverbs

1. Introduction

Superlative forms of adjectives and adverbs are used when an author or speaker likens or contrasts more than two persons, things, or actions. *Elative* usage is also common:

(EG 16)   "O *most worthy* king!"

2. Morphology

a. Adjectives

(1) Regular

    (a) In English superlative comparison is usually indicated by the addition of "-est" to the end of the regular adjective:

        (EG 17)   "fast," superlative: "fastest"

        (EG 18)   "high," superlative: "highest"

        (EG 19)   "long," superlative: "longest"

    (b) In Greek, ‑τατος, ‑τατη, ‑τατον added in place of the masculine singular nominative ς ending of the normal adjective performs the same function:

        (EG 20)   ἰσχυρός, superlative: ἰσχυρό<u>τατος</u>

        Some adjectives lengthen the *o* before the ‑τατος (when the previous syllable is short).

        (EG 21)   σοφός, superlative: σοφ<u>ώ</u>τατος

    (c) Third declension adjectives use the same ‑τατος, ‑τατη, ‑τατον endings, but these either are added directly to the stem (ἀληθέστατος, εὐθύτατος) or are preceded by εσ (ἀφρονέστατος). These are rare and in any case are easily recognized.

(2) Irregular

    (a) Some superlative formations are irregular:

        (EG 22)   "good," superlative: "best"

        (EG 23)   "bad," superlative: "worst"

        (EG 24)   "much," superlative: "most"

(b) In Greek, a number of irregular superlatives also occur (and, as with the English examples above, they occur with common words). Here, however, a common pattern of endings is followed. These superlatives end in ⁻ιστος, ⁻ιστη, ⁻ιστον and are declined like normal superlative (i.e., O and A declension) forms.

b. Adverbs

The *neuter accusative plural* of the superlative adjective is regularly used for the superlative adverb:

(EG 25)   ἰσχυρότατα = "most strongly"

E. Common Comparative and Superlative Adjectives

Positive	Comparative	Superlative
μέγας, etc.	μείζων ⁻ον	μέγιστος ⁻η ⁻ον
πολύς, etc.	πλείων ⁻ον	πλεῖστος ⁻η ⁻ον
ἀγαθός, etc.	κρείσσων ⁻ον	κράτιστος ⁻η ⁻ον
κακός, etc.	χείρων ⁻ον	ἐλάχιστος ⁻η ⁻ον

F. Vocabulary

ἤ (adv.): or; than

ἡδέως (adv.): gladly

ἰσχυρός ⁻ά ⁻όν: strong

μᾶλλον (adv.): more; rather (+ ἤ)

ὀλίγος ⁻η ⁻ον: few

παλαιός ⁻ά ⁻όν: old

πάντοτε (adv.): always

τότε (adv.): then

ὑγιής ⁻ές: healthy, well

χαρά ⁻ᾶς, f.: joy

χώρα ⁻ας: country, land, area

Do not forget μέγας, πᾶς, and πολύς from this chapter in the text, as well as the irregular comparative and superlative adjectives (section E) as vocabulary.

G. Exercise

Make the nominative masculine singular comparative and superlative adjective of ὀλίγος, παλαιός, ὑγιής.

H. Practice Sentences

1. Greek to English

a. οὐχ ἡδέως ἀπέδωκαν οἱ παλαιοὶ τὴν χώραν τοῖς ἐχθροῖς.

b. ἡ χαρὰ τῶν ἁγίων ἦν μείζων τῆς <u>λύπης</u> (cf. λυπέω) τῶν διακόνων τοῦ διαβόλου.

c. ἡ πᾶσα πόλις οὐκ ἠδυνήθη ἀποκτεῖναι πάντας τοὺς πονηροὺς λῃστάς.

d. ὀλίγοι ἰσχυρότεροι ἢ πολλοί, ὠφελοῦντος τοῦ θεοῦ.

e. ἀληθῶς οἱ ἀσθενεῖς ὑγιέστατοί εἰσιν, ἐὰν πιστεύ-ωσιν εἰς τὸν κύριον.

f. οἱ ὑγιεῖς ἐπεθύμησαν ταύτην τὴν γῆν μᾶλλον ἢ τὸν μέλλοντα αἰῶνα.

g. τότε οἱ μαθηταὶ ἠρώτησαν· πότε καταστήσεις τὴν βασιλείαν σου ἐν τῇ χώρᾳ ταύτῃ;

h. πολλοὶ ἤγγισαν θεραπευθῆναι, πλείονες δὲ πάντοτε ἐφοβήθησαν τοὺς Ἰουδαίους.

2. English to Greek

The true God is stronger than the gods of the Gentiles.

I. Bible Passages

John 13:16

Luke 1:32

Matthew 3:10

1 Corinthians 13:2

John 3:19–20

37

Case Usages

A. Introduction

In chapter 4 we introduced basic case usages. In this chapter, we will present a table of the most common usages, adding many not previously introduced. Note how frequently the uses correspond to what was said in chapter 5, B 2 b, concerning basic preposition usage. The vocative case is also introduced in this chapter.

B. Vocative Case

The vocative case is used for direct address.

(EG 1)   *"Slave,* come here!" ("Slave" is technically vocative.)

In Greek, vocative noun forms are the same as the nominative in the plurals of all declensions. Singular forms are the same for all neuter nouns and for feminines of the A declension. Masculine and feminine singular vocative forms of the O declension and slightly different, but they are easily recognizable by an ϵ final vowel.

(EG 2)   ἀπόστολε (vocative singular)

(EG 3)   παρθένε (vocative singular)

Masculines of the first declension have a short a in place of the η.

(EG 4)   προφῆτα (vocative singular)

The vocative of masculine and feminine third declension nouns in the singular is normally the same as the nominative, but some variations do occur:

(EG 5)   γύναι (vocative singular) (note accent)

(EG 6)   ἐλπί (vocative singular)

C. Nominative Case Usage

The nominative case is used for *subject* and *predicate* nouns and adjectives. In Koine Greek it is, however, often used *with the article* in place of the vocative in direct address.

(EG 7)   ναί, ὁ πατήρ.
          "Yes, *father*." (Matt. 11:26)

D. Genitive Case Usage

The genitive case is commonly used to express *possession* and *with some prepositions*. It is also used

1. to show *possession,* in the sense of *relationship,* sometimes with obvious words to be supplied from the context:

   (EG 8)   εἶδε τὸν Ἰησοῦν τὸν <u>τοῦ Ἰωσήφ</u>.
             He saw Jesus, the *son* of Joseph.

2. to express *separation* (though usually ἀπό or ἐκ is used):

   (EG 9)   ἀπήλθομεν <u>τῆς πόλεως</u>.
             We left the city.

3. in making *comparisons:*

   (EG 10)   ἄγγελοι κρείσσονες <u>δαιμονίων</u>.
             Angels [are] better *than* demons.

4. to indicate the *price* or worth of something:

   (EG 11)   ἠγόρασα τὰ πρόβατα <u>πολλοῦ ἀργυρίου</u>.
             I bought the sheep *for* much money.

5. to express the *idea of object* when the genitive noun stands as an object to a noun whose root is a verbal action:

   (EG 12)   ἡ πίστις <u>τοῦ εὐαγγελίου</u> σώζει, οὐκ ἔργα.
             Faith *in* the Gospel saves, not works. (Here, behind πίστις stands the verbal root πιστεύω and the idea of believing. "Gospel" [εὐαγγέλιον] is what is believed, not who does the believing.)

6. for the *direct object* of *some verbs,* especially verbs of sense (though not sight):

   (EG 13)   οἱ ὑπηρέται ἤκουσαν <u>τῆς φωνῆς</u>, εἶδον δὲ οὐδένα.
             The attendants heard *the voice,* but they saw no one.

7. to express *the time frame within which* something takes place:

   (EG 14)   οἱ κλέπται ἦλθον <u>νυκτός</u>.
             The thieves came *during* the night.

8. to express the *subject of a genitive absolute:*

   (EG 15)   ἀπελθόντος <u>αὐτου</u>, οἱ μαθηταὶ ἐκήρυσσον.
             After *he* had departed, the disciples began to preach.

E. Dative Case Usage

The dative case is commonly used to express the *indirect object* and *with some prepositions*. It is also used

1. to describe the *instrument or means* by which something is done:

   (EG 16)   οἱ ἄνθρωποι σῴζονται χάριτι.
              Men/people are saved *by* grace.

2. to delineate for whose *advantage* (or disadvantage) something is done:

   (EG 17)   οἱ μαθηταὶ συνήγαγον ἄρτους τοῖς ὄχλοις.
              The disciple gathered loaves of bread *for* the crowds.

3. to indicate with *respect* to what or whom something is said or done:

   (EG 18)   οἱ μὲν πονηροὶ ἰσχυροί εἰσιν σώματι, οἱ
              δὲ ἅγιοι ἰσχυροί εἰσι ψυχῇ.
              The evil men are strong *in* body, but the saints are
              strong *in* spirit.

4. to show the *measure of difference* with a comparative adjective or adverb:

   (EG 19)   αὕτη φρονιμωτέρα πολλῷ ἐστιν ἢ ἐγώ.
              This woman is *much* more intelligent than I.

5. for the *direct object of some verbs,* especially compounds:

   (EG 20)   ὑπήντησε τῷ σωτῆρι.
              He met the Savior.

6. to express a *point of time.*

   (EG 21)   ἀπέθανε τρίτῃ ὥρᾳ.
              He died *at* the third hour.

F. Accusative Case Usage

The accusative case is used to express most *direct objects* and *with some prepositions*. It is also used

1. to express the *subject of an infinitive:*

   (EG 22)   δεῖ ἡμᾶς φιλεῖν τὴν ἀλήθειαν.
              It is necessary that *we* love the truth.

2. *adverbially:*

   a. Often the neuter accusative singular of an adjective is used for the corresponding adverb.

(EG 23) οἱ ἱερεῖς <u>ταχὺ</u> ἐξῆλθον (ταχὺ instead of
ταχέως).
The priests came out *quickly*.

Note that the accusative is used to make comparative and superlative adverbs (see chapter 36, C 2 b and D 2 b).

b. Nouns are occasionally also used adverbially.

(EG 24) <u>δωρεὰν</u> ὁ θεὸς ἔπεμψε τὸν υἱὸν αὐτοῦ.
Freely God sent His son (δωρεά = a gift).

3. to express *extent of both time* and *place*.

a. Extent of time:

(EG 25) ὁ 'Ιησοῦς ἦν ἐπὶ τῷ σταυρῷ <u>ἒξ ὥρας</u>.
Jesus was on the cross *for* six hours.

b. Extent of place:

(EG 26) οἱ μαθηταὶ ἐπορεύθησαν <u>τέσσαρες</u>
<u>σταδίους</u>.
The disciples journeyed *for* four stades.

G. Vocabulary

ἀκοή ‐ῆς, f.: hearing; report

δεξιός ‐ά ‐όν: right[1]

ἔτος ‐ους, n.: year

λοιπός ‐ή ‐όν: remaining, left

μόνος ‐η ‐ον: alone; adverbial μόνον = only

τεσσαράκοντα: forty

ὑστερέω (R) + gen.: I lack; am less than, inferior to

χρόνος ‐ου, m.: time

ψυχή ‐ῆς, f.: soul, spirit

"Improper" prepositions (+ gen.):

ἔμπροσθεν: before, in the presence of

ἕνεκα: on account of

ἐνώπιον: before, in the presence of

ἔξω: outside

ἕως: until, up to

ὀπίσω: behind, after

χωρίς: apart from, without

H. Practice Sentences

1. Greek to English

a. ὦ δοῦλε τοῦ κυρίου, ὑστερεῖς τινος;

b. ἡ παλαιὰ γυνή, <u>Ἄννα</u>, οὐκ ἀφίστατο τοῦ ἱεροῦ πρὸ τοῦ τὸν Ἰωσὴφ παραστῆσαι τὸν Ἰησοῦν.

c. ἡ ἀκοὴ τοῦ θανάτου αὐτοῦ ἀπῆλθεν ἐπὶ πᾶσαν τὴν γῆν.

d. χωρὶς τῆς χάριτος οὐ μὴ δεξώμεθα ἄφεσιν ἁμαρτιῶν ἐνώπιον τοῦ Χριστοῦ, ὃς ἐκ δεξιῶν τοῦ θεοῦ κάθηται.

e. μετὰ τὴν ἀνάστασιν, ὁ Ἰησοῦς ὤφθη ὑπὸ τῶν μαθητῶν αὐτοῦ τεσσαράκοντα ἡμερῶν.

f. τῇ ψυχῇ ἰσχυρότερος πολλῷ εἶ, ἕνεκα τῆς χάριτος τοῦ θεοῦ.

g. τῇ τρίτῃ ἡμέρᾳ, ὁ Ἰησοῦς ἐπορεύθη μετὰ δύο μαθητῶν ἕως <u>Ἐμμαοῦς</u>.

h. ὁ βαπτιστὴς παρεγένετο ἔξω τῆς πόλεως καὶ ἐκήρυσσεν· ὁ ὀπίσω μου ἐρχόμενος ἔμπροσθέν μου γέγονεν.

i. οὐ πολὺν χρόνον περιεπάτει ὁ Ἰησοῦς κηρύσσων καὶ θεραπεύων, μόνον τρία ἔτη.

j. τὸ λοιπὸν² ἀποκαλύψω ὑμῖν τὰ μυστήρια τῆς βασιλείας.

2. English to Greek

For three days Jesus was lying in a tomb, even though He was the King of the earth.

I. Bible Passages

Matthew 27:28–29

James 1:22a . . . ἀκροαταί

John 3:1–2a . . . διδάσκαλος

Mark 5:36 (omit λαλούμενον)

Acts 28:12

Matthew 10:8

Notes

1. Note the common idiom with this adjective: ἐκ δεξιῶν = at the right hand.

2. Adverbial.

38

The Verb, Part 10:
The Optative Mood

A. Introduction

1. The optative is a fourth mood, which is less distinct than the subjunctive. Generally, it concerns the future, but it conveys not uncertainty to the extent of probability but uncertainty to the extend of mere *possibility*.

2. The function of the optative, extensive in classical Greek (see William W. Goodwin, *Greek Grammar*, London: MacMillian, 1963, para. 1322–23), is severely limited in the Koine in general and in the New Testament in particular. Still, it is not as rare as some feel, for it occurs over 70 times. As a result, its basic forms will be presented, to be learned more for recognition than for conjugation.

B. Paradigm Forms

1. λείπω

a. "Present"

	Active		Middle/Passive	
	Singular	Plural	Singular	Plural
1	λείποιμι	λείποιμεν	λειποίμην	λειποίμεθα
2	λείποις	λείποιτε	λείποιο	λείποισθε
3	λείποι	λείποιεν	λείποιτο	λείποιντο

b. "Aorist"

	Active		Middle	
	Singular	Plural	Singular	Plural
1	λίποιμι	λίποιμεν	λιποίμην	λιποίμεθα
2	λίποις	λίποιτε	λίποιο	λίποισθε
3	λίποι	λίποιεν	λίποιτο	λίποιντο

Passive

	Singular	Plural
1	λειφθείην	λειφθείημεν
2	λειφθείης	λειφθείητε
3	λειφθείη	λειφθείησαν

2. λύω

a. "Present"

	Active			Middle/Passive	
	Singular	Plural		Singular	Plural
1	λύοιμι	λύοιμεν		λυοίμην	λυοίμεθα
2	λύοις	λύοιτε		λύοιο	λύοισθε
3	λύοι	λύοιεν		λύοιτο	λύοιντο

b. "Aorist"

	Active			Middle	
	Singular	Plural		Singular	Plural
1	λύσαιμι	λύσαιμεν		λυσαίμην	λυσαίμεθα
2	λύσαις	λύσαιτε		λύσαιο	λύσαισθε
3	λύσαι	λύσαιεν		λύσαιτο	λύσαιντο

Passive

	Singular	Plural
1	λυθείην	λυθείημεν
2	λυθείης	λυθείητε
3	λυθείη	λυθείησαν

3. "To Be" (εἰμί)

	Singular	Plural
1	εἴην	εἴημεν
2	εἴης	εἴητε
3	εἴη	εἴησαν

Note: While classical Greek did use a future optative, these forms need not be learned for the New Testament.

C. Morphology

1. Stem

The appropriate stem of the word is used, unaugmented in the "aorist."

2. Connecting Vowel

As is appropriate for a separate mood, a separate connecting vowel, ι, is used. In most cases another short connecting vowel is inserted before the ι to produce a diphthong. When, however, the ι is added to forms whose stems end in a short vowel (the "aorist" passive, ⁻μι verbs, etc.), an η is added after the ι.

a. "Present" and strong "aorist" forms normally add *o* before *ι*.

b. Weak "aorists" use the characteristic *α* before *ι*.

c. The "aorist" passive retains its characteristic *ε* after the *θ* and thus adds *ιη* (cf. *εἰμί*).

d. The third plural active (cf. *λύοιεν, λύσαιεν*) has *ιε* instead of *ι*.

3. Endings

The endings for this mood are basically secondary. Note especially all middles and the "aorist" passive (plus the verb "to be"). Exceptions are

a. ‑*μι* in the first person singular "present" and "aorist" active;

b. ‑*o* in the second person singular "present" middle/passive and "aorist" middle.

4. Two Notes

a. An alternative weak "aorist" third person plural form is possible even in Koine: *λύσειαν*. This is very classical.

b. The final *οι* and *αι* of the third singular optative active forms are considered *long* for accenting purposes.

D. Tense

The "tense" of the optative indicates aspect/focus relative to action, not time. Review the principles of aspect in chapter 9.

E. Meaning

The optative, like the subjunctive (cf. chapter 28, E), does not have any specific meaning that may be attached to it at every occasion. The specific construction in which it occurs will determine the exact force and therefore the meaning.

F. Syntax

The optative, like the subjunctive, may be used either *independently* or *dependently*. In the New Testament, the independent usage is by far the more common. *μή*, not *οὐκ*, is the negative.

1. Independent Uses

a. The chief usage of the optative in the New Testament concerns *wishes*. It is used as a main verb of a clause to express a strong desire.

(EG 1)   εὕροι γυναῖκα.
         May he *find* a wife!

(EG 2)   νόμον οὖν καταργοῦμεν διὰ τῆς πίστεως;
         μὴ γένοιτο.
         "Do we, therefore, destroy the law through faith?
         May it not happen! " (Rom. 3:31)

(EG 3)   ὑμᾶς δὲ ὁ κύριος πλεονάσαι . . .
         "*May* the Lord *enrich* you . . ." (1 Thess. 3:12)

It may be noted that many "wishes" are stronger than simple
wishes and become *blessings,* especially when given by an
apostle.

(EG 4)   . . . ὁ θεὸς τῆς εἰρήνης ἁγιάσαι ὑμᾶς . . .
         ". . . *may* the God of peace *sanctify* you . . ."
         (1 Thess. 5:23)

b. The optative + ἄν is also used rather frequently by Luke *poten-
   tially,* i.e., to express a future action which "might" or "could"
   or "would" happen, depending on future circumstances. See
   Ernest de Witt Burton, *Syntax of the Moods and Tenses in New
   Testament Greek,* Third Edition, Edinburgh: T. & T. Clark,
   1898, reprinted 1973, para. 178–79.

(EG 5)   εὕροι ἄν γυναῖκα.
         He *might* (or *would,* or *could*) find a wife.

(EG 6)   τί ἄν θέλοι ὁ σπερμολόγος οὗτος λέγειν;
         What *would* this babbler wish to say? (Acts 17:18)

This usage can be viewed as the main clause of a conditional
sentence whose fulfillment is viewed as a remote possibility (the
"if" clause is [elliptically] assumed). See F 2 b below and chapter 39, D.

2. Dependent Uses

a. Introduction

In classical Greek, the optative was used quite commonly in dependent clauses. One of these uses will be encountered in chapter 42. The other, though rare in the New Testament, is introduced here because of its correspondence to the second independent usage detailed above (F 1 b).

b. The Optative in Conditional Sentences

In classical Greek, several uses of the optative in conditional
sentences were possible, but the most common used forms of
this mood in the "if" (εἰ) clause and the optative plus ἄν in the
main clause. Such a conditional sentence viewed its fulfillment
as a *mere possibility,* quite unlikely.

(EG 7) εἰ ὁ βασιλεὺς <u>ὠφελήσαι</u> αὐτόν, <u>εὕροι ἂν</u>
γυναῖκα.
If the king *should help* him, he *would find* a wife.

Note: The main clause of such a conditional sentence is the basis for the "potential optative" described in F 1 b above.

In two places in 1 Peter a form of this type of conditional sentence is used, but only the "if" (εἰ) clause contains the optative. In both, a present "tense" indicative mood main verb is assumed.

(EG 8) εἰ καὶ <u>πάσχοιτε</u> διὰ δικαιοσύνην,
μακάριοι.
"If you *should* even *suffer* on account of
righteousness, you are blessed." (1 Peter 3:14) See
also 1 Peter 3:17.

G. Vocabulary

αἰσχύνομαι . . . ἠσχύνθην: (I put to shame)[1]; pass.: I am
ashamed

ἀντί (prep. + gen.): in place of, on behalf of

ἀπέχω, etc.: I receive in full; I am distant (intrans.); middle: I
abstain from

εὐλογέω (R)[2]: I bless

μήποτε (conj.): lest (in order that not) (= ἵνα μή)

πληθύνω (Irreg.): I increase, multiply (trans.); pass.: I increase,
multiply (intrans.)

ταράσσω (R): I disturb, trouble; pass.: I am disturbed, troubled

ὑποτάσσω (r): I subject, subordinate; pass.: I am subject to; obey

φαίνω (Irreg.): (I bring to light)[1] (trans.); I shine (intrans.); pass.: I
appear

χωρίζω (R): I separate (trans.); pass.: I separate *(intrans.)*

H. Exercise

Parse the following:

1. γένοιτο   5. ποιήσαιτε   9. πίοιεν

2. πράξαις   6. φονεύσειαν   10. εἴη

3. σωθείη   7. φιλοῖμεν   11. φανείη

4. λάβοι   8. ἀγοράσαι

I. Practice Sentences

1. Greek to English

a. εὐλογήσαι ὁ κύριος καὶ φυλάξαι σε.

b. μὴ ταραχθείητε ψυχῇ διὰ τοὺς <u>πειρασμοὺς</u> τοῦ διαβόλου.

c. ἐν σαββάτῳ ὁ κύριος ἔλθοι ἂν πρὸς τὸ κρῖναι
πάντας τοὺς ἀνθρώπους.

d. φύγετε, μήποτε φονευθῆτε μαχαίρῃ.

e. οἱ ἐπιθυμοῦντες φανῆναι σοφοὶ ἀπέχουσι τὸν
μισθὸν αὐτῶν.

f. ὁ Ἰησοῦς ἀπέθανεν ἀνθ᾽ ἁμαρτωλῶν, νῦν δὲ τὸ
σῶμα αὐτοῦ, ὃ ἐστιν ἡ ἐκκλησία, ὑποτάσσεται
αὐτῷ.

g. εἰ σήμερον ἀποθάνοιμεν, ὁ θάνατος μὴ χωρίσαι ἂν
ἡμᾶς ἀπὸ τῆς ἀγάπης τοῦ σωτῆρος.

2. English to Greek

May you drink much wine and eat good bread!

J. Bible Passages

1 Peter 1:2b χάρις . . .

1 Thessalonians 3:11 ὁ θεός . . .

Romans 6:1–2a . . . γένοιτο

Matthew 19:6

Notes

1. This classical active meaning appears outside the New Testament and is reflected in the meaning of the passive.

2. εὐλογέω does not change initial ευ to ηυ when augmenting.

39

Conditional Sentences Contrary to Fact; Conspectus of Conditional Sentences

A. Introduction

1. We have studied a number of different types of conditional sentences heretofore, but all have dealt with reality or probability or at least possibility. We now come to conditional sentences that deal with ideas contrary to fact.

2. After we examine this final kind of conditional sentence, we will analyze the overall scheme of Greek conditional sentences.

B. Contrary to Fact Conditional Sentences

1. A contrary to fact conditional sentence imagines a situation that is definitely *impossible,* either in the present or in the past. In English, we use the subjunctive for such situations. If the hypothetical condition is in the present, we use the past subjunctive in the "if clause"; if it is in the past, we use the pluperfect subjunctive in that clause. In the main clause of both, "would" appears.

   (EG 1)   "If I *were* you, I *would* leave." = present contrary to fact

   (EG 2)   "If he *had come* then, he *would have* helped the virgin." = past contrary to fact

2. Greek usage is quite different.

   a. Greek does *not* use the subjunctive for conditional sentences contrary to fact. They deal neither with the future nor with uncertainty; instead, they deal with the past or present, and they contradict fact.

   b. Greek uses the indicative mood in a secondary "tense" for contrary to face conditionals, the *imperfect* for those dealing with the *present,* and the *aorist* for those dealing with the *past.* In

267

addition, it uses the particle ἄν in the main clause. (This particle is *not* now *used with the subjunctive or the optative*.)

(EG 3)   εἰ ἤμην σύ, ἀπηρχόμην ἄν.
If I *were* you, I *would* leave (cf. EG 1).

(EG 4)   εἰ τότε ἦλθεν, ὠφέλησεν ἄν τὴν παρθένον.
If he *had* come then, he *would* have helped the virgin (cf. EG 2).

Note again that only the simple indicative mood is used.

c. In contrary to fact conditional sentences, the negative in the "if" clause is μή, not οὐκ.

C. Conspectus of Conditional Sentences

Greek conditional sentences may be distinguished by the construction of first the *protasis* ("if" clause) and then the *apodosis* (main clause). At each dividing point, only two possibilities exist.

1. Step 1

a. If the protasis begins with ἐάν, the conditional sentence must either deal with the *future* (future more vivid: FMV) or give a *general truth* (present general: PG). (Cf. chapter 29, B 2 b.)

b. If the protasis begins with εἰ, the conditional sentence must either deal with a *particular* circumstance or situation (simple particular: SP; cf. chapter 29, B 2 b) or be contrary to fact (CTF; cf. B above). Either may deal with the present or the past.

2. Step 2

a. If the conditional sentence is either FMV or PG (i.e., has ἐάν in the protasis), then the apodosis will reveal the exact type.

(1) If the main verb is future (or its equivalent), it is FMV.

(2) If the main verb is present, it is PG.

b. If the conditional sentence is either SP or CTF (i.e. has εἰ in the protasis), then the apodosis will reveal the exact type.

(1) If the apodosis contains no ἄν, it is SP.

(2) If the apodosis contains ἄν, it is CTF.

3. Step 3

a. If the conditional sentence is SP, the "tense" of the verbs will reveal the time frame of the condition.

(1) If the verbs are in a secondary "tense," the condition is in the past.

(2) If the verbs are in the present "tense," the condition is present.

b. If the conditional sentence is CTF, the "tense" of the verbs will reveal the time frame of the condition.

(1) If the verbs are *imperfect,* the condition is *present.*

(2) If the verbs are *aorist,* the condition is *past.*

4. Mixed Conditional Sentences

Conditional sentences that are not purely one type or another also occur. Especially frequent is the use of the protasis of a simple particular (SP), either past or present, and the apodosis of a future more vivid (FMV).

(EG 5)   εἰ οὖν δοῦλοι Χριστοῦ ἐστε, σωθήσεσθε.
If, then, you are slaves of Christ, you will be saved.

(EG 6)   εἰ ὁ Ἰησοῦς ἀνέστησε τὸν υἱὸν τῆς χήρας, ἀναστήσει καὶ ἡμᾶς ἐν τῇ ἐσχάτῃ ἡμέρᾳ.
If Jesus raised the son of the widow, He will raise us also on the last day.

D. Conspectus Chart

The chart following contains a summary of C 1, 2, and 3, including examples. For completeness, examples using the optative mood are appended in the note.

Conditional Sentences

"If" clause = protasis
("Then") clause = apodosis

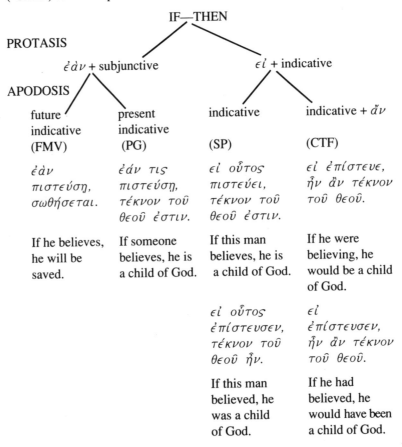

PROTASIS

             ἐάν + subjunctive   εἰ + indicative

APODOSIS

future indicative (FMV)	present indicative (PG)	indicative (SP)	indicative + ἄν (CTF)
ἐὰν πιστεύσῃ, σωθήσεται.	ἐάν τις πιστεύσῃ, τέκνον τοῦ θεοῦ ἐστιν.	εἰ οὗτος πιστεύει, τέκνον τοῦ θεοῦ ἐστιν.	εἰ ἐπίστευε, ἦν ἄν τέκνον τοῦ θεοῦ.
If he believes, he will be saved.	If someone believes, he is a child of God.	If this man believes, he is a child of God.	If he were believing, he would be a child of God.
		εἰ οὗτος ἐπίστευσεν, τέκνον τοῦ θεοῦ ἦν.	εἰ ἐπίστευσεν, ἦν ἄν τέκνον τοῦ θεοῦ.
		If this man believed, he was a child of God.	If he had believed, he would have been a child of God.

Note: A protasis with εἰ may take the optative mood. In this case, two options are available for the apodosis:

optative + ἄν (future less vivid: FLV; cf. chapter 38, F 2 b)
εἰ πιστεύσαι, σωθείη ἄν.
If he should believe, he would be saved.

imperfect indicative (past general)
εἰ τις πιστεύοι, τέκνον τοῦ θεοῦ ἦν.
If ever someone believed, he was a child of God.

E. Vocabulary

ἀδικία ⁻ας, f.: unrighteousness

ἀκροβυστία ⁻ας, f.: uncircumcision

ἐνδύω (R): I clothe (two objects possible) (cf. περιβάλλω)

θύω (R): I sacrifice, kill for sacrifice

> θυσία ⁻ας, f.: sacrifice

> θυσιαστήριον ⁻ου, n.: altar

ἰσχύω (R): I am strong; have validity, be in force

κόπτω (Irreg.): I cut; middle: I mourn

ποιμαίνω, ποιμανῶ, ἐποίμανα: I shepherd

σκανδαλίζω: (R): I cause to stumble; pass.: I take offense at

ψεύδομαι (M) (R): I lie, tell a falsehood

F. Exercise

Tell which kinds of conditional sentences the following must be, then translate them.

1. ἐὰν πράξῃς τοῦτο, ἁμαρτάνεις.

2. εἰ πράσσεις τοῦτο, ἁμαρτάνεις.

3. εἰ ἔπρασσες τοῦτο, ἡμάρτανες ἄν.

4. ἐὰν πράξῃς τοῦτο, ἁμαρτήσεις.

5. εἰ ἔπρασσες τοῦτο, ἡμάρτανες.

6. εἰ ἔπραξας τοῦτο, ἥμαρτες ἄν.

7. εἰ πράξαις τοῦτο, ἁμάρτοις ἄν.

G. Practice Sentences

1. Greek to English

Be sure to determine which kind of conditional sentence each example is (except c).

a. ἐὰν ψευδώμεθα, ἀρνούμεθα τὸν σωτῆρα τὸν ποι-
μαίνοντα ἡμᾶς.

b. εἰ περιτομὴ ἢ ἀκροβυστία ἴσχυεν, ὁ νόμος ἂν
ἔσῳζεν οὐδὲ τὸ εὐαγγέλιον.

c. οἱ κοπτόμενοι προσήνεγκον θυσίας τῷ θυσιαστηρίῳ
τῷ ἐν τῷ ἱερῷ, ἵνα ὁ θεὸς βοηθῇ αὐτοῖς.

d. ἐὰν σκανδαλίσωμεν τοῦτον τὸν ἀδελφόν, ἡ πίστις αὐτοῦ φθαρήσεται ὑπὸ τοῦ διαβόλου.

e. εἰ ἡ ἀδικία κατακρίνει, ἡ δικαιοσύνη σῴζει, καὶ ἡ δικαιοσύνη ἡ ἐν Χριστῷ.

f. εἰ οἱ ῞Ελληνες ἔθυσαν τῷ ἀληθεῖ θεῷ, τῶν <u>προσευχῶν</u> αὐτῶν οὗτος ἂν ἤκουσεν.

g. εἰ ὁ Χριστὸς ἐνέδυσε τὸν τελώνην δικαιοσύνην, οὗτος ἀπῆλθεν σὺν τῷ σωτῆρι αὐτοῦ εἶναι ἀποθανών.

h. εἰ ἔχεις πολὺ ἀργύριον, δυνήσῃ παραστῆσαι πολλὰς θυσίας.

2. English to Greek

If we were slaves of the devil, we would not have the hope of the resurrection.

H. Bible Passages

Galatians 3:28b–29 πάντες . . .

John 11:9b–10 ἐάν τις . . .

Matthew 9:21b ἐάν . . .

Galatians 1:10

Galatians 5:18

John 15:20b οὐκ . . . διώξουσιν

1 Corinthians 3:16–17a . . . θεός

1 Corinthians 2:7–8

Apocalypse 20:15

40

Reflexive and Reciprocal Pronouns; Further Uses of αὐτός

A. Introduction

Thus far we have had relative, personal, demonstrative, and interrogative pronouns. We now meet reflexive pronouns, in which the action of the verb is reflected back onto the subject, and reciprocal pronouns, which convey mutual action.

(EG 1)   "He saw *himself*" (reflexive).

(EG 2)   "They gave gifts to *one another*" (reciprocal).

Further uses of the personal pronoun form αὐτός will also be met, including, finally, uses of the nominative form.

B. Reflexive Pronouns

1. Forms

a. Singular

(1) First Person

		M	F	N
N		_____	_____	_____
G	(my own)	ἐμαυτοῦ	ἐμαυτῆς	ἐμαυτοῦ
D	(to myself)	ἐμαυτῷ	ἐμαυτῇ	ἐμαυτῷ
A	(myself)	ἐμαυτόν	ἐμαυτήν	ἐμαυτό

(2) Second Person

		M	F	N
N		_____	_____	_____
G	(your own)	σεαυτοῦ	σεαυτῆς	σεαυτοῦ
D	(to yourself)	σεαυτῷ	σεαυτῇ	σεαυτῷ
A	(yourself)	σεαυτόν	σεαυτήν	σεαυτό

(3) Third Person

		M	F	N
N	_____	_____	_____	_____
G	(his, her, its own)	ἑαυτοῦ	ἑαυτῆς	ἑαυτοῦ
D	(to him-, her-, itself)	ἑαυτῷ	ἑαυτῇ	ἑαυτῷ
A	(him-, her-, itself)	ἑαυτόν	ἑαυτήν	ἑαυτό

b. Plural (All Persons)

		M	F	N
N	_____	_____	_____	_____
G	(our, your, their own)	ἑαυτῶν	ἑαυτῶν	ἑαυτῶν
D	(to our-, your-, themselves)	ἑαυτοῖς	ἑαυταῖς	ἑαυτοῖς
A	(our-, your-, themselves)	ἑαυτούς	ἑαυτάς	ἑαυτά

2. Morphology

Reflexive pronouns follow the pattern of αὐτός, αὐτή, αὐτό. There are no nominative forms (see next section and D 2 c below).

3. Use

Reflexive pronouns reflect the action back onto the subject of the verb and may occur in any case but the nominative. Their person, gender, and number will agree with that of the subject.

(EG 3)   εἶδεν ἑαυτόν.
He saw *him*self.

(EG 4)   εἶδεν ἑαυτήν.
She saw *her*self.

(EG 5)   εἶδες σεαυτόν.
You saw *your*self.

(EG 6)   εἶδον ἐμαυτόν.
I saw *my*self.

(EG 7)   ἔπεμψε δῶρα ἑαυτῷ.
He sent gifts *to him*self.

(EG 8)   ἔπεμψαν δῶρα ἑαυτοῖς.
They sent gifts *to them*selves.

(EG 9)   ἔπεμψαν τὰ δῶρα ἑαυτῶν.
They sent *their own* gifts.

C. Reciprocal Pronouns

1. Forms (Plural Only)

		M	F	N
N	_____	_____	_____	_____
G	(one another's)	ἀλλήλων	ἀλλήλων	ἀλλήλων
D	(to one another)	ἀλλήλοις	ἀλλήλαις	ἀλλήλοις
A	(one another)	ἀλλήλους	ἀλλήλας	ἀλλήλα

2. Morphology

The forms of the reciprocal pronoun follow the pattern of αὐτός and the reflexive pronoun (in the plural).

3. Use

The reciprocal pronoun is used when action undertaken by a group of people is mutual or when people in a group act on each other. Often the translation "one another" is the best.

(EG 10) οἱ ἵπποι εἶδον <u>ἀλλήλους</u> ἐν τῷ ποταμῷ.
I see the son *himself.*
The horses saw *one another* in the river.

(EG 11) ἔδωκαν δῶρα <u>ἀλλήλοις</u>.
They gave gifts *to one another.*

D. Further Uses of αὐτός, αὐτή, αὐτό

1. Introduction

Thus far we have used αὐτός as the personal pronoun, and *this is by far its most common use.* Two other uses do occur, however. In both, αὐτός (and all its forms) functions as an *adjective;* it modifies a noun of the same gender, number, and case. Such a noun is always arthrous (with its article).

2. Use

a. If αὐτός occurs in *attributive* position to a noun and its article, it carries the meaning "same."

(EG 12) βλέπω <u>τὸν αὐτὸν</u> υἱόν.
I see the *same* son.

(EG 13) ἔπεμψα δῶρα <u>τῇ αὐτῇ</u> γυναικί.
I sent gifts to the *same* woman.

b. If αὐτός occurs in *predicate* position to a noun and its article, it carries the meaning "-self." (In this position, it *intensifies* the meaning of the noun it modifies.)

(EG 14) βλέπω τὸν υἱὸν <u>αὐτόν</u>.
I see the son *himself.*

(EG 15)   ἔπεμψα δῶρα τῇ γυναικὶ <u>αὐτῇ</u>.
          I sent gifts to the woman *herself.*

It may be noted that both types of attributive and predicate position may be used.

(EG 16)   βλέπω τὸν υἱὸν <u>τὸν αὐτόν</u>.
          I see the *same* son.

(EG 17)   ἔπεμψα δῶρα <u>αὐτῇ</u> τῇ γυναικί.
          I sent gifts to the woman *herself.*

c. The nominative form of *αὐτός* is used in the ways that we have just detailed, or it may be used alone. When it is used *alone,* it functions also as an intensifier (cf. previous section) and also means "-self." Actually, this is precisely the same use as the full predicate position usage (previous section) because, technically, it is in predicate position to the unexpressed subject of the verb.

(EG 18)   ὁ <u>αὐτὸς</u> υἱὸς βλέπει με.
          The *same* son sees me.

(EG 19)   ὁ υἱὸς <u>αὐτὸς</u> βλέπει με.
          The son *himself* sees me.

(EG 20)   <u>αὐτὸς</u> βλέπει με.
          He *himself* sees me.

Note: Because *αὐτός* in the nominative functions technically as an adjective, it may be used with any *person.*

(EG 21)   <u>αὐτὸς</u> (ἐγὼ) βλέπω σε.
          I *myself* see you. (Cf. EG 20.)

(EG 22)   <u>αὐτοὶ</u> (ὑμεῖς) βλέπετε ἡμᾶς.
          You *yourselves* see us. (Cf. EGs 21 and 20.)

d. Conspectus of the Uses of *αὐτός*

We may summarize the uses of *αὐτός* with the following chart, according to its appearance in a sentence:

(1) *Alone* (without a noun and article agreeing with it)

    (a) Nominative case = "-self" (cf. EG 20)

    (b) Oblique cases (genitive, dative, accusative) = third person personal pronoun (most common usage—cf. chapter 10)

(2) *With a noun and article* agreeing with it

    (a) Predicate position = "-self" (cf. EG 19)

    (b) Attributive position = "same" (cf. EG 18)

E. Vocabulary

ἀρέσκω, ἀρέσω, ἤρεσα + dat.: I please

ἕκαστος ⁻η ⁻ον: each

θλῖψις ⁻εως, f.: tribulation

ποῖος ⁻α ⁻ον (interrogative): What sort?

    οἷος ⁻α ⁻ον (relative): the sort that

        τοιοῦτος ⁻αύτη ⁻οῦτο (demonstrative): this sort

πόσος ⁻η ⁻ον (interrogative): How much (pl.: many)?

    ὅσος ⁻η ⁻ον (relative): as much as (pl.: many)

        τοσοῦτος ⁻αύτη ⁻οῦτο (demonstrative): this much (pl.: many)

ῥῆμα ⁻ατος, n.: utterance

ῥύομαι (M) (R): I rescue

στηρίζω, στηρίξω[1] (R): I make firm, support

ταπεινόω (R): I humble; pass: I am humble

τέ (enclitic): and (sometimes with καί)

ὑψόω (R): I exalt, raise up

Do not forget the reflexive and reciprocal pronouns as vocabulary.

F. Exercise

Translate the following sentences into Greek, using reflexive and reciprocal pronouns and αὐτός.

1. We see ourselves.
2. You (pl.) see yourselves.
3. They see themselves.
4. I send this to myself.
5. You send this to yourself.
6. He sends this to himself.
7. You (pl.) send this to yourselves.
8. We see one another.
9. You (pl.) see one another.
10. We send this to one another.
11. The same shepherd sees me.
12. The shepherd himself sees me.
13. I myself see you.
14. You yourself see me.

G. Practice Sentences

1. Greek to English

a. πόσοι σωθήσονται; ὅσοι ὑπομενοῦσιν τοὺς πειρασ- μοὺς τοῦ <u>Σατανᾶ</u>.

b. ποίους ἰχθύας ἔχεις;

c. ὅσοι πιστεύουσιν εἰς τὸν Χριστὸν (τοσοῦτοι) οὐ μὴ αἰσχυνθῶσιν ἐν τῇ θλίψει.

d. εἰ ἕκαστος ἑαυτὸν δοξάζει, οὐδεὶς ἀρέσκει τῷ θεῷ.

e. πάντες οἱ ὑψοῦντες ἑαυτοὺς ταπεινωθήσονται, ἀλλ' ὁ θεὸς ῥύσεται τοὺς πτωχοὺς καὶ ἀσθενεῖς.

f. εἰ ἠδυνήθης στηρίξασθαι σεαυτόν, ἰσχυρότερός μου ἦς ἄν.

g. οἱ μαθηταί τε καὶ αἱ γυναῖκες ἐμνήσθησαν τῶν ῥημάτων τοῦ κυρίου, καὶ ἐλάλησαν αὐτὰ ἀλλήλοις.

h. πᾶσαι αἱ γυναῖκες ἔδωκαν τῷ πατρὶ αὐτῶν τὸ αὐτὸ δῶρον.

i. φονεύσαντες τὸν διάκονον αὐτοῦ, οἱ στρατιῶται ἀπέκτειναν τὸν βασιλέα αὐτόν.

j. οἷός ἐστιν ἀνήρ, τοιοῦτος ὁ υἱὸς αὐτοῦ.

2. English to Greek

If he humbles himself, I will do the same (thing).

H. Bible Passages

Matthew 4:6a . . . κάτω

John 6:52

Matthew 1:21

Mark 3:23–26

John 17:19

1 Peter 4:1

Note

---

1. More regular forms with σ (cf. ἐστήρισα) also occur.

41

Miscellanea 4

A. Introduction

In this chapter a number of constructions will be introduced that, while not necessarily infrequent, are nevertheless either exceptions or additions to normal usage. No new morphology need be learned.

B. Participle Usage

A number of uses of the participle move beyond the basic principles and usage introduced in chapters 20–22. Note that all are in predicate position.

1. Supplementary

At times the participle *supplements* something else in the sentence, usually the direct object. Here the participle is very closely linked to its referent and is normally "present tense."

(EG 1)   εἴδομεν τὸν διάκονον <u>γράφοντα</u> τὸ βιβλίον.
We saw the servant *writing* the book.

While this example sentence may mean: "We saw the servant *while he was writing* the book," often the participle in such cases is *not* circumstantial, giving further information about the circumstances surrounding the seeing, but *supplementary,* i.e., *supplementing the object* and *actually part of it.* Another example:

(EG 2)   οἱ ὄχλοι ἤκουσαν τοὺς μαθητὰς <u>λαλοῦντας</u> ἐν ταῖς γλώσσαις ἑαυτῶν.
The crowds heard the disciples *speaking* in their own tongues.

Note that verbs of perception are regularly involved. See also Ernest de Witt Burton, *Syntax of the Moods and Tenses in New Testament Greek*, para. 146.

2. Periphrastic

We have met the periphrastic use of the participle in the perfect and pluperfect middle/passive forms of the verb (cf. chapters 25 and 26). Such constructions, i.e., the participle with a form of the verb "to be," became common in Koine Greek, especially to express the "continuous action" sense of the imperfect . In these cases, the *participle* is put into the "*present* tense" and the *verb "to be"* into the *imperfect,* according to the person and number of the subject. (The participle agrees with the verb "to be" in number.) Translate literally.

(EG 3)   ὁ Πέτρος ἦν διδάσκων τὸν λαόν.
         Peter *was teaching* the people.

(EG 4)   οἱ ἱερεῖς ἦσαν διώκοντες τοὺς πιστούς.
         The priests *were persecuting* the faithful.

Mark often uses this construction, preserving the imperfect forms for the other five uses of the imperfect (See, e.g., Mark 1:21–22.)

Note: Periphrastic constructions may also occur with future forms of the verb "to be," conveying continuous action in the future.

3. "Aorist" Participle Conveying Action *Contemporaneous* with the Main Verb

In chapter 21 (G) we indicated that the so-called "aorist" participle, generally conceived of as conveying action in *time previous* to that of the main verb, does not contradict the basic concept of aspect set forth in this text, namely, that the "aorist" stem conveys a focus on the action. This is borne out by the fact that the "aorist" participle may occasionally convey action that occurs *at the same time as* the main verb. In these instances, the action is generally *identical* to the action of the main verb.

(EG 5)   ἀλλὰ λήμψεσθε δύναμιν, ἐπελθόντος τοῦ
         ἁγίου πνεύματος ἐφ᾽ ὑμᾶς.
         But you will receive power *when* the Holy Spirit comes on you (i.e., "in the act of" the Holy Spirit coming on you). (Acts 1:8)

The idea is certainly *not* that, first the disciples will receive the Holy Spirit, and then *afterward* they will receive power. The coming of the Holy Spirit *is* the giving of power.

The most frequent use of this construction is in the rather Semitic idiom "He answered and said":

(EG 6)   ἀποκριθεὶς εἶπεν.

This is *not* to be translated: "*After* he had answered, he said." The answering and the saying constitute the same act.

See also Burton, *Moods and Tenses,* para. 132–51.

C. τοῦ + the Infinitive

The infinitive is sometimes used *with the genitive neuter singular article, τοῦ*. In such cases it normally conveys *purpose*.

(EG 7)   οἱ λῃσταὶ ἦλθον <u>τοῦ ἀποκτεῖναι</u> τοὺς πλουσίους.
The bandits came *(in order) to kill* the rich people.

Some authors also use this construction in object and epexegetical clauses.

(EG 8)   θέλει <u>τοῦ ἰδεῖν</u> τὸν ἰχθύν.
He desires *to see* the fish.

(EG 9)   ἕτοιμός εἰμι <u>τοῦ ἀκοῦσαι</u> τῆς φωνῆς τοῦ θεοῦ.
I am ready *to hear* the voice of God.

D. Multiplication of Negatives

In Greek, negatives do not generally cancel one another out. Normally, they "heap up" and make the thought more negative. The second and succeeding negative in such constructions will be compound.

(EG 10)   <u>οὐ</u> λέγει τοῦτο <u>οὐδείς</u>.
No one *says* this.

(EG 11)   <u>μὴ</u> αἰτήσητε <u>μηδένα</u> ποιεῖν <u>μηδέν</u>.
Do *not* ask *any*one to do *any*thing.

E. Questions Introduced by οὐκ or μή (οὐχί or μήτι)

Often a question *expects* a positive or negative answer. In these instances, it is introduced by

1. οὐκ (οὐχί) if it expects a positive answer;

2. μή (μήτι) if it expects a negative answer.

   (EG 12)   <u>οὐχὶ</u> ὁ διδάσκαλός εἰμι τῶν μαθητῶν μου;
               I *am* the teacher of my students, *am I not?* (Expected answer: "Yes!")

   (EG 13)   <u>μήτι</u> ὁ δοῦλος ὑπὲρ τὸν δεσπότην;
               The slave is *not* above the master, *is he?* (Expected answer: "No!")

A genuine inquiry is not introduced by these negatives.

Note the use of μή with the *indicative* mood here.

F. Vocabulary

δέω (Irreg.): I bind

κτίσις ⁻εως, f.: creation, creature

μήτι
οὐχί } (adv.): not (strong, or used to introduce questions)

ξένος ⁻η ⁻ον: foreign

σπουδάζω (R): I hasten

στόμα ⁻ματος, n.: mouth

τέλος ⁻ους, n.: end; goal

ὑπάρχω, etc.: I exist (really)[1]

φημί:[2] I say

G. Practice Sentences

1. Greek to English

a. ὁ στρατιώτης ἐσπούδασεν ἆραι τὸν δοῦλον τὸν δεδεμένον ἐκ τοῦ στόματος τοῦ θηρίου.

b. ἔφη ὁ Ἰησοῦς ὅτι τὰ ὑπάρχοντα ἡμῶν οὐκ βοηθήσει ἡμῖν ἐπὶ τῷ τέλει τοῦ κόσμου.

c. ὁ σωτὴρ ἐρύσατο καὶ τοὺς ἀνθρώπους καὶ πᾶσαν τὴν κτίσιν, ἐγερθεὶς ἐκ νεκρῶν.

d. οὐχὶ μαθητὴς εἶ;

e. οἱ ξένοι προσῆλθον τῷ Ἰησοῦ καὶ ἐπηρώτησαν· μήτι ὁ σωτὴρ ὁ μέλλων φαίνεσθαι καταβέβηκεν ἀπὸ τοῦ οὐρανοῦ;

f. ἐν τῷ θεᾶσθαι τοὺς μαθητὰς τὸν κύριον περιπα⁻ τοῦντα παρὰ τὴν θάλασσαν, ἦμεν διδάκοντες τοὺς ὄχλους.

g. αἱ γυναῖκες ἐφοβοῦντο διὰ τὸ τοὺς τελώνας ἔρχεσθαι τοῦ ἐρωτῆσαι πόσον οἶνον ἔχουσιν.

h. οὐδεὶς οὐκέτι εἶπεν οὐδὲν κατὰ τοῦ δεσπότου.

2. English to Greek

I saw you writing an epistle to the church in the big city.

H. Bible Passages

Acts 1:11b οὖτος . . . (ὃν τρόπον = ὡς)

Luke 4:20

1 Thessalonians 1:6–7

Luke 1:76–77

Mark 15:4–5

John 4:29

1 Corinthians 9:1

Mark 16:8

Notes

1. τὰ ὑπάρχοντα is the common phrase for one's possessions.

2. This verb, used only in the present and imperfect indicative, is conjugated like ἵστημι: φημί, φής, φησί; φαμέν, φατέ, φασί. It is enclitic in the present indicative. The third singular imperfect, ἔφη, is an alternative to εἶπεν, especially in Acts and Matthew.

42

Miscellanea 5

A. Introduction

In our last chapter we encounter several new features of the Greek language, as well as several uses that look like one thing but are actually another ("deceiving constructions").

B. New Words and Constructions

1. Indirect Discourse

a. Introduction

Two moods/forms of the verb outside the indicative are used at times in indirect discourse. *In these uses only,* the so-called "tense" of the forms indicates *time* and *not* aspect or focus relative to action.

b. The Infinitive in Indirect Discourse

The infinitive may be used without ὅτι to convey reported speech. As already noted, in this construction the "tense" of the infinitive conveys, not aspect, but time, specifically, the time of the corresponding indicative mood form in the direct statement.

(EG 1)   ὁ μαθητὴς εἶπεν τὸν Ἰησοῦν ἐκεῖ εἶναι.
The disciple said that Jesus *was* there. (The actual statement was, ὁ Ἰησοῦς ὧδέ ἐστιν.)

(EG 2)   ὁ μαθητὴς εἶπεν τὸν Ἰησοῦν θεραπεῦσαι τοὺς ἀσθενεῖς.
The disciple said that Jesus *had healed* the sick. (The actual statement was, ὁ Ἰησοῦς ἐθεράπευσε τοὺς ἀσθενεῖς.)

c. The Optative in Indirect Discourse

A classical usage of the optative, found only in Luke in the NT, is as a replacement for an indicative mood[1] form in indirect discourse *after a main verb in a secondary "tense."* When this occurs, the so-called "tense" of the optative reflects the "tense" of the indicative mood form that it replaces. As with the infinitive in indirect discourse, in this construction, the "tense" of the optative conveys time, not aspect/focus relative to action.

(EG 3)   εἶπεν ὅτι *ἴδοι* τὸν πατέρα.
He said that he *had seen* the father.

(EG 4)   καὶ διελογίζετο ποταπὸς *εἴη* ὁ ἀσπασμὸς
οὗτος.
And she [Mary] began to consider what sort of
greeting this *was*. (Luke 1:29b)

The actual thought of Mary in EG 4 was ποταπός *ἐστιν* ὁ
ἀσπασμὸς οὗτος;

2. The Possessive Adjective

The normal way to express personal possession is through the
genitive case of the personal pronoun.

(EG 5)   βλέπεις τοὺς δούλους *μου*.
You see *my* slaves.

(EG 6)   ἀπέκτειναν τὸν πατέρα *ἡμῶν*.
They killed *our* father.

Greek may, however, use possessive adjectives for the first and
second persons. These follow the normal adjective pattern (O declension for masculine and neuter, A declension for feminine) and
are *emphatic*.

Singular	Plural
1 ἐμός -ή -όν	ἡμέτερος -α -ον
2 σός, σή, σόν	ὑμέτερος -α -ον

Such adjectives are always used in attributive position with an
arthrous noun.

(EG 7)   βλέπεις τοὺς *ἐμοὺς* δούλους.
You see *my* slaves! (Cf. EG 5.)

(EG 8)   ἀπέκτειναν τὸν *ἡμέτερον* πατέρα.
They killed *our* father! (Cf. EG 6.)

Note that the number of the ending depends on the number of the
noun modified, not on the number of the person of the adjective. In
EG 7, even though ἐμούς refers to only one person, it is plural because "slaves" is plural. Likewise, in EG 8 ἡμέτερον, though
plural in thought, has a singular ending, because only one father is
involved.

C. Deceiving Constructions

All of the following constructions have been encountered before but with a different meaning.

1. ἐν + Dative for Means.

Often the dative of means will be preceded by ἐν (reflecting the Semitic use of בְּ). It must be translated not "in" but "by" or "with."

(EG 9)   οἱ λῃσταὶ ἀπεκτάνθησαν ἐν λίθοις.
            The bandits were killed *by* stones.

2. ἐάν = ἄν

ἄν has been used in indefinite clauses with the subjunctive in future or general contexts. (See chapter 29, B 2). Sometimes ἐάν is used not only for εἰ + ἄν, but also in place of simple ἄν with relative pronouns or adverbs of place.

(EG 10)   ὃς ἐὰν ἔλθῃ πρὸς τὸν Ἰησοῦν σωθήσεται.
            Who*ever* comes to Jesus will be saved.

(EG 11)   ἀκολουθοῦσιν αὐτῷ ὅπου ἐὰν πορευθῇ.
            They follow him wher*ever* he goes.

3. ὅτι and εἰ to Introduce *Direct* Discourse

Occasionally ὅτι and εἰ, instead of introducing indirect discourse, are used like quotation marks to introduce direct statements or questions. This construction can be detected when indirect discourse makes little sense.

(EG 12)   ὁ Ἰησοῦς εἶπεν ὅτι ἀπελεύσομαι πρὸς
            τὸν πατέρα μου.
            Jesus said, "*I* will go away to My Father."

(EG 13)   οἱ μαθηταὶ ἠρώτησαν εἰ βασιλεύσομεν ἐν
            τῇ βασιλείᾳ;
            The disciples asked, "Will *we* reign in the Kingdom?"

Note that indirect discourse is extremely unlikely in either case.

4. Improper Use of the Genitive Absolute

We have said (chapter 22, A 2 a) that a genitive absolute should be "absolute," i.e., that its subject should not appear in any major way in the main clause. Occasionally, this rule is violated, however, especially in the Gospel narratives. In such cases, the subject of the genitive absolute *does* appear in the main clause.

(EG 14)   λαλήσαντος τοῦ Ἰησοῦ, οἱ μαθηταὶ
            προσῆλθον αὐτῷ.
            After *Jesus* had spoken, the disciples came to *Him*.

EG 14 "should" have been written: οἱ μαθηταὶ προσῆλθον τῷ Ἰησοῦ λαλήσαντι.

(EG 15)   ὑποστρεψάντων <u>τῶν ἀποστόλων</u>, ὁ ’Ιησοῦς
προσεκαλέσατο <u>αὐτούς</u>.
After the *apostles* had returned, Jesus summoned
them.

EG 15 "should" have been written: ὁ ’Ιησοῦς προσεκαλέσατο
τοὺς ἀποστόλους ὑποστρέψαντας.

D. Vocabulary

αἰώνιος ⁻ον: eternal (same ending for masc. and fem.)

ἄχρι(ς)
μέχρι(ς) } (conj. and improper prep.): until, as far as (= ἕως)

βαστάζω (R): I carry, bear

ἐντέλλομαι (M) (Irreg.): I command

ἐπεί (conj.): because, since; when

ἰάομαι (⁻άσομαι) (M) (R): I heal

ἴδιος ⁻α ⁻ον: one's own

κράζω (Irreg.) I cry out, yell

μνημονεύω (R): I remember (+ gen. or acc.)

ναός ⁻οῦ, m.: temple

οἰκία ⁻ας, f.: house

ὅλος ⁻η ⁻ον: whole[2]

ὅστις, ἥτις, ὅ τι: whoever (= ὅς ἄν); who (= ὅς, ἥ, ὅ)

παιδίον ⁻ου, n.: child

πίμπλημι (Irreg.): I fill

πλῆθος ⁻ους, n.: multitude, crowd

πρίν (conj.): before (usually + infinitive, often with ἤ)

ὑπηρέτης ⁻ου, m.: attendant, servant

E. Practice Sentences

1. Greek to English

a. ὅστις δέχεται τοιοῦτο παιδίον διὰ Χριστὸν κληρο⁻
νομήσει τὴν αἰώνιον ζωήν.

b. ἐστῶτος τοῦ ’Ιησοῦ πρὸ τοῦ ναοῦ, δεσπότης τις
προσῆλθεν αὐτῷ καὶ ἔφη τὸν μαθητὴν ἰάσασθαι τὸν
ὑπηρέτην αὐτοῦ.

c. συνήχθη πλῆθος ἔξω τῆς οἰκίας, πρὶν ἢ τὸν Ἰησοῦν δύνασθαι ὑποστρέψαι εἰς τὴν κώμην τὴν ἰδίαν.

d. ὁ πονηρὸς προφήτης ἐνετείλατο ἵνα πάντες βαστάσωσιν τὰ ὑπάρχοντα εἰς τὴν ἔρημον καὶ ἐκεῖ μείνωσιν ἄχρις ἂν ὁ καιρὸς πλησθῇ.

e. ὃς ἐὰν πειράζῃ σωθῆναι ἐν ἔργοις ἀπολεῖται.

f. ὁ τελώνης ἐπορεύθη μέχρι τῶν ὁρῶν, τοῦ φυγεῖν ἀπὸ τῶν στρατιωτῶν τοῦ βασιλέως.

g. ὅλος ὁ ὄχλος ἠρώτησε τὸν διδάσκαλον εἰ λίποι ἀργύριον τοῖς τυφλοῖς καὶ χωλοῖς.

h. ὁ προφήτης ἔκραξεν ἐν μεγάλῃ φωνῇ καὶ εἶπεν ὅτι μνημονεύετε τὰς ἐπαγγελίας αἳ ἐδόθησαν τοῖς ὑμετέροις πατράσιν.

2. English to Greek

The attendant said that Jesus would judge the wicked. (Use φημί and, in indirect discourse, an infinitive.)

F. Bible Passages

Matthew 16:13

John 17:17

Acts 21:33a . . . εἴη

Romans 5:8–9

Matthew 5:19

Matthew 27:43 (+ 38–42, 44)

Matthew 12:9–10

Matthew 8:5–7

Matthew 27:27

Acts 5:24

Notes

1. Occasionally a subjunctive will be replaced by an optative, in which case the stem of the optative will reflect the stem of the corresponding subjunctive. Then, of course, no time is conveyed.

2. This word normally occurs in predicate position to an arthrous noun.

Answer Key

Every other answer is given, unless otherwise indicated.

Note: In the translation sections, words in parentheses ( ) are alternative renderings, while words in brackets [ ] are implied and may or must be supplied in English.

Chapter 1

F. Exercises

1. Which letter comes after each of the following in the alphabet?
   $\beta : \gamma$ $\pi : \rho$ $\nu : \xi$ $\tau : \upsilon$

2. Short vowels: ϵ, o (all given)
   Variable vowels: a, ι, υ (all given)

3. κ = voiceless   guttural
   θ = aspirate   dental
   χ = aspirate   guttural

4. Divide the following words into syllables:

   a. ἀ / λη / θής   g. κα / τα / στή / σον / ται
   c. δου / λεύ / ω   i. φευ / ξό / με / θα
   e. οἶ / κος

Chapter 2

C. Exercises

1. Accent the following verb forms:

   a. βλέπομεν   g. παρακαλέσεται
   c. γραφέσθω   i. λύετε
   e. ἀναγινώσκω   k. ἐπιγινώσκεις

2. Accent the following noun forms:

a. λόγος	c. ἄνθρωπος	e. δῶρον
λόγῳ	ἀνθρώπου	δώρου
λόγοις	ἄνθρωποι	δώρῳ
λόγοι	ἀνθρώπους	δῶρα
λόγους	ἄνθρωπον	δώροις
λόγων	ἀνθρώπων	δώρων

289

Chapter 3

I. Exercises

1. Divide the forms by stem, connecting vowel, and ending.

   a. λύ/ο / μεν   e. λύ/ε / τε   i. λύ/ουσιν

   c. λυ/ό / μεθα   g. λύ/ω   k. λύ/ο / μαι

2. Primary middle endings:

   ⁻μαι   ⁻μεθα
   ⁻η   ⁻σθε   (all given)
   ⁻ται   ⁻νται

J. Practice Sentences

1. Greek to English

   a. You lead.
   c. He (she, it) hears.
   e. I wash myself.
   g. They write for themselves.
   i. You leave for yourself.
   k. He (she, it) steals for himself.
   m. We heal.

2. English to Greek

   a. κλέπτομεν   i. γράφουσι(ν)
   c. νίπτει   k   βλέπεις
   e. σῴζει   m. λύω
   g. ἀκούει

Chapter 4

H. Exercise

Give the dative singular and accusative plural of the nouns in the vocabulary.

Dative Singular	Accusative Plural
ἀγγέλῳ	ἀγγέλους
ἀνθρώπῳ	ἀνθρώπους
ἀργυρίῳ	ἀργύρια
δαιμονίῳ	δαιμόνια
εὐαγγελίῳ	εὐαγγέλια
ἱματίῳ	ἱμάτια
νόμῳ	νόμους
παρθένῳ	παρθένους
σημείῳ	σημεῖα

I. Practice Sentences

1. Greek to English

   a. I heal diseases.
   c. A demon leaves a child.
   e. We see signs.
   g. Apostles write good news (a gospel) to a brother.

2. English to Greek

   a. *θεραπεύει νόσους.*
   c. *τέκνα πέμπουσιν ἱμάτια ἀδελφοῦ.*

Chapter 5

D. Exercises

1. Give gender, number, and case.

	Gender	*Number*	*Case*
a.	F	P	Dat.
c.	F	P	Dat.
e.	F	P	Nom.
g.	M	S	Nom.
i.	F	P	Acc.
	F	S	Gen.

2. Give the genitive singular, dative singular, and accusative plural.

	a. *προφήτης*	c. *δόξα*
Gen. S.	*προφήτου*	*δόξης*
Dat. S.	*προφήτῃ*	*δόξῃ*
Acc. Pl.	*προφήτας*	*δόξας*

E. Practice Sentences

1. Greek to English

   a. Virgins (maidens) send loaves of bread into villages.
   c. A slave leads children out of a village towards a lake (sea).
   e. Days of apostles abound in love and glory.
   g. God (A god) sends for Himself truth and righteousness to men (people).

2. English to Greek

   a. *προφῆται βλέπουσι πλοῖα ἐν κώμαις.*
   c. *ἀπόστολοι πέμπουσιν ἄρτον ἐκκλησίαις.*

Chapter 6

E. Exercise

Decline the given phrases through each case in singular and plural:

	Singular	Plural
1. Nom.	ἡ πρώτη κώμη	αἱ πρῶται κῶμαι
Gen.	τῆς πρώτης κώμης	τῶν πρώτων κωμῶν
Dat.	τῇ πρώτῃ κώμῃ	ταῖς πρώταις κώμαις
Acc.	τὴν πρώτην κώμην	τὰς πρώτας κώμας

	Singular	Plural
3. Nom.	ἡ ἁγία παρθένος	αἱ ἅγιαι παρθένοι
Gen.	τῆς ἁγίας παρθένου	τῶν ἁγίων παρθένων
Dat.	τῇ ἁγίᾳ παρθένῳ	ταῖς ἁγίαις παρθένοις
Acc.	τὴν ἁγίαν παρθένον	τὰς ἁγίας παρθένους

F. Practice Sentences

1. Greek to English

   a. The first apostles and the last prophets proclaim the good news (Gospel) to the world.

   c. The evil demons leave for themselves the beautiful virgins (maidens) in the small village.

   e. The Son of Man leads the just (righteous) and good child out of ^a _λ house into the church (assembly).

2. English to Greek

   a. ὁ προφήτης πείθει τὴν καρδίαν τοῦ ἁγίου μαθητοῦ.

   c. ὁ ἀγαθὸς υἱὸς βλέπει τὸν ἄρτον τοῦ Ἰησοῦ καὶ πέμπει ἀργύριον μικρᾷ κώμῃ (πρὸς μικρὰν κώμην).

Chapter 7

E. Exercises

1. Give the second person singular future indicative active:

   a. ἀκούσεις   c. ἀγοράσεις

   Give the third person singular future indicative middle:

   a. ἀκούσεται   c. ἀγοράσεται

2. Give the third person plural future indicative:

   a. βήσονται   e. δέξονται
   c. πίονται   g. προσ‑εύξονται

F. Practice Sentences

1. Greek to English

    a. The love of the churches increases and will increase.

    b. *She will go into the first village and will buy loaves of bread,*

    c. I will pray to Jesus and He will hear.

    d. *We will drink wine with the good workers, and we will keep*

    e. Do you (pl.) know the truth of God? You (pl.) will know on the *the last words* day of the Son of Man. *of the prophets.*

    g. I will teach *the children* the truths of the Gospel.

    i. Will the bad children receive beautiful gifts? They will not get gifts.

    f. The holy virgins work in the small village, and they walk in the commandments of God.

2. English to Greek

    h. The disciples of Jesus will flee into the temple, for the evil prophets are persecuting holy people.

    a. τὰ ἔργα τοῦ νόμου οὐ σώσουσιν ἀνθρώπους· τὸ δῶρον τοῦ θεοῦ σῴζει ἀπὸ δαιμονίων.

Chapter 8

G. Exercise

Give the third person singular present, future, and aorist indicative active and middle.

Active

Present	Future	Aorist
ἁμαρτάνει	ἁμαρτήσει	ἥμαρτε(ν)
εὑρίσκει	εὑρήσει	εὗρε(ν)
τίκτει	———————	ἔτεκε(ν)
σῴζει	σώσει	ἔσωσε(ν)

Middle

Present	Future	Aorist
ἁμαρτάνεται	ἁμαρτήσεται	ἥμάρτετο
εὑρίσκεται	εὑρήσεται	εὗρετο
τίκτεται	τέξεται	ἐτέκετο
σῴζεται	σώσεται	ἐσώσατο

H. Practice Sentences

1. Greek to English

    a. The virgin bore Jesus, and Joseph carried the child into Egypt.

    b. *The disciples fled from the rich workers, but they fell into the lake.*

    c. I sinned, but I will receive righteousness from the Lord.

    e. We bought *loaves of* bread and wine, and with the virgins (maidens) we went into the temple, and there we ate and drank.

    g. I (they) left the slaves in the house, and (but) I (they) led the sheep into the village.

    d. The law will not save, but the promise of the Gospel will persuade evil hearts.

    f. He prayed and he healed the disease of the good slave, and he said "You suffered, but now you will abound in the works of the Lord.

2. English to Greek

a. ὁ ἔσχατος προφήτης ἐκήρυξε τὴν ἐπαγγελίαν ἀνθρώποις.

h. The slaves found the beautiful cloak of the virgin and the money, but they took the money.

Chapter 9

D. Exercise

Give the corresponding imperfect for each verb form in the translation
section in chapter 8.

a. ἔτικτε(ν)   c. ἡμάρτανον   e. ἠγοράζομεν   g. ἔλειπον
   ἔφερε(ν)   ἐδεχόμην   ἠρχόμεθα   ἦγον
                                   ἠσθίομεν
                                   ἐπίνομεν

E. Practice Sentences

1. Greek to English

   a. The virgins (maidens) were washing (used to wash) themselves
      in the field.
      b. The disciples saw the Lord with the slaves.
   c. The Word of the Kingdom was purifying (began to purify) evil
      hearts. *d. The robbers used to find money in the Church, but they found wine.*
   e. Jesus went away into Galilee, and there He began to preach (was
      preaching) the Gospel and began to heal (was healing) diseases.
      f. Jesus was speaking beautiful parables, but the crowd were not listen
   g. The apostles used to write holy books and send [them] to the
      churches.
      h. A robber drove the sheep away from the village into the desert, and there they died.

2. English to Greek

   a. ἐθεραπεύετε τέκνα.
   c. ἀπ-ήλθομεν καὶ ἠκούομεν τοὺς λόγους τοῦ θεοῦ.

Chapter 10

G. Exercise

1. I see you.
3. You see me.
5. I know your brother.
7. I see a prophet and I know him.
9. I see him.
11. I see it.
13. I am sending the cloak to her.
15. I am sending the cloak to them.
17. I am coming (going) to you (pl.).

H. Practice Sentences

1. Greek to English

   a. When did the teachers discover the tax collector and release him?

   b. *Where was the devil revealing the mystery of his Kingdom?*

   c. How did Jesus go away into the heavens (heaven)?

   d. *The evil teachings of the Sanhedrin will not persuade me.*

   e. The last apostles died before the day of the Lord.

   f. *The robbers were fleeing from me into the desert, but I drove them out of it toward you.*

   g. The rich tax collector was dying because he was not eating, neither was he drinking (because he did not try to eat . . . or, because he habitually did not eat . . .).

   h. *In the temple, the disciples saw a virgin and he sent her a gift.*

   i. *You* (pl.) do not know us, but *we* know you (pl.)

2. English to Greek

   a. ἠκούσαμεν τὰς διδαχὰς τῶν πονηρῶν προφητῶν, οὐ δὲ δεχόμεθα αὐτάς.

Chapter 11

H. Exercises

1.

	"Tense"	Voice
a.	Aor.	P
c.	Impf.	A
e.	F	P
g.	Impf.	P
i.	Aor.	P
k.	Impf.	A
m.	Impf.	P
o.	F	P
q.	Pres.	A
s.	Aor.	A

2. Translation into Greek

a.	ἐλήμφθην	k.	ἐδόξαζες
c.	ἔλεγον	m.	ἠκούεσθε
e.	σωθήσῃ	o.	θεραπευθήσομαι
g.	ἐβαπτιζόμην	q.	εὑρίσκει
i.	ἐφονεύθη	s.	ἀπ-ελύσαμεν

I. Practice Sentences

1. Greek to English

   a. Jesus was baptized by John in the river.

   b. *The robbers were slain by the soldiers with swords.*

   c. Today I will go up into the church, and there I will greet the holy apostles and prophets.

   d. *The Good News of the Kingdom will be heard in the villages, for the disciples will go into them and they will preach it.*

e. Jesus was seen by His disciples, as He was being carried into
heaven.

d. The workers of the temple were being slain by evil men with stone

g. The teachers of the village were healed by Jesus and they re-
gained their sight. Therefore, the crowds began to come to Him
and say, "When will You heal also our slaves?"

2. English to Greek

h. as the soldiers were guarding the boats

a. γνώσεσθε τὴν ἀλήθειαν τοῦ θεοῦ καὶ ἀπο-καλύψετε
αὐτήν.

for themselves, the robbers stole their money and their swords,

Chapter 12

D. Exercises

1. Attributive or predicate position?

a. A, P. The wise slave is blind.
c. A, P. The wise slave is blind.
e. P. The slave is *wise*.

2. Translate the following:

a. I see the good [men] (or) [people].
c. I see the [men] [who are] in the desert.

E. Practice Sentences

1. Greek to English

a. The Jews were sinful (sinners), but they came to the wise
apostle. *b. Jesus began healing the lame, and the deaf and the blind.*

c. The poor are blessed, because they will receive the kingdom of
God. *d. On the last day, will go out of the tombs. The faithful will go with the Lord, the unfaithful*

e. I bought the horse in the village. *will go away with the devi*

g. You (pl.) did the evil thing (deed). Therefore, you (pl.) will suf-
fer with the people in the desert. *h. The rich men saw the poor women in the field and they send for themse*

i. The workmen [who were] in the fields found the money and *wine*
carried it to the virgins (maidens) [who were] in the temple. *bread to the*

2. English to Greek

οἱ τυφλοὶ ἔπασχον, αἱ δὲ πλούσιαι αἱ ἐν τῇ κώμῃ
ἤγαγον αὐτοὺς πρὸς τὸν Ἰησοῦν.

f. I bought the horse that was in the village.

j. The hostile soldiers will become disciples of Jesus Christ.

Chapter 13

L. Exercises

1. Short Sentences

a. You (pl.) went beyond the river.

c. You (pl.) went around the church.

e. You (pl.) went through the field.

g. You (pl.) spoke on behalf of the poor.

i. You (pl.) spoke against the Lord.

2. Adverbs

a. $\tau\upsilon\phi\lambda\hat{\omega}\varsigma$ c. $\chi\omega\lambda\hat{\omega}\varsigma$

M. Practice Sentences

1. Greek to English

a. Peace and love will increase in the church.

b. *In the beginning Jesus was teaching the crowds with parables.*

c. We used to have sheep in our village, but the robbers led them away through the field around the lakes.

e. ~~Because~~ *On account* of the law, the Jews did not used to work on the Sabbath.

g. Jesus said: "I have other sheep. I know *them*, and they know *Me*."

i. On the last day Jesus will come down out of heaven and [will] prepare life for the saints and death for the evil ones.

2. English to Greek

$\dot{o}$ $'I\eta\sigma o\hat{u}\varsigma$ $\dot{\alpha}\pi\text{-}\acute{e}\theta\alpha\nu\epsilon\nu$ $\dot{u}\pi\grave{e}\rho$ $\tau\hat{\omega}\nu$ $\dot{\alpha}\mu\alpha\rho\tau\omega\lambda\hat{\omega}\nu$ $\tauo\hat{u}$ $\kappa\acuteo\sigma\muou.$

Chapter 14

F. Exercises

1. Parse and translate the following:

	Person	*Number*	*"Tense"*	*Mood*	*Voice*
a.	2	P	Pres.	Ind.	A
c.	3	S	Pres.	Ind.	M/P
e.	2	P	Aor.	Ind.	A
g.	1/3	S/P	Impf.	Ind.	A
i.	3	P	Aor.	Ind.	A

a.   You (pl.) inherit.

c.   He calls for himself (is being called).

e.   You (pl.) built.

g.   I (they) were seeking.

i.   They requested.

2. Put forms from F 1 in the corresponding imperfect "tense."

   a. *ἐκληρονομεῖτε*
   c. *ἐφωνεῖτο*
   e. *ᾠκοδομεῖτε*

G. Practice Sentences

1. Greek to English

   a. With a small voice God called the prophet.

   c. The poor people ask (are asking) for loaves of bread, and they will receive them.

   e. As Jesus was speaking to the crowds, the disciples were seeking (began to seek) wine in the village.

   g. The tax collector did evil things (deeds), but *we* love the truth of God.

2. English to Greek

   φιλοῦμεν τὸν θεὸν καὶ κληρονομήσομεν τὴν ζωὴν τὴν ἐν οὐρανῷ.

Chapter 15

D. Exercise

Fill in the proper form of the relative pronoun:

1. *ὅν*
3. *οὗ*

E. Practice Sentences

1. Greek to English

   a. (But) Jesus took along Peter and John and went away into a holy place.

   c. The crowds marveled at the teachings that they began to hear (were hearing) from Jesus.

   e. The lame man was sitting at the door of the house [that was] at the side of the road and continued to ask for money (used to sit . . . and ask).

   g. The Baptist appeared beside the river and began to preach in the presence of sinful people (sinners).

2. English to Greek

   ὁ δοῦλος ὃν φιλεῖς ἔκλαυσεν ἐπὶ τοῦ δεσπότου αὐτοῦ.

Chapter 16

G. Exercise

Give the "present" and "aorist" active, middle, and passive infinitives of the following:

	1. "Present"	"Aorist"
Active	πέμπειν	πέμψαι
Middle	πέμπεσθαι	πέμψασθαι
Passive	πέμπεσθαι	πεμφθῆναι

	3. "Present"	"Aorist"
Active	σώζειν	σῶσαι
Middle	σώζεσθαι	σώσασθαι
Passive	σώζεσθαι	σωθῆναι

	5. "Present"	"Aorist"
Active	φέρειν	ἐνεγκεῖν
Middle	φέρεσθαι	ἐνεγκέσθαι
Passive	φέρεσθαι	ἐνεχθῆναι

H. Practice Sentences

1. Greek to English

a. The prophet went (came) to see the people and to speak the truth. [continue to]

c. This is good, that we love God and keep His commandments.

e. I am not suitable (able) to teach the disciple whom you sent.

g. The disciples began to preach the gospel, but the Jews ordered them to be driven out of the temple.

i. We ought to love our enemies, for (because) Jesus died to save them, too. [continue to / try to]

k. This is the hour of death. Therefore, it is time to repent.

2. English to Greek

ὁ Ἰησοῦς ἐκέλευσε τοὺς μαθητὰς ἐλθεῖν (ἔρχεσθαι) εἰς τὸν κόσμον καὶ κηρῦξαι (κηρύσσειν) τὸ εὐαγγέλιον ἀνθρώποις.

Chapter 17

D. Exercise

	1	3	5	7	9	11
"Tense"	"Aor."	"Pres."	"Aor."	"Pres."	"Aor."	"Aor."
Voice	P	M/P	M	A	M	P

E. Practice Sentences

1. Greek to English

   a. Jesus came into the world to help sinners.

   c. Because Jesus had healed their eyes, the blind [men] saw again.

   e. The fruit of the first tree is good, but the fruit of the second is bad.

   g. While he was going again into the house in which he (had) left the holy book, he saw other disciples.

   i. Before John began to preach by the side of the river, Jesus had (did) not yet appeared (appear) in the presence of the people.

2. English to Greek

   μετὰ τὸ λιπεῖν τὸν μαθητὴν τὸν δοῦλον αὐτοῦ ἐν τῇ κώμῃ, ἦλθεν εἰς τὸν ἀγρόν.

Chapter 18

F. Exercise

Dative Singular	Accusative Singular	Dative Plural
1. *αἵματι*	*αἷμα*	*αἵμασι(ν)*
3. *εἰκόνι*	*εἰκόνα*	*εἰκόσι(ν)*
5. *ποδί*	*πόδα*	*ποσί(ν)*

G. Practice Sentences

1. Greek to English

   a. Jesus washed the feet of the disciples.

   c. Evil spirits did not have (were not in possession of) power to rule in that age.

   e. Flesh and blood will not inherit the kingdom of heaven.

   g. The soldier found the blood of the enemies (enemy), but they did not see the bodies.

2. English to Greek

   τοῦτό ἐστι τὸ σῶμα καὶ τὸ αἷμα τοῦ σωτῆρος ἡμῶν [τοῦ] Ἰησοῦ Χριστοῦ.

Chapter 19

D. Exercise

Dative Singular	Accusative Singular	Dative Plural
1. *ἀναστάσει*	*ἀνάστασιν*	*ἀναστάσεσι(ν)*
3. *γραμματεῖ*	*γραμματέα*	*γραμματεῦσι(ν)*
5. *ταχεῖ*	*ταχύν*	*ταχέσι(ν)*

E. Practice Sentences

1. Greek to English

   a. The Savior will come in order to save also the Gentiles.

   c. After the tax collector had stolen a swift horse, he departed straightway (i.e., immediately).

   e. There is not a true image of God, for we see Him by faith and not with our eyes.

2. English to Greek

   ὁ 'Ιησοῦς ἦλθεν (εἰς τὸ) θεραπεῦσαι (θεραπεύειν) τὰς νόσους τῶν ἀσθενῶν καὶ κηρῦξαι (κηρύσσειν) τοῖς βασιλεῦσι καὶ ἄρχουσιν (πρὸς τοὺς βασιλεῖς καὶ ἄρχοντας).

Chapter 20

I. Exercises

1.	Gender	Number	Case	"Tense"	Voice
a.	M	P	Nom.	"Pres."	A
c.	M/N	S	Gen.	"Pres."	A
e.	F	S	Nom.	"Pres."	A
g.	N	P	Nom./Acc.	"Pres."	M/(P)
i.	M	S	Acc.	"Pres."	M/(P)
	N	S	Nom./Acc.	"Pres."	M/(P)
k.	M/N	S	Gen.	"Pres."	M/P

2. εἰσ-ερχόμενος πάλιν εἰς τὸν οἶκον ἐν ᾧ ἔλιπε τὸ ἅγιον βιβλίον εἶδεν ἄλλους μαθητάς.

J. Practice Sentences

1. Greek to English

   a. While He was going up to Jerusalem, Jesus began (continued) to teach the Twelve.

   c. Because they were being pursued by the leader, the rich tax collectors carried their money into the desert.

   e. The people(s) marveled at the truths that were being revealed in the ten parables.

g. The Sanhedrin ordered the four disciples to be released, because they were no longer preaching the gospel.

2. English to Greek   *for themselves*

γράφοντες ἐπιστολὰς οἱ μαθηταὶ εἶδον τὸν κύριον.

Chapter 21

I. Exercises

1.
	Gender	Number	Case	"Tense"	Voice
a.	M	P	Nom.	"Aor."	A
c.	M/N	S	Gen.	"Aor."	A
e.	F	S	Gen.	"Aor."	A
g.	M	S	Nom.	"Aor."	M
i.	F	S	Acc.	"Aor."	A
k.	M	S	Nom.	"Aor."	A

2. Give the "aorist" forms of chapter 20, I 2:

a. λύσαντες

c. φιλήσαντος

J. Practice Sentences

1. Greek to English

a. The robbers slaughtered the priest, because (after) he had found their money.

c. After they had given thanks, the shepherds ate bread and drank water on the mountain.

e. The true light of the world did not hate those who hated (were hating) Him.

g. The people who had suffered badly went out to Jesus, after (because) He had approached their city.

i. Christ is the elect son of God.

2. English to Greek

ἰδόντες τὸ τέκνον, ἠλέησαν τοὺς ἐν τῇ κώμῃ.

Chapter 22

D. Exercises

1. Which of the following sentences would be translated with a genitive absolute in Greek?

a, b, d, f, h (all given)

2.

	Masculine	Feminine
a. Gen. Sing.	φονευθέντος	φονευθείσης
Acc. Pl.	φονευθέντας	φονευθείσας
c. Gen. Sing.	πραχθέντος	πραχθείσης
Acc. Pl.	πραχθέντας	πραχθείσας

E. Practice Sentences

1. Greek to English

   a. Because (after) signs had appeared in the darkness, the shepherds glorified God.

   c. The foolish men said: "Hair is a member of the body."

   e. The lame man went away into the villages in order to make known the grace of God, after (because) he had been healed by the disciples.

   g. After Mary had given birth to the holy child, Joseph prepared to go away into Galilee, but an angel said to him: "It is necessary to flee into Egypt, for Herod is about to seek your son in order to kill Him. But after the king dies (has died), you will take the child and Mary and [will] go up into the land of Israel.

2. English to Greek

   πεμφθέντος τοῦ μαθητοῦ εἰς τὰς κώμας, ὁ Ἰησοῦς εἶπε τοῖς ἱερεῦσιν.

Chapter 23

I. Exercises

1. ἀκολουθῶ αὐτῷ.
3. πιστεύω εἰς αὐτόν.
5. ὑπ-ήκουσεν αὐτῷ.
7. προσ-ῆλθον τῷ θεῷ.

J. Practice Sentences

1. Greek to English

   a. The bad men said: "The books were written by the prophet [who was] in the desert."

   c. And it came to pass that Jesus touched the hand of the mother and commanded her to bear witness to the sign that He had done, and she obeyed Him.

   e. After the father had carried (brought) his son to the Lord, He [the Lord] commanded him to believe His word.

2. English to Greek

ἡ γυνὴ ἡ ἁψαμένη τοῦ ἱματίου τοῦ 'Ιησοῦ ἐμαρ-
τύρησε τῇ ἀληθείᾳ.

Chapter 24

F. Exercise

1. τίς ἐποίησε ταῦτα;
3. ἐπι-στρέφομαι.
5. ἐπορεύθη.
7. ἐφοβήθην τὴν γυναῖκα.

G. Practice Sentences

1. Greek to English

   a. And it came to pass that someone called the prophet. He [the prophet] heard the voice and said: "Who is here?" But no one said a word.

   c. The women journeyed to the tomb, and there they began to mourn.

   e. After she had touched the clothing of Jesus, the mother became frightened and tried to hide in the crowd.

   g. The man turned around and did not try to follow the Lord.

2. English to Greek

   πορευθεὶς πρὸς τὴν κώμην, ὁ πατὴρ προσ-ήνεγκε τὸν
   υἱὸν αὐτοῦ τῷ σωτῆρι.

Chapter 25

E. Exercises

1. Give the fifth principal part of the verbs in chart in section D.

ἦγμαι	δεδίδαγμαι
κέκλεμμαι	πεφύλαγμαι
πέπεμμαι	τέταγμαι

2.

	Person	Number	"Tense"	Mood	Voice	1st Prin. Part
a.	3	S	Pf.	Ind.	M/P	διδάσκω
c.	2	S	Pf.	Ind.	M/P	πέμπω
e.	1	P	Pf.	Ind.	M/P	ἄγω
g.	2	P	Pf.	Ind.	M/P	κλέπτω
i.	2	S	Pf.	Ind.	A	πίνω
k.	3	P	Pf.	Ind.	M/P	στρέφω

	Gender	Number	Case	"Tense"	Voice	1st Prin. Part
m.	M	S	N	"Pf."	A	φυλάσσω

F. Practice Sentences

1. Greek to English

   a. God will save those [who are] sealed by the blood of the Savior.

   c. I have heard the Gospel and have seen the things [that were] done by Jesus.

   e. The robber seized the crown [that was] fashioned for the king, but even though he [had] fled, he was found by the soldiers.

   g. The women left in the desert are dying, because they do not have bread and water.

2. English to Greek

   οἱ ἡγιασμένοι φιλοῦσιν καὶ τοὺς μισοῦντας αὐτούς.

Chapter 26

E. Exercises

1. Give the corresponding pluperfect from exercise E 2 in chapter 25.

   a. ἐδεδίδακτο
   c. ἐπέπεμψο
   h. ἐγέγραπτο
   j. εἰρήκειμεν

2. Translate the following:

   a. He says that he works (is working) in the Kingdom.
   c. He said that he was working in the Kingdom.
   e. He says that he will work in the Kingdom.
   g. He says that he was working in the Kingdom.

F. Practice Sentences

1. Greek to English

   a. He said that he had come in through the open(ed) door.

   c. Those who deny the Master will be slain, but those who confess that Jesus is Lord will come (go) into the Kingdom.

   e. Because Jesus was walking on (over) the water(s), the disciples thought that they were seeing an evil spirit.

   g. After he had heard that the servants were afraid of the Jews, Paul comforted them with the promises of the Gospel.

2. English to Greek

   οἱ προφῆται ἔδοξαν ὅτι ὁ βασιλεῦς ἦλθεν (εἰσ-ῆλθεν) εἰς τὸ ἱερόν.

Chapter 27

D. Exercise

	1	3	5
Second Principal Part	βελῶ	βαρῶ	βενῶ
Third Principal Part	ἔβειλα	ἔβαρα	ἔβεινα

E. Practice Sentences

1. Greek to English

   a. After He had been raised (had risen) from the dead, Jesus went up into heaven.

   c. [And] the Lord said that those who judged others would be condemned.

   e. The sower went out to sow in the field.

   g. After (because) the houses of the village had been destroyed by the evil men, the saints endured evil things.

2. English to Greek

   ὁ ʼΙησοῦς κατ-έβη πρὸς τὴν γῆν, εἰς (πρὸς) τὸ σῶσαι τοὺς ὑπὸ τὴν κρίσιν τοῦ διαβόλου.

Chapter 28

J. Exercises

1. Give the third singular and second plural "present" and "aorist" subjunctive of each vocabulary verb:

	"Present"	"Aorist"
3/S	ἀνα-γινώσκῃ	ἀνα-γνῷ
2/P	ἀνα-γινώσκητε	ἀνα-γνῶτε
3/S	ἐπι-γινώσκῃ	ἐπι-γνῷ
2/P	ἐπι-γινώσκητε	ἐπι-γνῶτε
3/S	παρ-έρχηται	παρ-έλθῃ
2/P	παρ-έρχησθε	παρ-έλθητε

2. Parse the following:

	Person	*Number*	*"Tense"*	*Mood*	*Voice*
a.	1	P	Aor.	S	A
c.	2	P	Aor.	S	A
e.	2	P	Aor.	S	M
g.	1	P	Aor.	S	A
i.	2	S	Aor.	S	P
k.	2	S	Aor.	S	A

K. Practice Sentences

1. Greek to English

   a. The prophets said, "Let us read the words of the Law to the people."

   c. After He had got into the boat, Jesus announced that He knew the heart of man.

   e. The Law shall surely not pass away before Jesus comes down again to judge the earth.

   g. On the third day Jesus rose (was raised), and after He had commanded the disciples to travel to the ends of the earth, He was taken up into the clouds.

2. English to Greek

   μὴ πιστεύσῃς τοῖς πονηροῖς προφήταις, οὐ μὴ γὰρ λάβωνται ⟨τὴν⟩ ἀληθῆ ζωήν.

Chapter 29

D. Exercises

1. Sentences a–e of chapter 16, H 1, substituting ἵνα clauses for the infinitives.

   a. ὁ προφήτης ἦλθεν ἵνα ἴδῃ τὸν λαὸν καὶ ⟨ἵνα⟩ λα-λήσῃ τὴν ἀλήθειαν.

   c. τοῦτό ἐστιν ἀγαθόν, ἵνα φιλῶμεν τὸν θεὸν καὶ ⟨ἵνα⟩ τηρῶμεν τὰς ἐντολὰς αὐτοῦ.

   e. οὐχ ἱκανός εἰμι ἵνα διδάξω τὸν μαθητὴν ὃν ἔπεμψας.

2. False

E. Practice Sentences

1. Greek to English   [for himself]

   a. If someone confesses his sins, he receives forgiveness from the Father. ʌ

   c. When Mary conceived her first child, Joseph did not believe that she was still a virgin.

   e. Where (wherever) your treasure is, there your heart will be.

   g. We are worthy to be called sons of God.

   i. The bride of Christ, who (which) is the church, will endure until her bridegroom comes again.

2. English to Greek

μὴ ἐξ-έλθῃς ἵνα ἴδῃς τὰ σημεῖα τὰ γενομένα (γε-
γενημένα) (γεγονότα) ἐν τῷ οὐρανῷ.

Chapter 30

F. Exercise

Parse the following:

	Person	Number	"Tense"	Mood	Voice
1.	1	S	Aor.	Ind.	A
3.	1	P	Aor.	Ind.	M
5.	3	S	Pres.	Ind./S	A
7.	1	P	Pres.	Ind./S	A
9.	2	P	F	Ind.	A
11.	3	S	Aor.	Ind.	A

13. Participle: masculine or neuter, singular, genitive, "present," active

15. Infinitive: "present," active

G. Practice Sentences

1. Greek to English

   a. Let us love (We love) God because He loved us in Christ.

   c. After he had labored in the field, the slave sat down in the house.

   e. If you (pl.) live in Christ, you will also reign with Him.

   g. After he had begotten the child, the father worried about him (it).

   i. The Greeks asked if the true Savior had come into the world.

2. English to Greek

   οἱ ἄνδρες φιλοῦσι τὰς γυναῖκας, ἀλλ᾽ ὁ θεὸς ἀγαπᾷ
   ἡμᾶς ἐν Χριστῷ.

Chapter 31

F. Exercises

1. The Third Singular Active

	Indicative	Subjunctive
"Present"	πληροῖ	πληροῖ
Imperfect	ἐπλήρου	_____
Future	πληρώσει	_____
"Aorist"	ἐπλήρωσε	πληρώσῃ
"Perfect"	πεπλήρωκε	[πεπληρώκῃ]
Pluperfect	ἐπεπληρώκει	_____

2. Parse the following:

	Person	*Number*	*"Tense"*	*Mood*	*Voice*
a.	3	S	Pres.	Ind./S	A
c.	2	P	"Aor."	S	P
e.	3	P	Aor.	Ind.	A
g.	1	P	"Pres."	S	A
i.	2	P	Aor.	Ind.	P
k.	3	S	Pf.	Ind.	A

G. Practice Sentences

1. Greek to English

   a. God earnestly desired to justify sinners.

   c. The kingdom of God is similar to the shepherd as he keeps (guards, watches) his sheep.

   e. After they had led Jesus out of the city, the soldiers lifted up a cross and on it they crucified the Lord.

   g. By (means of) the resurrection Jesus has made perfect the salvation prepared for the saints.

   i. The Lord likened the kingdom of heaven to a treasure hidden in a field.

2. English to Greek

   ὁ Ἰησοῦς ἐσταυρώθη ὑπὸ τοῦ ἡγεμόνος, εἰπὼν τὴν ἀλήθειαν.

Chapter 32

I. Exercise

Parse the following:

	Person	Number	"Tense"	Mood	Voice
1.	2	P	"Aor."	Imv.	A
3.	2	S	"Aor."	Imv.	A
5.	2	S	"Pres."	Imv.	M/P
7.	2	P	"Aor."	S	P
9.	2	S	"Aor."	Imv.	A
11.	2	S	"Pres."	Imv.	M/P
13.	3	P	Aor.	Ind.	A
15.	3	S	"Pres."	Imv.	A

J. Practice Sentences

1. Greek to English

   a. Return [in]to your village and announce the good news to the poor [people].

   c. Go quickly and help the father whose daughter is dying.

   e. Let the children always help the widows, and let the widows never look down on the young virgins (maidens).

   g. Love (pl.) the brothers and sisters and do not do evil to those who hate you.

2. English to Greek

   μὴ καταφρονεῖτε τῶν ἐχόντων χρείας, ἀλλ᾽ ὠφελεῖτε αὐτούς.

Chapter 33

F. Exercises

1. Parse—finite verb forms:

	Person	Number	"Tense"	Mood	Voice
a.	3	S	Pres.	Ind.	A
c.	2	S	"Pres."	S	A
e.	1	S	F	Ind.	A
g.	3	S	Impf.	Ind.	A
i.	3	S	Aor.	Ind.	A
k.	3	S	Pres.	Ind.	A
m.	1	S	Aor.	Ind.	A
o.	1	P	"Aor."	S	A

2. Parse—infinitives and participles:

	Gender	Number	Case	"Tense"	Voice	
a.	M	P	A	"Pres."	A	participle
c.	M	S	N	"Aor."	A	participle
e.	N	P	N/A	"Aor."	A	participle
	M	S	A	"Aor."	A	participle
g.				"Aor."	A	infinitive
i.				"Pres."	A	infinitive
k.				"Aor."	A	infinitive

G. Practice Sentences

1. Greek to English

   a. God gives good gifts to those who ask.

   c. After he had laid his hands on the head of Timothy, Paul returned to the holy city.

   e. Jesus forgave the sins of the tax collector, and he brought others to the Lord, in order that He [the Lord] might forgive them also.

   g. The deaf man whom the Lord had healed neither glorified God nor gave money to the poor.

   i. Let no one ever impose evil laws on you (pl.).

2. English to Greek

   ὁ δεσπότης ἔδωκεν ἄρτον τῷ δούλῳ αὐτοῦ, ὃς ἔθηκε αὐτὸν εἰς τὴν χεῖρας τοῦ κυρίου.

Chapter 34

F. Exercises

1. Parse—finite verb forms:

	Person	Number	"Tense"	Mood	Voice
a.	1	P	Pres.	Ind.	M/P
c.	1	S	Pres.	Ind.	M/P
e.	1	P	F	Ind.	M
g.	3	P	Impf.	Ind.	M/P
i.	1	S	Perf.	Ind.	M/P
k.	1	S	Aor.	Ind.	P
m.	1	P	Aor.	Ind.	P
o.	2	P	Aor.	Ind.	P

2. Parse—infinitives and participles:

	Gender	Number	Case	"Tense"	Voice	
a.	M	S	N	"Pres."	M/P	participle
c.	M/N	S	G	"Aor."	P	participle
e.	N/M	P	N	"Aor."	P	participle
g.				"Aor."	M	infinitive
i.				"Aor."	P	infinitive
k.				"Pres."	M/P	infinitive

G. Practice Sentences

1. Greek to English

   a. Paul commanded Timothy to entrust the Gospel to faithful teachers.

   c. God convenanted (made) a new covenant with the people (nation), because they had not obeyed His first commandments.

   e. The apostle circumcised Timothy, but Titus was not circumcised.

   g. Circumcision does not save the Jew, and wisdom [does] not [save] the Greek.

   i. New horses will be given to the poor [people] in the villages.

2. English to Greek

   αἱ χεῖρες τῶν ἀποστόλων ἐπετέθησαν ἐπὶ τῶν κεφαλῶν τῶν ἁγίων.

Chapter 35

F. Exercises

1. Parse—finite forms:

	Person	Number	"Tense"	Mood	Voice
a.	1	S	Pres.	Ind.	M/P
c.	2	S	F	Ind.	A
e.	1	S	Aor.	Ind.	P
g.	1	S	"Aor."	S	A
i.	1	S	Plpf.	Ind.	A
k.	3	S	Perf.	Ind.	A
m.	1	P	Aor.	Ind.	A
o.	1	S	F	Ind.	P

a.	intrans.		i.	intrans.
c.	trans.		k.	intrans.
e.	intrans. (trans.)		m.	intrans.
g.	intrans.		o.	intrans. (trans.)

2. Parse—infinitives and participles:

	Gender	Number	Case	"Tense"	Voice	
a.	M	S	N	"Pres."	A	participle
c.	M	S	N	"Aor."	P	participle
e.	M	S	N	"Pres."	M/P	participle
g.	M	S	N	"Perf."	A	participle
	N	S	N/A	"Perf."	A	participle
i.				"Pres."	A	infinitive
k.				"Aor."	A	infinitive
m.				"Perf."	A	infinitive

a.	trans.		i.	trans.
c.	intrans. (trans.)		k.	trans.
e.	intrans.		m.	intrans.
g.	intrans. (trans.)			

G. Practice Sentences

1. Greek to English

   a. Jesus stood in the presence of the governor and answered nothing (gave no answer).

   c. Paul established deacons and elders in the churches of Asia.

   e. The words of Jesus amazed the crowds, with the result that they (these people) said that He was beside Himself (mad, crazy).

   g. Even though (while, because) He is sitting on the throne in heaven, our Lord is able to continue to guard [for Himself] His children well.

   i. Never allow (Stop allowing) the devil to draw you (pl.) away from the truth.

2. English to Greek

   ἔστημεν πρὸ τοῦ κυρίου καὶ ἠρωτήσαμεν περὶ τοῦ πατρὸς ἡμῶν.

Chapter 36

G. Exercise

Give the nominative masculine singular comparative and superlative adjective forms:

	Comparative	Superlative
ὀλίγος	ὀλιγώτερος	ὀλιγώτατος
ὑγιής	ὑγιέστερος	ὑγιέστατος

H. Practice Sentences

1. Greek to English

   a. The old people (men) did not give the land back to the enemy (enemies) gladly.

   c. The whole city was not able to kill all the evil robbers.

   e. Truly, the weak are most healthy, if they believe in the Lord.

   g. Then the disciples asked, "When will you establish Your kingdom in this land?"

2. English to Greek

   ὁ ἀληθὴς θεός ἐστιν ἰσχυρότερος τῶν θεῶν τῶν ἐθνῶν (ἢ οἱ θεοὶ τῶν ἐθνῶν).

Chapter 37

H. Practice Sentences

1. Greek to English

   a. O slave of the Lord, do you lack something (are you inferior to anyone)?

   c. The report of his death went out over all the earth (land).

   e. After the resurrection, Jesus was seen by His disciples during a 40-day period.

   g. On the third day, Jesus journeyed with two disciples as far as Emmaus.

   i. Not for a long (much) time was Jesus walking around preaching and healing, only for three years.

2. English to Greek

   τρεῖς ἡμέρας ὁ Ἰησοῦς ἔκειτο ἐν μνημείῳ, ὢν ὁ βασιλεὺς τῆς γῆς.

Chapter 38

H. Exercise

Parse the following:

	Person	*Number*	*"Tense"*	*Mood*	*Voice*
1.	3	S	"Aor."	O	M
3.	3	S	"Aor."	O	P
5.	2	P	"Aor."	O	A
7.	1	P	"Pres."	O	A
9.	3	P	"Aor."	O	A
11.	3	S	"Aor."	O	P

I. Practice Sentences

1. Greek to English

   a. May the Lord bless [you] and keep you.

   c. The Lord might come to judge all men on the Sabbath.

   e. Those who earnestly desire to appear wise receive their reward in full.

   g. If we should die today, death would not separate us from the love of the Savior.

2. English to Greek

   πίοις (πίνοις) πολὺν οἶνον καὶ φάγοις (ἐσθίοις) ἀγαθόν ἄρτον.

Chapter 39

F. Exercise

Conditional sentences—type and translation:

1. *Present General*: If you [ever] do this, you sin.

3. *Contrary to Fact, Present*: If you were doing this, you would be sinning.

5. *Simple Particular, Past*: If you were doing this, you were sinning.

7. *Future Less Vivid*: If you should do this, you would sin.

G. Practice Sentences

1. Greek to English

   a. If we lie, we deny the Savior, who shepherds us. (PG)

   c. Those who were mourning brought sacrifices to the altar [that was] in the temple, in order that God might come to their aid (help them).

   e. If unrighteousness condemns, righteousness saves, even the righteousness [that is] in Christ. (SP, present)

   g. If Christ clothed the tax collector with righteousness, he went away (departed) to be with his Savior after he [had] died. (SP, past)

2. English to Greek

   εἰ ἦμεν δοῦλοι τοῦ διαβόλου, οὐκ ἂν εἴχομεν τὴν ἐλπίδα τῆς ἀναστάσεως.

Chapter 40

F. Exercise

Translation using pronouns:

  1. βλέπομεν ἑαυτούς.
  3. βλέπουσιν ἑαυτούς.
  5. πέμπεις τοῦτο σεαυτῷ.
  7. πέμπετε τοῦτο ἑαυτοῖς.
  9. βλέπετε ἀλλήλους.
 11. ὁ αὐτὸς ποιμήν βλέπει με.
 13. αὐτὸς βλέπω σε.

G. Practice Sentences

  1. Greek to English

   a. How many will be saved? As many as will endure the temptations of Satan.

   c. As many as believe in Christ [so many] shall surely not be put to shame in the tribulation.

   e. All who exalt themselves will be humbled, but God will rescue the poor and weak.

   g. Both the disciples and the women remembered the utterances of the Lord, and they spoke them to one another.

   i. After they had slain his servant, the soldiers killed the king himself.

  2. English to Greek

   ἐὰν ταπεινώσῃ ἑαυτόν, ποιήσω (πράξω) τὸ αὐτό.

Chapter 41

G. Practice Sentences

  1. Greek to English

   a. The soldier hastened to lift the bound servant up out of the mouth of the wild beast.

   c. The Savior rescued both people and all creation by rising from the dead.

   e. The foreigners came to Jesus and asked, "The Savior who is about to appear has not come down from heaven, has He?"

   g. The women were afraid because the tax collectors were coming to ask how much wine they had.

2. English to Greek

εἶδόν σε γράφοντα ἐπιστολὴν τῇ ἐκκλησίᾳ (τῇ) ἐν τῇ μεγάλῃ πόλει.

Chapter 42

E. Practice Sentences

1. Greek to English

   a. Whoever receives such [sort of] a little child for the sake of Christ will inherit eternal life.

   c. A crowd gathered outside the house, before Jesus was able to return to His own village.

   e. Whoever tries to be saved by works will perish.

   g. The whole crowd asked the teacher if he had left money for the blind and lame.

2. English to Greek

   ὁ ὑπηρέτης ἔφη τὸν Ἰησοῦν κρινεῖν τοὺς πονηρούς.

Paradigms

A. Nouns

1. O or Second Declension

a. Masculine and Feminine

	Singular	Plural
N	λόγος	λόγοι
G	λόγου	λόγων
D	λόγῳ	λόγοις
A	λόγον	λόγους

b. Neuter

	Singular	Plural
N	τέκνον	τέκνα
G	τέκνου	τέκνων
D	τέκνῳ	τέκνοις
A	τέκνον	τέκνα

2. A or First Declension

a. Feminine

(1) α Pattern (2) η Pattern

	Singular	Plural		Singular	Plural
N	ἡμέρα	ἡμέραι		ἀγάπη	ἀγάπαι
G	ἡμέρας	ἡμερῶν		ἀγάπης	ἀγαπῶν
D	ἡμέρᾳ	ἡμέραις		ἀγάπῃ	ἀγάπαις
A	ἡμέραν	ἡμέρας		ἀγάπην	ἀγάπας

(3) Hybrid Pattern

	Singular	Plural
N	δόξα	δόξαι
G	δόξης	δοξῶν
D	δόξῃ	δόξαις
A	δόξαν	δόξας

b. Masculine

	Singular	Plural
N	προφήτης	προφῆται
G	προφήτου	προφητῶν
D	προφήτῃ	προφήταις
A	προφήτην	προφήτας

3. Third Declension

a. Consonantal Stem

(1) Masculine and Feminine

(a) Standard

	Singular	Plural
N	σωτήρ	σωτῆρες
G	σωτῆρος	σωτήρων
D	σωτῆρι	σωτῆρσι(ν)
A	σωτῆρα	σωτῆρας

(b) Monosyllable

	Singular	Plural
N	σάρξ	σάρκες
G	σαρκός	σαρκῶν
D	σαρκί	σαρξί(ν)
A	σάρκα	σάρκας

(2) Neuter

	Singular	Plural
N	πνεῦμα	πνεύματα
G	πνεύματος	πνευμάτων
D	πνεύματι	πνεύμασι(ν)
A	πνεῦμα	πνεύματα

b. Vowel Stem

(1) Feminine

	Singular	Plural
N	πόλις	πόλεις
G	πόλεως	πόλεων
D	πόλει	πόλεσι(ν)
A	πόλιν	πόλεις

(2) Masculine

	Singular	Plural
N	βασιλεύς	βασιλεῖς
G	βασιλέως	βασιλέων
D	βασιλεῖ	βασιλεῦσι(ν)
A	βασιλέα	βασιλεῖς / βασιλέας

c. Sigma Stem: Neuter

	Singular	Plural
N	ἔθνος	ἔθνη
G	ἔθνους	ἐθνῶν
D	ἔθνει	ἔθνεσι(ν)
A	ἔθνος	ἔθνη

d. Syncopated (Major)

(1) γυνή

	Singular	Plural
N	γυνή	γυναῖκες
G	γυναικός	γυναικῶν
D	γυναικί	γυναιξί(ν)
A	γυναῖκα	γυναῖκας

(2) ἀνήρ

	Singular	Plural
N	ἀνήρ	ἄνδρες
G	ἀνδρός	ἀνδρῶν
D	ἀνδρί	ἀνδράσι(ν)
A	ἄνδρα	ἄνδρας

(3) πατήρ

	Singular	Plural
N	πατήρ	πατέρες
G	πατρός	πατέρων
D	πατρί	πατράσι(ν)
A	πατέρα	πατέρας

B. The Article

	Singular		
	M	F	N
N	ὁ	ἡ	τό
G	τοῦ	τῆς	τοῦ
D	τῷ	τῇ	τῷ
A	τόν	τήν	τό

	Plural		
	M	F	N
N	οἱ	αἱ	τά
G	τῶν	τῶν	τῶν
D	τοῖς	ταῖς	τοῖς
A	τούς	τάς	τά

C. Adjectives

1. O (Second) Declension

a. Feminine Singular: η Pattern

Singular

	M	F	N
N	ἀγαθός	ἀγαθή	ἀγαθόν
G	ἀγαθοῦ	ἀγαθῆς	ἀγαθοῦ
D	ἀγαθῷ	ἀγαθῇ	ἀγαθῷ
A	ἀγαθόν	ἀγαθήν	ἀγαθόν

Plural

	M	F	N
N	ἀγαθοί	ἀγαθαί	ἀγαθά
G	ἀγαθῶν	ἀγαθῶν	ἀγαθῶν
D	ἀγαθοῖς	ἀγαθαῖς	ἀγαθοῖς
A	ἀγαθούς	ἀγαθάς	ἀγαθά

b. Feminine Singular: α Pattern

Singular

	M	F	N
N	δίκαιος	δικαία	δίκαιον
G	δικαίου	δικαίας	δικαίου
D	δικαίῳ	δικαίᾳ	δικαίῳ
A	δίκαιον	δικαίαν	δίκαιον

Plural

	M	F	N
N	δίκαιοι	δίκαιαι	δίκαια
G	δικαίων	δικαίων	δικαίων
D	δικαίοις	δικαίαις	δικαίοις
A	δικαίους	δικαίας	δίκαια

2. Third Declension

a. Consonantal Stem

	Singular		Plural	
	M/F	N	M/F	N
N	ἄφρων	ἄφρον	ἄφρονες	ἄφρονα
G	ἄφρονος	ἄφρονος	ἀφρόνων	ἀφρόνων
D	ἄφρονι	ἄφρονι	ἄφροσι(ν)	ἄφροσι(ν)
A	ἄφρονα	ἄφρον	ἄφρονας	ἄφρονα

Note: This pattern is also used for irregular comparative forms (cf. μείζων).

b. Sigma Stem

	Singular		Plural	
	M/F	**N**	**M/F**	**N**
N	ἀληθής	ἀληθές	ἀληθεῖς	ἀληθῆ
G	ἀληθοῦς	ἀληθοῦς	ἀληθῶν	ἀληθῶν
D	ἀληθεῖ	ἀληθεῖ	ἀληθέσι(ν)	ἀληθέσι(ν)
A	ἀληθῆ	ἀληθές	ἀληθεῖς	ἀληθῆ

c. Vowel Stem

	Singular		
	M	**F**	**N**
N	εὐθύς	εὐθεῖα	εὐθύ
G	εὐθέος	εὐθείας	εὐθέος
D	εὐθεῖ	εὐθείᾳ	εὐθεῖ
A	εὐθύν	εὐθεῖαν	εὐθύ

	Plural		
	M	**F**	**N**
N	εὐθεῖς	εὐθεῖαι	εὐθέα
G	εὐθέων	εὐθειῶν	εὐθέων
D	εὐθέσι(ν)	εὐθείαις	εὐθέσι(ν)
A	εὐθεῖς	εὐθείας	εὐθέα

3. Irregular (Major)

a. μέγας

	Singular		
	M	**F**	**N**
N	μέγας	μεγάλη	μέγα
G	μεγάλου	μεγάλης	μεγάλου
D	μεγάλῳ	μεγάλῃ	μεγάλῳ
A	μέγαν	μεγάλην	μέγα

	Plural		
	M	**F**	**N**
N	μεγάλοι	μεγάλαι	μεγάλα
G	μεγάλων	μεγάλων	μεγάλων
D	μεγάλοις	μεγάλαις	μεγάλοις
A	μεγάλους	μεγάλας	μεγάλα

b. πολύς

	Singular		
	M	**F**	**N**
N	πολύς	πολλή	πολύ
G	πολλοῦ	πολλῆς	πολλοῦ
D	πολλῷ	πολλῇ	πολλῷ
A	πολύν	πολλήν	πολύ

		Plural	
	M	F	N
N	πολλοί	πολλαί	πολλά
G	πολλῶν	πολλῶν	πολλῶν
D	πολλοῖς	πολλαῖς	πολλοῖς
A	πολλούς	πολλάς	πολλά

c. πᾶς

		Singular	
	M	F	N
N	πᾶς	πᾶσα	πᾶν
G	παντός	πάσης	παντός
D	παντί	πάσῃ	παντί
A	πάντα	πᾶσαν	πᾶν

		Plural	
	M	F	N
N	πάντες	πᾶσαι	πάντα
G	πάντων	πασῶν	πάντων
D	πᾶσι(ν)	πάσαις	πᾶσι(ν)
A	πάντας	πάσας	πάντα

D. Pronouns

1. Personal

a. First Person

	Singular	Plural
N	ἐγώ	ἡμεῖς
G	ἐμοῦ / μου	ἡμῶν
D	ἐμοί / μοι	ἡμῖν
A	ἐμέ / με	ἡμᾶς

b. Second Person

	Singular	Plural
N	σύ	ὑμεῖς
G	σοῦ / σου	ὑμῶν
D	σοί / σοι	ὑμῖν
A	σέ / σε	ὑμᾶς

c. Third Person

		Singular	
	M	F	N
N	αὐτός	αὐτή	αὐτό
G	αὐτοῦ	αὐτῆς	αὐτοῦ
D	αὐτῷ	αὐτῇ	αὐτῷ
A	αὐτόν	αὐτήν	αὐτό

Plural

	M	F	N
N	αὐτοί	αὐταί	αὐτά
G	αὐτῶν	αὐτῶν	αὐτῶν
D	αὐτοῖς	αὐταῖς	αὐτοῖς
A	αὐτούς	αὐτάς	αὐτά

2. Demonstrative

a. οὗτος

Singular

	M	F	N
N	οὗτος	αὕτη	τοῦτο
G	τούτου	ταύτης	τούτου
D	τούτῳ	ταύτῃ	τούτῳ
A	τοῦτον	ταύτην	τοῦτο

Plural

	M	F	N
N	οὗτοι	αὗται	ταῦτα
G	τούτων	τούτων	τούτων
D	τούτοις	ταύταις	τούτοις
A	τούτους	ταύτας	ταῦτα

b. ἐκεῖνος

Singular

	M	F	N
N	ἐκεῖνος	ἐκείνη	ἐκεῖνο
G	ἐκείνου	ἐκείνης	ἐκείνου
D	ἐκείνῳ	ἐκείνῃ	ἐκείνῳ
A	ἐκεῖνον	ἐκείνην	ἐκεῖνο

Plural

	M	F	N
N	ἐκεῖνοι	ἐκεῖναι	ἐκεῖνα
G	ἐκείνων	ἐκείνων	ἐκείνων
D	ἐκείνοις	ἐκείναις	ἐκείνοις
A	ἐκείνους	ἐκείνας	ἐκεῖνα

3. Relative

	Singular				Plural		
	M	F	N		M	F	N
N	ὅς	ἥ	ὅ	N	οἵ	αἵ	ἅ
G	οὗ	ἧς	οὗ	G	ὧν	ὧν	ὧν
D	ᾧ	ᾗ	ᾧ	D	οἷς	αἷς	οἷς
A	ὅν	ἥν	ὅ	A	οὕς	ἅς	ἅ

4. Interrogative

	Singular		Plural	
	M/F	N	M/F	N
N	τίς	τί	τίνες	τίνα
G	τίνος	τίνος	τίνων	τίνων
D	τίνι	τίνι	τίσι(ν)	τίσι(ν)
A	τίνα	τί	τίνας	τίνα

5. Reflexive

a. Singular

(1) First Person

	M	F	N
N	———	———	———
G	ἐμαυτοῦ	ἐμαυτῆς	ἐμαυτοῦ
D	ἐμαυτῷ	ἐμαυτῇ	ἐμαυτῷ
A	ἐμαυτόν	ἐμαυτήν	ἐμαυτό

(2) Second Person

	M	F	N
N	———	———	———
G	σεαυτοῦ	σεαυτῆς	σεαυτοῦ
D	σεαυτῷ	σεαυτῇ	σεαυτῷ
A	σεαυτόν	σεαυτήν	σεαυτό

(3) Third Person

	M	F	N
N	———	———	———
G	ἑαυτοῦ	ἑαυτῆς	ἑαυτοῦ
D	ἑαυτῷ	ἑαυτῇ	ἑαυτῷ
A	ἑαυτόν	ἑαυτήν	ἑαυτό

b. Plural (All Persons)

	M	F	N
N	———	———	———
G	ἑαυτῶν	ἑαυτῶν	ἑαυτῶν
D	ἑαυτοῖς	ἑαυταῖς	ἑαυτοῖς
A	ἑαυτούς	ἑαυτάς	ἑαυτά

6. Reciprocal (Plural Only)

	M	F	N
N	———	———	———
G	ἀλλήλων	ἀλλήλων	ἀλλήλων
D	ἀλλήλοις	ἀλλήλαις	ἀλλήλοις
A	ἀλλήλους	ἀλλήλας	ἀλλήλα

E. Numerals

1. One

	M	F	N
N	εἷς	μία	ἕν
G	ἑνός	μιᾶς	ἑνός
D	ἑνί	μιᾷ	ἑνί
A	ἕνα	μίαν	ἕν

2. Three

	M/F	N
N	τρεῖς	τρία
G	τριῶν	τριῶν
D	τρισί(ν)	τρισί(ν)
A	τρεῖς	τρία

3. Four

	M/F	N
N	τέσσαρες	τέσσαρα
G	τεσσάρων	τεσσάρων
D	τέσσαρσι(ν)	τέσσαρσι(ν)
A	τέσσαρας	τέσσαρα

F. Verbs: Finite and Infinitive[1]

---

1. For participles, see the charts in the next section (G).

   Forms in brackets are extremely rare in the NT but may be encountered in other κοινή Greek literature.

1. Regular, Weak: λύω

Aspect/focus:	Connection				
Common name:	"Present"		"Future"[2]		
Principal part:	1st		2nd		(6th)
Stem:	λυ-		λυσ-		λυθησ-
Voice:	Active	Middle/Passive	Active	Middle	Passive

Mood:

Indicative

Non-past time

λύω	λύομαι	λύσω	λύσομαι	λυθήσομαι
λύεις	λύῃ	λύσεις	λύσῃ	λυθήσῃ
λύει	λύεται	λύσει	λύσεται	λυθήσεται
λύομεν	λυόμεθα	λύσομεν	λυσόμεθα	λυθησόμεθα
λύετε	λύεσθε	λύσετε	λύσεσθε	λυθήσεσθε
λύουσι(ν)	λύονται	λύσουσι(ν)	λύσονται	λυθήσονται

Past time

(Imperfect)

ἔλυον	ἐλυόμην
ἔλυες	ἐλύου
ἔλυε(ν)	ἐλύετο
ἐλύομεν	ἐλυόμεθα
ἐλύετε	ἐλύεσθε
ἔλυον	ἐλύοντο

Subjunctive

λύω	λύωμαι
λύῃς	λύῃ
λύῃ	λύηται
λύωμεν	λυώμεθα
λύητε	λύησθε
λύωσι(ν)	λύωνται

Optative

λύοιμι	λυοίμην	[λύσοιμι	λυσοίμην	λυθησοίμην
λύοις	λύοιο	λύσοις	λύσοιο	λυθήσοιο
λύοι	λύοιτο	λύσοι	λύσοιτο	λυθήσοιτο
λύοιμεν	λυοίμεθα	λύσοιμεν	λυσοίμεθα	λυθήσοιμεθα
λύοιτε	λύοισθε	λύσοιτε	λύσοισθε	λυθήσοισθε
λύοιεν	λύοιντο	λύσοιεν	λύσοιντο	λυθήσοιντο]

Imperative

2s	λῦε	λύου
3s	λυέτω	λυέσθω
2p	λύετε	λύεσθε
3p	λυέτωσαν	λυέσθωσαν

Infinitive	λύειν	λύεσθαι	[λύσειν	λύσεσθαι	λυθήσεσθαι]

2. See footnote 1, chapter 9.

Aspect/focus:	Action			Result	
Common name:	"Aorist"			"Perfect"	
Principal part:	3rd		6th	4th	5th
Stem:	λυσ-		λυθη-	λελυκ-	λελυ-
Voice:	Active	Middle	Passive	Active	Middle/Passive

Mood:

Indicative — Non-past time

	Active	Middle	Passive	Active	Middle/Passive
				λέλυκα	λέλυμαι
				λέλυκας	λέλυσαι
				λέλυκε(ν)	λέλυται
				λελύκαμεν	λελύμεθα
				λελύκατε	λέλυσθε
				λελύκασι(ν)	λέλυνται

(Pluperfect)

Indicative — Past time

	Active	Middle	Passive	Active	Middle/Passive
	ἔλυσα	ἐλυσάμην	ἐλύθην	ἐλελύκειν	ἐλελύμην
	ἔλυσας	ἐλύσω	ἐλύθης	ἐλελύκεις	ἐλέλυσο
	ἔλυσε(ν)	ἐλύσατο	ἐλύθη	ἐλελύκει	ἐλέλυτο
	ἐλύσαμεν	ἐλυσάμεθα	ἐλύθημεν	ἐλελύκειμεν	ἐλελύμεθα
	ἐλύσατε	ἐλύσασθε	ἐλύθητε	ἐλελύκειτε	ἐλέλυσθε
	ἔλυσαν	ἐλύσαντο	ἐλύθησαν	ἐλελύκεισαν	ἐλέλυντο

Subjunctive

	Active	Middle	Passive	Active	Middle/Passive
	λύσω	λύσωμαι	λυθῶ	λελύκω	λελυμένος ὦ
	λύσῃς	λύσῃ	λυθῇς	λελύκῃς	λελυμένος ᾖς
	λύσῃ	λύσηται	λυθῇ	λελύκῃ	λελυμένος ᾖ
	λύσωμεν	λυσώμεθα	λυθῶμεν	λελύκωμεν	λελυμένοι ὦμεν
	λύσητε	λύσησθε	λυθῆτε	λελύκητε	λελυμένοι ἦτε
	λύσωσι(ν)	λύσωνται	λυθῶσι(ν)	λελύκωσι(ν)	λελυμένοι ὦσι(ν)

Optative

	Active	Middle	Passive	Active	Middle/Passive
	λύσαιμι	λυσαίμην	λυθείην	[λελύκοιμι	λελυμένος εἴην
	λύσαις	λύσαιο	λυθείης	λελύκοις	λελυμένος εἴης
	λύσαι	λύσαιτο	λυθείη	λελύκοι	λελυμένος εἴη
	λύσαιμεν	λυσαίμεθα	λυθείημεν	λελύκοιμεν	λελυμένοι εἴημεν
	λύσαιτε	λύσαισθε	λυθείητε	λελύκοιτε	λελυμένοι εἴητε
	λύσαιεν	λύσαιντο	λυθείησαν	λελύκοιεν	λελυμένοι εἴησαν]

Imperative

	Active	Middle	Passive	Active	Middle/Passive
2s	λῦσον	λῦσαι	λύθητι	λέλυκε	λέλυσο
3s	λυσάτω	λυσάσθω	λυθήτω	λελυκάτω	λελύσθω
2p	λύσατε	λύσασθε	λύθητε	λελύκατε	λέλυσθε
3p	λυσάτωσαν	λυσάσθωσαν	λυθήτωσαν	λελυκάτωσαν	λελύσθωσαν

Infinitive

	Active	Middle	Passive	Active	Middle/Passive
	λῦσαι	λύσασθαι	λυθῆναι	λελυκέναι	λελύσθαι

2. Irregular, Strong: λείπω

Aspect/focus:	Connection				
Common name:	"Present"		"Future"		
Principal part:	1st		2nd		(6th)
Stem:	λειπ-		λειψ-		λειφθησ-
Voice:	Active	Middle/ Passive	Active	Middle	Passive

Mood:

Indicative — Non-past time

λείπω	λείπομαι	λείψω	λείψομαι	λειφθήσομαι
λείπεις	λείπῃ	λείψεις	λείψῃ	λειφθήσῃ
λείπει	λείπεται	λείψει	λείψεται	λειφθήσεται
λείπομεν	λειπόμεθα	λείψομεν	λειψόμεθα	λειφθησόμεθα
λείπετε	λείπεσθε	λείψετε	λείψεσθε	λειφθήσεσθε
λείπουσι(ν)	λείπονται	λείψουσι(ν)	λείψονται	λειφθήσονται

Indicative — Past time (Imperfect)

ἔλειπον	ἐλειπόμην
ἔλειπες	ἐλείπου
ἔλειπε(ν)	ἐλείπετο
ἐλείπομεν	ἐλειπόμεθα
ἐλείπετε	ἐλείπεσθε
ἔλειπον	ἐλείποντο

Subjunctive

λείπω	λείπωμαι
λείπῃς	λείπῃ
λείπῃ	λείπηται
λείπωμεν	λειπώμεθα
λείπητε	λείπησθε
λείπωσι(ν)	λείπωνται

Optative

λείποιμι	λειποίμην	[λείψοιμι	λειψοίμην	λειφθησοίμην
λείποις	λείποιο	λείψοις	λείψοιο	λειφθήσοιο
λείποι	λείποιτο	λείψοι	λείψοιτο	λειφθήσοιτο
λείποιμεν	λειποίμεθα	λείψοιμεν	λειψοίμεθα	λειφθήσοιμεθα
λείποιτε	λείποισθε	λείψοιτε	λείψοισθε	λειφθήσοισθε
λείποιεν	λείποιντο	λείψοιεν	λείψοιντο	λειφθήσοιντο]

Imperative

2s	λεῖπε	λείπου
3s	λειπέτω	λειπέσθω
2p	λείπετε	λείπεσθε
3p	λειπέτωσαν	λειπέσθωσαν

Infinitive

λείπειν	λείπεσθαι	[λείψειν	λείψεσθαι	λειφθήσεσθαι]

Aspect/focus:	Action			Result	
Common name:	"Aorist"			"Perfect"	
Principal part:	3rd		6th	4th	5th
Stem:	λιπ-		λειφθη-	λελοιπ-	λελειπ-
Voice:	Active	Middle	Passive	Active	Middle/Passive

Mood:

Indicative — Non-past time

	Active	Middle	Passive	Active	Middle/Passive
				λέλοιπα	λέλειμμαι
				λέλοιπας	λέλειψαι
				λέλοιπε(ν)	λέλειπται
				λελοίπαμεν	λελείμμεθα
				λελοίπατε	λέλειφθε
				λελοίπασι(ν)	λελειμμένοι ἐισί(ν)

(Pluperfect)

Indicative — Past time

	Active	Middle	Passive	Active	Middle/Passive
	ἔλιπον	ἐλιπόμην	ἐλείφθην	ἐλελοίπειν	ἐλελείμμην
	ἔλιπες	ἐλίπου	ἐλείφθης	ἐλελοίπεις	ἐλέλειψο
	ἔλιπε(ν)	ἐλίπετο	ἐλείφθη	ἐλελοίπει	ἐλέλειπτο
	ἐλίπομεν	ἐλιπόμεθα	ἐλείφθημεν	ἐλελοίπειμεν	ἐλελείμμεθα
	ἐλίπετε	ἐλίπεσθε	ἐλείφθητε	ἐλελοίπειτε	ἐλέλειφθε
	ἔλιπον	ἐλίποντο	ἐλείφθησαν	ἐλελοίπεισαν	λελειμμένοι ἦσαν

Subjunctive

	Active	Middle	Passive	Active	Middle/Passive
	λίπω	λίπωμαι	λειφθῶ	λελοίπω	λελειμμένος ὦ
	λίπῃς	λίπῃ	λειφθῇς	λελοίπῃς	λελειμμένος ᾖς
	λίπῃ	λίπηται	λειφθῇ	λελοίπῃ	λελειμμένος ᾖ
	λίπωμεν	λιπώμεθα	λειφθῶμεν	λελοίπωμεν	λελειμμένοι ὦμεν
	λίπητε	λίπησθε	λειφθῆτε	λελοίπητε	λελειμμένοι ἦτε
	λίπωσι(ν)	λίπωνται	λειφθῶσι(ν)	λελοίπωσι(ν)	λελειμμένοι ὦσι(ν)

Optative

	Active	Middle	Passive	Active	Middle/Passive
	λίποιμι	λιποίμην	λειφθείην	[λελοίποιμι	λελειμμένος εἴην
	λίποις	λίποιο	λειφθείης	λελοίποις	λελειμμένος εἴης
	λίποι	λίποιτο	λειφθείη	λελοίποι	λελειμμένος εἴη
	λίποιμεν	λιποίμεθα	λειφθείημεν	λελοίποιμεν	λελειμμένοι εἴημεν
	λίποιτε	λίποισθε	λειφθείητε	λελοιποιτε	λελειμμένοι εἴητε
	λίποιεν	λίποιντο	λειφθείησαν	λελοίποιεν	λελειμμένοι εἴησαν\

Imperative

	Active	Middle	Passive	Active	Middle/Passive
2s	λίπε	λιποῦ	λείφθητι	λέλοιπε	λέλειψο
3s	λιπέτω	λιπέσθω	λειφθήτω	λελοιπάτω	λελείφθω
2p	λίπετε	λίπεσθε	λείφθητε	λελοίπατε	λέλειφθε
3p	λιπέτωσαν	λιπέσθωσαν	λειφθήτωσαν	λελοιπάτωσαν	λελείφθωσαν

Infinitive

	Active	Middle	Passive	Active	Middle/Passive
	λιπεῖν	λιπέσθαι	λειφθῆναι	λελοιπέναι	λελεῖφθαι

3. Liquid: φθείρω: 2nd, 3rd, and (Strong) 6th Principal Parts

Aspect/focus:
Common name: "Future"
Principal part: 2nd   (6th)
Stem: φθερω⁻   φθαρησ⁻
Voice: Active   Middle   Passive

Mood:

	Active	Middle	Passive
Indicative — Non-past time	φθερῶ	φθεροῦμαι	φθαρήσομαι
	φθερεῖς	φθερῇ	φθαρήσῃ
	φθερεῖ	φθερεῖται	φθαρήσεται
	φθεροῦμεν	φθερούμεθα	φθαρησόμεθα
	φθερεῖτε	φθερεῖσθε	φθαρήσεσθε
	φθεροῦσι(ν)	φθεροῦνται	φθαρήσονται

Indicative — Past time

Subjunctive

Optative   (Rare)

Imperative

Infinitive   [φθερεῖν   φθερεῖσθαι   φθαρήσεσθαι]

Aspect/focus:		Action	
Common name:		"Aorist"	
Principal part:		3rd	6th
Stem:		φθειρ-	φθαρη-
Voice:	Active	Middle	Passive

Mood:

		Active	Middle	Passive
Indicative	Non-past time			
	Past time	ἔφθειρα	ἐφθειράμην	ἐφθάρην
		ἔφθειρας	ἐφθείρω	ἐφθάρης
		ἔφθειρε(ν)	ἐφθείρατο	ἐφθάρη
		ἐφθείραμεν	ἐφθειράμεθα	ἐφθάρημεν
		ἐφθείρατε	ἐφθείρασθε	ἐφθάρητε
		ἔφθειραν	ἐφθείραντο	ἐφθάρησαν
Subjunctive		φθείρω	φθείρωμαι	φθαρῶ
		φθείρῃς	φθείρῃ	φθαρῇς
		φθείρῃ	φθείρηται	φθαρῇ
		φθείρωμεν	φθειρώμεθα	φθαρῶμεν
		φθείρητε	φθείρησθε	φθαρῆτε
		φθείρωσι(ν)	φθείρωνται	φθαρῶσι(ν)
Optative		φθείραιμι	φθειραίμην	φθαρείην
		φθείραις	φθείραιο	φθαρείης
		φθείραι	φθείραιτο	φθαρείη
		φθείραιμεν	φθειραίμεθα	φθαρείημεν
		φθείραιτε	φθείραισθε	φθαρείητε
		φθείραιεν	φθείραιντο	φθαρείησαν
Imperative	**2s**	φθεῖρον	φθεῖραι	φθάρητι
	3s	φθειράτω	φθειράσθω	φθαρήτω
	2p	φθείρατε	φθείρασθε	φθάρητε
	3p	φθειράτωσαν	φθειράσθωσαν	φθαρήτωσαν
Infinitive		φθεῖραι	φθείρασθαι	φθαρῆναι

4. Contract(ed)

a. φιλέω

Aspect/focus:	Connection				
Common name:	"Present"			"Future"	
Principal part:	1st		2nd		(6th)
Stem:	φιλε⁻		φιλησ⁻		φιληθησ⁻
Voice:	Active	Middle/ Passive	Active	Middle	Passive

Mood:

Indicative — Non-past time

Active	Middle/Passive	Active	Middle	Passive
φιλῶ	φιλοῦμαι	φιλήσω	φιλήσομαι	φιληθήσομαι
φιλεῖς	φιλῇ	φιλήσεις	φιλήσῃ	φιληθήσῃ
φιλεῖ	φιλεῖται	φιλήσει	φιλήσεται	φιληθήσεται
φιλοῦμεν	φιλούμεθα	φιλήσομεν	φιλησόμεθα	φιληθησόμεθα
φιλεῖτε	φιλεῖσθε	φιλήσετε	φιλήσεσθε	φιληθήσεσθε
φιλοῦσι(ν)	φιλοῦνται	φιλήσουσι(ν)	φιλήσονται	φιληθήσονται

Indicative — Past time **(Imperfect)**

Active	Middle/Passive
ἐφίλουν	ἐφιλούμην
ἐφίλεις	ἐφιλοῦ
ἐφίλει	ἐφιλεῖτο
ἐφιλοῦμεν	ἐφιλούμεθα
ἐφιλεῖτε	ἐφιλεῖσθε
ἐφίλουν	ἐφιλοῦντο

Subjunctive

Active	Middle/Passive
φιλῶ	φιλῶμαι
φιλῇς	φιλῇ
φιλῇ	φιλῆται
φιλῶμεν	φιλώμεθα
φιλῆτε	φιλῆσθε
φιλῶσι(ν)	φιλῶνται

Optative

Active	Middle/Passive	Active	Middle	Passive
φιλοῖμι	φιλοίμην	[φιλήσοιμι	φιλησοίμην	φιληθησοίμην
φιλοῖς	φιλοῖο	φιλήσοις	φιλήσοιο	φιληθήσοιο
φιλοῖ	φιλοῖτο	φιλήσοι	φιλήσοιτο	φιληθήσοιτο
φιλοῖμεν	φιλοίμεθα	φιλήσοιμεν	φιλησοίμεθα	φιληθησοίμεθα
φιλοῖτε	φιλοῖσθε	φιλήσοιτε	φιλήσοισθε	φιληθήσοισθε
φιλοῖεν	φιλοῖντο	φιλήσοιεν	φιλήσοιντο	φιληθήσοιντο]

Imperative

	Active	Middle/Passive
2s	φίλει	φιλοῦ
3s	φιλείτω	φιλείσθω
2p	φιλεῖτε	φιλεῖσθε
3p	φιλείτωσαν	φιλείσθωσαν

Infinitive	φιλεῖν	φιλεῖσθαι	[φιλήσειν	φιλήσεσθαι	φιληθήσεσθαι]

Aspect/focus:	Action			Result	
Common name:	"Aorist"			"Perfect"	
Principal part:	3rd		6th	4th	5th
Stem:	φιλησ-		φιληθη-	πεφιληκ-	πεφιλη-
Voice:	Active	Middle	Passive	Active	Middle/ Passive

Mood:

Indicative — Non-past time

				πεφίληκα	πεφίλημαι
				πεφίληκας	πεφίλησαι
				πεφίληκε(ν)	πεφίληται
				πεφιλήκαμεν	πεφιλήμεθα
				πεφιλήκατε	πεφίλησθε
				πεφιλήκασι(ν)	πεφίληνται

(Pluperfect)

Indicative — Past time

Active	Middle	Passive	Active	Middle/Passive
ἐφίλησα	ἐφιλησάμην	ἐφιλήθην	ἐπεφιλήκειν	ἐπεφιλήμην
ἐφίλησας	ἐφιλήσω	ἐφιλήθης	ἐπεφιλήκεις	ἐπεφίλησο
ἐφίλησε(ν)	ἐφιλήσατο	ἐφιλήθη	ἐπεφιλήκει	ἐπεφίλητο
ἐφιλήσαμεν	ἐφιλησάμεθα	ἐφιλήθημεν	ἐπεφιλήκειμεν	ἐπεφιλήμεθα
ἐφιλήσατε	ἐφιλήσασθε	ἐφιλήθητε	ἐπεφιλήκειτε	ἐπεφίλησθε
ἐφίλησαν	ἐφιλήσαντο	ἐφιλήθησαν	ἐπεφιλήκεισαν	ἐπεφίληντο

Subjunctive

φιλήσω	φιλήσωμαι	φιληθῶ	πεφιλήκω	πεφιλημένος ὦ
φιλήσῃς	φιλήσῃ	φιληθῇς	πεφιλήκῃς	πεφιλημένος ᾖς
φιλήσῃ	φιλήσηται	φιληθῇ	πεφιλήκῃ	πεφιλημένος ᾖ
φιλήσωμεν	φιλησώμεθα	φιληθῶμεν	πεφιλήκωμεν	πεφιλημένοι ὦμεν
φιλήσητε	φιλήσησθε	φιληθῆτε	πεφιλήκητε	πεφιλημένοι ἦτε
φιλήσωσι(ν)	φιλήσωνται	φιληθῶσι(ν)	πεφιλήκωσι(ν)	πεφιλημένοι ὦσι(ν)

Optative

φιλήσαιμι	φιλησαίμην	φιληθείην	[πεφιλήκοιμι	πεφιλημένος εἴην
φιλήσαις	φιλήσαιο	φιληθείης	πεφιλήκοις	πεφιλημένος εἴης
φιλήσαι	φιλήσαιτο	φιληθείη	πεφιλήκοι	πεφιλημένος εἴη
φιλήσαιμεν	φιλησαίμεθα	φιληθείημεν	πεφιλήκοιμεν	πεφιλημένοι εἴημεν
φιλήσαιτε	φιλήσαισθε	φιληθείητε	πεφιλήκοιτε	πεφιλημένοι εἴητε
φιλήσαιεν	φιλήσαιντο	φιληθείησαν	πεφιλήκοιεν	πεφιλημένοι εἴησαν]

Imperative

	Active	Middle	Passive	Active	Middle/Passive
2s	φίλησον	φίλησαι	φιλήθητι	πεφίληκε	πεφίλησο
3s	φιλησάτω	φιλησάσθω	φιληθήτω	πεφιληκάτω	πεφιλήσθω
2p	φιλήσατε	φιλήσασθε	φιλήθητε	πεφιλήκατε	πεφίλησθε
3p	φιλησάτωσαν	φιλησάσθωσαν	φιληθήτωσαν	πεφιληκάτωσαν	πεφιλήσθωσαν

Infinitive

φιλῆσαι	φιλήσασθαι	φιληθῆναι	πεφιληκέναι	πεφιλῆσθαι

b. τιμάω

Aspect/focus:	Connection				
Common name:	"Present"			"Future"	
Principal part:	1st		2nd		(6th)
Stem:	τιμα⁻		τιμησ⁻		τιμηθησ⁻
Voice:	Active	Middle/Passive	Active	Middle	Passive

Mood:

Indicative

Non-past time

τιμῶ	τιμῶμαι	τιμήσω	τιμήσομαι	τιμηθήσομαι
τιμᾷς	τιμᾷ	τιμήσεις	τιμήσῃ	τιμηθήσῃ
τιμᾷ	τιμᾶται	τιμήσει	τιμήσεται	τιμηθήσεται
τιμῶμεν	τιμώμεθα	τιμήσομεν	τιμησόμεθα	τιμηθησόμεθα
τιμᾶτε	τιμᾶσθε	τιμήσετε	τιμήσεσθε	τιμηθήσεσθε
τιμῶσι(ν)	τιμῶνται	τιμήσουσι(ν)	τιμήσονται	τιμηθήσονται

Past time

(Imperfect)

ἐτίμων	ἐτιμώμην
ἐτίμας	ἐτιμῶ
ἐτίμα	ἐτιμᾶτο
ἐτιμῶμεν	ἐτιμώμεθα
ἐτιμᾶτε	ἐτιμᾶσθε
ἐτίμων	ἐτιμῶντο

Subjunctive

τιμῶ	τιμῶμαι
τιμᾷς	τιμᾷ
τιμᾷ	τιμᾶται
τιμῶμεν	τιμώμεθα
τιμᾶτε	τιμᾶσθε
τιμῶσι(ν)	τιμῶνται

Optative

τιμῷμι	τιμώμην	[τιμήσοιμι	τιμησοίμην	τιμηθησοίμην
τιμῷς	τιμῷο	τιμήσοις	τιμήσοιο	τιμηθήσοιο
τιμῷ	τιμῷτο	τιμήσοι	τιμήσοιτο	τιμηθήσοιτο
τιμῷμεν	τιμώμεθα	τιμήσοιμεν	τιμησοίμεθα	τιμηθησοίμεθα
τιμῷτε	τιμῷσθε	τιμήσοιτε	τιμήσοισθε	τιμηθήσοισθε
τιμῷεν	τιμῷντο	τιμήσοιεν	τιμήσοιντο	τιμηθήσοιντο]

Imperative

2s	τίμα	τιμῶ
3s	τιμάτω	τιμάσθω
2p	τιμᾶτε	τιμᾶσθε
3p	τιμάτωσαν	τιμάσθωσαν

Infinitive	τιμᾶν	τιμᾶσθαι	[τιμήσειν	τιμήσεσθαι	τιμηθήσεσθαι]

Aspect/focus:	Action			Result	
Common name:	"Aorist"			"Perfect"	
Principal part:	3rd		6th	4th	5th
Stem:	τιμησ-		τιμηθη-	τετιμηκ-	τετιμη-
Voice:	Active	Middle	Passive	Active	Middle/ Passive

Mood:

Indicative

Non-past time

				τετίμηκα	τετίμημαι
				τετίμηκας	τετίμησαι
				τετίμηκε(ν)	τετίμηται
				τετιμήκαμεν	τετιμήμεθα
				τετιμήκατε	τετίμησθε
				τετιμήκασι(ν)	τετίμηνται

(Pluperfect)

Past time

ἐτίμησα	ἐτιμησάμην	ἐτιμήθην	ἐτετιμήκειν	ἐτετιμήμην
ἐτίμησας	ἐτιμήσω	ἐτιμήθης	ἐτετιμήκεις	ἐτετίμησο
ἐτίμησε(ν)	ἐτιμήσατο	ἐτιμήθη	ἐτετιμήκει	ἐτετίμητο
ἐτιμήσαμεν	ἐτιμησάμεθα	ἐτιμήθημεν	ἐτετιμήκειμεν	ἐτετιμήμεθα
ἐτιμήσατε	ἐτιμήσασθε	ἐτιμήθητε	ἐτετιμήκειτε	ἐτετίμησθε
ἐτίμησαν	ἐτιμήσαντο	ἐτιμήθησαν	ἐτετιμήκεισαν	ἐτετίμηντο

Subjunctive

τιμήσω	τιμήσωμαι	τιμηθῶ	τετιμήκω	τετιμημένος ὦ
τιμήσῃς	τιμήσῃ	τιμηθῇς	τετιμήκῃς	τετιμημένος ᾖς
τιμήσῃ	τιμήσηται	τιμηθῇ	τετιμήκῃ	τετιμημένος ᾖ
τιμήσωμεν	τιμησώμεθα	τιμηθῶμεν	τετιμήκωμεν	τετιμημένοι ὦμεν
τιμήσητε	τιμήσησθε	τιμηθῆτε	τετιμήκητε	τετιμημένοι ἦτε
τιμήσωσι(ν)	τιμήσωνται	τιμηθῶσι(ν)	τετιμήκωσι(ν)	τετιμημένοι ὦσι(ν)

Optative

τιμήσαιμι	τιμησαίμην	τιμηθείην	[τετιμήκοιμι	τετιμημένος εἴην
τιμήσαις	τιμήσαιο	τιμηθείης	τετιμήκοις	τετιμημένος εἴης
τιμήσαι	τιμήσαιτο	τιμηθείη	τετιμήκοι	τετιμημένος εἴη
τιμήσαιμεν	τιμησαίμεθα	τιμηθείημεν	τετιμήκοιμεν	τετιμημένοι εἶμεν
τιμήσαιτε	τιμήσαισθε	τιμηθείητε	τετιμήκοιτε	τετιμημένοι εἶητε
τιμήσαιεν	τιμήσαιντο	τιμηθείησαν	τετιμήκοιεν	τετιμημένοι εἶησαι]

Imperative

2s	τίμησον	τίμησαι	τιμήθητι	τετίμηκε	τετίμησο
3s	τιμησάτω	τιμησάσθω	τιμηθήτω	τετιμηκάτω	τετιμήσθω
2p	τιμήσατε	τιμήσασθε	τιμήθητε	τετιμήκατε	τετίμησθε
3p	τιμησάτωσαν	τιμησάσθωσαν	τιμηθήτωσαν	τετιμηκάτωσαν	τετιμήσθωσαν

Infinitive τιμῆσαι τιμήσασθαι τιμηθῆναι τετιμηκέναι τετιμῆσθαι

c. *δηλόω*

Aspect/focus:	Connection				
Common name:	"Present"		"Future"		
Principal part:	1st		2nd		(6th)
Stem:	*δηλο-*		*δηλωσ-*		*δηλωθησ-*
Voice:	Active	Middle/ Passive	Active	Middle	Passive

Mood:

Indicative — Non-past time

δηλῶ	*δηλοῦμαι*	*δηλώσω*	*δηλώσομαι*	*δηλωθήσομαι*
δηλοῖς	*δηλοῖ*	*δηλώσεις*	*δηλώσῃ*	*δηλωθήσῃ*
δηλοῖ	*δηλοῦται*	*δηλώσει*	*δηλώσεται*	*δηλωθήσεται*
δηλοῦμεν	*δηλούμεθα*	*δηλώσομεν*	*δηλωσόμεθα*	*δηλωθησόμεθα*
δηλοῦτε	*δηλοῦσθε*	*δηλώσετε*	*δηλώσεσθε*	*δηλωθήσεσθε*
δηλοῦσι(ν)	*δηλοῦνται*	*δηλώσουσι(ν)*	*δηλώσονται*	*δηλωθήσονται*

Indicative — Past time (Imperfect)

ἐδήλουν	*ἐδηλούμην*
ἐδήλους	*ἐδηλοῦ*
ἐδήλου	*ἐδηλοῦτο*
ἐδηλοῦμεν	*ἐδηλούμεθα*
ἐδηλοῦτε	*ἐδηλοῦσθε*
ἐδήλουν	*ἐδηλοῦντο*

Subjunctive

δηλῶ	*δηλῶμαι*
δηλοῖς	*δηλοῖ*
δηλοῖ	*δηλῶται*
δηλῶμεν	*δηλώμεθα*
δηλῶτε	*δηλῶσθε*
δηλῶσι(ν)	*δηλῶνται*

Optative

δηλοῖμι	*δηλοίμην*	[*δηλώσοιμι*	*δηλωσοίμην*	*δηλωθησοίμην*
δηλοῖς	*δηλοῖο*	*δηλώσοις*	*δηλώσοιο*	*δηλωθήσοιο*
δηλοῖ	*δηλοῖτο*	*δηλώσοι*	*δηλώσοιτο*	*δηλωθήσοιτο*
δηλοῖμεν	*δηλοίμεθα*	*δηλώσοιμεν*	*δηλωσοίμεθα*	*δηλωθησοίμεθα*
δηλοῖτε	*δηλοῖσθε*	*δηλώσοιτε*	*δηλώσοισθε*	*δηλωθήσοισθε*
δηλοῖεν	*δηλοῖντο*	*δηλώσοιεν*	*δηλώσοιντο*	*δηλωθήσοιντο*]

Imperative

2s	*δήλου*	*δηλοῦ*
3s	*δηλούτω*	*δηλούσθω*
2p	*δηλοῦτε*	*δηλοῦσθε*
3p	*δηλούτωσαν*	*δηλούσθωσαν*

Infinitive *δηλοῦν*   *δηλοῦσθαι*   [*δηλώσειν*   *δηλώσεσθαι*   *δηλωθήσεσθαι*]

Aspect/focus:	Action			Result	
Common name:	"Aorist"			"Perfect"	
Principal part:	3rd		6th	4th	5th
Stem:	δηλωσ-		δηλωθη-	δεδηλωκ-	δεδηλω-
Voice:	Active	Middle	Passive	Active	Middle/Passive

Mood:

Indicative — Non-past time

				Active	Middle/Passive
				δεδήλωκα	δεδήλωμαι
				δεδήλωκας	δεδήλωσαι
				δεδήλωκε(ν)	δεδήλωται
				δεδηλώκαμεν	δεδηλώμεθα
				δεδηλώκατε	δεδήλωσθε
				δεδηλώκασι(ν)	δεδήλωνται

(Pluperfect)

Indicative — Past time

Active	Middle	Passive	Active	Middle/Passive
ἐδήλωσα	ἐδηλωσάμην	ἐδηλώθην	ἐδεδηλώκειν	ἐδεδηλώμην
ἐδήλωσας	ἐδηλώσω	ἐδηλώθης	ἐδεδηλώκεις	ἐδεδήλωσο
ἐδήλωσε(ν)	ἐδηλώσατο	ἐδηλώθη	ἐδεδηλώκει	ἐδεδήλωτο
ἐδηλώσαμεν	ἐδηλωσάμεθα	ἐδηλώθημεν	ἐδεδηλώκειμεν	ἐδεδηλώμεθα
ἐδηλώσατε	ἐδηλώσασθε	ἐδηλώθητε	ἐδεδηλώκειτε	ἐδεδήλωσθε
ἐδήλωσαν	ἐδηλώσαντο	ἐδηλώθησαν	ἐδεδηλώκεισαν	ἐδεδήλωντο

Subjunctive

Active	Middle	Passive	Active	Middle/Passive
δηλώσω	δηλώσωμαι	δηλωθῶ	δεδηλώκω	δεδηλωμένος ὦ
δηλώσῃς	δηλώσῃ	δηλωθῇς	δεδηλώκῃς	δεδηλωμένος ᾖς
δηλώσῃ	δηλώσηται	δηλωθῇ	δεδηλώκῃ	δεδηλωμένος ᾖ
δηλώσωμεν	δηλωσώμεθα	δηλωθῶμεν	δεδηλώκωμεν	δεδηλωμένοι ὦμεν
δηλώσητε	δηλώσησθε	δηλωθῆτε	δεδηλώκητε	δεδηλωμένοι ἦτε
δηλώσωσι(ν)	δηλώσωνται	δηλωθῶσι(ν)	δεδηλώκωσι(ν)	δεδηλωμένοι ὦσι(ν)

Optative

Active	Middle	Passive	Active	Middle/Passive
δηλώσαιμι	δηλωσαίμην	δηλωθείην	[δεδηλώκοιμι	δεδηλωμένος εἴην
δηλώσαις	δηλώσαιο	δηλωθείης	δεδηλώκοις	δεδηλωμένος εἴης
δηλώσαι	δηλώσαιτο	δηλωθείη	δεδηλώκοι	δεδηλωμένος εἴη
δηλώσαιμεν	δηλωσαίμεθα	δηλωθείημεν	δεδηλώκοιμεν	δεδηλωμένοι εἴημεν
δηλώσαιτε	δηλώσαισθε	δηλωθείητε	δεδηλώκοιτε	δεδηλωμένοι εἴητε
δηλώσαιεν	δηλώσαιντο	δηλωθείησαν	δεδηλώκοιεν	δεδηλωμένοι εἴησαι]

Imperative

	Active	Middle	Passive	Active	Middle/Passive
2s	δήλωσον	δήλωσαι	δηλώθητι	δεδήλωκε	δεδήλωσο
3s	δηλωσάτω	δηλωσάσθω	δηλωθήτω	δεδηλωκάτω	δεδηλώσθω
2p	δηλώσατε	δηλώσασθε	δηλώθητε	δεδήλωκατε	δεδήλωσθε
3p	δηλωσάτωσαν	δηλωσάσθωσαν	δηλωθήτωσαν	δεδηλωκάτωσαν	δεδηλώσθωσαν

Infinitive

Active	Middle	Passive	Active	Middle/Passive
δηλῶσαι	δηλώσασθαι	δηλωθῆναι	δεδηλωκέναι	δεδηλῶσθαι

5. ⁻μι

a. δίδωμι: 1st and 3rd (+ 6th) Principal Parts

Aspect/focus: Connection
Common name: "Present"
Principal part: 1st
Stem: διδο⁻

Voice:	Active	Middle/Passive
Mood:		

Indicative

Non-past time

	Active	Middle/Passive
	δίδωμι	δίδομαι
	δίδως	δίδοσαι
	δίδωσι(ν)	δίδοται
	δίδομεν	διδόμεθα
	δίδοτε	δίδοσθε
	διδόασι(ν)	δίδονται

(Imperfect)

Past time

	Active	Middle/Passive
	ἐδίδουν	ἐδιδόμην
	ἐδίδους	ἐδίδοσο
	ἐδίδου	ἐδίδοτο
	ἐδίδομεν	ἐδιδόμεθα
	ἐδίδοτε	ἐδίδοσθε
	ἐδίδοσαν	ἐδίδοντο

Subjunctive

	Active	Middle/Passive
	διδῶ	διδῶμαι
	διδῷς	διδῷ
	διδῷ	διδῶται
	διδῶμεν	διδώμεθα
	διδῶτε	διδῶσθε
	διδῶσι(ν)	διδῶνται

Optative

	Active	Middle/Passive
	[διδοίην	διδοίμην
	διδοίης	διδοῖο
	διδοίη	διδοῖτο
	διδοίημεν	διδοίμεθα
	διδοίητε	διδοῖσθε
	διδοίησαν	διδοῖντο]

Imperative

	Active	Middle/Passive
2s	δίδου	δίδοσο
3s	διδότω	διδόσθω
2p	δίδοτε	δίδοσθε
3p	διδότωσαν	διδόσθωσαν

Infinitive διδόναι   δίδοσθαι

Aspect/focus:		Action	
Common name:		"Aorist"	
Principal part:	3rd		6th
Stem:	δο⁻		δοθη⁻
Voice:	Active	Middle	Passive

Mood:

		Active	Middle	Passive
Indicative — Non-past time				
Indicative — Past time		ἔδωκα	ἐδόμην	ἐδόθην
		ἔδωκας	ἔδου	ἐδόθης
		ἔδωκε(ν)	ἔδοτο	ἐδόθη
		ἐδώκαμεν / ἔδομεν	ἐδόμεθα	ἐδόθημεν
		ἐδώκατε / ἔδοτε	ἔδοσθε	ἐδόθητε
		ἔδωκαν / ἔδοσαν	ἔδοντο	ἐδόθησαν
Subjunctive		δῶ	δῶμαι	δοθῶ
		δῷς	δῷ	δοθῇς
		δῷ	δῶται	δοθῇ
		δῶμεν	δώμεθα	δοθῶμεν
		δῶτε	δῶσθε	δοθῆτε
		δῶσι(ν)	δῶνται	δοθῶσι(ν)
Optative		δοίην	[δοίμην	δοθείην
		δοίης	δοῖο	δοθείης
		δοίη / δῴη	δοῖτο	δοθείη
		δοίημεν	δοίμεθα	δοθείημεν
		δοίητε	δοῖσθε	δοθείητε
		δοίησαν	δοῖντο	δοθείησαν]
Imperative	**2s**	δός	δοῦ	δόθητι
	3s	δότω	δόσθω	δοθήτω
	2p	δότε	δόσθε	δόθητε
	3p	δότωσαν	δόσθωσαν	δοθήτωσαν
Infinitive		δοῦναι	δόσθαι	δοθῆναι

b. τίθημι: 1st and 3rd (+ 6th) Principal Parts

Aspect/focus:	Connection	
Common name:	"Present"	
Principal part:	1st	
Stem:	τιθε-	
Voice:	**Active**	**Middle/ Passive**

Mood:

Indicative

Non-past time

τίθημι	τίθεμαι
τίθης	τίθεσαι
τίθησι(ν)	τίθεται
τίθεμεν	τιθέμεθα
τίθετε	τίθεσθε
τιθέασι(ν)	τίθενται

(Imperfect)

Past time

ἐτίθην	ἐτιθέμην
ἐτίθεις	ἐτίθεσο
ἐτίθει	ἐτίθετο
ἐτίθεμεν	ἐτιθέμεθα
ἐτίθετε	ἐτίθεσθε
ἐτίθεσαν	ἐτίθεντο

Subjunctive

τιθῶ	τιθῶμαι
τιθῇς	τιθῇ
τιθῇ	τιθῆται
τιθῶμεν	τιθώμεθα
τιθῆτε	τιθῆσθε
τιθῶσι(ν)	τιθῶνται

Optative

[τιθείην	τιθείμην
τιθείης	τιθεῖο
τιθείη	τιθεῖτο
τιθείημεν	τιθείμεθα
τιθείητε	τιθεῖσθε
τιθείησαν	τιθεῖντο]

Imperative

2s	τίθει	τίθεσο
3s	τιθέτω	τιθέσθω
2p	τίθετε	τίθεσθε
3p	τιθέτωσαν	τιθέσθωσαν

Infinitive	τιθέναι	τίθεσθαι

Aspect/focus:			Action		
Common name:			"Aorist"		
Principal part:		**3rd**		**6th**	
Stem:		*θε⁻*		*τεθη⁻*	
Voice:	Active		Middle	Passive	

Mood:

		Active	Middle	Passive
Indicative	Non-past time			
	Past time	*ἔθηκα*	*ἐθέμην*	*ἐτέθην*
		ἔθηκας	*ἔθου*	*ἐτέθης*
		ἔθηκε(ν)	*ἔθετο*	*ἐτέθη*
		ἐθήκαμεν / ἔθεμεν	*ἐθέμεθα*	*ἐτέθημεν*
		ἐθήκατε / ἔθετε	*ἔθεσθε*	*ἐτέθητε*
		ἔθηκαν / ἔθεσαν	*ἔθεντο*	*ἐτέθησαν*
Subjunctive		*θῶ*	*θῶμαι*	*τεθῶ*
		θῇς	*θῇ*	*τεθῇς*
		θῇ	*θῆται*	*τεθῇ*
		θῶμεν	*θώμεθα*	*τεθῶμεν*
		θῆτε	*θῆσθε*	*τεθῆτε*
		θῶσι(ν)	*θῶνται*	*τεθῶσι(ν)*
Optative		*[θείην*	*θείμην*	*τεθείην*
		θείης	*θεῖο*	*τεθείης*
		θείη	*θεῖτο*	*τεθείη*
		θείημεν	*θείμεθα*	*τεθείημεν*
		θείητε	*θεῖσθε*	*τεθείητε*
		θείησαν	*θεῖντο*	*τεθείησαν]*
Imperative	**2s**	*θές*	*θοῦ*	*τέθητι*
	3s	*θέτω*	*θέσθω*	*τεθήτω*
	2p	*θέτε*	*θέσθε*	*τέθητε*
	3p	*θέτωσαν*	*θέσθωσαν*	*τεθήτωσαν*
Infinitive		*θεῖναι*	*θέσθαι*	*τεθῆναι*

c. ἵστημι: 1st, 3rd (Both Weak and Strong), and 4th (+ 6th) Principal Parts

Aspect/focus:	Connection
Common name:	"Present"
Principal part:	1st
Stem:	ἰστα-
Voice:	Active	Middle/ Passive

Mood:

Indicative

Non-past time

Active	Middle/Passive
ἵστημι	ἵσταμαι
ἵστης	ἵστασαι
ἵστησι(ν)	ἵσταται
ἵσταμεν	ἱστάμεθα
ἵστατε	ἵστασθε
ἱστᾶσι(ν)	ἵστανται

(Imperfect)

Past time

Active	Middle/Passive
ἵστην	ἱστάμην
ἵστης	ἵστασο
ἵστη	ἵστατο
ἵσταμεν	ἱστάμεθα
ἵστατε	ἵστασθε
ἵστασαν	ἵσταντο

Subjunctive

Active	Middle/Passive
ἱστῶ	ἱστῶμαι
ἱστῇς	ἱστῇ
ἱστῇ	ἱστῆται
ἱστῶμεν	ἱστώμεθα
ἱστῆτε	ἱστῆσθε
ἱστῶσι(ν)	ἱστῶνται

Optative

Active	Middle/Passive
[ἱσταίην	ἱσταίμην
ἱσταίης	ἱσταῖο
ἱσταίη	ἱσταῖτο
ἱσταίημεν	ἱσταίμεθα
ἱσταίητε	ἱσταῖσθε
ἱσταίησαν	ἱσταῖντο]

Imperative

	Active	Middle/Passive
2s	ἵστη	ἵστασο
3s	ἱστάτω	ἱστάσθω
2p	ἵστατε	ἵστασθε
3p	ἱστάτωσαν	ἱστάσθωσαν

Infinitive ἱστάναι ἵστασθαι

Aspect/focus:	Action			Result	
Common name:	"Aorist"			"Perfect"	
Principal part:	3rd		6th	4th	5th
Stem:	στησ⁻	στα⁻	σταθη⁻	ἑστηκ⁻	ἑστα⁻
Voice:	Active: Weak	Active: Strong	Passive	Active	Middle/Passive

Mood:

Indicative — Non-past time

			ἕστηκα	
			ἕστηκας	
			ἕστηκε(ν)	(Rare)
			ἑστήκαμεν	
			ἑστήκατε	
			ἑστήκασι(ν)	

(Pluperfect)

Indicative — Past time

Active: Weak	Active: Strong	Passive	Active
ἔστησα	ἔστην	ἐστάθην	εἱστήκειν
ἔστησας	ἔστης	ἐστάθης	εἱστήκεις
ἔστησε(ν)	ἔστη	ἐστάθη	εἱστήκει
ἐστήσαμεν	ἔστημεν	ἐστάθημεν	εἱστήκειμεν
ἐστήσατε	ἔστητε	ἐστάθητε	εἱστήκειτε
ἔστησαν	ἔστησαν	ἐστάθησαν	εἱστήκεισαν

Subjunctive

στήσω	στῶ	σταθῶ	
στήσῃς	στῇς	σταθῇς	
στήσῃ	στῇ	σταθῇ	(Rare)
στήσωμεν	στῶμεν	σταθῶμεν	
στήσητε	στῆτε	σταθῆτε	
στήσωσι(ν)	στῶσι(ν)	σταθῶσι(ν)	

Optative

[στήσαιμι	σταίην	σταθείην	
στήσαις	σταίης	σταθείης	
στήσαι	σταίη	σταθείη	(Rare)
στήσαιμεν	σταίημεν	σταθείημεν	
στήσαιτε	σταίητε	σταθείητε	
στήσαιεν	σταίησαν	σταθείησαν]	

Imperative

2s	στῆσον	στῆθι / στά	στάθητι	
3s	στησάτω	στήτω	σταθήτω	(Rare)
2p	στήσατε	στῆτε	στάθητε	
3p	στησάτωσαν	στήτωσαν	σταθήτωσαν	

Infinitive

στῆσαι	στῆναι	σταθῆναι	ἑστάναι

d. $\epsilon i \mu i$: 1st and 2nd Principal Parts

Aspect/focus:	Connection	
Common name:	"Present"	"Future"
Principal part:	1st	2nd
Stem:	$\dot{\epsilon}\sigma^-$	$\dot{\epsilon}\sigma^-$
Voice:	Active	Middle

Mood:

Indicative

Non-past time

$\epsilon i \mu i$	$\ddot{\epsilon}\sigma o\mu\alpha\iota$
$\epsilon \hat{\iota}$	$\ddot{\epsilon}\sigma\eta$
$\dot{\epsilon}\sigma\tau i(\nu)$	$\ddot{\epsilon}\sigma\tau\alpha\iota$
$\dot{\epsilon}\sigma\mu\dot{\epsilon}\nu$	$\dot{\epsilon}\sigma\dot{o}\mu\epsilon\theta\alpha$
$\dot{\epsilon}\sigma\tau\dot{\epsilon}$	$\ddot{\epsilon}\sigma\epsilon\sigma\theta\epsilon$
$\epsilon i \sigma i(\nu)$	$\ddot{\epsilon}\sigma o\nu\tau\alpha\iota$

(Imperfect)

Past time

$\ddot{\eta}\mu\eta\nu$
$\hat{\eta}s$
$\hat{\eta}\nu$
$\hat{\eta}\mu\epsilon\nu$
$\hat{\eta}\tau\epsilon$
$\hat{\eta}\sigma\alpha\nu$

Subjunctive

$\hat{\omega}$
$\hat{\eta}s$
$\hat{\eta}$
$\hat{\omega}\mu\epsilon\nu$
$\hat{\eta}\tau\epsilon$
$\hat{\omega}\sigma\iota(\nu)$

Optative

$\epsilon \ddot{\iota}\eta\nu$
$\epsilon \ddot{\iota}\eta s$
$\epsilon \ddot{\iota}\eta$ (Rare)
$\epsilon \ddot{\iota}\eta\mu\epsilon\nu$
$\epsilon \ddot{\iota}\eta\tau\epsilon$
$\epsilon \ddot{\iota}\eta\sigma\alpha\nu$

Imperative

2s	$\ddot{\iota}\sigma\theta\iota$
3s	$\ddot{\epsilon}\sigma\tau\omega$
2p	$[\ddot{\epsilon}\sigma\tau\epsilon]$
3p	$\ddot{\epsilon}\sigma\tau\omega\sigma\alpha\nu$

Infinitive $\epsilon \hat{\iota}\nu\alpha\iota$ $[\ddot{\epsilon}\sigma\epsilon\sigma\theta\alpha\iota]$

see also p. 365

6. βαίνω: 3rd Principal Part

Aspect/focus: Action
Common name: "Aorist"
Principal part: 3rd
Stem: βα⁻
Voice: Active

Mood:

Indicative

Non-past time

Past time

ἔβην
ἔβης
ἔβη
ἔβημεν
ἔβητε
ἔβησαν

Subjunctive

βῶ
βῇς
βῇ
βῶμεν
βῆτε
βῶσι(ν)

Optative

(Rare)

Imperative

2s	βῆθι / βά
3s	βάτω
2p	βάτε
3p	βάτωσαν

Infinitive   βῆναι

7. γινώσκω: 3rd Principal Part

Aspect/focus:	**Action**
Common name:	**"Aorist"**
Principal part:	**3rd**
Stem:	**γνο⁻**
Voice:	**Active**

Mood:

Indicative	Non-past time	
	Past time	ἔγνων
		ἔγνως
		ἔγνω
		ἔγνωμεν
		ἔγνωτε
		ἔγνωσαν
Subjunctive		γνῶ
		γνῷς
		γνῷ
		γνῶμεν
		γνῶτε
		γνῶσι(ν)
Optative		(Rare)
Imperative	2s	γνῶθι
	3s	γνώτω
	2p	γνῶτε
	3p	γνώτωσαν
Infinitive		γνῶναι

8. οἶδα: 4th Principal Part

Aspect/focus:	**Result = Connection**
Common name:	**"Perfect" = "Present"**
Principal part:	**4th**
Stem:	εἰδ-
Voice:	**Active**

Mood:

Indicative

Non-past time

οἶδα
οἶδας
οἶδε(ν)
οἴδαμεν
οἴδατε
οἴδασι(ν)

Past time

(Pluperfect = Imperfect)

ᾔδειν
ᾔδεις
ᾔδει
ᾔδειμεν
ᾔδειτε
ᾔδεισαν

Subjunctive

εἰδῶ
εἰδῇς
εἰδῇ
εἰδῶμεν
εἰδῆτε
εἰδῶσι(ν)

Optative

(Rare)

Imperative

2s	ἴσθι
3s	ἴστω
2p	ἴστε
3p	ἴστωσαν

Infinitive εἰδέναι

G. Participles

1. Regular Verb, Weak: λύω

a. Focus upon Connection / "Present"

(1) Active

Singular

	M	F	N
N	λύων	λύουσα	λῦον
G	λύοντος	λυούσης	λύοντος
D	λύοντι	λυούσῃ	λύοντι
A	λύοντα	λύουσαν	λῦον

Plural

	M	F	N
N	λύοντες	λύουσαι	λύοντα
G	λυόντων	λυουσῶν	λυόντων
D	λύουσι(ν)	λυούσαις	λύουσι(ν)
A	λύοντας	λυούσας	λύοντα

(2) Middle/Passive

Singular

	M	F	N
N	λυόμενος	λυομένη	λυόμενον
G	λυομένου	λυομένης	λυομένου
D	λυομένῳ	λυομένῃ	λυομένῳ
A	λυόμενον	λυομένην	λυόμενον

Plural

	M	F	N
N	λυόμενοι	λυόμεναι	λυόμενα
G	λυομένων	λυομένων	λυομένων
D	λυομένοις	λυομέναις	λυομένοις
A	λυομένους	λυομένας	λυόμενα

[b. "Future"

(1) Active

Singular

	M	F	N
N	λύσων	λύσουσα	λῦσον
G	λύσοντος	λυσούσης	λύσοντος
D	λύσοντι	λυσούσῃ	λύσοντι
A	λύσοντα	λύσουσαν	λῦσον

Plural

	M	F	N
N	λύσοντες	λύσουσαι	λύσοντα
G	λυσόντων	λυσουσῶν	λυσόντων
D	λύσουσι(ν)	λυσούσαις	λύσουσι(ν)
A	λύσοντας	λυσούσας	λύσοντα

(2) Middle

Singular

	M	F	N
N	λυσόμενος	λυσομένη	λυσόμενον
G	λυσομένου	λυσομένης	λυσομένου
D	λυσομένῳ	λυσομένῃ	λυσομένῳ
A	λυσόμενον	λυσομένην	λυσόμενον

Plural

	M	F	N
N	λυσόμενοι	λυσόμεναι	λυσόμενα
G	λυσομένων	λυσομένων	λυσομένων
D	λυσομένοις	λυσομέναις	λυσομένοις
A	λυσομένους	λυσομένας	λυσόμενα

(3) Passive

(Rare)]

c. Focus on the Action / "Aorist"

(1) Active

Singular

	M	F	N
N	λύσας	λύσασα	λῦσαν
G	λύσαντος	λυσάσης	λύσαντος
D	λύσαντι	λυσάσῃ	λύσαντι
A	λύσαντα	λύσασαν	λῦσαν

Plural

	M	F	N
N	λύσαντες	λύσασαι	λύσαντα
G	λυσάντων	λυσασῶν	λυσάντων
D	λύσασι(ν)	λυσάσαις	λύσασι(ν)
A	λύσαντας	λυσάσας	λύσαντα

(2) Middle

Singular

	M	F	N
N	λυσάμενος	λυσαμένη	λυσάμενον
G	λυσαμένου	λυσαμένης	λυσαμένου
D	λυσαμένῳ	λυσαμένῃ	λυσαμένῳ
A	λυσάμενον	λυσαμένην	λυσάμενον

Plural

	M	F	N
N	λυσάμενοι	λυσάμεναι	λυσάμενα
G	λυσαμένων	λυσαμένων	λυσαμένων
D	λυσαμένοις	λυσαμέναις	λυσαμένοις
A	λυσαμένους	λυσαμένας	λυσάμενα

(3) Passive

Singular

	M	F	N
N	λυθείς	λυθεῖσα	λυθέν
G	λυθέντος	λυθείσης	λυθέντος
D	λυθέντι	λυθείσῃ	λυθέντι
A	λυθέντα	λυθεῖσαν	λυθέν

Plural

	M	F	N
N	λυθέντες	λυθεῖσαι	λυθέντα
G	λυθέντων	λυθεισῶν	λυθέντων
D	λυθεῖσι(ν)	λυθείσαις	λυθεῖσι(ν)
A	λυθέντας	λυθείσας	λυθέντα

d. Focus upon Result / "Perfect"

(1) Active

Singular

	M	F	N
N	λελυκώς	λελυκυῖα	λελυκός
G	λελυκότος	λελυκυίας	λελυκότος
D	λελυκότι	λελυκυίᾳ	λελυκότι
A	λελυκότα	λελυκυῖαν	λελυκός

Plural

	M	F	N
N	λελυκότες	λελυκυῖαι	λελυκότα
G	λελυκότων	λελυκυιῶν	λελυκότων
D	λελυκόσι(ν)	λελυκυίαις	λελυκόσι(ν)
A	λελυκότας	λελυκυίας	λελυκότα

(2) Middle/Passive

Singular

	M	F	N
N	λελυμένος	λελυμένη	λελυμένον
G	λελυμένου	λελυμένης	λελυμένου
D	λελυμένῳ	λελυμένῃ	λελυμένῳ
A	λελυμένον	λελυμένην	λελυμένον

Plural

	M	F	N
N	λελυμένοι	λελυμέναι	λελυμένα
G	λελυμένων	λελυμένων	λελυμένων
D	λελυμένοις	λελυμέναις	λελυμένοις
A	λελυμένους	λελυμένας	λελυμένα

2. Irregular Verb, Strong: λείπω

a. Focus upon Connection / "Present"

(1) Active

Singular

	M	F	N
N	λείπων	λείπουσα	λεῖπον
G	λείποντος	λειπούσης	λείποντος
D	λείποντι	λειπούσῃ	λείποντι
A	λείποντα	λείπουσαν	λεῖπον

Plural

	M	F	N
N	λείποντες	λείπουσαι	λείποντα
G	λειπόντων	λειπουσῶν	λειπόντων
D	λείπουσι(ν)	λειπούσαις	λείπουσι(ν)
A	λείποντας	λειπούσας	λείποντα

(2) Middle/Passive

Singular

	M	F	N
N	λειπόμενος	λειπομένη	λειπόμενον
G	λειπομένου	λειπομένης	λειπομένου
D	λειπομένῳ	λειπομένῃ	λειπομένῳ
A	λειπόμενον	λειπομένην	λειπόμενον

Plural

	M	F	N
N	λειπόμενοι	λειπόμεναι	λειπόμενα
G	λειπομένων	λειπομένων	λειπομένων
D	λειπομένοις	λειπομέναις	λειπομένοις
A	λειπομένους	λειπομένας	λειπόμενα

[b. "Future"

(1) Active

Singular

	M	F	N
N	λείψων	λείψουσα	λεῖψον
G	λείψοντος	λειψούσης	λείψοντος
D	λείψοντι	λειψούσῃ	λείψοντι
A	λείψοντα	λείψουσαν	λεῖψον

Plural

	M	F	N
N	λείψοντες	λείψουσαι	λείψοντα
G	λειψόντων	λειψουσῶν	λειψόντων
D	λείψουσι(ν)	λειψούσαις	λείψουσι(ν)
A	λείψοντας	λειψούσας	λείψοντα

(2) Middle

Singular

	M	F	N
N	λειψόμενος	λειψομένη	λειψόμενον
G	λειψομένου	λειψομένης	λειψομένου
D	λειψομένῳ	λειψομένη	λειψομένῳ
A	λειψόμενον	λειψομένην	λειψόμενον

Plural

	M	F	N
N	λειψόμενοι	λειψόμεναι	λειψόμενα
G	λειψομένων	λειψομένων	λειψομένων
D	λειψομένοις	λειψομέναις	λειψομένοις
A	λειψομένους	λειψομένας	λειψόμενα

(3) Passive

(Rare)]

c. Focus on the Action / "Aorist"

(1) Active

Singular

	M	F	N
N	λιπών	λιποῦσα	λιπόν
G	λιπόντος	λιπούσης	λιπόντος
D	λιπόντι	λιπούσῃ	λιπόντι
A	λιπόντα	λιποῦσαν	λιπόν

Plural

	M	F	N
N	λιπόντες	λιποῦσαι	λιπόντα
G	λιπόντων	λιπουσῶν	λιπόντων
D	λιποῦσι(ν)	λιπούσαις	λιποῦσι(ν)
A	λιπόντας	λιπούσας	λιπόντα

(2) Middle

Singular

	M	F	N
N	λιπόμενος	λιπομένη	λιπόμενον
G	λιπομένου	λιπομένης	λιπομένου
D	λιπομένῳ	λιπομένη	λιπομένῳ
A	λιπόμενον	λιπομένην	λιπόμενον

Plural

	M	F	N
N	λιπόμενοι	λιπόμεναι	λιπόμενα
G	λιπομένων	λιπομένων	λιπομένων
D	λιπομένοις	λιπομέναις	λιπομένοις
A	λιπομένους	λιπομένας	λιπόμενα

(3) Passive

Singular

	M	F	N
N	λειφθείς	λειφθεῖσα	λειφθέν
G	λειφθέντος	λειφθείσης	λειφθέντος
D	λειφθέντι	λειφθείσῃ	λειφθέντι
A	λειφθέντα	λειφθεῖσαν	λειφθέν

Plural

	M	F	N
N	λειφθέντες	λειφθεῖσαι	λειφθέντα
G	λειφθέντων	λειφθεισῶν	λειφθέντων
D	λειφθεῖσι(ν)	λειφθείσαις	λειφθεῖσι(ν)
A	λειφθέντας	λειφθείσας	λειφθέντα

d. Focus upon Result / "Perfect"

(1) Active

Singular

	M	F	N
N	λελοιπώς	λελοιπυῖα	λελοιπός
G	λελοιπότος	λελοιπυίας	λελοιπότος
D	λελοιπότι	λελοιπυίᾳ	λελοιπότι
A	λελοιπότα	λελοιπυῖαν	λελοιπός

Plural

	M	F	N
N	λελοιπότες	λελοιπυῖαι	λελοιπότα
G	λελοιπότων	λελοιπυιῶν	λελοιπότων
D	λελοιπόσι(ν)	λελοιπυίαις	λελοιπόσι(ν)
A	λελοιπότας	λελοιπυίας	λελοιπότα

(2) Middle/Passive

Singular

	M	F	N
N	λελειμμένος	λελειμμένη	λελειμμένον
G	λελειμμένου	λελειμμένης	λελειμμένου
D	λελειμμένῳ	λελειμμένῃ	λελειμμένῳ
A	λελειμμένον	λελειμμένην	λελειμμένον

Plural

	M	F	N
N	λελειμμένοι	λελειμμέναι	λελειμμένα
G	λελειμμένων	λελειμμένων	λελειμμένων
D	λελειμμένοις	λελειμμέναις	λελειμμένοις
A	λελειμμένους	λελειμμένας	λελειμμένα

3. Liquid Verb: φθείρω

[a. "Future"

(1) Active

Follows the pattern of focus upon connection / "present" participles of -έω contract verbs.

(2) Middle

Follows the pattern of focus upon connection / "present" participles of -έω contract verbs.

(3) Passive

(Rare)]

b. Focus on the Action / "Aorist"

(1) Active

Singular

	M	F	N
N	φθείρας	φθείρασα	φθεῖραν
G	φθείραντος	φθειράσης	φθείραντος
D	φθείραντι	φθειράσῃ	φθείραντι
A	φθείραντα	φθείρασαν	φθεῖραν

Plural

	M	F	N
N	φθείραντες	φθείρασαι	φθείραντα
G	φθειράντων	φθειρασῶν	φθειράντων
D	φθείρασι(ν)	φθειράσαις	φθείρασι(ν)
A	φθείραντας	φθειράσας	φθείραντα

(2) Middle

Singular

	M	F	N
N	φθειράμενος	φθειραμένη	φθειράμενον
G	φθειραμένου	φθειραμένης	φθειραμένου
D	φθειραμένῳ	φθειραμένη	φθειραμένῳ
A	φθειράμενον	φθειραμένην	φθειράμενον

Plural

	M	F	N
N	φθειράμενοι	φθειράμεναι	φθειράμενα
G	φθειραμένων	φθειραμένων	φθειραμένων
D	φθειραμένοις	φθειραμέναις	φθειραμένοις
A	φθειραμένους	φθειραμένας	φθειράμενα

(3) Passive

Singular

	M	F	N
N	φθαρείς	φθαρεῖσα	φθαρέν
G	φθαρέντος	φθαρείσης	φθαρέντος
D	φθαρέντι	φθαρείσῃ	φθαρέντι
A	φθαρέντα	φθαρεῖσαν	φθαρέν

Plural

	M	F	N
N	φθαρέντες	φθαρεῖσαι	φθαρέντα
G	φθαρέντων	φθαρεισῶν	φθαρέντων
D	φθαρεῖσι(ν)	φθαρείσαις	φθαρεῖσι(ν)
A	φθαρέντας	φθαρείσας	φθαρέντα

4. Contract(ed) Verb

a. φιλέω

(1) Focus upon Connection / "Present"

(a) Active

Singular

	M	F	N
N	φιλῶν	φιλοῦσα	φιλοῦν
G	φιλοῦντος	φιλούσης	φιλοῦντος
D	φιλοῦντι	φιλούσῃ	φιλοῦντι
A	φιλοῦντα	φιλοῦσαν	φιλοῦν

Plural

	M	F	N
N	φιλοῦντες	φιλοῦσαι	φιλοῦντα
G	φιλούντων	φιλουσῶν	φιλούντων
D	φιλοῦσι(ν)	φιλούσαις	φιλοῦσι(ν)
A	φιλοῦντας	φιλούσας	φιλοῦντα

(b) Middle/Passive

Singular

	M	F	N
N	φιλούμενος	φιλουμένη	φιλούμενον
G	φιλουμένου	φιλουμένης	φιλουμένου
D	φιλουμένῳ	φιλουμένῃ	φιλουμένῳ
A	φιλούμενον	φιλουμένην	φιλούμενον

Plural

	M	F	N
N	φιλούμενοι	φιλούμεναι	φιλούμενα
G	φιλουμένων	φιλουμένων	φιλουμένων
D	φιλουμένοις	φιλουμέναις	φιλουμένοις
A	φιλουμένους	φιλουμένας	φιλούμενα

(2) Other stems follow the regular (weak) pattern of λύω.

b. *τιμάω*

  (1) Focus upon Connection / "Present"

    (a) Active

Singular

	M	F	N
N	τιμῶν	τιμῶσα	τιμῶν
G	τιμῶντος	τιμώσης	τιμῶντος
D	τιμῶντι	τιμώσῃ	τιμῶντι
A	τιμῶντα	τιμῶσαν	τιμῶν

Plural

	M	F	N
N	τιμῶντες	τιμῶσαι	τιμῶντα
G	τιμώντων	τιμωσῶν	τιμώντων
D	τιμῶσι(ν)	τιμώσαις	τιμῶσι(ν)
A	τιμῶντας	τιμώσας	τιμῶντα

    (b) Middle/Passive

Singular

	M	F	N
N	τιμώμενος	τιμωμένη	τιμώμενον
G	τιμωμένου	τιμωμένης	τιμωμένου
D	τιμωμένῳ	τιμωμένῃ	τιμωμένῳ
A	τιμώμενον	τιμωμένην	τιμώμενον

Plural

	M	F	N
N	τιμώμενοι	τιμώμεναι	τιμώμενα
G	τιμωμένων	τιμωμένων	τιμωμένων
D	τιμωμένοις	τιμωμέναις	τιμωμένοις
A	τιμωμένους	τιμωμένας	τιμώμενα

(2) Other stems follow the regular (weak) pattern of λύω.

c. *δηλόω*

  (1) Focus upon Connection / "Present"

    (a) Active

Singular

	M	F	N
N	δηλῶν	δηλοῦσα	δηλοῦν
G	δηλοῦντος	δηλούσης	δηλοῦντος
D	δηλοῦντι	δηλούσῃ	δηλοῦντι
A	δηλοῦντα	δηλοῦσαν	δηλοῦν

	M	**F**	**N**
		Plural	
N	δηλοῦντες	δηλοῦσαι	δηλοῦντα
G	δηλούντων	δηλουσῶν	δηλούντων
D	δηλοῦσι(ν)	δηλούσαις	δηλοῦσι(ν)
A	δηλοῦντας	δηλούσας	δηλοῦντα

(b) Middle/Passive

	M	**F**	**N**
		Singular	
N	δηλούμενος	δηλουμένη	δηλούμενον
G	δηλουμένου	δηλουμένης	δηλουμένου
D	δηλουμένῳ	δηλουμένῃ	δηλουμένῳ
A	δηλούμενον	δηλουμένην	δηλούμενον
		Plural	
N	δηλούμενοι	δηλούμεναι	δηλούμενα
G	δηλουμένων	δηλουμένων	δηλουμένων
D	δηλουμένοις	δηλουμέναις	δηλουμένοις
A	δηλουμένους	δηλουμένας	δηλούμενα

(2) Other stems follow the regular (weak) pattern of λύω.

5. -μι Verb

a. δίδωμι (1st and 3rd Principal Parts)

(1) Focus upon Connection / "Present"

(a) Active

	M	**F**	**N**
		Singular	
N	διδούς	διδοῦσα	διδόν
G	διδόντος	διδούσης	διδόντος
D	διδόντι	διδούσῃ	διδόντι
A	διδόντα	διδοῦσαν	διδόν
		Plural	
N	διδόντες	διδοῦσαι	διδόντα
G	διδόντων	διδουσῶν	διδόντων
D	διδοῦσι(ν)	διδούσαις	διδοῦσι(ν)
A	διδόντας	διδούσας	διδόντα

(b) Middle/Passive

	M	**F**	**N**
		Singular	
N	διδόμενος	διδομένη	διδόμενον
G	διδομένου	διδομένης	διδομένου
D	διδομένῳ	διδομένῃ	διδομένῳ
A	διδόμενον	διδομένην	διδόμενον

Plural

	M	F	N
N	διδόμενοι	διδόμεναι	διδόμενα
G	διδομένων	διδομένων	διδομένων
D	διδομένοις	διδομέναις	διδομένοις
A	διδομένους	διδομένας	διδόμενα

(2) Focus on the Action / "Aorist"

   (a) Active

Singular

	M	F	N
N	δούς	δοῦσα	δόν
G	δόντος	δούσης	δόντος
D	δόντι	δούσῃ	δόντι
A	δόντα	δοῦσαν	δόν

Plural

	M	F	N
N	δόντες	δοῦσαι	δόντα
G	δόντων	δουσῶν	δόντων
D	δοῦσι(ν)	δούσαις	δοῦσι(ν)
A	δόντας	δούσας	δόντα

   (b) Middle

Singular

	M	F	N
N	δόμενος	δομένη	δόμενον
G	δομένου	δομένης	δομένου
D	δομένῳ	δομένῃ	δομένῳ
A	δόμενον	δομένην	δόμενον

Plural

	M	F	N
N	δόμενοι	δόμεναι	δόμενα
G	δομένων	δομένων	δομένων
D	δομένοις	δομέναις	δομένοις
A	δομένους	δομένας	δόμενα

   (c) Passive (6th Principal Part)

      (Normal)

b. τίθημι (1st and 3rd Principal Parts)

(1) Focus upon Connection / "Present"

(a) Active

Singular

	M	F	N
N	τιθείς	τιθεῖσα	τιθέν
G	τιθέντος	τιθείσης	τιθέντος
D	τιθέντι	τιθείσῃ	τιθέντι
A	τιθέντα	τιθεῖσαν	τιθέν

Plural

	M	F	N
N	τιθέντες	τιθεῖσαι	τιθέντα
G	τιθέντων	τιθεισῶν	τιθέντων
D	τιθεῖσι(ν)	τιθείσαις	τιθεῖσι(ν)
A	τιθέντας	τιθείσας	τιθέντα

(b) Middle/Passive

Singular

	M	F	N
N	τιθέμενος	τιθεμένη	τιθέμενον
G	τιθεμένου	τιθεμένης	τιθεμένου
D	τιθεμένῳ	τιθεμένῃ	τιθεμένῳ
A	τιθέμενον	τιθεμένην	τιθέμενον

Plural

	M	F	N
N	τιθέμενοι	τιθέμεναι	τιθέμενα
G	τιθεμένων	τιθεμένων	τιθεμένων
D	τιθεμένοις	τιθεμέναις	τιθεμένοις
A	τιθεμένους	τιθεμένας	τιθέμενα

(2) Focus on the Action / "Aorist"

(a) Active

Singular

	M	F	N
N	θείς	θεῖσα	θέν
G	θέντος	θείσης	θέντος
D	θέντι	θείσῃ	θέντι
A	θέντα	θεῖσαν	θέν

Plural

	M	F	N
N	θέντες	θεῖσαι	θέντα
G	θέντων	θεισῶν	θέντων
D	θεῖσι(ν)	θείσαις	θεῖσι(ν)
A	θέντας	θείσας	θέντα

(b) Middle

Singular

	M	F	N
N	θέμενος	θεμένη	θέμενον
G	θεμένου	θεμένης	θεμένου
D	θεμένῳ	θεμένῃ	θεμένῳ
A	θέμενον	θεμένην	θέμενον

Plural

	M	F	N
N	θέμενοι	θέμεναι	θέμενα
G	θεμένων	θεμένων	θεμένων
D	θεμένοις	θεμέναις	θεμένοις
A	θεμένους	θεμένας	θέμενα

(c) Passive (6th Principal Part)

(Normal)

c. ἵστημι (1st, 3rd, and 4th Principal Parts)

(1) Focus upon Connection / "Present"

(a) Active

Singular

	M	F	N
N	ἱστάς	ἱστᾶσα	ἱστάν
G	ἱστάντος	ἱστάσης	ἱστάντος
D	ἱστάντι	ἱστάσῃ	ἱστάντι
A	ἱστάντα	ἱστᾶσαν	ἱστάν

Plural

	M	F	N
N	ἱστάντες	ἱστᾶσαι	ἱστάντα
G	ἱστάντων	ἱστασῶν	ἱστάντων
D	ἱστᾶσι(ν)	ἱστάσαις	ἱστᾶσι(ν)
A	ἱστάντας	ἱστάσας	ἱστάντα

(b) Middle/Passive

Singular

	M	F	N
N	ἱστάμενος	ἱσταμένη	ἱστάμενον
G	ἱσταμένου	ἱσταμένης	ἱσταμένου
D	ἱσταμένῳ	ἱσταμένῃ	ἱσταμένῳ
A	ἱστάμενον	ἱσταμένην	ἱστάμενον

Plural

	M	F	N
N	ἱστάμενοι	ἱστάμεναι	ἱστάμενα
G	ἱσταμένων	ἱσταμένων	ἱσταμένων
D	ἱσταμένοις	ἱσταμέναις	ἱσταμένοις
A	ἱσταμένους	ἱσταμένας	ἱστάμενα

(2) Focus on the Action / "Aorist"

    (a) Active: Weak

Singular

	M	F	N
N	στήσας	στήσασα	στῆσαν
G	στήσαντος	στησάσης	στήσαντος
D	στήσαντι	στησάσῃ	στήσαντι
A	στήσαντα	στήσασαν	στῆσαν

Plural

	M	F	N
N	στήσαντες	στήσασαι	στήσαντα
G	στησάντων	στησασῶν	στησάντων
D	στήσασι(ν)	στησάσαις	στήσασι(ν)
A	στήσαντας	στησάσας	στήσαντα

    (b) Active: Strong

Singular

	M	F	N
N	στάς	στᾶσα	στάν
G	στάντος	στάσης	στάντος
D	στάντι	στάσῃ	στάντι
A	στάντα	στᾶσαν	στάν

Plural

	M	F	N
N	στάντες	στᾶσαι	στάντα
G	στάντων	στασῶν	στάντων
D	στᾶσι(ν)	στάσαις	στᾶσι(ν)
A	στάντας	στάσας	στάντα

    (c) Middle

    (Rare)

    (d) Passive (6th Principal Part)

    (Normal)

(3) Focus upon Result / "Perfect"

    (a) Active: Weak

Singular

	M	F	N
N	ἑστηκώς	ἑστηκυῖα	ἑστηκός
G	ἑστηκότος	ἑστηκυίας	ἑστηκότος
D	ἑστηκότι	ἑστηκυίᾳ	ἑστηκότι
A	ἑστηκότα	ἑστηκυῖαν	ἑστηκός

Plural

	M	F	N
N	ἑστηκότες	ἑστηκυῖαι	ἑστηκότα
G	ἑστηκότων	ἑστηκυιῶν	ἑστηκότων
D	ἑστηκόσι(ν)	ἑστηκυίαις	ἑστηκόσι(ν)
A	ἑστηκότας	ἑστηκυίας	ἑστηκότα

(b) Active: Strong

Singular

	M	F	N
N	ἑστώς	ἑστῶσα	ἑστός
G	ἑστῶτος	ἑστώσης	ἑστῶτος
D	ἑστῶτι	ἑστώσῃ	ἑστῶτι
A	ἑστῶτα	ἑστῶσαν	ἑστός

Plural

	M	F	N
N	ἑστῶτες	ἑστῶσαι	ἑστῶτα
G	ἑστώτων	ἑστωσῶν	ἑστώτων
D	ἑστῶσι(ν)	ἑστώσαις	ἑστῶσι(ν)
A	ἑστῶτας	ἑστώσας	ἑστῶτα

(c) Middle/Passive (5th Principal Part)

(Rare)

d. εἰμί (1st Principal Part)

(1) Focus upon Connection / "Present"

Singular

	M	F	N
N	ὤν	οὖσα	ὄν
G	ὄντος	οὔσης	ὄντος
D	ὄντι	οὔσῃ	ὄντι
A	ὄντα	οὖσαν	ὄν

Plural

	M	F	N
N	ὄντες	οὖσαι	ὄντα
G	ὄντων	οὐσῶν	ὄντων
D	οὖσι(ν)	οὔσαις	οὖσι(ν)
A	ὄντας	οὔσας	ὄντα

(2) "Future"

(Rare)

6. βαίνω: Focus on the Action / "Aorist" Active

Singular

	M	F	N
N	βάς	βᾶσα	βάν
G	βάντος	βάσης	βάντος
D	βάντι	βάσῃ	βάντι
A	βάντα	βᾶσαν	βάν

Plural

	M	F	N
N	βάντες	βᾶσαι	βάντα
G	βάντων	βασῶν	βάντων
D	βᾶσι(ν)	βάσαις	βᾶσι(ν)
A	βάντας	βάσας	βάντα

7. γινώσκω: Focus on the Action / "Aorist" Active

Singular

	M	F	N
N	γνούς	γνοῦσα	γνόν
G	γνόντος	γνούσης	γνόντος
D	γνόντι	γνούσῃ	γνόντι
A	γνόντα	γνοῦσαν	γνόν

Plural

	M	F	N
N	γνόντες	γνοῦσαι	γνόντα
G	γνόντων	γνουσῶν	γνόντων
D	γνοῦσι(ν)	γνούσαις	γνοῦσι(ν)
A	γνόντας	γνούσας	γνόντα

8. οἶδα: Focus upon Result / "Perfect" = Focus upon Connection / "Present"

a. Active

Singular

	M	F	N
N	εἰδώς	εἰδυῖα	εἰδός
G	εἰδότος	εἰδυίας	εἰδότος
D	εἰδότι	εἰδυίᾳ	εἰδότι
A	εἰδότα	εἰδυῖαν	εἰδός

Plural

	M	F	N
N	εἰδότες	εἰδυῖαι	εἰδότα
G	εἰδότων	εἰδυιῶν	εἰδότων
D	εἰδόσι(ν)	εἰδυίαις	εἰδόσι(ν)
A	εἰδότας	εἰδυίας	εἰδότα

b. Middle/Passive (5th Principal Part)

(Rare)

Principal Parts

1	2	3	4	5	6
ἀγγέλλω	ἀγγελῶ	ἤγγειλα	ἤγγελκα	ἤγγελμαι	ἠγγέλην
ἄγω	ἄξω	ἤγαγον	ἦχα	ἦγμαι	ἤχθην
αἴρω	ἀρῶ	ἦρα	ἦρκα	ἦρμαι	ἤρθην
ἀκούω	ἀκούσω	ἤκουσα	ἀκήκοα	ἤκουσμαι	ἠκούσθην
ἁμαρτάνω	ἁμαρτήσω	ἥμαρτον	ἡμάρτηκα	ἡμάρτημαι	ἡμαρτήθην
ἀνοίγω	ἀνοίξω	ἀνέῳξα	ἀνέῳχα	ἀνέῳγμαι	ἀνεῴχθην
ἀποθνῄσκω	ἀποθανοῦμαι	ἀπέθανον	τέθνηκα		
ἀποκτείνω	ἀποκτενῶ	ἀπέκτεινα			ἀπεκτάνθην
ἀπόλλυμι	ἀπολῶ	ἀπώλεσα	ἀπολώλεκα		
ἀπόλλυμαι	ἀπολοῦμαι	ἀπωλόμην	ἀπόλωλα		
ἀποστέλλω	ἀποστελῶ	ἀπέστειλα	ἀπέσταλκα	ἀπέσταλμαι	ἀπεστάλην
βαίνω	βήσομαι	ἔβην	βέβηκα		
βάλλω	βαλῶ	ἔβαλον	βέβληκα	βέβλημαι	ἐβλήθην
γίνομαι	γενήσομαι	ἐγενόμην	γέγονα	γεγένημαι	ἐγενήθην
γινώσκω	γνώσομαι	ἔγνων	ἔγνωκα	ἔγνωσμαι	ἐγνώσθην
γράφω	γράψω	ἔγραψα	γέγραφα	γέγραμμαι	ἐγράφην

1	2	3	4	5	6
δέω	δήσω	ἔδησα	δέδεκα	δέδεμαι	ἐδέθην
διδάσκω	διδάξω	ἐδίδαξα	δεδίδαχα	δεδίδαγμαι	ἐδιδάχθην
δίδωμι	δώσω	ἔδωκα (δο-)	δέδωκα	δέδομαι	ἐδόθην
διώκω	διώξω	ἐδίωξα	δεδίωχα	δεδίωγμαι	ἐδιώχθην
ἐγείρω	ἐγερῶ	ἤγειρα		ἐγήγερμαι	ἠγέρθην
ἐντέλλομαι	ἐντελοῦμαι	ἐνετειλάμην		ἐντέταλμαι	
ἔρχομαι	ἐλεύσομαι	ἦλθον	ἐλήλυθα		
εὑρίσκω	εὑρήσω	εὗρον	εὕρηκα	εὕρημαι	εὑρέθην
ἔχω	ἕξω	ἔσχον	ἔσχηκα		
ἵημι	ἥσω	ἧκα (ἑ-)	εἷκα	εἷμαι	ἕθην
ἵστημι	στήσω	ἔστησα / ἔστην	ἕστηκα	ἕσταμαι	ἐστάθην
καλέω	καλέσω	ἐκάλεσα	κέκληκα	κέκλημαι	ἐκλήθην
κλέπτω	κλέψω	ἔκλεψα	κέκλοφα	κέκλεμμαι	ἐκλέφθην
κόπτω	κόψω	ἔκοψα	(κέκοφα)	κέκομμαι	ἐκόπην
κράζω	κράξω	ἔκραξα	κέκραγα		
κρίνω	κρινῶ	ἔκρινα	κέκρικα	κέκριμαι	ἐκρίθην
κρύπτω	κρύψω	ἔκρυψα	(κέκρυφα)	κέκρυμμαι	ἐκρύβην
λαμβάνω	λήμψομαι	ἔλαβον	εἴληφα	εἴλημμαι	ἐλήμφθην
λέγω	ἐρῶ	εἶπον	εἴρηκα	εἴρημαι	ἐρρήθην / ἐρρέθην
λείπω	λείψω	ἔλιπον	λέλοιπα	λέλειμμαι	ἐλείφθην
λύω	λύσω	ἔλυσα	λέλυκα	λέλυμαι	ἐλύθην
μανθάνω	μαθήσομαι	ἔμαθον	μεμάθηκα		
μένω	μενῶ	ἔμεινα	μεμένηκα		

1	2	3	4	5	6
δράω	ὄψομαι	εἶδον	ἑώρακα	(ἑώραμμαι)	ὤφθην
πάσχω	πείσομαι	ἔπαθον	πέπονθα		
πείθω	πείσω	ἔπεισα	πέποιθα	πέπεισμαι	ἐπείσθην
πέμπω	πέμψω	ἔπεμψα	πέπομφα	πέπεμμαι	ἐπέμφθην
περιτέμνω	περιτεμῶ	περιέτεμον	περιτέτμηκα	περιτέτμημαι	περιετμήθην
πίμπλημι	(πλήσω)	ἔπλησα			ἐπλήσθην
πίνω	πίομαι	ἔπιον	πέπωκα		ἐπόθην
πίπτω	πεσοῦμαι	ἔπεσον	πέπτωκα		
πλήθυνω	πληθυνῶ	ἐπλήθυνα			ἐπληθύνθην
πράσσω	πράξω	ἔπραξα	πέπραχα	πέπραγμαι	ἐπράχθην
σπείρω	σπερῶ	ἔσπειρα		ἔσπαρμαι	ἐσπάρην
στρέφω	στρέψω	ἔστρεψα	ἔστροφα	ἔστραμμαι	ἐστράφην
σώζω	σώσω	ἔσωσα	σέσωκα	σέσωσμαι	ἐσώθην
τάσσω	τάξω	ἔταξα	τέταχα	τέταγμαι	ἐτάχθην
τίθημι	θήσω	ἔθηκα (θε-)	τέθεικα	τέθειμαι	ἐτέθην
τίκτω	τέξομαι	ἔτεκον			ἐτέχθην
φαίνω	φανοῦμαι	ἔφανα			ἐφάνην
φέρω	οἴσω	ἤνεγκον	ἐνήνοχα	ἐνήνεγμαι	ἠνέχθην
φεύγω	φεύξομαι	ἔφυγον	πέφευγα		
φθείρω	φθερῶ	ἔφθειρα	ἔφθαρκα	ἔφθαρμαι	ἐφθάρην
φυλάσσω	φυλάξω	ἐφύλαξα	πεφύλαχα	πεφύλαγμαι	ἐφυλάχθην

Common Irregular Stems and Their First Principal Parts

Note: Be sure to check the principal parts chart on the preceding pages to see which principal part each form may represent. Entries totally in parentheses (cf. last entry) are augmented stems whose unaugmented forms, which are also given, are difficult to identify.

ἀγαγ‑:	cf. ἄγω	κεκλη(κ)‑:	cf. καλέω
ἀν‑εωγ‑:	cf. ἀν‑οίγω	κλαυσ‑:	cf. κλαίω
ἀρ‑:	cf. αἴρω	κλη‑:	cf. καλέω
βη‑:	cf. βαίνω	λαβ‑:	cf. λαμβάνω
βησ‑:	cf. βαίνω	λημψ‑:	cf. λαμβάνω
γεγενη‑:	cf. γίνομαι	μαθ‑:	cf. μανθάνω
γεν‑:	cf. γίνομαι	οἰσ‑:	cf. φέρω
γνω‑:	cf. γινώσκω	ὀφ‑:	cf. ὁράω
δειξ‑:	cf. δείκνυμι	ὀψ‑:	cf. ὁράω
δο‑:	cf. δίδωμι	παθ‑:	cf. πάσχω
δωκ‑:	cf. δίδωμι	πεπεισ‑:	cf. πείθω
δωσ‑:	cf. δίδωμι	πεπονθ‑:	cf. πάσχω
ἐγνωκ‑:	cf. γίνωσκω	πεποιθ‑:	cf. πείθω
(εἰδ‑:	stem = ἰδ‑; cf. ὁράω)	πεσ‑:	cf. πίπτω
εἰληφ(φ)‑:	cf. λαμβάνω	πι‑:	cf. πίνω
εἰπ‑:	cf. λέγω	πλησ‑:	cf. πίμπλημι
εἰρη(κ)‑:	cf. λέγω	‑σταλ‑:	cf. ‑στέλλω
εἰστηκ‑:	cf. ἵστημι	σπαρ‑:	cf. σπείρω
ἐληλυθ‑:	cf. ἔρχομαι	στα‑:	cf. ἵστημι
ἐλευσ‑:	cf. ἔρχομαι	σταθ‑:	cf. ἵστημι
ἐλθ‑:	cf. ἔρχομαι	στη‑:	cf. ἵστημι
ἐνεγκ‑:	cf. φέρω	στησ‑:	cf. ἵστημι
ἐξ‑:	cf. ἔχω	στραφ‑:	cf. στρέφω
ἐρ‑:	cf. λέγω	σχ‑:	cf. ἔχω
ἑστηκ‑:	cf. ἵστημι	τεθ‑:	cf. τίθημι
εὑρ‑:	cf. εὑρίσκω	τεθει(κ)‑:	cf. τίθημι
εὑρη(κ)‑:	cf. εὑρίσκω	τεθνηκ‑:	cf. ἀπο‑θνήσκω
ἡκ‑:	cf. ἵημι	τεκ‑:	cf. τίκτω
(ἤγαγ‑:	stem = ἀγαγ‑; cf. ἄγω)	φα‑:	cf. φημί
(ἤλθ‑:	stem = ἐλθ; cf. ἔρχομαι)	φαγ‑:	cf. ἐσθίω
(ἤνεγκ‑:	stem = ἐνεγκ‑; cf. φέρω)	φαν‑:	cf. φαίνω
(ἤρ‑:	stem = ἀρ‑; cf. αἴρω)	φθαρ(κ)‑:	cf. φθείρω
ἰδ‑:	cf. ὁράω	φυγ‑:	cf. φεύγω
θηκ‑:	cf. τίθημι	(ὠφ‑:	stem = ὀφ‑; cf. ὁράω)
θησ‑:	cf. τίθημι		

Vocabulary

The number in parentheses following each entry indicates the chapter in which the word was introduced.

ἀγαθός -ή -όν: good (6)

ἀγαλλιάω (-άσω) (R): I rejoice, exult (usually deponent) (30)

ἀγαπάω (R): I love (30)

ἀγάπη -ης, f.: love (5)

ἀγγέλλω (Irreg.): I announce (27)

ἄγγελος -ου, m.: angel; messenger (4)

ἁγιάζω (R): I make holy, sanctify (25)

ἅγιος -α -ον: holy (6)

ἀγοράζω (R): I buy (7)

ἀγρός -οῦ, m.: field; countryside (9)

ἄγω (Irreg.): I lead; drive (3)

ἀδελφός -οῦ, m.: brother (4)

ἀδικία -ας, f.: unrighteousness (39)

αἷμα -ατος, n.: blood (18)

αἴρω (Irreg.): I take up; carry away (27)

αἰσχύνομαι . . . ᾐσχύνθην: (I put to shame); pass.: I am ashamed (38)

αἰτέω (R): I request (14)

αἰών -ῶνος, m.: age, aeon (18)

αἰώνιος -ον: eternal (same ending for masc. and fem.) (42)

ἀκολουθέω (R) + dat.: I follow (23)

ἀκοή -ῆς, f.: hearing; report (37)

ἀκούω (r): I hear (3)

ἀκροβυστία ‑ας, f.: uncircumcision (39)

ἀλήθεια ‑ας, f.: truth (5)

ἀληθής ‑ές: true (19)

ἀλλά (conj.): but (~~strong~~) *emphatic* (8)

ἀλλήλων (reciprocal pron.): one another's (40)

ἄλλος ‑η ‑ο: other (13)

ἁμαρτάνω (Irreg.): I sin (8)

ἁμαρτία ‑ας, f.: sin (13)

ἁμαρτωλός ‑ή ‑όν: sinful (12)

ἀναβαίνω (Irreg.): I go up (11)

ἀναβλέπω (R): I look up; regain sight (11)

ἀναγινώσκω (Irreg.): I read (28)

ἀνάστασις ‑εως, f.: resurrection (19)

ἀνήρ, ἀνδρός, m.: man (male); husband (23)

ἄνθρωπος ‑ου, m.: person, man (generic) (4)

ἀνίστημι (Irreg.): trans.: I raise; intrans.: I stand up, rise (35)

ἀνοίγω (Irreg.): I open (26)

ἀντί (prep. + gen.): in place of, on behalf of (38)

ἄξιος ‑α ‑ον: worthy (6)

ἀπάγω (Irreg.): I drive, lead away (9)

ἀπέρχομαι (Irreg.): I go (come) away (9)

ἀπέχω (Irreg.): I receive in full; I am distant (intrans.); middle: I abstain from (38)

ἀπό (prep. + gen.): from (5)

ἀποδίδωμι (Irreg.): I give back; middle: I sell (33)

ἀποθνῄσκω (Irreg.): I die (9)

ἀποκαλύπτω (R): I reveal (10)

ἀποκρίνομαι . . . ἀπεκρίθην (P): I answer (24)

ἀποκτείνω (Irreg.): I kill (27)

ἀπόλλυμι (Irreg): I destroy; lose; middle: I perish; am being lost (34)

ἀπολύω (R): I release; dismiss (10)

ἀποστέλλω (Irreg.): I send out (27)

ἀπόστολος ⁻ου, m.: apostle, ambassador (4)

ἅπτομαι (M)(R) + gen.: I touch (23)

ἀργύριον ⁻ου, n.: silver, money (4)

ἀρέσκω, ἀρέσω, ἤρεσα + dat.: I please (40)

ἀρνέομαι (M)(R): I deny (26)

ἄρτος ⁻ου, m.: bread (pl. loaves of bread) (4)

ἀρχή ⁻ῆς, f.: beginning (13)

ἄρχω (R): I rule; middle: I begin (16)

ἄρχων ⁻οντος, m.: ruler (18)

ἀσθενής ⁻ές: weak, sick (19)

ἀσπάζομαι (M)(R): I greet (11)

αὐξάνω, αὐξήσω (R): I increase (transitive and intransitive) (7)

αὐτός, ⁻ή, ⁻ό (pers. pron): he; she; it; pl: they (10)

ἄφεσις ⁻εως, f.: forgiveness (29)

ἀφίημι (Irreg.): I forgive; allow; leave (33)

ἀφίστημι (Irreg.): trans. I draw away; intrans.: I depart, withdraw (35)

ἄφρων ⁻ον: foolish (19)

ἄχρι(ς) (conj. and improper prep.): until, as far as (42)

βαίνω (Irreg.): I go, step, walk (7)

βάλλω (Irreg.): I throw; put (27)

βαπτίζω (R): I baptize; wash (ritual) (11)

βασιλεία ⁻ας, f.: kingdom (9)

βασιλεύς ⁻έως, m.: king (19)

βασιλεύω (R): I rule (15)

βαστάζω (R): I carry, bear (42)

βιβλίον ⁻ου, n.: book (9)

βλέπω (R): I see (3)

βοηθέω (R) + dat.: I come to the aid of, help (32)

βούλομαι . . . ἐβουλήθην (P): I want (24)

γαμέω (R): I marry (15)

γάρ (conj.—postpositive): because, for (7)

γεννάω (R): I beget (30)

γῆ, γῆς, f.: earth; land (14)

γίνομαι (M) (Irreg.): I become; am (12)

γινώσκω (Irreg.): I know (7)

γνωρίζω (R): I make known (22)

γραμματεύς ⁻έως, m.: scribe (19)

γράφω (r): I write (3)

γυνή, γυναικός, f.: woman; wife (23)

δαιμόνιον ⁻ου, n.: demon (4)

δέ (conj.—postpositive): and; but (weak) (8) *unemphatic*

δεῖ: It is necessary (16)

δείκνυμι, δείξω (R): I show (34)

δέκα: ten (20)

δένδρον ⁻ου, n.: tree (17)

δεξιός ⁻ά ⁻όν: right (37)

δεσπότης ⁻ου, m.: master (13)

δεύτερος ⁻α ⁻ον: second (17)

δέχομαι (M) (R): I receive (7)

δέω (Irreg.): I bind (41)

δηλόω (R): I make plain (31)

διά (prep.)   + gen.: through (local and means)
              + acc.: on account of (13)

διάβολος -ου, m.: devil (10)

διαθήκη ⁻ης, f.: covenant; testament (34)

διάκονος ⁻ου, m.: servant; deacon (35)

διατάσσω (r) (+ dat.): I command, direct (23)

διατίθεμαι (M) (Irreg.): I make a covenant with (+ dat. or with
              πρός + acc.) (34)

διδάσκαλος ⁻ου, m.: teacher (10)

διδάσκω, διδάξω (r): I teach (7)

διδαχή ⁻ῆς, f.: teaching (10)

δίδωμι (Irreg.): I give (33)

δίκαιος ⁻α ⁻ον: just, righteous (6)

δικαιοσύνη ‑ης, f.: righteousness, justice (5)

δικαιόω (R): I justify, make righteous legally (31)

διώκω (r): I pursue; persecute (7)

δοκέω, δόξω (R): I think; third singular may be intransitive and
impersonal = It seems (26)

δοκιμάζω (R): I test for approval; approve (25)

δόξα ‑ης, f.: glory (5)

δοξάζω (R): I glorify (5)

δοῦλος ‑ου, m.: slave, servant (4)

δύναμαι, δυνήσομαι . . . ἠδυνήθην: I am able (conjugated as
is ἵσταμαι) (35)

δύο: two (22)

δώδεκα: twelve (20)

δῶρον ‑ου, n.: gift (7)

ἑαυτοῦ, ‑ῆς, ‑οῦ (refl. pron.): his, her, its own (40)

ἑαυτῶν (refl. pron.): our, your, their own (40)

ἐάω, ἐάσω, εἴασα: I allow (30)

ἐγγίζω (R): I draw near, approach (21)

ἐγείρω (Irreg.): I rouse (the dead), raise; pass.: I rise (27)

ἐγώ, ἐμοῦ, ἐμοί, ἐμέ (pers. pron.): I (10)

ἔθνος ‑ους, n.: nation (pl. Gentiles) (19)

εἰ (conj.): if (29)

εἰκών ‑όνος, f.: image (18)

εἰμί, ἔσομαι: I am (12)

εἰρήνη ‑ης, f.: peace (13)

εἰς (prep. + acc.): into; for (purpose, result) (5)

εἷς, μία, ἕν: one (24)

ἐκ (prep. + gen.): out of (ἐξ before a vowel following) (5)

ἕκαστος ‑η ‑ον: each (40)

ἐκεῖ (adv.): there (8)

ἐκεῖνος ‑η ‑ο: that (pl. those) (13)

ἐκκλησία ‑ας, f.: church; assembly (5)

ἐκλεκτός -ή -όν: elect (21)

ἐλέγχω (R): I convict; convince; reprove (34)

ἐλεέω (R): I pity, have mercy on (21)

ἐλεύθερος -α -ον: free (29)

Ἕλλην -ηνος, m.: Greek (18)

ἐλπίζω (R): I hope (16)

ἐλπίς -ίδος, f.: hope (18)

ἐμαυτοῦ, -ῆς, -οῦ (refl. pron.): my own (40)

ἐμβαίνω (Irreg.): I get into (a boat), embark (28)

ἔμπροσθεν: before, in the presence of (37)

ἐν (prep. + dat.): in; on (temporal, not local); among (group of
                people) (5)

ἐνδύω (R): I clothe (two objects possible) (39)

ἕνεκα: on account of (37)

ἐντέλλομαι (M) (Irreg.): I command (42)

ἐντολή -ῆς, f.: commandment (5)

ἐνώπιον: before, in the presence of (37)

ἔξεστι(ν): It is possible; lawful (16)

ἐξίστημι (Irreg.): trans.: I amaze; intrans.: I am beside myself; am
                amazed (35)

ἐξουσία -ας, f.: power, authority (15)

ἔξω: outside (37)

ἑορτή -ῆς, f.: feast (29)

ἐπαγγελία -ας, f.: promise (8)

ἐπεί (conj.): because, since; when (42)

ἐπί (prep.) + gen.: on; in the time of; in the presence of
                + dat.: at
                + acc.: on; over (15)

ἐπιγινώσκω (Irreg.): I know thoroughly (28)

ἐπιθυμέω (R): I desire earnestly, crave (15)

ἐπιστολή -ῆς, f.: epistle (20)

ἐπιστρέφω (r): I turn toward, turn around (trans.);
                pass.: I turn toward, turn around (intrans.) (24)

ἐπιτάσσω (r) (+ dat.): I command, direct (23)

ἐπιτίθημι (Irreg.): I lay on, impose (33)

ἐπιτιμάω (R) + dat.: I rebuke (30)

ἑπτά: seven (20)

ἐργάζομαι (M) (R): I work (7)

ἐργάτης ‾ου, m.: workman (7)

ἔργον ‾ου, n.: work (7)

ἔρημος ‾ου, f.:desert (9)

ἔρχομαι (Irreg.): I come, go (8)

ἐρωτάω (R): I inquire (30)

ἐσθίω (Irreg.): I eat (8)

ἔσχατος ‾η ‾ον: last (6)

ἔτι (adv.): still, yet (20)

ἑτοιμάζω (R): I prepare (13)

ἔτος ‾ους, n.: year (37)

εὐαγγέλιον ‾ου, n.: Gospel, good news (4)

εὐθέως (adv.): straightway, immediately (19)

εὐθύς ‾εῖα ‾ύ: straight (19)

εὐλογέω (R): I bless (38)

εὑρίσκω (Irreg.): I find (8)

εὐχαριστέω (R): I give thanks (21)

ἐχθρός ‾ά ‾όν: hostile, enemy (12)

ἔχω (Irreg.): I have (imperfect = εἶχον) (13)

ἕως (conj.): until (29)

ἕως: until, up to (37)

ζάω (R): I live (30)

ζητέω (R): I seek (14)

ζωή ‾ῆς, f.: life (13)

ἤ (adv.): or; than (36)

ἡγεμών ‾όνος, m.: leader (18)

ἡδέως (adv.): gladly (36)

ἡμεῖς, ἡμῶν, ἡμῖν, ἡμᾶς (pers. pron.): we (10)

ἡμέρα ‾ας, f.: day (5)

θάλασσα ⁻ης, f.: sea, lake (5)

θάνατος ⁻ου, m.: death (13)

θαυμάζω (R): (intrans.) I wonder at, marvel (15)

θεάομαι (⁻άσομαι) (M) (R): I look at (30)

θέλω, θελήσω, ἠθέλησα: I desire (imperfect = ἤθελον) (13)

θεός ⁻οῦ, m.: God, god (4)

θεραπεύω (R): I heal (3)

θερίζω (R): I reap, harvest (28)

θηρίον ⁻ου, n.: wild beast (33)

θησαυρός ⁻οῦ, m.: treasure (29)

θλῖψις ⁻εως, f.: tribulation (40)

θρίξ, τριχός, f.: hair (strand) (pl. = head of hair) (22)

θρόνος ⁻ου, m.: throne (35)

θυγάτηρ, θυγατρός, f.: daughter (28)

θύρα ⁻ας, f.: door (15)

θυσία ⁻ας, f.: sacrifice (39)

θυσιαστήριον ⁻ου, n.: altar (39)

θύω (R): I sacrifice, kill for sacrifice (39)

ἰάομαι (⁻άσομαι) (M) (R): I heal (42)

ἴδιος ⁻α ⁻ον: one's own (42)

ἱερεύς ⁻έως, m.: priest (19)

ἱερόν ⁻οῦ, n.: temple (7)

ἵημι (Irreg.): I send (33)   ; *Joshua*

ʼΙησοῦς ⁻οῦ, m.: Jesus (6)

ἱκανός ⁻ή ⁻όν: suitable, adequate, able (16)

ἱμάτιον ⁻ου, n.: cloak, piece of clothing (pl. clothing) (4)

ἵνα (conj.): (that) (29)

ʼΙουδαῖος ⁻α ⁻ον: Jewish (12)

ἵππος ⁻ου: m.: horse (12)   < *ἵστημι : I stand*

ἰσχυρός ⁻ά ⁻όν: strong (36)   *(trans. and intrans.) (3*

ἰσχύω (R): I am strong; have validity, be in force (39)

ἰχθύς ⁻ύος, m.: fish (acc. sing. = ἰχθύν) (22)

καθαρίζω (R): I purify (9)

κάθημαι (M): I am seated, sit (35)

καθίζω (R): I sit; sit down (15)

καθίστημι (Irreg.): trans.: I establish; intrans.: I am established (35)

καθώς (adv.): just as (13)

καί (conj.): and, also, even (4)

καινός -ή -όν: new (different) (34)

καιρός -οῦ, m.: due time, season (16)

κακός -ή -όν: bad (6)

καλέω (Irreg.): I call (26)

καλός -ή -όν: beautiful; noble (6)

καρδία -ας, f.: heart (6)

καρπός -οῦ, m.: fruit (17)

κατά (prep.)   + gen.: against; down
                    + acc.: according to (13)

καταβαίνω (Irreg.): I go down (13)

κατακρίνω (Irreg.): I condemn (27)

καταργέω (R): I abolish, nullify (29)

καταρτίζω (R): I fashion, create (25)

καταφρονέω (R) + gen.: I despise (32)

κατοικέω (R): I inhabit, dwell in (+ ἐν) (29)

καυχάομαι (-άσομαι) (M) (R): I boast (30)

κεῖμαι (M): I lie, recline (34)

κελεύω (R): I order (16)

κεφαλή -ῆς, f.: head (22)

κηρύσσω (R): I proclaim (3)

κλαίω, κλαύσω (R): I weep (15)

κλέπτω (r): I steal (3)

κληρονομέω (R): I inherit (14)

κοινόω (R): I make common, defile (31)

κοινωνία -ας, f.: fellowship; participation (31)

κοπιάω (-άσω) (R): I toil, labor (30)

κόπτω (Irreg.): I cut; middle: I mourn (39)

κόσμος ⁻ου, m.: world (6)

κράζω (Irreg.) I cry out, yell (42)

κρατέω (R) + gen.: I seize; arrest (25)

κρίνω (Irreg.): I judge (27)

κρίσις ⁻εως, f.: judgment (27)

κριτής ⁻οῦ, m.: judge (27)

κρύπτω (r): I hide (something); pass.: I hide (intrans.) (24)

κτίσις ⁻εως, f.: creation, creature (41)

κύριος ⁻ου, m.: lord, the Lord (8)

κώμη ⁻ης, f.: village (5)

κωφός ⁻ή ⁻όν: deaf, mute (dumb) (12)

λαλέω (R): I speak (openly) (14)

λαμβάνω (Irreg.): I get; take (7)

λαός ⁻οῦ, m.: people (16)

λατρεύω (R) + dat.: I worship (25)

λέγω (Irreg.): I say (8)

λείπω (Irreg.): I leave (behind); abandon (3)

λῃστής ⁻οῦ, m.: robber, bandit (9)

λίθος ⁻ου, m.: stone (11)   ) *account as*

λογίζομαι (M) (R): I reckon (26)

                                      λ . *reason*

λόγος ⁻ου, m.: word; account (4)

λοιπός ⁻ή ⁻όν: remaining, left (37)

λυπέω (R): I grieve, cause to mourn; pass.: I mourn (24)

λύω (R): I loose; break (3)

μαθητής ⁻οῦ, m.: disciple (5)

μακάριος ⁻α ⁻ον: blessed (12)

μᾶλλον (adv.): more; rather (+ ἤ) (36)

μανθάνω (Irreg.): I learn (26)

μαρτυρέω (R) + dat.: I bear witness to (23)

μάχαιρα ⁻ης, f.: sword (11)

μέγας, μεγάλη, μέγα: great (36)

μέλλω, μελλήσω: I am going (to), about (to) (imperfect = ἤμελλον) (16)

μέλος ⁻ους, n.: member (22)

μέν (particle—postpositive): (on the one hand) (13)

μένω (Irreg.): I remain (27)

μεριμνάω (R): I worry (about) (30)

μετά (prep.) + gen.: with
                      + acc.: after (13)

μετανοέω (R): I repent (14)

μέχρι(ς) (conj. and improper prep.): until, as far as (42)

μή (adv.): not (with verb forms other than the indicative) (16); introduces questions expecting a negative answer (41)

μηκέτι (adv.): no longer (20)

μήποτε (conj.): lest (in order that not) (= ἵνα μή) (38)

μήτηρ, μητρός, f.: mother (23)

μήτι (adv.): not (strong, or introduces questions expecting a negative answer) (41)

μικρός ⁻ά ⁻όν: small (6)

μιμνήσκομαι . . . ἐμνήσθην (P) + gen.: I remember (26)

μισέω (R): I hate (21)

μισθός ⁻οῦ, m.: pay, wages (28)

μνημεῖον ⁻ου, n.: tomb (12)

μνημονεύω (R): I remember (+ gen. or acc.) (42)

μόνος ⁻η ⁻ον: alone; adverbial μόνον = only (37)

μυστήριον ⁻ου, n.: mystery (10)

ναός ⁻οῦ, m.: temple (42)

νεκρός ⁻ά ⁻όν: dead (12)

νέος ⁻α ⁻ον: new (34)

νεφέλη ⁻ης, f.: cloud (28)

νηστεύω (R): I fast (17)

νίπτω (R): I wash (3)

νόμος ⁻ου, m.: law (4)

νόσος ⁻ου, f.: disease (4)

νύμφη ‑ης, f.: bride (15)

νυμφίος ‑ου, m.: groom (15)

νῦν (adv.): now (8)

νύξ, νυκτός, f.: night (18)

ξένος ‑η ‑ον: foreign (41)

ὁδός ‑οῦ, f.: road, way (15)

οἶδα (perf.): I know (ᾔδειν, pluperfect = I knew) (26)

οἰκία ‑ας, f.: house (42)

οἰκοδομέω (R): I build (14)

οἶκος ‑ου, m.: house; household (6)

οἶνος ‑ου, m.: wine (7)

οἷος ‑α ‑ον (relative pron.): the sort that (40)

ὀλίγος ‑η ‑ον: few (36)

ὅλος ‑η ‑ον: whole (42)

ὅμοιος ‑α ‑ον + dat.: like, similar (to) (31)

ὁμοιόω (R) (+ dat.) I make like, liken (31)   *; pass.: be like*

ὁμολογέω (R): I confess (26)

ὀπίσω: behind, after (37)

ὅπου (conj.): where (29)

ὅπως (conj.): (in order) that (29)

ὁράω (Irreg.): I see (9)

ὀργή ‑ῆς, f.: wrath (17)

ὄρος ‑ους, n.: mountain (19)

ὅς, ἥ, ὅ (relative pron.): who, which (15)

ὅσος ‑η ‑ον (relative pron.): as much as (pl.: many) (40)

ὅστις, ἥτις, ὅ τι: whoever (= ὅς ἄν); who (= ὅς, ἥ, ὅ) (42)

ὅτε (conj.): when (29)

ὅτι (conj.): because (10); that (introducing indirect discourse or
            thought) (26)

οὐδέ (adv.): and not; neither, nor (10)

οὐκ (adv): not (οὐ before consonant, οὐχ before aspirated vowel)
          (6); introduces questions expecting a postive answer (41)

οὐκέτι (adv.): no longer (20)

οὖν (conj.—postpositive): therefore; then (11)

οὔπω (adv.): not yet (17)

οὐρανός ‑οῦ, m.: heaven; sky (10)

οὖς, ὠτός, n.: ear (32)

οὔτε . . . οὔτε; neither . . . nor (22)

οὗτος, αὕτη, τοῦτο: this (pl. these) (13)

οὕτως (adv.): in this way; so (13)

οὐχί (adv.): not (strong, or introduces questions expecting a postive
                answer) (41)

ὀφείλω: I owe; I ought (+ infinitive) (16)

ὀφθαλμός ‑οῦ, m.: eye (17)

ὄχλος ‑ου, m.: crowd (9)

παιδίον ‑ου, n.: child (42)

παῖς, παιδός, m., f.: child (32)

παλαιός ‑ά ‑όν: old (36)

πάλιν (adv.): again; back (17)

πάντοτε (adv.): always (36)

παρά (prep.)   + gen.: away from (the side of)
               + dat.: at (the side of)
               + acc.: to (the side of) (15)

παραβολή ‑ῆς, f.: parable (9)

παραγίνομαι (Irreg.): I am present; appear (15)

παραδίδωμι (Irreg.): I hand over; betray (33)

παρακαλέω (Irreg.): I exhort; comfort; encourage (26)

παραλαμβάνω (Irreg.): I take along; receive (15)

παρατίθημι (Irreg.): I set before, middle: I entrust (34)

παρέρχομαι (Irreg.): I pass by; pass away (28)

παρθένος ‑ου, f.: virgin, maiden (4)

παρίστημι (Irreg.): trans.: I present; intrans.: I am present; stand
                by (35)

πᾶς, πᾶσα, πᾶν: all; every; whole (36)

πάσχω (Irreg.): I suffer (8)

πατήρ, πατρός, m.: father (23)

πείθω (r): I persuade (6)

πειράζω (R): I tempt, try; attempt (22)

πέμπω (r): I send (3)

πέντε: five (20)

περί (prep.)   + gen.: concerning
                      + acc.: around (13)

περιβάλλω (Irreg.): I throw around, clothe (two objects possible);
                      middle: I clothe myself (27)

περιπατέω (R): I walk; conduct my life (21)

περισσεύω (R): I abound (5)

περιτέμνω (Irreg.): I circumcise (34)

περιτομή -ῆς, f.: circumcision (34)

πίμπλημι (Irreg.): I fill (42)

πίνω (Irreg.): I drink (7)

πίπτω (Irreg.): I fall (8)

πιστεύω (R) + dat.: I believe; with εἰς + acc. = I believe *in* (23)

πίστις -εως, f.: faith (19)

πιστός -ή -όν: faithful (12)

πλανάω (R): I lead astray; pass.: I err , wander (30)

πλῆθος -ους, n.: multitude, crowd (42)

πληθύνω (Irreg.): I increase, multiply (trans.); pass.: I increase,
                      multiply (intrans.) (38)

πληρόω (R): I fill (acc. = thing filled, gen. = contents) (31)

πλήρωμα -ατος, n.: fulness (31)

πλοῖον -ου, n.: boat (4)

πλούσιος -α -ον: rich (6)

πνεῦμα -ατος, n.: spirit; breath (18)

ποιέω (R): I make; do (14)

ποιμαίνω, ποιμανῶ, ἐποίμανα: I shepherd (39)

ποιμήν -ένος, m.: shepherd (18)

ποῖος -α -ον (interrogative pron.): What sort? (40)

πόλις -εως, f.: city (19)

πολύς, πολλή, πολύ: much; pl.: many (36)

πονηρός ‑ά ‑όν: evil, wicked (6)

πορεύομαι (P) (R): I journey (24)

πορνεία ‑ας, f.: unchastity, immorality (17)

πόσος ‑η ‑ον (interrogative pron.): How much (pl.: many)? (40)

ποταμός ‑οῦ, m.: river (11)

πότε (adv.): When? (10)

ποῦ (adv.): Where? (10)

πούς, ποδός, m.: foot (18)

πράσσω (r): I do, act (12)

πρεσβύτερος ‑ου, m.: elder (35)

πρίν (conj.): before (usually + infinitive, often with ἤ) (42)

πρό (prep. + gen.): before (of time and space) (10)

πρόβατον ‑ου, n.: sheep (8)

πρός (prep. + acc.): to, toward (5)

προσέρχομαι (Irreg.) (+ dat.): I come (go) to (23)

προσεύχομαι (M) (R): I pray (7)

προσέχω (Irreg.) (+ dat.): I give heed to, pay attention to (32)

προσκαλέομαι (M) (Irreg.): I summon (26)

προσκυνέω (R) (+ dat.): I worship; prostrate myself before (23)

προστάσσω (r) (+ dat.): I command, direct (23)

προσφέρω (Irreg.) (+ dat.): I bear (carry) to (23)

πρόσωπον ‑ου, n.: face (17)

προφήτης ‑ου, m.: prophet (5)

πρῶτος ‑η ‑ον: first (6)

πτωχός ‑ή ‑όν: poor (12)

πῦρ, πυρός, n.: fire (32)

πῶς (adv.): How? (10)

ῥῆμα ‑ατος, n.: utterance (40)

ῥύομαι (M) (R): I rescue (40)

σάββατον ‑ου, n.: Sabbath; week (11)

σάρξ, σαρκός, f.: flesh (18)

σεαυτοῦ, ‑ῆς, ‑οῦ (refl. pron.): your own (40)

σημεῖον ⁻ου, n.: sign (4)

σήμερον (adv.): today (11)

σκανδαλίζω: (R): I cause to stumble; pass.: I take offense at (39)

σκότος ⁻ους, n.: darkness (22)

σοφός ⁻ή ⁻όν: wise (12)

σπείρω (Irreg.): I sow (27)

σπουδάζω (R): I hasten (41)

σταυρός ⁻οῦ, m.: cross (31)

σταυρόω (R): I crucify (31)

στέφανος ⁻ου, m.: crown (14)

στηρίζω, στηρίξω (R): I make firm, support (40)

στόμα ⁻ματος, n.: mouth (41)

στρατιώτης ⁻ου, m.: soldier (11)

στρέφω (r): I turn (trans.); pass.: I turn (intrans.) (24)

σύ, σοῦ, σοί, σέ (pers. pron.): you (sing.) (10)

συλλαμβάνω (Irreg.): I seize; conceive a child (29)

σύν (prep. + dat.): with (in the company of) (5)

συνάγω (Irreg.): I gather (trans.); pass.: I gather, assemble (intrans.)
　　　　　　(24)

συνέδριον ⁻ου, n.: Sanhedrin (10)

συνίημι (Irreg.): I understand (33)

σφραγίζω (R): I seal (25)

σῴζω (r): I save⟨, *rescue*⟩ (3)

σῶμα ⁻ατος, n.: body (18)

σωτήρ ⁻ῆρος, m.: savior (18)

ταπεινόω (R): I humble; pass: I am humble (40)

ταράσσω (R): I disturb, trouble; pass.: I am disturbed, troubled (38)

τάσσω (r): I arrange; command, direct (23)

ταχύς ⁻εῖα ⁻ύ: swift (19)

τέ (enclitic): and (sometimes with καί) (40)

τέκνον ⁻ου, n.: child (4)

τέλειος ⁻α ⁻ον: complete, perfect, mature (31)

τελειόω (R): I make complete, perfect (31)

τέλος ⁻ους, n.: end; goal (41)

τελώνης ⁻ου, m.: tax collector (10)

τεσσαράκοντα: forty (37)

τέσσαρες ⁻α: four (third declension) (20)

τηρέω (R): I keep, observe (laws) (14)

τίθημι (Irreg.): I place, set (33)

τιμάω (R): I honor (30)

τιμή ⁻ῆς, f.: honor; price, value (30)

τίς, τί (interrog. pron.): Who? Which? What? (24)

τις, τι (indef. pron.): someone, something, anyone, anything (24)

τίκτω (Irreg.): I bear (a child) (8)

τοιοῦτος ⁻αύτη ⁻οῦτο (demonstrative pron.): this sort (40)

τόπος ⁻ου, m.: place (15)

τοσοῦτος ⁻αύτη ⁻οῦτο (demonstrative pron.): this much (pl.: many) (40)

τότε (adv.): then (36)

τρεῖς, τρία: three (third declension) (20)

τρίτος ⁻η ⁻ον,: third (28)

τυφλός ⁻ή ⁻όν: blind (12)

ὑγιής ⁻ές: healthy, well (36)

ὕδωρ, ὕδατος, n.: water (21)

υἱός ⁻οῦ, m.: son (6)

ὑμεῖς, ὑμῶν, ὑμῖν, ὑμᾶς (pers. pron.): you (pl.) (10)

ὑπάγω (Irreg.): I depart (intrans.) (32)

ὑπακούω (r) (+ dat.): I obey (23)

ὑπαντάω (R) (+ dat.): I meet (32)

ὑπάρχω (R): I exist (really) (41)

ὑπέρ (prep.)   + gen.: on behalf of
              + acc.: beyond (13)

ὑπηρέτης ⁻ου, m.: attendant, servant (42)

ὑπό (prep.)   + gen.: by (agent)
             + acc.: under (13)

ὑπομένω (Irreg.): I endure (27)

ὑποστρέφω (r): I return; turn back (intrans.) (32)

ὑποτάσσω (r): I subject, subordinate; pass.: I am subject to; obey (38)

ὑστερέω (R) + gen.: I lack; am less than, inferior to (37)

ὑψόω (R): I exalt, raise up (40)

φαίνω (Irreg.): (I bring to light) (trans.); I shine (intrans.); pass.: I appear (38)

φέρω (Irreg.): I bear, carry, take along (8)

φεύγω (Irreg.): I flee (7)

φημί: I say (41)

φθείρω (Irreg.): I corrupt, destroy (27)

φιλέω (R): I love (14)

φοβέω (R): I frighten, cause to fear; pass.: I am frightened; fear (24)

φονεύω (R): I slay, murder (11)

φυλάσσω (r): I guard; keep (7)

φωνέω, (R): I call (with animals = "I make a sound") (14)

φωνή -ῆς, f.: voice; call (14)

φῶς, φωτός, n.: light (21)

χαίρω . . . ἐχάρην: I rejoice (32)

χαρά -ᾶς, f.: joy (36)

χαρίζομαι (M) (R): I grant; forgive (21)

χάρις -ιτος, f.: grace (acc. sing. = χάριν) (22)

χείρ, χειρός, f.: hand (dat. pl. = χερσί) (22)

χήρα -ας, f.: widow (32)

χρεία -ας, f.: need (16)

χρόνος -ου, m.: time (37)

χωλός -ή -όν: lame (12)

χώρα -ας: country, land, area (36)

χωρίζω (R): I separate (trans.); pass.: I separate (38) (intrans.)

χωρίς: apart from, without (37)

ψεύδομαι (M) (R): I lie, tell a falsehood (39)

ψυχή -ῆς, f.: soul, spirit (37)

ὧδε (adv): here (20)

ὥρα ‑ας, ῑ.: hour (16)

ὡς (conj.): as (time, manner) (11)

ὥστε (conj.): so that (result) (16)

ὠφελέω (R): I help (17)

Index

Note: Capitalized words or phrases have their own entry in the index.